Olivier Duplâtre and Pierre-Yves Modicom (Eds.)
Adverbs and Adverbials

Trends in Linguistics
Studies and Monographs

Editors
Chiara Gianollo
Daniël Van Olmen

Editorial Board
Walter Bisang
Tine Breban
Volker Gast
Hans Henrich Hock
Karen Lahousse
Natalia Levshina
Caterina Mauri
Heiko Narrog
Salvador Pons
Niina Ning Zhang
Amir Zeldes

Editor responsible for this volume
Chiara Gianollo

Volume 371

Adverbs and Adverbials

Categorial Issues

Edited by
Olivier Duplâtre and Pierre-Yves Modicom

DE GRUYTER
MOUTON

ISBN 978-3-11-163177-6
e-ISBN (PDF) 978-3-11-076797-1
e-ISBN (EPUB) 978-3-11-076801-5
ISSN 1861-4302

Library of Congress Control Number: 2022932366

Bibliographic information published by the Deutsche Nationalbibliothek
The Deutsche Nationalbibliothek lists this publication in the Deutsche Nationalbibliografie;
detailed bibliographic data are available on the Internet at http://dnb.dnb.de.

© 2024 Walter de Gruyter GmbH, Berlin/Boston
This volume is text- and page-identical with the hardback published in 2022.
Typesetting: Integra Software Services Pvt. Ltd.

www.degruyter.com

Contents

List of abbreviations —— VII

Olivier Duplâtre & Pierre-Yves Modicom
Introduction – Adverbs and adverbials: Categorial issues —— 1

I Delimitational approaches

1 Consistency of the class

Romain Delhem
The incoherence of the English adverb class —— 33

Christina Sanchez-Stockhammer & Antony Unwin
The subcategorization of English adverbs: A feature-based clustering approach —— 55

2 Margins of the class

Ignazio Mauro Mirto
Proteus: Adverbial multi-word expressions in Italian and their cognate counterparts in *–mente* —— 87

Marius Albers
Prenominal adverbs in German? The cases of *auf* and *zu* —— 109

II Classificational approaches

3 Adverbial scope: beyond the low / high dichotomy

Aquiles Tescari Neto
'Sentence adverbs' don't exist! —— 139

Fryni Kakoyianni-Doa
Formal and functional features of modal adverbs in French and Modern Greek —— 167

Jian Courteaud Zhang
Different types of subject-oriented adverbials in French and in Mandarin Chinese: A contrastive study —— 195

4 **The case of domain adverb(ial)s**

Martina Werner & Nina C. Rastinger
Domain adverbials and morphology: The rivalry between *-mäßig* and *-technisch* in German —— 229

Anna-Maria De Cesare
Framing, segmenting, indexing: **Towards a functional account of Romance domain adverbs in written texts** —— 249

List of contributors —— 277

Index —— 279

List of abbreviations

ADV	adverb
AFF	affirmation
COMP	comparative
COND	conditional
DA	domain adverbial
DAT	dative
DIR	directive
F	feminine gender
FUT	future
GOV.PREP	governed preposition
LOC	locative
M	masculine gender
NT	neutral gender
N	noun
NEG	negation/denial
NOM	nominative
NP	noun phrase
PL	plural
PRES	present
QA	qualitative adverbial
RA	relational adjective
SA	sentence adverb
SBJV	subjunctive
SG	singular
V	verb

Olivier Duplâtre & Pierre-Yves Modicom
Introduction – Adverbs and adverbials: Categorial issues

1 Looking for a definition of adverbs

1.1 Doomed at birth? The emergence of adverbs in grammaticography

The theory of parts-of-speech is both one of the most fundamental issues of any syntactic description or any syntactic theory, and one of the trickiest for anyone defending a cross-linguistic, comparative approach (Haspelmath 2001: 16538). A first major question, common to language-specific and cross-linguistic research, is whether parts-of-speech are essentially word-classes or functional classes. Directly pertaining to this matter is the question of the polycategoriality and/or polyfunctionality of items that seem to belong to several classes. Depending on the positions adopted in this debate, the respective relevance of semantic, syntactic and morphological criteria needs to be considered differently. From a cross-linguistic perspective, syntactic and above all morphological tests are put into jeopardy even more directly. As a result the degree of language-specific variation, the extent of flexibility required in classifications and the respective role of functional and formal criteria are still major issues for any theory of parts-of-speech.

Among the word-classes of traditional grammar, there is one which appears to be even less satisfactory than the other ones: the adverb. The concept of "adverb" (Lat. *adverbium*) has been coined as a loan translation from Greek *epirrhêma (ἐπίρρημα)*. This concept goes back to Dionysius Thrax (2nd century BCE), who defined it as "something that applies to a verb" in the penultimate chapter of his *Τέχνη Γραμματική* (chapter 24 following Davidson's 1874 rendition, chapter 19 in Uhlig's 1883 version). The definition of adverbs has been shaky and ambiguous from the beginning. For instance, there are two interpretations for the origin and the name of the Greek concept of *épirrhêma*. The first one is positional (De Benedetto 1959: 111): "adverbs" either immediately follow or precede the verb. The other one is semantic: based on the meaning of the preposition *kata* (*kata rhematos legomenon*), Lallot (1998: 221–222) claims that the *épirrhêma* is said (*legomenon*) of (*kata*) the rheme (*rhematos*). In other words: the *épirrhêma* is a predication on

---

Olivier Duplâtre, Sorbonne Université, olivier-duplatre@wanadoo.fr
Pierre-Yves Modicom, Université Bordeaux-Montaigne, pymodicom.ling@yahoo.fr

https://doi.org/10.1515/9783110767971-001

the rheme. While he also defended the view that Greek adverbs had a special slot immediately before the verb, Apollonius Dyscolus (2nd century CE) claims that the *épirrhêma* is predicated on the verb, or rather on some or all finite marks on the verb (*katêgoroũsa tõn ễn toĩs rhếmasin ẻnklíseôn kathólou ễ merisôs*, Apollonius Dyscolus 2021:76). But the most blatant issue with adverbs is the extreme heterogenity of the class, of which Dionysius Thrax was already well aware:

> An Adverb is an indeclinable part of speech, said of a verb or added to a verb. Of the Adverbs, some are Simple, and others Compound; simple, as πάλαι; compound, as πρόπαλαι. Some are indicative of time, as νῦν, τότε, αὖθις: to these we must subordinate as species those that connote particular times or seasons, as σήμερον, αὔριον, τόφρα, τέως, πηνίκα. Some indicate manner, as καλῶς, σοφῶς, δυνατῶς; some, quality, as πύξ, λάξ, βοτρυδόν, ἀγεληδόν; some, quantity, as πολλάκις, ὀλιγάκις, μυριάκις; some, number, as δίς, τρίς, τετράκις; some, place, as ἄνω, κάτω – of these there are three kinds, those signifying *in* a place, those signifying *to* a place, and those signifying *from* a place, as οἴκοι, οἴκαδε, οἴκοθεν. Some Adverbs signify a wish, as εἴθε, αἴθε, ἄβαλε; some express horror, as παπαί, ἰού, φεῦ; some, denial or negation, as οὔ, οὐχί, οὐ δῆτα, οὐδαμῶς; some, agreement, as ναί, ναίχι; some, prohibition, as μή, μὴ δῆτα, μηδαμῶς; some, comparison or similarity, as ὥς, ὥσπερ, ἠΰτε, καθά, καθάπερ; some, surprise, as βαβαί; some, probability, as ἴσως, τάχα, τυχόν; some, order, as ἑξῆς, ἐφεξῆς, χωρίς; some, congregation, as ἄρδην, ἅμα, ἤλιθα; some, command, as εἶα, ἄγε, φέρε; some, comparison, as μᾶλλον, ἧττον; some, interrogation, as πόθεν, ποῦ, πηνίκα, πῶς; some, vehemence, as σφόδρα, ἄγαν, πάνυ, μάλιστα; some, coincidence, as ἅμα, ὁμοῦ, ἄμυδις; some are deprecative, as μά; some are asseverative, as νή; some are positive, as ἀγνωστέον, γραπτέον, πλευστέον; some express ratification, as δηλαδή; and some enthusiasm, as εὐοῖ, εὐάν. (Thrax & Davidson 1874: 337–338)[1]

The starting point of Dionysus Thrax is a morphosyntactic definition of the adverb. In his work, semantics is essentially reduced to the question of incidence. In a nutshell, Dionysus's theory of adverbial incidence is that adverbs predicate a property onto the verb. Other semantic features (circumstantiality, manner, etc.) do not belong to the definition and are considered as secondary accidents to the *épirrhêma*: after the primary accident, the so-called *figura* in Latin grammars (some *épirrhêma* are simple, others are compound), there follows a long enumeration of the various semantic fields in which the *épirrhêma* occurs. In the mainstream reception of Dionysus Thrax however, the adverb is not defined functionally as a predication on the verb, but morphosyntactically, as a part of speech that may be pre- or postponed to the verb. The cause for this evolution may be found in the Latin interpretation and translation of *épirrhêma*: "adverbium praeponitur et postponitur verbo" (Macrobius 1848: 263).

---

[1] We quote from the 1874 English translation by Thomas Davidson for the *Journal of Speculative Philosophy*.

Latin grammar has also endowed the *épirrhêma* with a semantic dimension. Among the grammarians who played a major role in this Latin reception, one should name Remmius Palæmon (in his reconstructed *Ars grammatica*) and his successors, like Charisius, but also Donatus (*Ars Minor, Ars Maior*) and Diomedes (Swiggers & Wouters 2002: 295). All of them indicate that the adverb explains and completes the verb (*adverbium est pars orationis quae adiecta verbo significationem eius explanat atque implet*). Such a definition[2] was contradicted by the fact that an adverb or a so called one could occur alone (Pinkster 1972: 136–141). This issue is also addressed by Apollonius Dyscolus (2021: 78–79) in his major treaty on Greek adverbs. Apollonius makes a distinction between adverbs which are directly associated to a verb and adverbs for which grammarians had to postulate an underlying verbal assertion which the adverb modifies in a further step. Apollonius's hypothesis was mostly motivated by his wish to maintain the parallelism adjective/noun, adverb/verb (Brocquet 2005: 128). Priscian also drew a parallel with adjectives and claimed that the meaning of the adverb is added to that of the verb (*Adverbium est pars orationis indeclinabilis, cujus significatio verbis adicitur*). As Pinkster points out, the ancient grammarians were used to "describ[ing] parts of speech in terms of relationship between categories and not in terms of their function in a sentence." (Pinkster 2005: 180). Still, Priscian's definition paves the way for functional conceptions. The adverb does not complete or explain the verb any more, its signification is only added, which means that the adverb is ready to become a modifier. The notion of verbal incidence plays a cardinal role alongside the criterion of invariability. However, the limits of the verbal incidence thesis quickly become apparent. First, it is well-known that adverbs can be incident to adjectives (example 1) or to other adverbs (example 2).

(1) Since Sylvia Plath died in 1963, she's been turned into a *crudely tragic* symbol.
(bbc.com, July 21st, 2021)

(2) Rawls never wrote about himself, and *virtually never* gave interviews.
(The Guardian, Nov. 17th, 2002)

This fact led some scholars to enlarge the etymological definition of the adverb inasmuch as *verbum* may not only signifies *verb*, but *word*. This was done for instance by 18th century Cartesian grammarian Beauzée, who held that "adverbs complete the meaning of adjectives or even of other adverbs as often as the meaning of verbs" (Beauzée 1767: 548–549).

---

[2] Note that it bears some similarity with modern definitions of manner adverbials which are claimed to expand Aktionsart features of the verb (Dik 1997: 228).

On the other hand, even an adverb that seems to be incident to a verb may actually be incident to a higher node in the syntactic structure of the verbal clause, such as a complex made up of the verb and one of its arguments, or the VP as a whole, or even higher functional levels, as is most notably the case for "sentence adverbs" or "high adverbs". This high degree of variation regarding the real level of incidence of adverbs is a major issue for any syntactic theory and has enjoyed renewed interest over the last 25 years. Most significantly, it has played a prominent role in the constitution of the "cartographic approach" in the field of Generative Grammar (Cinque 1999). As early as 1990, Dik et al. (1990) developed a functional view drawing on a similar intuition: the clause is structured as a cascade of successive predicative operations, for which the verbal categories are grammatical operators, whereas adverbs and adverbials are lexical satellites, located at different representational levels and thus incident to different syntactic units within the verbal clause.

The question of syntactic incidence within the shell structure of the VP goes along with considerations on the relationship between adverbs and the hierarchy of "functional heads" or grammatical categories such as aspect, tense or mood. This way of thinking bears striking similarities with insights from Apollonius (2021: 80–81), who developed a fine-grained account of how adverbs may be incident either to the verbal root or to verbal flections, with some adverbs being associated to tense, while others apply to mood or even to personal agreement morphemes. According to Apollonius, selectional restrictions imposed on adverbs by inflectional categories show that temporal adverbs were predicated on tense markers and that adverbs which would now be called illocutionary were predicated on mood (see Dumarty 2021: 202–204 for a general discussion and 222–233 for a case-by-case analysis of Apollonius's claims). Apollonius thus paved the way for further accounts distinguishing between different levels of adverbial scope within the VP itself.

1.2 Adverbs: A superfluous class? Issues in contemporary theories

Indeed, if we look at contemporary research on adverbs, it seems that, far from advancing towards a more precise, consensual definition of the adverb, we are faced with an even greater level of heterogeneity. The formal and functional heterogeneity of this class makes it "the least satisfactory of all" according to Quirk et al. (1972: 267). A similar view is expressed by Gleason (1965: 129):

> The traditional „adverbs" are a miscellaneous lot, having very little if anything in common. Some fit part of the definition, but not other parts. Some fit the whole definition but far exceed its limits. The linguist almost invariably divides this assemblage into several groups which are not related to one another. (Gleason 1965: 129)

Some scholars are even tempted to define adverbs negatively, i.e. to drop the idea of finding a unitary, consistent definition for the class:

> Indeed, it is tempting to say simply that the adverb is an item that does not fit the definitions for other parts of speech/word classes. (Quirk et al. 1972: 267)

> Thus, resorting to the notion of adverb as a distinct word-class may be a matter of mere expedience, aimed at maintaining a relatively stable number of parts of speech in the face of the multiplicity of non-flectional morpheme and lexeme classes in Standard Average European languages. (Rauh 2015: 38)

Finding a universally valid definition of adverbs seems to be an almost impossible task. This can lead to the conclusion that "adverbs" are not a typologically relevant category. In this respect, "adverbs" illustrate how a eurocentric conception of parts of speech is a cross-linguistically inadequate descriptive tool. This was already suggested by Hopper & Thompson (1984: 747):

> To the extent that forms can be said to have an a-priori existence outside of discourse, they are characterizable as acategorial; i.e., their categorical classification is irrelevant. Categoriality – the realization of a form as either a N or a V – is imposed on the form by discourse. Yet we have also seen that the noun/verb distinction is apparently universal: there seem to be no languages in which all stems are indifferently capable of receiving all morphology appropriate for both N's and V's. This suggests that the continua which in principle begin with acategoriality, and which end with fully implemented nounhood or fully implemented verbhood, are already partly traversed for most forms. (Hopper & Thompson 1984: 747)

Given the problems raised above, it appears that the prominence of adverbs in Standard Average European should not lead us into abusive generalizations: a cross-linguistic survey suggests that the class of "adverbs", however fuzzy and all-encompassing, is superfluous for the description of certain (types of) languages. For instance, Hengeveld & Valstar (2010: 6), drawing on a system of four basic, functionally defined parts of speech (heads vs modifiers; within referential vs predicative phrases), show that the Krongo language does not show any specialized part of speech for modifiers, thus eliminating the adverb (as a part of speech for modifiers within a predicative phrase). Krongo uses only subordinate verbal phrases as modifiers. In this language, there might be something like an adverbial function ("modifier of a predicate phrase"), but no corresponding word-class. Hengeveld (1992a, b and 2004) defends the view that there is a cross-linguistic hierarchy of parts of speech, meaning that not all "big four" classes are equally likely to be found across languages:

Head of predicate phrase > head of referential phrase > modifier of referential phrase > modifier of predicate phrase.

In this hierarchy, adverbs occupy the lowest position (i.e. if there is a class of adverbs in a given language, that language must also display the other three classes, while the opposite is not true). On the other hand, this hierarchical approach is not necessary if we enlarge Croft's conception of modification and couple it with a radical view on word-classes. For instance, we may consider that subordinate clauses in Krongo correspond to a morphologically marked adverb, the unmarked item being absent in that language.

In his radical attempt at deconstructing presupposed categories, Croft (1991) sketches a threefold distinction for parts-of-speech which leaves aside the adverb. He distinguishes between three discourse functions: reference, predication and modification. These functions are prototypically filled by "nouns", "verbs" and "adjectives". More precisely, nouns, verbs and adjectives are unmarked items, resulting from the combination of reference, predication and modification with objects, actions and properties, respectively. Marked items (for instance deadjectival nouns, predicate adjectives) proceed from one of the other combinations between form and function. But what about adverbs? Croft does not treat them explicitly, but admits that modification of a predicate would also have to be represented in a theory devoted to parts-of-speech (Croft 2001: 94).

This enlargement of the discourse function of modification is taken up by Haser & Kortmann (2006: 68), who claim that prototypical adverbs, much like prototypical adjectives, can be defined as items that provide modification by a property, the difference being that prototypical adjectives modify referents and prototypical adverbs modify predicates. This could mean that the adverbial class is reduced to manner adverbs, at the expense of, say, adverbs of space and time. Manner adverbs would be then the unmarked items, whereas prepositional phrases (see for example *mit schnellem Schritt/with quick steps* in German), nominal phrases (see for example *schnellen Schrittes/with quick steps* in German) or even converbs would be marked items (see Hallonsten Halling 2018: 38). In this framework, adverbs are essentially conceived of on the basis of adjectives, raising the question whether adverbs are really a primary word-class. However, one may want to maintain the idea that the modifiers of predicates are not secondary to the modifiers of referential phrases, i.e. that "adverbs" are not secondary to "adjectives". According to Hallonsten Halling (2018: 96), "the languages that have adverbs but lack adjectives are genealogically unrelated and geographically distant. This shows that it is not necessary for a language to have adjectives in order for it to have adverbs, as earlier argued by Hengeveld (1992b, 2013)."

Another proposal for a revision of "word-classes" on a non-eurocentric base has been made by Haspelmath (2012), drawing on insights from Croft (2001). It is striking to see that here also, the proposed model leaves adverbs aside. Haspelmath argues that questions such as "Is there a noun/adjective distinction in language

X or Y?" are wrongly formulated since they presuppose clear-cut cross-linguistic definitions of word-classes, which are ultimately language-specific. Instead, he proposes to go back to the mostly implicit view behind traditional definitions of word-classes and to examine roots, not words, on a semantic (ontological) basis, looking for "root-groupings" such as "thing-roots", "action-roots" and "property-roots". The second set of comparative concepts advocated for in his paper are defined on a functional basis. Haspelmath calls them "referential roots", "predicate roots" and "attribute roots", i.e. roots that are specialized for one of those three functions and usually need further material (e.g. additional affixes) to be used in the other two functions. Both sets of comparative concepts intend to rescue the concepts of nouns, verbs and adjectives, based on the premise that "things-roots" tend to be "referential roots" as well, while "action-roots" are often "predicative roots" and "property-roots" are "attribute roots". But what about adverbs? What would be the ontological base for a comparative concept replacing this category, alongside with "things", "actions" and "properties"? Could it be "circumstance"? Or perhaps "manner"? And what about the functional concept corresponding to the class? Should we look for "adjunct roots"?

Considering this extreme fuzziness, some grammarians have looked for a renewed definition of adverbs based on prototypical features (Ramat & Ricca 1994). A possible outcome of this strain of thought is to sketch a hierarchy of adverbial classes, distinguishing central subclasses (e.g. manner adverbs) and peripheral subclasses, which would be "less adverbial" than others (e.g. sentence adverbials). But which criteria should be chosen to define the prototype of the adverb? Should frequency data play a role in this definition? Should one take some semantic features as more prototypical than others? Can the manner adverb constitute the prototype? Should we follow Hengeveld's position (1992a and b, 2004) that the only way to come up with typological generalizations is to focus on manner adverbs?

1.3 Looking for a functional alternative: Adverbials

Hengeveld (1992 and subsequent) and Hengeveld & Valstar (2010) use the definition of "modifier of a predicate phrase" as a functional cue leading to the identification of "adverbs" in given languages (provided that there exists a corresponding word-class in this language). This actually means that we first define a function (which shall henceforth be called "adverbial") and that "adverbs", if there are any, are those lexemes which are specialized for this function. Other scholars have chosen to do away with the category of adverb and to concentrate (almost) exclusively on the functional category of adverbial (Nølke 1990, Pittner 1999), with the latter being defined in a purely syntactic way if necessary (Chomsky 1965, Steinitz 1969). Similarly, some linguists take the adverbial as the more basic notion and derive the notion of adverb from it (Maienborn & Schäfer 2019).

However the notion of "adverbial" is not very clear either (Eisenberg 2013: 212). Its boundaries are probably just as fuzzy as those of the word-class "adverb". If the concept of "adverbial" encompasses all phrases that are not positively defined as belonging to another specific type of sentential component (Nølke 1990: 17), this means that any type of circumstantial, be it an adjective, a prepositional phrase, a subordinated clause, etc., falls into this category. Further, the question of the syntactic domain of adverbials and of their semantic scope is as difficult as it ever was for adverbs: should we really lump together in one category manner adverbials, speaker-oriented modal adverbials, evaluative adverbials, circumstantials, or even discourse markers?

Due to the syntactic tests used to isolate them (e.g. commutation, coordination, ellipsis) the definition of adverbials can be a test case for both constituency grammars, dependency grammars and valency theory. For instance, should we draw a line between adjuncts and adverbials? Dionysius Thrax makes a difference between "adverbs" and "conjunctions", i.e. particles and discourse connectives. The last chapter of the Τέχνη Γραμματική is devoted to these "conjunctions". Dionysius Thrax shows that semantically, particles and discourse connectives do not predicate "properties". From a syntactic point of view, they are not constituents, either. Yet, Dionysus regards negations as "adverbs", and also counts affirmative νή as an adverb, while today's dictionaries treat it as a particle. Are all adverbials and/or "adverbs" full constituents, or should we acknowledge the existence of cliticized or particulized "deficient adverbs" (Cardinaletti & Starke 1999: 97–102)? If so, should we still count them as adverbials?

Another major issue undermining the categorial homogeneity of adverbials is the distinction between bound and unbound adverbials or, to use a generative terminology, between central and peripheral adverbials. This distinction has been popularized for adverbial clauses, by Haegeman (2012), among others. Central adverbial clauses are modifiers within the VP. Among other properties, they can be negated, receive contrastive focus, and can be the answers to *wh*-questions. Peripheral adverbial clauses, on the other hand, are located within the illocutionary layer of the clause: they cannot be focused upon, nor can they be negated, and there is no corresponding *wh*-word.

(3) a. We went to England for the first time *as our children were still small*.
    b. We went to England for the first *not as our children were still small*, but only later.

Note that (3a) can also be an answer to the question "When did you go to England for the first time?". By contrast, (4a) is neither an answer to "When didn't you want to make the journey to England?", nor to "Why didn't you want to make the journey to England?":

(4) a. *As our children were still small,* we didn't want to make the journey to England.
 b. **Not as our children were still small,* we didn't want to make the journey to England.

Further properties such as the possibility of using discourse particles in peripheral, but not in central clause suggest that peripheral clauses are indeed illocutionarily autonomous. If we consider the fact that speaker-oriented adverbs tend to exhibit similar properties (see for instance Ernst 2009 on their behaviour with respect to negation, or Pérennec 2002 for questions), an important issue is whether this functional dichotomy between two sorts of adverbials is relevant only for adverbial clauses. Shouldn't we also look for a similar division between two groups of lexical adverbs?

2 Adverbs as lexical class: Delimitational and classificational issues

Delimitational approaches, either from a formal or from a functional point of view, often point out that it is sometimes hard to distinguish between adverbs and particles, adverbs and interjections, adverbs and discourse markers, even in languages where the tradition of "parts of speech" is supposed to guarantee strict borders between well-established categories. But the most salient issue in delimitational research is probably the relationship between adverbs and adverbial adjectives. If we assume that adverbials in sentences such as (5) and (6) are adjectives fulfilling an adverbial function, the class of adverbs has to undergo a strong reduction.

(5) Lo saben *seguro.*
 'They *certainly* know it.'

(6) Er singt *gut.*
 'He sings *well.*'

But the fuzziness of the adjective-adverb boundary also involves morphological issues: is it enough to have an "adverbial morpheme" distinguishing "adverbs" from corresponding adjectives? Or should we refrain from immediately reading these morphemes as derivational affixes yielding lexical adverbs? Two striking examples are the derivative adverbial suffixes of Latin -*e*, -*o* and Greek -*ôs*, which are broadly similar to inflectional endings, which raises the question as to whether adverbial derivation can always be separated from adjective flection (Haspelmath 1995). This question was already raised by Greek grammarians. For instance, a large part of Apollonius's treaty is devoted to the analysis of adverbial morphology, trying to determine which suffixes have to be traced back to marks of declension, and which adverbial forms are actually verbs or nouns (see especially Apollonius 2021: 84–107).

This issue becomes even more striking if we follow a radical diachronic view underlining the adjectival component of Romance lexemes ending in -*ment(e)* or English so-called adverbs in -*ly*. Haspelmath claims:

> For example, if the English adverb-forming suffix -*ly* is regarded as an inflectional suffix, then *quickly* is an inflected adverb form of the (adjectival) lexeme *quick*, hence it is an adjective. But if the suffix -*ly* is regarded as a derivational form, then quickly is a derived adverb lexeme. It turns out that there is no good general way of distinguishing between the two kinds of processes [. . .], so we cannot make this distinction the basis of our definition. Another serious problem is that there is no good general way of distinguishing inflectional affixes from separate clitic words. (Haspelmath 2012: 123)

Following this strain of thought, most "manner adverbs" would be discarded from the lexical class, and the notion of "adverbs" would be almost reserved to deictic adverbs of time and space and, depending on the author, to some grammatical forms used as a basis for (more or less lexicalized) adverbial constructions. Among these "adverbial" grammatical(ized) items, we could count the English suffix -*ly* (originally a noun, today a derivational suffix for both adjectives and adverbs, see Pittner 2015) or Romance -*ment*, -*mente* (also a former noun, see Lehmann 2015: 93 among many others). The same questions can be raised for gerunds and especially converbs in languages where converb derivation is highly productive (Haspelmath & König 1995): should they be regarded as deverbal adverbs? How do we distinguish between inflection, subordination and derivation in the case of gerunds and converbs? It is unclear whether the notions of "adverb" or "adverbial" really help to capture what is going on at all, since some differences at play within the derivational or inflectional procedures described above seem to permeate these classical categories.

For instance, in German, most adjectives can play the role of manner adverbials (Schäfer 2008). But in some cases, modal adverbials turn out to be originally epistemic modal adjectives having undergone functional specialisation. Today, a form like *vermutlich*, "plausible, plausibly" is no longer in use as an adjective. Adjectival uses of *offenbar* "manifest, manifestly" as NP-modifier are still marginally attested in the German Reference Corpus (DeReKo), but adverbial and predicative uses make up the vast majority of tokens. It appears that an adjective can turn into an adverb and all but lose its NP-modifying usage without any morphological altering. Yet, High German has also developed a derivation path resorting to a grammaticalized noun (-*weise*) meaning 'manner' and giving rise to a morphologically distinct class of "adverbs". This morphological opposition, which is strongly reminiscent of the Romance data observed by Schneider, Pollin, Gerhalter & Hummel (2020), also has a functional correlate: many *weise*-adverbials are not licit as proper manner adverbials (see overview in Elsner 2015), whereas most adjective-adverbs are ruled out from higher adverbial functions, with functionally specialized epistemic modals like *offenbar* and *vermutlich* being the main exceptions (which means that forms used as sentence adverbials still tend to be disprefered for NP-modifying functions).

At this stage, the morphological examination of adverbs raises several major issues pertaining to the consistency of the class: the different morphological classes of adverbs do not correspond to the different adverbial functions. At the same time, many forms appear to be morphologically ambiguous between adverbs and adjectives or adverbs and prepositions.

The first two chapters of this volume explore these mismatches between morphology and functions from a corpus-based perspective, taking Present-Day English as target of their study. With the help of a statistical study carried out with the software R, **Romain Delhem** ("The incoherence of the English adverb class") redefines on the morphosyntactic level the class of English adverbs. Two series of adverbs are eliminated: place adverbs, such as *here, there, abroad, ahead, home, downstairs* or *forward* move to the class of prepositions, which confirms the analysis of Huddleston & Pullum (2002). Flat adverbs, i.e. adverbs with a form identical to that of an adjective, join the class of adjectives. Finally, the third class includes adverbs expressing manner, frequency, time, modality, degree, etc. Romain Delhem assumes that the coherence of this class could be ensured by derived adjectives in *-ly* and units having the same function. Whereas Romain Delhem relies on morpho-syntactic criteria to carry out his statistical analysis of English adverbs, **Christina Sanchez-Stockhammer and Antony Unwin** ("The subcategorization of English adverbs: A feature-based clustering approach") use new morpho-semantic criteria such as the formation of the adverb, its capacity to give rise to other terms, its origin and its age. Their innovative clustering approach makes it possible to isolate three adverbial classes: adverbs in *-ly*, adverbs without suffixation that can be decomposed, such as *away, forward, anywhere*, etc., adverbs that cannot be decomposed, such as *out, next, so, then*, etc.

The adjective/adverb interface is an issue per se. Special attention has to be paid to the competition between "adverbial adjectives" (*seguro, gut,* see ex. 5 and 6), adjectives that have re-lexicalized as adverbs (*offenbar, vermutlich*) and adverbs derived from adjectives (using *-ly*, *-mente*, *-erweise*), which seem to compete for adverbial functions. This field has been extensively studied in Romance in the last years from a diachronic perspective (see especially the studies in Hummel & Valera 2017 as well as contributions by Hummel 2018, Gerhalter 2020 and Schneider, Pollin, Gerhalter & Hummel 2020). Hummel (2019) distinguishes between three competing ways of forming adverbs in the history of Romance: the use of adverbial adjectives (*seguro*, "surely, for sure"); suffix derivation (*seguramente*, "surely, for sure"); prepositional constructions (*de seguro*, "surely, for sure"). What are the parameters of variation at stake in the choice of one strategy or another? Are these determined by usage conditions, possibly linked to larger language change phenomena? Are there language-internal, synchronic biases? Are they linked to the level of incidence of the adverbial? What can morphology (e.g. agreement) teach us here? These issues are addressed by the contribution of **Ignazio Mirto** ("Proteus: Adverbial multi-word expressions in Italian and their cognate counterparts in *–mente*"), who is concerned with Italian *-mente* adverbials and their multiword counterparts (e.g. *lussuosamente* vs. *di lusso*, both meaning "lavishly"). Mirto shows both the truth-conditional interchangeability of both morphological types and their distributional differences as well as their semantic idiosyncrasies (under special consideration of subject-orientation). Inflection plays a major role in his reflection, which leads to a reassessment of morphosyntactic procedures in the functional examination of modifiers, at reasonable distance from traditional parts-of-speech classifications.

The very notion of "modification" needs to be re-examined in the light of such fuzziness. Should modification be conceived of as a (secondary) predication or as a phenomenon of attribution? Here also, adjectives offer an interesting parallel, and the comparison between both can be insightful, especially when adjectives compete with adverbs. . . or where morphological adverbs (or limit cases between adverbs and prepositions such as German *auf*) appear to gain access to adjectival functions. For instance, in (7), *auf* would most classically be analysed as a directional particle meaning "above". In (8), *auf* is a particle meaning "open" in a resultative construction.

(7) Er packte den Schläfer unter der Achsel und riss ihn *auf*.
    'He seized the sleeper under the armpits and drew him up.'   (*Digitales Wörterbuch der Deutschen Gegenwartssprache*, August 13th, 2021)

(8) Feuerwehreinsatz: Katze   dreht   das   Wasser   auf
    fire-brigade-intervention: cat   turns   the   water   up
    'Fire brigade intervenes: The cat had opened the stop cock.' (*Hannoversche Allgemeine Zeitung*, January 29th, 2018, retrieved August 13th, 2021)

In (9), which is non-standard but colloquially attested, it is an NP-internal modifier, and inflected as such:[3]

(9) Billigere   Lösung   ist   auffes   Fenster
    cheaper.F   solution(F) is   auf-NT   window(NT)
    'The cheaper solution is an open window.'
        (https://narkive.com/1sPiPR9C.4, dated 2010, retrieved August 13th, 2021)

These phenomena are at the heart of the chapter written by **Marius Albers** ("Prenominal adverbs in German? The verbal particles of *auf* 'open' and *zu* 'closed'"): according to Marius Albers, the inflection of the verbal particles *auf* and *zu* is made possible by the fact that they can be used predicatively, the predicative use paving then the way to an attributive one. These particles are thus much more akin to adjectives than adverbs and represent, according to the author, a particular use of a polyfunctional adjective. The evolution of adverbs into adjectives in German raises major questions as to the respective status of both classes, since it suggests that the border between adjectives and adverbs is open in both directions, against the common assumption that there is a hierarchy in the class of German modifiers and that adverbs are a secondary group. Further, it appears that adjectival uses of adverbs have developed from resultative constructions where the adverbial constituent fulfilled a predicative function that is typical for satellite-framed languages (Talmy 1991). This opens the way to new research about the link between the great typological divide first observed by Talmy in the expression of movement and issues of part-of-speech flexibility, where the syntactic type of motion expression determines which kinds of conversion are possible.

3 Semantics and syntax: Beyond manner and circumstances

3.1 Splitting "manner adverbs"

The result of inquiries looking for a consistent definition of adverbs as wordclass is that items classified as adverbs actually have to be separated into several homogeneous groups. As a consequence, the delimitational enterprise leads to

---

[3] Example (9) is taken from an internet forum. Participants are discussing about the most convenient ways to smoke in closed spaces.

renewed interest in functional classifications. Within the set of adverbial functions, the notion of "manner adverb(ial)" plays a central, if not prototypical role in research on adverbs and adverbials, both from a formal point of view (*-ly*, *-erweise* or *-mente* are all semantically related to the marking of "manner") and from a semantic perspective. In a discussion on the different meanings encoded by converbs (i.e. adverbial constructions of verbal lexemes), König (1995) posits a general domain of circumstantial relations as semantically central for their interpretation. Within this domain, König (1995: 66) argues for a sharp distinction between "manner" and "attendant circumstance". Manner describes "two aspects of or dimensions of only one event", whereas "two independent events or actions are involved" in the case of "attendant circumstance" (König 1995: 65–66). The articulation of manner and circumstances appears to be a central issue for any semantic view on the cohesion of "adverbs" as a class.

So-called "manner adverbs" in *-ly* (English), *-ment* (French) or *-mente* (other Romance languages) can often be used as "sentence adverbs" or as assertive adverbs. In other words: classificational research must address the question of the relationship between the semantic domain of adverbials and their level of incidence. "Manner" is normally a determination of the process, and thus "adverbials of manner" should be modifiers of the VP. "High adverbials" on the other hand are modifiers of a higher layer. For instance, French *diplomatiquement*, 'diplomatically', can be used as a VP-internal modifier of manner:

(10) Elle a oublié de répondre *diplomatiquement*.
'She forgot to answer diplomatically, she forgot to make a diplomatic answer.'

But it can also be used as domain adverbial, with a partly circumstantial reading:

(11) *Diplomatiquement*, ne pas répondre était une bonne solution.
'From a diplomatic point of view, not to answer was a good idea.'

Finally, given that *diplomatiquement* can bear a latent evaluative value paraphrasable as "skilfully, though not necessarily honestly", it is possible to force a speaker-oriented reading of the adverb when it is detached to the left. This interpretation is easily accessible if the adverb is intensified, which would be clumsy with a domain adverbial, since they are supposed to be ungradable:

(12) *Très diplomatiquement*, elle a oublié de répondre.
'She forgot to answer, which I think was a very skilful decision.'

Incidence and scope variations are not compatible with the claim that *-ly* or *-mente* adverbials form a homogeneous group. Which are the levels that should be taken into consideration for a more fine-grained taxonomy? For instance, can syntax help differentiate between low and high adverbs? Or between low and high adverbial positions that can be occupied by the same lexical items? Or is the interpretation of adverbs forced by other factors such as the lexical meaning of the derivation root, or maybe the meaning of the verbal predicate?

3.2 "High adverbs"

Positional criteria can help distinguish subclasses of adverb(ial)s. Just as for peripheral adverbial clauses, these apparent "manner adverbs" can actually modify the illocutionary layer of the clause rather than the predication.

(13) *Bêtement*, il a répondu au juge.
      '*Stupidly*, he gave an answer to the judge.'   (evaluative, wide scope:
             he gave an answer to the judge, and that was stupid of him)

(14) Il a répondu *bêtement* au juge.
      'He gave a *stupid* answer to the judge.'   (manner adverbial, narrow scope)

In this case, they are to be considered as illocutionary modifiers, raising a new series of questions about incidence, scope and semantic orientation. Adverbs taking wide scope are traditionally called "sentence adverbs": an adverb, according to the traditional definition, is due to modify not only a verb, an adjective, another adverb, but also a larger unit, including the propositional content of the whole clause. Sentence adverbs are said to scope over the propositional content and to express the speaker's position relative to this content. Since they do not participate in the propositional content itself, they cannot be clefted and are not licit under the scope of the propositional negation. But this adverbial class leaves aside Greenbaum's style disjuncts (1969: 81–93) as well as the so-called domain adverbs, since both do not express any commitment of the speaker to the content. Besides, as **Aquiles Tescari Neto** points out ("Sentence adverbs don't exist!"), the propositional content is not necessarily the only relevant level of incidence for these adverbs. For instance, in example (15), depending on the prosody of the clause, *provavelmente* can take scope directly and solely over the propositional content (paraphrase 15a) or be associated with a specific constituent under contrastive stress (15b):

(15a) A Maria   cantou   provavelmente   para   o patrão
       The Maria sang   probably   for   the boss
       'Maria sang probably for her boss.'
                              (quoted from Tescari-Neto: this volume)

(15b) a. It is likely that Maria sang for her boss.
       b. It is likely for her boss that Maria sang.

This leads to the conclusion that the syntactic status of an adverb is independent from its domain of modification: sentence adverbs do not correspond to a category *per se*, but to a constructional phenomenon or a function. In languages such as English and French, this function is mainly assumed by an homogeneous morphological class. But, as shown by **Fryni Kakoyianni-Doa** ("Formal and functional features of modal adverbs in French and Modern Greek"), a comparative study of modal adverbs reveals that the suffixation of this adverbial subgroup is more diverse in Modern Greek. On the contrary, French and Modern Greek share much more similarities on the syntactic level. This finding tends to confirm the hypothesis according to which modal adverbs, and more generally sentence adverbs, are in fact functions.

Adverbial orientation is a very important criterion: it makes it possible to draw a border between adverbs expressing circumstances of time, place, cause, purpose, etc., which have no orientation, and subject-oriented adverbs and speaker-oriented adverbs. It also makes it possible to differentiate speaker-oriented adverbs, i.e. adverbs expressing the position of the speaker towards the propositional content, from subject-oriented adverbs. According to Jackendoff (1972), speaker-oriented adverbs are distinguished from manner adverbs by the fact that S' contains the surface subject and is embedded in an attributive structure containing the adjective and a reference, which may be implicit, to the speaker:

(16) *Evidently*, Frank is avoiding us.
      'It is evident (to me) that Frank is avoiding us.'

(17) *Happily*, Frank is avoiding us.
      'I am happy that Frank is avoiding us.'   (Jackendoff 1972: 69)

Subject-oriented adverbs are distinguished from manner adverbs by the fact that S' is embedded in an attributive structure containing the corresponding adjective and a nominal phrase representing the surface subject (18b to 18d, compared to the investigated adverbial construction, represented in 18a):

(18) a. Carefully, clumsily(,) John spilled the beans.
　　 b. John was careful to spill the beans.
　　 c. It was clumsy of John to spill the beans.
　　 d. John was clumsy in spilling the beans.　　　　(Jackendoff 1972: 70)

However, the notion of orientation raises a syntactic problem: a subject-oriented adverb, whether it is an agent-oriented adverb or a mental attitude adverb (Ernst 2002), says something about the subject. Speaker-oriented adverbs, on the other hand, do not necessarily say much about the "speaker", i.e. the bearer of the illocutionary act: « the status of the speaker variable in (16) and (17) is not the same. Unlike (17), example (16) cannot be paraphrased as "I am evident that Frank is avoiding us". Similarly, (19) cannot be paraphrased as "I am unfortunate that Frank is avoiding us", but only as "It is unfortunate that Frank is avoiding us:"

(19) *Unfortunately*, Frank is avoiding us.

Is it the speaker who uses the adverb to say something about the propositional content – or rather the epistemic judge? Or another bearer of propositional attitudes (Gévaudan 2011)? The answer is certainly not the same for all "speaker-oriented" adverbs, which probably have to be split into a series or even a cascade of functional subcategories, as proposed by Greenbaum for more than half a century (Greenbaum 1969, under special consideration of fronted and detached adverbs in English). This enterprise has been pursued independently by many scholars. The study of Cinque (1999) on the functional hierarchy of adverbial heads played a major role in the renewed interest in adverbial syntax in the last twenty years. Functional semantics have also delivered valuable criticisms of speaker-orientation, e.g. Franckel & Paillard (2008) and Paillard (2017), on French.

3.3 Agent- and subject-orientation: From semantic orientation to syntactic hierarchy

"Subject-orientation" is an even trickier category than speaker orientation. Ernst (2002) distinguishes agent-oriented adverbs from mental attitude adverbs:

(20)　Rudely, she left.　　　　　　　　　　　　　　　　(Ernst 2002: 57)

(21)　John wisely got out of bed.　　　　　　　　　　　(Ernst 2002: 55)

(22) John wisely lay on the bed. (Ernst 2002: 55)

(23) She calmly had left the room. (Ernst 2002: 63)

In the first case, the agent is the entity controlling the process, i.e. the entity that can "choose not to do some action, enter into a state, etc." (Ernst 2002: 55). In the second case, the subject is not the agent, but the experiencer, i.e. the entity having during the process the state of mind expressed by the adverb.

The first type of adverb differs from the manner adverb (*She left rudely*) in that the latter describes a way of doing the action denoted by the verb (*leave, get out*) or of being in the space (*lay*), but not a property of the agent during the action or the position. The second type differs from the manner adverb (*she had left the room calmly*) in that the subject does have the state of mind expressed by the adverb during the process, whereas this is not the case for the manner adverb (Ernst 2002: 66). In other words, one can leave a room calmly, without being calm during the process of leaving. This description, however, raises two problems. First of all, it is not clear whether the controller is both responsible for the process (action or position) and its continuation. Ernst uses the example of position (*John wisely lay on the bed*) to enlarge the notion of agent, but he indicates at the same time that the agent is not responsible for this position. In the former cases (*rudely, she left*; *John wisely got out of bed*), on the other hand, the agent is at the origin of the process and is responsible for its continuation too. Moreover, how can we distinguish the agent from the experiencer in *She had calmly left the room*, knowing that the subject is also the controller of the process? In addition to the notion of orientation, we face a second problem: How can the notion of control be defined in such a way as to distinguish the agent from the experiencer?

However limited and insufficient, the notion of "orientation" should not be rejected altogether, since it is very useful to distinguish manner adverbs. As Guimier (1991: 33) pointed out, in (24) *inutilement* 'in vain' is "attracted to the verb":

(24) Pierre travaille *inutilement*.
 'Peter works in vain.'

But in (25), *joyeusement* 'happily' is "attracted to the subject":

(25) Pierre travaille *joyeusement*.
 'Peter works with glee.'

Finally, in (26), *méticuleusement* 'carefully' is "attracted to the verb and the subject":

(26) Pierre travaille *méticuleusement*.
    'Peter works carefully.'

Unlike the subject-oriented adverb as defined by Ernst, the manner adverb does not relate exclusively to the subject, it also has a relationship with the predicate. It would therefore be tempting to establish a functional classification of manner adverbs:
a. The adverb is attracted to the subject, as in (25);
b. It is attracted to the verb, as in (24);
c. These forces of attraction balance each other, as in (26).

This double attraction, the fact that the manner adverb oriented towards the subject does not relate exclusively to the subject and the fact, by symmetry, that the manner adverb oriented towards the verb does not relate exclusively to the verb, make it possible to assume that the manner adverb is defined by a double relation: a relation of determination allowing one to subcategorize the action performed by the subject (relation to the verb), a relation of predication allowing one to attribute a property to the subject within the framework set by the predicate (relation to the subject). These fine-grained distinctions are at the heart of **Jian Courteaud Zhang**'s contribution on subject-oriented adverbials in Chinese, which is elaborated from a contrastive perspective ("Different types of subject-oriented adverbials in French and in Mandarin Chinese: a contrastive study"). Zhang also addresses important methodological issues for the cross-linguistic comparison of manner adverbials, sentence adverbials and semantic phenomena of subject-orientation, such as the value of classical syntactic tests that are used in several Standard Average European languages but which cannot be applied to Chinese. However, drawing on semantic and information-structural tests, Zhang manages to isolate three cross-linguistic classes of subject-oriented adverbials with different incidence properties (subject-predicate manner adverbials, subject-oriented sentence adverbials and subject-describing adverbials).

Such fine-grained descriptions make it possible to classify adverbs according to their distance from the lowest hierarchy node of the VP, and to account for functional changes due to their syntactic position in the hierarchical structure of the clause, very much in the spirit of both Dik et al. (1990) and Cinque (1999) and exemplified in this volume by the contribution of Aquiles Tescari-Neto (see above). Indeed, the elements found on the different layers are not fixed. The adverbials of instrument for example (Duplâtre 2021), are very close to manner, in that they presuppose a controller. They can even create the illusion of manner when manner is not made explicit. This phenomenon is due to the fact that manner is presupposed by action verbs (cf. Dik 1997: 228). Thus, when the slot reserved for manner is empty, i.e when manner is not realized on the surface, heterogeneous elements such as instrumental indications, but also indications of place (27), time (28), or frequency (29), etc., can occupy the slot left vacant.

(27) a. Il dort *à même le sol*.
 'He sleeps *directly on the floor*.'
 b. Il dort *à la dure*.
 'He sleeps *in the tough way*.' (i.e. without a bed)

(28) a. Ils ont agi *de nuit*.
 'They acted *nightly / by night*.'
 b. Ils ont agi *nuitamment*.
 'They acted *nightly / by night*.'

(29) a. Il boit *tous les jours*.
 'He drinks *every day*.'
 b. Il boit *quotidiennement*.
 'He drinks *everyday*.'

Unlike English *nightly*, French *nuitamment* does not only mean "during the night", but also "in secret" (Nilsson-Ehle 1941: 206–207). Thus, this adverb, which *a priori* expresses time, can, given that the controller chooses precisely to carry out the action at night, be transformed into a manner adverb and provide indications about the subject and the action carried out. This semantic shift can also be observed with French adverbs such as *brusquement* 'abruptly', which are transformed into aspectual complements (Duplâtre 2021):

(30) a. Il me parla *brusquement*.
 'He spoke to me abruptly.'
 b. Il partit *brusquement*.
 'He left abruptly.'

Finally, *brusquement* can be used to mark discourse-relative temporality ('then, all of a sudden'), which corresponds to an even higher position in the functional hierarchy:

c. Le ciel était serein; *brusquement*, l'orage éclata.
'The sky was serene; *suddenly*, the storm broke out.'

3.4 Domain adverbs and adverbials

Domain adverbials are free from any selectional restriction between them and the rest of the verb phrase. In Germanic and Romance, they are usually placed at the beginning of the utterance and are often detached from the rest of the clause. From a semantic point of view, they are used to restrict the content of the clause only to the frame of validity which they denote. As Maienborn & Schäfer (2019) point out, the content of the clause with the adverb/adverbial does not entail the content of the clause without the adverbial. Thus, it would probably be more accurate to call these adverbials "adverbials of relative validation". For instance, in the Spanish example below (ex. 31), the speaker states that selling football player Lionel Messi in the Summer of 2020 would have been the right thing to do from an economic (here: financial) point of view for his employer. However, this does not mean that it was the right thing to do in general:

(31)   Económicamente hubiera sido deseable vender a Messi en verano.
'Economically, it would have been preferable to sell Messi this Summer.'
(*El Periódico*, Dec. 3rd, 2020)

By contrast, in example (32), *económicamente* is constructed as a VP-internal manner adverbial depending from the verb *apoyar*, "to support":

(32)   La 'caja de solidaridad', creada por las entidades soberanistas en el 2017 y reconvertida en una fundación dedicada a recoger fondos para apoyar económicamente a investigados judicialmente por el 'procés', ya se está movilizando.
'The 'solidarity office', which was created by sovereignist entities in 2017 and reconverted into a foundation that raises funds aimed at supporting economically those who have been charged by the judiciary power in the circumstances of the independence process, has already begun to mobilize.'
(*El Periódico*, July 6th, 2021)

Domain adverb(ial)s and framesetting adverb(ial)s raise challenging questions as to the scope of adverbials and the relevance of the distinction between sentence adverbials or wide-scope adverbials and circumstantial adjuncts. As was already pointed out by Charolles (1997), many framesetters tend to be recruited from domains like space, time or conditions, which are also among the classical domains denoted by circumstantial adjuncts. But according to him, framesetting adverbials take scope over the whole utterance, not only the predicate, and they sometimes introduce text sequences that can encompass several utterances. In English and in Romance languages, many domain adverbials are formally akin to "manner adverbials", since they are formed with suffixes such as -*ly* or -*mente*. Once again, syntactic position helps discriminate between various interpretations, e.g. between the two readings of *económicamente* (Spanish, "economically") in the examples above.

The contribution by **Martina Werner and Nina C. Rastinger** takes a morphological stance on this issue and investigates two derivation patterns that seem to be specialized for domain adverbials ("Domain adverbials and morphology: the rivalry between -*mäßig* and -*technisch* in German"). Superficially, -*mäßig* and -*technisch* form denominal adjectives, but the authors show that they have developed an adverbial usage that is restricted to domain adverbials in the case of -*technisch*, whereas -*mäßig*-formations display uses as domain adverbials and as qualitative adverbials. Their corpus study also reveals that -*technisch* is the more productive suffixoid, so that German seems to be developing a conventionalized formation pattern that is reserved for domain adverbials designating a notional domain to which the validity of the predicate is restricted.

The syntax of domain adverbials and the absence of selectional restrictions between them and the content of the clause, point to an "outsider status" for adverbials, which are not integrated into the core structure of the verbal phrase. This is in line with the terminological choices made by scholars for whom adverbials express a point of view (Mørdrup 1976, Molinier & Lévrier 2000) or designate a limit (Nilsson-Ehle 1941, Bartsch 1972, Nøjgaard 1993), a frame (Schlyter 1977) or a domain (Bellert 1977, Nolke 1990, Guimier 1996, Ernst 2004, Maienborn & Schäfer 2019, Grübl 2020, De Cesare et al. 2020): the meaning of the domain adverbial is not part of the state of affairs denoted by the clause. It helps characterise the mental space against the background of which that very state of affairs is set (Fauconnier 1984). In Cognitive Grammar terms (Langacker 1987), domain adverbials are used to *ground* a propositional unit made up of the predicate, its arguments, circumstantial adjuncts, and possibly even (some) epistemic modals. According to Duplâtre (2018), domain adverbials are secondary predicates mapped onto the clausal unit as a whole. In turn, this operation yields a new, complex discourse unit, of which the domain adverbial is a part.

A major question to solve here is the definition of what is to be called a "domain of validity". Some scholars lump together all adverbs/adverbials expressing not only a notional domain, but also a point of view, a frame or a limit (Charolles 1997, Franckel & Paillard 2008). Thus, the proposed adverbial class

would include English items like *politically, botanically, linguistically*, but also *personally, in my opinion, essentially, in practice, in a sense*, etc. At least at first glance, the result is a rather heterogeneous class, and further internal distinctions are needed, as demonstrated by Grübl (2020). The contribution by **Anna-Maria De Cesare** ("*Framing, segmenting, indexing:* Towards a functional account of Romance domain adverbs in written texts") addresses a broad range of phenomena and extensively discusses previous accounts in the literature. This chapter offers a comprehensive synthesis, according to which it is possible to distinguish three main classes within this broad set:
- domain adverbs expressing a notional domain;
- viewpoint adverbs or adverbials, which in addition to domain adverbs/adverbials, include adverbs such as *personally* and adverbial expressions such as *in my opinion*;
- limitative adverbs, which, besides domain adverbs, encompass terms such as *essentially, globally, strictly* and adverbial expressions such as *in theory, in a sense*, etc.

4 Concluding remarks

The studies presented in this volume present converging cross-linguistic data to suggest that traditional definitions insisting on morphological invariability and dependency from the verb or the verbal phrase should be taken with much caution. The same holds for binary distinctions such as predicate adverb vs. sentence adverb or for labels that may be erroneously taken as homogeneous categories, such as "subject-oriented adverbs" or "domain adverbs". However, there are also converging signals that adverbial morphology is not a jungle void of any regularity: there are indeed language-specific morphological types of adverbs corresponding to homogenous functional sets, as shown by Delhem and Sanchez-Stockhammer & Unwin on English, but also to some extent by Courteaud Zhang, who shows that in Chinese, morphosyntactic procedures at the interface of syntax and derivation are used to distinguish thoroughly between subject-oriented sentence adverbials and all kinds of predicate-internal subject-oriented adverbials. At the micro-functional level, Werner & Rastinger demonstrate the rise of a specialized formation pattern for adverbials of notional domain in German. In all three languages, morphological regularities can be studied while keeping some distance towards traditional parts-of-speech models. This emancipation of adverbial morphology from parts-of-speech distinctions is also highlighted in the contribution by Ignazio Mirto, who lays the foundation of paradigms of competing morphosyntactic procedures corresponding to neighbouring functional properties. The determination of a specific word-class of "adverbs" should not be the starting point of the study; it is much rather a possible result of the analysis of sets of morphosyntactic properties associated with semantic regularities. For this reason, it is highly important to establish a set of cross-linguistically valid syntactic tests. The contrastive contributions by Kakoyanni-Doa and Courteaud Zhang, addressing Greek and Chinese respectively, both discard several usual tests of Romance and Germanic adverbial research, but they also confirm that the various functional types of adverbials can be distinguished alongside properties located at the interface of syntax and information-structure (most prominently negation, focalization, interrogation).

All these data suggest that functional semantics are the starting point. In other words: adverbials should be used as the more basic concept, before determining whether a functional (sub-)class has partly conventionalized into a lexical class. Adverbs form an unstable, secondary part-of-speech even in languages that supposedly display a morphological class of adverbials, as shown by Albers's study of how stable German adverbs can be re-adjectivized under the pressure of ambiguous constructions: it is not only adverbs that arise from the specialization of adjectival forms; morphologically simple adverbs can fall into the adjectival category where they had never belonged. Thus, there is no unidirectional movement towards the establishing of a barrier between adjectives and adverbs.

Among the semantic regularities that can be observed, a common denominator is the notion of attribution onto the predication. This attribution may take the form of proper determination, but also of secondary predication, either onto a constituent of the proposition or onto the predication as a whole, operating from different levels. The contributions by Tescari-Neto and Kakoyanni-Doa highlight the fact that notions such as "sentence adverbials" or "modal adverbials" should be taken *cum grano salis*, yet they also isolate stable semantic properties as well as a shared position in the functional hierarchy of the clause. Chinese may be radically different in its morphosyntactic characteristics, yet here, too, a thin line of semantic properties linked to incidence but not reducible to it can be distinguished along lines that are similar to those of Romance, for instance. The same is true for "domain adverbials", as was shown by Werner & Rastinger, who were able to isolate a formally consistent set of adverbials of notional domain, and by De Cesare, whose syntactic and semantic study paves the way to a clearcut, three-way functional typology of domain adverbials. As a result, it appears that adverbs become a problem only if their categorial definition and their classification is taken for granted from the beginning. Starting from a comparative concept of adverbial modification, more fine-grained functional and formal sets of properties emerge, which do not define one "part-of-speech", but several functional classes that bear a family resemblance and display noticeable similarities throughout language families. It is hard to claim that any other "word-class" is significantly more consistent than that from a cross-linguistic point of view. In this respect, adverbs do not make up a "dustbin category": they only invite us to more humility in the definition of categories in general.

References

Apollonius Dyscolus [Apollonius Dyscole]. 2021. *Traité des adverbes: Introduction générale, édition critique, traduction française et commentaire par Lionel Dumarty*. Paris: Vrin.
Bartsch, Renate. 1972. *Adverbialsemantik*. Frankfurt am Main: Athenäum Verlag.
Beauzée, Nicolas. 1767. *Grammaire générale*. Tome 1. Paris: Barbou.
Bellert, Irena. 1977. On semantic and distributional properties of sentential adverbs. *Linguistic Inquiry* 8(2). 337–351.
Broquet, Sylvain. 2005. Apollonius Dyscole et l'adverbe. *Histoire Épistémologie Language* 27(2). 121–140.
Cardinaletti, Anna & Michal Starke. 1999. A typology of structural deficiency: on the three grammatical classes. In Henk Van Riemsdijk (ed.), *Eurotyp*. Volume 5/Part 1: *Clitics in the Languages of Europe*, 145–234. Berlin: De Gruyter.
Charolles, Michel. 1997. L'encadrement du discours: Univers, champs, domaines et espaces. *Cahiers de Recherche Linguistique LANDISCO* 6. 1–73.
Chomsky, Noam. 1965. *Aspects of the theory of syntax*. Cambridge/Massachusetts: The M.I.T. Press.
Cinque, Guglielmo. 1999. *Adverbs and functional heads*. Oxford: Oxford University Press.
Croft, William. 1990. *Syntactic Categories and Grammatical Relations*. Chicago and London: The University of Chicago Press.
Croft, William. 2001. *Radical Construction Grammar*. Oxford: Oxford University Press.
De Cesare, Anna-Maria, Ana Albom, Doria Cimmino & Marta Lupica Spagnolo. 2020. Domain adverbials in the news. A corpus-based contrastive study of English, German, French, Italian and Spanish. *Languages in Contrast* 20(1). 31–57
Di Benedetto, Vincenzo. 1959. Dioniso Trace et la Techne a lui attribuita. *Annali della Scuola Normale Superiore di Pisa* 2(27). 169–210.
Dik, Simon C., Kees Hengeveld, Elseline Vester & Co Vet. 1990. The hierarchical structure of the clause and the typology of adverbial satellites. In Jan Nuyts, Machtelt Bolkestein, & Co Vet (eds.), *Layers and levels of representation in language theory: A functional view*, 25–70. Amsterdam: John Benjamins.
Dik, Simon C. 1997. *The Theory of Functional Grammar. First Part: The Structure of the Clause*. 2nd ed. Berlin/New York: De Gruyter.
Duplâtre, Olivier. 2018. *Incidence de second degré et adverbe. Utilité de cette notion dans la redéfinition syntaxique de l'adverbe*. Sorbonne Université: Habilitation thesis.

Duplâtre, Olivier. 2021. Un constituant invisible obligatoire. In Catherine Moreau & Jean Albrespit, *Complément, complémentation, complétude-2 – Du lacunaire au complet* (= Travaux linguistiques du CERLICO 32), 85–99. Rennes: Presses Universitaires de Rennes.

Dumarty, Lionel. 2021. Commentaire. In Apollonius Dyscole, *Traité des adverbes: Introduction générale, édition critique, traduction française et commentaire par Lionel Dumarty*, 185–509. Paris: Vrin.

Eisenberg, Peter. 2013. *Grundriss der deutschen Grammatik: Der Satz*. Stuttgart: Metzler.

Elsner, Daniela. 2013. Adverbial morphology in German: Formations with -*weise*/-*erweise*. In Karin Pittner, Daniela Elsner & Fabian Barteld (eds.), *Adverbs: functional and diachronic aspects*, 101–132. Amsterdam: John Benjamins.

Ernst, Thomas. 2002. *The syntax of adjuncts*. Cambridge University Press.

Ernst, Thomas. 2004. Domain adverbs and the syntax of adjuncts. In Jennifer R. Austin, Stefan Engelberg & Gisa Rauh (eds.), *Adverbials: The interplay between meaning, context, and syntactic structure*, 103–129. Amsterdam: John Benjamins.

Ernst, Thomas. 2009. Speaker-oriented adverbs. *Natural Language and Linguistic Theory* 27. 497–544.

Fauconnier, Gilles. 1984. *Espaces mentaux. Aspects de la construction du sens dans les langues naturelles*. Paris: Les éditions de minuit.

Franckel, Jean-Jacques & Denis Paillard. 2008. Mots du discours, adéquation et point de vue: l'exemple de *réellement, en réalité, en effet, effectivement*. *Estudos Linguísticos/Linguistic Studies* (Lisboa) 2. 255–274.

Gerhalter, Katharina. 2020. *Paradigmas y polifuncionalidad. La diacronía de preciso / precisamente, justo / justamente, exacto / exactamente y cabal / cabalmente*. Berlin/Boston: De Gruyter.

Gévaudan, Paul. 2011. Sprachliche Modalität zwischen Illokution und Polyphonie. *Romanistisches Jahrbuch* 61. 31–66.

Gleason, Henry Allan. 1965. *Linguistics and English grammar*. New York: Holt, Rinehart and Winston.

Greenbaum, Sidney. 1969. *Studies in English* adverbial *usage*. London: Longman.

Grübl, Klaus. 2020. What are 'domain adverbs' and what functions do they have? Paper presented in the online Conference Adverbs and Adverbials: Categorial Issues, org. by Olivier Duplâtre and Pierre-Yves Modicom, 2.10.2020.

Guimier, Claude. 1991. Peut-on définir l'adverbe? In Claude Guimier & Pierre Larcher (eds.), *Les États de l'adverbe*, 11–34. Rennes: Presses Universitaires de Rennes.

Guimier, Claude. 1996. *Les adverbes du français. Le cas des adverbes en -ment*. Paris: Ophrys.

Haegeman, Liliane. 2012. *Adverbial clauses, main clause phenomena and the composition of the left periphery*. Oxford: Oxford University Press.

Hallonsten Halling, Pernilla. 2018. Adverbs: A typological study of a disputed category. Dissertation. Stockholm University.

Haser, Verena & Bernd Kortmann. 2006. Adverbs. In Keith Brown (ed.), *Encyclopedia of language and linguistics*, 66–69. Boston: Elsevier.

Haspelmath, Martin. 1995. Word-class-changing inflection and morphological theory. *Yearbook of Morphology 1995*. 43–66.

Haspelmath, Martin. 2001. Word classes and parts of speech. In Neil J. Smelser & Paul B. Baltes (eds.), *Encyclopedia of the Social and Behavioral Sciences*, 16538–16545. Oxford: Pergamon.

Haspelmath, Martin. 2012. How to compare major word-classes across the world's languages. *UCLA Working Papers in Linguistics, Theories of Everything* 17(16). 109–130.
Haspelmath, Martin & Ekkehard König (eds.). 1995. *Converbs in Cross-Linguistic Perspective: Structure and Meaning of Adverbial Verb Forms – Adverbial Participles, Gerunds*. Berlin: De Gruyter.
Hengeveld, Kees. 1992a. Parts of speech. In Michael Fortescue, Peter Harder & Lars Kristoffersen (eds.), *Layered Structure and Reference in a Functional Perspective*, 29–53. (Papers from the functional grammar conference in Copenhagen 1990). Amsterdam: John Benjamins.
Hengeveld, Kees. 1992b. *Non-verbal predication: theory, typology, diachrony*. Berlin: Mouton de Gruyter.
Hengeveld, Kees, Jan Rijkhoff & Anna Siewierska. 2004. Parts-of-speech systems and word order. *Journal of Linguistics* 40. 527–570.
Hengeveld, Kees & Marieke Valstar. 2010. Parts-of-speech systems and lexical subclasses. *Linguistics in Amsterdam* 3(1). 2–25.
Hengeveld, Kees. 2013. Parts-of-speech systems as a basic typological determinant. In Jan Rijkhoff & Eva van Lier (eds.), *Flexible word classes: Typological studies of underspecified parts of speech*, 31–55. Oxford: Oxford University Press.
Hopper, Paul J. & Sandra A. Thompson. 1984. The discourse basis for lexical categories in universal grammar. *Language* 60/4. 703–752.
Hummel, Martin & Salvador Valera (eds.). 2017. *Adjective Adverb Interfaces in Romance*. Amsterdam: John Benjamins.
Hummel, Martin. 2018. La structure 'verbe + adjectif'. Parler vrai, dire juste, faire simple et compagnie. *Revue Romane* 53(2). 261–296.
Hummel, Martin. 2019. The Third Way: Prepositional Adverbials in the Diachrony of Romance. *Romanische Forschungen* 131(2). 145–185.
Jackendoff, Ray S. 1972. *Semantic interpretation in generative grammar*. Cambridge/Massachusetts/London: The MIT Press.
Lallot, Jean. 2003. *La Grammaire de Denys le Thrace*. 2nd ed. Paris: CNRS Éditions.
Lehmann, Christian. 2015. *Thoughts on grammaticalization*. Revised edition. Berlin: Language Science Press.
Lyons, John. 1968. *Introduction to theoretical linguistics*. Cambridge University Press.
Macrobius, Ambrosius Theodorus. 1848. De Differentiis et Societatibus Graeci Latinique Verbi. In Ludovicus Ianus [Ludwig von Jan] (ed.), *Macrobii Ambrosii Theodosii Opera quae supersunt, I*. 227–277. Quedlinburg: Gottfried Basse Verlag.
Maienborn, Claudia & Martin Schäfer. 2019. Adverbs and adverbials. In Claudia Maienborn, Klaus von Heusinger & Paul Portner (eds.), *Semantics – Lexical Structures and Adjectives*, 477–514. Berlin: De Gruyter.
Molinier, Christian & Françoise Lévrier. 2000. *Grammaire des adverbes. Description des formes en -ment*. Genève/Paris: Droz.
Mørdrup, Ole. 1976. *Une analyse non-transformationnelle des adverbes en -ment*. (Études romanes de l'Université de Copenhague 11). Copenhagen: Akademisk forlag.
Nilsson-Ehle, Hans. 1941. *Les Adverbes en -ment compléments d'un verbe en français moderne*. Lund: Gleerup/Copenhagen: Munksgaard.
Nølke, Henning. 1990. Les adverbiaux contextuels: problèmes de classification. *Langue française* 88. 12–27.

Nøjgaard, Morten. 1992/1993/1995. *Les Adverbes français – Essai de description fonctionnelle*. Copenhagen: Munksgaard.
Paillard, Denis. 2017. Scène énonciative et types de marqueurs discursifs. *Langages* 207. 17–32.
Pérennec, Marcel. 2002. *Sur le texte: énonciation et mots du discours en allemand contemporain*. Lyon: Presses Universitaires de Lyon.
Pinkster, Harm. 1972. *On Latin Adverbs*. Amsterdam: North-Holland Publishing Company.
Pinkster, Harm. 2005. *Histoire Épistémologie Langage* 27(2). 179–180.
Pittner, Karin. 1999. *Adverbiale im Deutschen: Untersuchungen zu ihrer Stellung und Interpretation*. Tübingen: Stauffenburg.
Pittner, Karin. 2015. Between inflection and derivation: Adverbial suffixes in English and German. In Karin Pittner, Daniela Elsner & Fabian Barteld (eds.), *Adverbs: functional and diachronic aspects*, 133–156. Amsterdam: John Benjamins.
Quirk, Randolph, Sidney Greenbaum, Geoffrey Leech & Jan Svartvik. 1972. *A comprehensive Grammar of English*. London: Longman.
Ramat, Paolo & Davide Ricca. 1994. Prototypical adverbs: On the scalarity/radiality of the notion Adverb. *Rivista di Linguistica*. 289–326.
Rauh, Gisa. 2015. Adverbs as a linguistic category (?). In Karin Pittner, Daniela Elsner & Fabian Barteld (eds.), *Adverbs: functional and diachronic aspects*, 19–45. Amsterdam: John Benjamins.
Schäfer, Martin. 2008. *Deutsche adverbiale Adjektive oder was es heißt, ein Adverbial der Art und Weise zu sein*. Manuscript, Unpublished. Leipzig. URL: https://tinyurl.com/7smsxuxu (last retrieved Sept. 21st, 2021).
Schlyter, Suzanne. 1977. *La place des adverbes en -ment en français*. Universität Konstanz. Dissertation.
Schmöe, Friederike. 2002. *Das Adverb – Zentrum und Peripherie einer Wortklasse*. Wien: Praesens.
Schneider, Gerlinde, Christopher Pollin, Katharina Gerhalter & Martin Hummel. 2020. *Adjective-Adverb Interfaces in Romance*. Open-Access Database (=AAIF-Database). http://gams.uni-graz.at/context:aaif (last retrieved Sept. 21st, 2021).
Talmy, Leonard. 1991. Path to realization: A typology of event conflation. *Berkeley Working Papers in Linguistics*. 480–519.

I Delimitational approaches

1 Consistency of the class

Romain Delhem
The incoherence of the English adverb class

Abstract: The various grammatical descriptions of English do not agree on the limits of the adverb class, which is often seen as a residual category. In order to give it some more coherence, a multivariate analysis of English units based on morphosyntactic criteria was carried out, in accordance with the idea that a word class should only include units that are similar enough. After comparing those units with other word classes, the results show that place adverbs should instead be classified as prepositions, and flat adverbs as adjectives, thus bringing greater coherence to the remaining English adverb class, whose prototypes are manner, frequency and modality adverbs.

Keywords: Adjectives, adverbs, prepositions, statistical clustering, taxonomy

Introduction

Every description of the English language uses word classes to categorize units; word classes (or *lexical categories*, or *parts of speech*) are, according to Huddleston & Pullum (2002: 20), one of the axioms of syntactical analysis. Among these classes, the label 'adverb' is used by almost every reference grammar dealing with English (e.g. Huddleston & Pullum 2002; Quirk *et al.* 1985), although Fries (1952) is an exception.

However, there is unanimous recognition in these works that the class is an extremely heterogeneous one, because it is made up of all the units that linguists have no good reason to classify otherwise. Let us take the following example, taken from the Corpus of Contemporary American English (COCA):

(1) And they **also** believed in something **very** important – that when you've worked **hard**, and done **well**, and you **finally** walked through that doorway of opportunity, you don't slam it shut behind you. (*Applause*.) **No** – you reach **back**, and you give other folks the same chances that helped you succeed.
⟨COCA 2012: BLOG⟩

Romain Delhem, Université Clermont Auvergne, romain.delhem@uca.fr

The seven units in bold are classified as adverbs by most authors, but differ in three respects:
(i) They have different forms: some are monomorphemic (*also*, *very*, *no*, *back*), some are morphologically complex (*finally*), while others share their form with an adjective (*hard* and *well*).
(ii) They have different distributions: some only modify verbs (*hard*, *back*), some only modify adjectives and adverbs (*very*) and others can modify units that belong to all these categories (*finally*).
(iii) They have different meanings: they express manner (*hard*, *well*), time (*finally*), place (*back*), degree (*very*), addition (*also*) and negation (*no*).

According to Haspelmath (2001: 16543), "adverbs are the most problematic major word class because they are extremely heterogeneous in all languages", including English. The problem is that not only does this word class exhibit heterogeneity among its members, but its very limits are not agreed upon by all linguists. Thus, in some works (e.g. Fries 1952; Huddleston & Pullum 2002), units such as *very* and *back* would not be grouped with adverbs but would either be put in another class or attributed a distinct class altogether.

The goal of this article is to assess the validity of the adverb class and its limits by comparing different arguments and classification methods. After briefly reviewing the place of adverbs in various accounts of the English language (§1), I will describe different ways of establishing word classes and argue for an approach in which word classes are used only if some units are sufficiently similar (§2). Following these guidelines, I will put forward a multivariate analysis of the 200 most frequently used units that are classified as adverbs (§3). The results show that the class is indeed very heterogeneous, and a comparison with other word classes calls for a recategorization of a considerable number of those units (§4).

1 Adverbs in grammatical descriptions of English

As mentioned earlier, adverbs have been renowned for being an extremely heterogeneous class. At least since the *Art of Grammar* in the 2nd century BCE, attributed to Dionysus Thrax (Davidson 1874: 14–15), adverbs (ἐπίρρημα, literally 'on a verb') have been defined as invariable units that modify verbs. This extremely broad definition essentially makes adverbs "a miscellaneous or residual category – the category to which words are assigned if they do not satisfy the more specific criteria for nouns, verbs, adjectives, prepositions, and conjunctions" (Huddleston & Pullum 2002: 563). This led several linguists to try to reduce the extension of the category so as to make it more coherent. Some accounts of the adverb category thus depart, sometimes greatly, from traditional description, but linguists disagree over which units should be recategorized.

Table 1 below shows how some invariable units are classified in reference grammar books. Note that some authors (like Eastwood 2002) were not included because most of them exactly follow Quirk *et al.*'s (1985) classification.

Table 1: Classification of degree, manner and place elements in grammatical descriptions of English.

	very	slowly	abroad
Jespersen (1924)		particle	
Fries (1952)	group D	class 4	
Quirk *et al.* (1985)		adverb	
Huddleston & Pullum (2002)	adverb		preposition
Kolln & Funk (2012)	qualifier	adverb	

Among units that are traditionally classified as adverbs are also the deictic time elements *today*, *tomorrow*, *yesterday* and *tonight*. Most authors consider them adverbs because they are invariable and express time. On the other hand, Payne & Huddleston (2002: 429) rather classify them as pronouns, since they can appear in subject function, have a genitive form and are unable to take determiners.

As Table 1 shows, three cases may be distinguished according to whether manner elements (*slowly*) are grouped with degree elements (*very*), place elements (*abroad*), or both. Adverbs in traditional accounts of English grammar, such as Quirk *et al.* (1985), tend to constitute a very large category comprising invariable elements that do not have any complement. This broad classification was questioned in at least two ways. Fries (1952)[1] and Kolln & Funk (2012) choose to place degree elements in a distinct category (*intensifiers* or *qualifiers*). They do so on distributional grounds: units like *very* and *rather* cannot modify verbs, only adjectives and adverbs. On the other hand, manner and place elements can modify verbs, which is enough to put them in the same category.

Conversely, Huddleston & Pullum (2002) choose to remove from the adverb class many units traditionally called *place adverbs* and *time adverbs* and to group them together with prepositions. They argue that these units have the same distribution as prepositions and preposition phrases, as shown in (2).

---

[1] Fries (1952) makes a distinction between *classes*, i.e. open word classes, and *groups*, i.e. closed word classes. They are differentiated with numbers and letters, respectively.

(2) a. Economists **abroad** ⟨outside the country /   [modifier in NP]
 *externally⟩ will continue to demand austerity
 and further unemployment. ⟨COCA 1990: SPOK⟩
 b. Someone else put it **there** ⟨near the entrance /   [complement of *put*]
 *adjacently⟩. ⟨COCA 2015: TV⟩
 c. I need to talk to Kyle right **now** ⟨after the show /   [modification by
 *immediately⟩. ⟨COCA 2010: TV⟩   *right*]

Their only difference resides in their complementation, which is not a good argument in favor of a separate category, according to Huddleston & Pullum.[2] In this respect, they follow Burton-Roberts (1991) and Lee (1998), who coined the term *intransitive preposition* for such cases. As a consequence, they leave within the adverb category all the units that can fill the function of units formed from adjectives by adding *-ly*.

What can be learned from these different accounts is that linguists almost always use a distinct category of units that can modify verbs, and this category always includes elements that express the way an action is carried out. If one accepts to call this category 'adverbs' (or another term like 'class 4', *à la* Fries), then adverbs seem to have those manner elements as central members. However, apart from those prototypical elements, the boundaries of this class are far from consensual, which is mainly due to the way word classes are established in general.

2 Word classes and their delimitation

2.1 Top-down and bottom-up approaches

As far as I know, all syntactic analyses of the English language posit the existence of word classes. Along with constituents and syntactic functions, word classes are part of the axioms of syntax (Huddleston & Pullum 2002: 20): if these three concepts are not accepted, then no syntactic analysis is apparently possible.

Even within theoretical approaches which argue that syntax is not distinct from morphology or the lexicon, like constructionist approaches, word classes

---

2 The authors argue, for instance, that *know* can be complemented by a noun phrase, a clause or nothing but is not thought to belong to three different classes, whereas *before* has the same possibilities of complementation and is traditionally treated as a preposition, a conjunction and an adverb, respectively.

are used. Langacker (2008: 93–103) uses them because they have a conceptual foundation, while other constructionists like Goldberg (2006: 51) consider them essential to explain why constructional slots accept some kinds of units but not others. These classes are generally needed in linguistic analysis to predict the morphosyntactic behavior of specific units and are probably somehow interiorized by speakers (cf. Berko 1958 and the "*wug* test"[3]). However, the way those units should be grouped together is not agreed upon among linguists.

Word classes have traditionally been inherited from Greek and Latin grammatical description. Since then, they have barely changed, apart from the substantive class, which was divided into nouns and adjectives, and the determinative[4] class, which was expanded or created altogether. Most grammatical works use between 8 and 10 classes and assume that all words must fall into one of them (Huddleston & Pullum 2002: 21–22). In this sort of "top-down" approach, the linguist thus establishes a set of limited, pre-defined categories. The inventory of the linguistic units of a given language is divided *a priori* and every linguistic unit is then assigned to (preferably) one category. The problem with the top-down approach is that it cannot account for non-prototypical members of a class, or unclassifiable units:

(3) a. Brothers and sisters, our Lord Jesus Himself warned us, "Beware of false prophets who come in sheep's clothing," for inwardly, they are ravenous wolves. ‹COCA 2017: MOV›
 b. I'm a nice person! And anyone who doesn't think so can have a sock in the eye. ‹COCA 2012: BLOG›

The unit *beware* is usually classified as a verb (Huddleston & Pullum 2002: 1186; Quirk et al. 1985: 152) despite the fact that it is highly defective synchronically; indeed, it can only be encountered in a plain form and in directive contexts (i.e. in imperative constructions and after strong deontic modals):

---

3 In this test, children are presented with a nonsense word, *wug*, in a nominal context. Older children spontaneously use a plural suffix (*wugs*) when faced with a plural syntactic context (*there are two___*). This shows that speakers can spontaneously apply a certain number of grammatical processes to a word once they have identified it as a noun, for instance.
4 I follow Huddleston & Pullum (2002: 24-25), who clearly distinguish *determinatives* (a word class) and *determiners* (a syntactic function). These two concepts mainly overlap, but some determinatives can be used as heads of NPs (**this** *is it*) while some determiners are not determinatives (**Sandra's** *car*).

(4) a. I can only warn you, not teach you. **Beware** of what you dream for. ‹COCA 2004: MOV›
b. Santorum (and most of the Rs from top to bottom as well) should **beware** of squirrels and chipmunks. ‹COCA 2012: WEB›
c. *He has **bewared** of pickpockets.

Verbs are the only category whose members can enter into those syntactic contexts as well, hence the classification of *beware*; but if one chooses to follow it, then one has to admit that *beware* is at best a highly non-prototypical verb. Because word classes help predict the morphosyntactic behavior of a given unit, it will be necessary to add a large set of exceptions for *beware* so as to explain why it lacks some typical verbal forms.

In example [3ii], *so* functions as a complement of *think* and replaces a clause whose propositional content is identical to a previous clause; it is the equivalent of *anyone who doesn't think [(that) I'm a nice person]*. This prompted Quirk *et al.* (1985: 880–881) to call it "pro-clause *so*". It is difficult to assign pro-clause *so* a word class: other adverbs cannot be used as complements of epistemic verbs, and pronouns can function as subjects, which is not the case of pro-clause *so*. This prompts Huddleston & Pullum (2002: 1536) to state that it would be unproductive to artificially assign a word class to this unit. Therefore, working with a limited number of pre-established word classes can be problematic, because a few exceptional units might not be subject to the rules applying to the category they are assigned to by default, and because some units may have a unique syntactic behavior.

Conversely, one could classify units not by using predefined categories, but by observing recurrent behavior among linguistic units – a "bottom-up" approach. In this case, such units are compared according to the grammatical properties they exhibit and are only grouped together if they manifest the same set of (morphological, syntactic or semantic) properties in full or in a non-negligible part. In that case a small word class is created and if the same conditions apply, it can further integrate other units or fuse with other classes to create a larger category.

This approach thus leaves the door open for unclassified units, like pro-clause *so*. It makes it also possible for a unit to be gradient (Aarts 2007), i.e. to exhibit properties from several categories. The unit *near*, for instance, has both adjectival and prepositional properties:
- Like other adjectives, it has a comparative and superlative form (*nearer, nearest*), it can be derived into an adverb (*nearly*) and it can be modified by degree units (**very** *near, near* **enough,** **as** *near* **as possible**);
- Like other prepositions, it is complemented by NPs (*near* **the building**), it can function as a complement of motion verbs (**put** *it* / **go** *near the door*) and it can be modified by *right* (**right** *near the entrance*).

The bottom-up approach also relies on generalization (Crystal 1967: 26–27): a word class is created and used only if it is powerful enough to account for the morphosyntactic behavior or the semantic content of a given linguistic unit.

Because of this, I think it preferable to adopt a bottom-up approach when studying word classes. Such categories are not objective or directly observable: they are abstract constructs used by linguists to facilitate grammatical description. Since they are merely the result of an operation of categorization based on analogy, they should be used not as an end in itself, but to describe a language more efficiently when a number of units exhibit certain properties that are relevant to grammatical description.

2.2 Lumpers and splitters

As mentioned earlier, small classes can be fused together if the resulting category is believed to be relevant enough for grammatical description. Systematic fusion of classes may therefore result in a limited number of categories. There is a great deal of variation among classifications, however; Table 2 below expands on Table 1 and shows how linguists classify various invariable units of English.

Table 2: Invariable word classes in grammatical descriptions of English.

	very	slowly	abroad	from	while	whether	and	oh
Jespersen (1924)	particle							
Fries (1952)	group D	class 4		group F		group J	group E	group K
Quirk et al. (1985)	adverb			preposition	conjunction			interjection
Biber et al. (2002)	adverb			preposition	subordinator		coordinator	insert
Huddleston & Pullum (2002)	adverb			preposition		subordinator	coordinator	interjection
Kolln & Funk (2012)	qualifier	adverb		preposition	conjunction	expletive	conjunction	interjection

As Table 2 shows, there is no consensus on the way English invariable units should be classified. Linguists use from one (Jespersen) to six categories (Fries and Kolln & Funk) to describe them. Although these linguists presumably have access to the same data, i.e. how linguistic units behave and combine with other units, they chose different classifications. In scientific disciplines involving classification, a distinction is often made between *lumpers* and *splitters*. The former tend to establish very large categories, while the latter prefer smaller and more numerous classes; in Table 2, Jespersen and Fries could be seen as typical examples of a lumper and a splitter, respectively. Both approaches have their advantages and drawbacks.

Lumping tends to emphasize common characteristics between units. By taking into account only a small number of criteria to classify units (only less than a dozen), lumpers allow for less cumbersome grammatical systems. The problem with lumping is that the classes are so large that they become almost useless. Knowing that a unit is a particle (in Jespersen's terms) only gives an indication on its morphological behavior, not its syntactic behavior. In order to account for specific properties, a lumper will have to rely heavily on subclasses.

Conversely, splitting consists in translating any difference in behavior into a distinct class. For instance, the fact that some degree elements cannot modify verbs is a sufficient reason to create a specific class for splitters. This allows for a more precise system in which each class is homogeneous because its members exhibit the same morphosyntactic behavior. However, there is theoretically no limit to how many distinct classes one can create. Any difference might trigger the partition of a category, leading to a very complex descriptive system that might be hard to handle, especially for learners.

Choosing one approach over the other therefore depends on whether one wants to draw attention to the similarities or the differences between units. In the former case, the system will achieve generality; in the latter, it will achieve accuracy. At first sight, one could just say that the choice between broad and narrow categories is not a real one. For instance, despite their differences, lexical verbs and auxiliary verbs are often ultimately thought to belong to the same class because they have properties that distinguish them quite sharply from other classes. Therefore, there is no contradiction in saying that adverbs, prepositions, conjunctions and interjections are subclasses of "invariable units" or "particles" (or that "invariable units" is the superclass encompassing adverbs, prepositions, conjunctions and interjections). After all, this choice is only about what one's preferred scale of analysis is.

Yet another problem arises with linguists who choose an intermediate number of categories. Indeed, a similar number of classes does not ensure that these classes will include the exact same members. For instance, Biber et al. (2002) and Huddleston & Pullum (2002) have opted for five classes of invariable units, but the authors give those classes different boundaries. In particular, Huddleston & Pullum's preposition class is more extensive than Biber et al.'s because they gave priority to a different set of grammatical properties.

Variation in classification results from the fact that linguists choose to weigh their criteria of classification differently. In the end, the boundaries of the word classes one uses depend on the properties that are deemed more relevant than others; they are therefore the result of a completely subjective choice.

2.3 A third way of classifying

There is probably no right answer to how far one should split or lump word classes, because it depends on the scale of analysis that a linguist will choose. What can be solved in a less subjective way is which units one should group together in priority.

In line with the theoretical principles exposed in §2, I propose a third way of classifying units, which is often called *clustering*. Under this approach, the categorization of units is done step by step. If units A and B have more in common than do A and C or B and C, then any group that one might want to create will include A and B before anything else. This means that no priority is given to any property: they all equally participate in determining how close or far two units are. Thus a common way to mark a complement (e.g. with a specified preposition like *of*) is given the same weight as a common inflectional suffix (e.g. a plural marker). Any weighting of a property would have been a necessarily subjective choice, hence a debatable one.

Note that this approach does not dictate HOW MANY common characteristics are needed for several units to be considered part of the same class. This is up to the linguist and the way they conceptualize categories. What this approach allows for is ending up having the same subcategories when breaking down large categories. With this method, a word class will be a set of units which will be close enough to each other and/or far enough away from other groups. This means that there will be potential isolates, i.e. units that will be so far from others that they cannot be readily categorized (e.g. pro-clause *so*), and potential hybrids, i.e. units that will lie between classes (e.g. *near*).

Since one may potentially compare a large number of units according to a large number of grammatical properties, it is preferable to use an automated way of establishing word classes that follows the principles exposed above. I will now present a statistical method of clustering linguistic units that I will apply to English units traditionally classified as adverbs.

3 A multivariate analysis of English adverbs

3.1 Criteria of distinction

As mentioned earlier, adverbs are extremely heterogeneous and linguists choose to classify them very differently. My goal here is to try to minimize the subjectivity of such classifications and to group together units that behave in an identical or very similar way.

To do so, I listed as many criteria of variation as possible that are displayed by units traditionally called 'adverbs' in English. I used three main types of criteria:
- The morphology of the units, i.e. their internal structure and their potential (inflectional or derivational) affixes;
- Their syntactic distribution (Creissels 2006: 16), also known as their passive valence (Iordanskaja & Mel'čuk 2009), i.e. the syntactic contexts they can be put into;
- The range of their dependents, also known as their active valence, i.e. their potential complements and modifiers.

The decision to exclude the semantic category of adverbs as a criterion of distinction was based on two observations.
(i) There is no right answer as to what level of precision is needed. Speed adverbs (*fast*, *rapidly*, *slowly*) are for instance classified as manner adverbs by Mittwoch et al. (2002: 670); one can either annotate them as manner adverbs, which denies their semantic and syntactic specificity, or as speed adverbs, which involves trying to find a semantic subcategory for all manner adverbs.
(ii) More often than not, adverbs can have several interpretations: *truly*, for instance, can express manner (*I will speak truly*), degree (*I do not truly understand what this is about*), modality (*this is truly a miracle*) and illocution (*I truly do not expect you to come*), which makes it hard to assign a definite category to this adverb.

Although semantic categories will not be used as criteria of distinction, a semantic classification will be applied at the end of the analysis to see whether morphosyntactic subcategories of adverbs have a semantic basis. If two criteria yielded the same results for all units (see §3.2), then they were fused together or one of them was removed. Initially, for instance, *too* ~ and *very* ~ were used as criteria (where ~ replaces the adverb under consideration), but any adverb that could be used in one of these contexts could be used in the other. The former was removed in favor of the latter. Another case was the initial position of adverbs in the sentence: a distinction was initially drawn between integrated and detached initial adverbs. However, those criteria virtually yielded the same results, probably because usage fluctuates in written corpora as to whether a comma should be inserted or not.

This resulted in 39 criteria of distinction, which are listed below:

MORPHOLOGY

Internal structure:
structure ⟨X·ly⟩, where X is an existing adjective
structure ⟨X·Y⟩, where X and Y are any identifiable elements

Inflected forms: comparative (~*er than*)
Derived forms: privative (*in*~,[5] *un*~)
adverb (~*ly*)

SYNTACTIC DISTRIBUTION

Can function as complement of:[6]
be
become
behave
go and *put*
last$_V$
until

Can be a particle (i.e. can occur between a verb and its NP object or after the NP object)

Can function as a modifier or supplement of:[7]
– verbs:
  initial position, prosodic detachment (~, S V X)
  initial position, compulsory subject-auxiliary inversion (~ Aux S V)[8]
  central position (S Aux ~ V)
  final position (S V X ~)
  final position, prosodic detachment (S V X, ~)
– adjectives:
  attributive position (*the ~ good thing*)
  predeterminer position (~ *good a thing*)
– prepositions
– nouns:
  post-head position (*the room ~ is large*)
  pre-head position[9] (*the very ~ thing*)

---

5 The criterion *in*~ covers cases in which the nasal consonant assimilates with the first consonant of the base, thus becoming /m/, /ŋ/ or /ɪ/ (as in the pair *regularly~irregularly*).

6 These units are the only ones in English that accept adverbs as complements. More specifically, *behave* and *last* are one of the few English verbs that accept manner adverbs and time adverbs as complements, respectively.

7 Note that "modifier of adverbs" was not used as a criterion. Most of the time, when two adverbs occur in a row, the first one (the modifier) will be a degree adverb, so there will not be much variation. Moreover, the modification of an adverb by another adverb is already covered by several criteria in the third category (*dependents*). Maintaining a similar criterion in the second category would have resulted in a duplicate.

8 In some cases, preposed adverbs can trigger **optional** subject-auxiliary inversion (e.g. *Thus did he break with a family tradition*). This kind of construction is however very formal and subject to a lot of variation among speakers.

9 The pre-head position is typical of adjectives. This criterion is concerned with adverbs which have the same form as adjectives, also called *flat adverbs*.

DEPENDENTS	Can have as complements:	NPS PPS headed by a specified preposition (*for*, *from*, *of*, *to*, *with*) *that* and bare content clauses *to*-infinitive clauses gerund-participial (*-ing*) clauses
	Can have as modifiers:	degree modifiers (*as ~ as possible*, *more ~ than*, *very ~*) typical modifiers of prepositions (*right ~*) NPS (*3 days ~*)

3.2 Corpus and method

Once the various criteria of distinction were established, I selected the 200 units labeled as adverbs that appear most frequently in the COCA. In some cases, the tagging was erroneous (*for*, *of*) but the historical preposition is actually part of a polylexemic adverb (*for example*, *kind of*, *of course*, *sort of*); those four polylexemic adverbs were included in the list.[10]

Among those 200 units, a distinction was made between homonyms, i.e. units which have the exact same form but whose senses are unrelated (at least synchronically) in a way that allows them to be analyzed as several linguistic units. To do so, Blank's (2003: 270–271) typology of polysemy was used: if two senses of a unit are not related by one of the seven polysemy links (metaphoric, co-hyponymous, taxonomic, metonymic, auto-converse, antiphrastic, antilogic), then they can be considered homonyms, even if they have a common etymology.[11] Based on these criteria, I found four potentially homonymous units: *so* (expressing degree or result), *still* (expressing aspect or concession), *too* (expressing degree or addition) and *yet* (expressing aspect or concession).

The COCA was then checked for every morphosyntactic context given in §3. In a spreadsheet, the adverbs (rows) were then annotated according to whether they could appear in each of these contexts (columns). The spreadsheet was imported

---

10 One argument in favor of analyzing those as polylexemic units is the fact that they will often undergo phonetic reduction: [fɹɡˈzæmpɫ], [ˈkʰaɪn(d)ə], [ˈfkʰɔːɹs], [ˈsɔːɹɹə].
11 The noun *box*, for instance, has two senses that are etymologically related, as in *box₁ tree* and *a box₂ of chocolate*. Historically, containers were typically made out of box wood: *box₂* was therefore metonymically derived from *box₁*. Nowadays, boxes (containers) are far more frequently made out of other materials, so that the original link that existed between those two senses has disappeared, making them homonyms.

to R and the *daisy* function was used to automatically calculate the Gower distance between each unit. If two units have the exact same properties, they are at a distance of zero; if they differ according to 4 properties, they are at a distance of 4, and so on. The result is a large matrix that shows these distances, like a table of distances between cities on a map – with the difference that these are not physical distances, but abstract ones.

Following the bottom-up approach that was advocated in §2, clusters of adverbs were created through agglomerative hierarchical clustering. Each adverb was initially considered as a cluster (i.e., a class); an algorithm then combined, step by step, the two clusters (adverbs or groups of adverbs) that were the most similar into a new, larger cluster. The operation was repeated until all points formed one single cluster, thus forming a dendrogram (average linkage clustering, cophenetic coefficient 0.85). The elbow method was used to determine that the optimal number of classes for the adverbs under consideration was 4.

Those distances were then modeled using a multidimensional scaling process: this is a method that makes it possible to represent the distance between each point (i.e. each unit) on a two- or three-dimensional space in order to better visualize it. Since the distances are not physical, the representation is necessarily imperfect and some data will not be represented on a two-dimensional plane. The SMACOF (*scaling by majorizing a convex function*) algorithm is used to minimize this loss of information. The result is a map composed of 200 points that represent the 200 units. These points are more or less close to one another and this spatial proximity conveys a proximity in the properties of these units. This representation can therefore help determine whether adverbs are a homogeneous class or not, whether there are clear groups and whether some adverbs can be considered hybrids or isolates.

4 Results and discussion

4.1 Adverbs as a heterogeneous category

The result of the analysis carried out is the two-dimensional space in Figure 1 below:

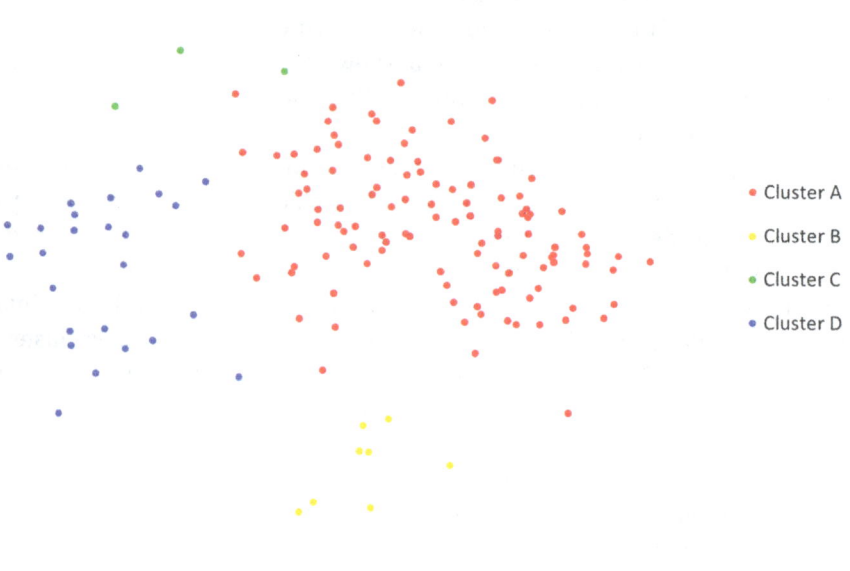

Figure 1: Two-dimensional scaling of adverb units, using SMACOF algorithm, colored by cluster.

As mentioned earlier, since multidimensional scaling consists in representing a certain number of dimensions of variations with only two dimensions, this representation is necessarily imperfect. The proportion of information thus lost is called the *stress*. Here the stress is 11,07%, which means that to accurately represent the remaining 11,07% information, more than two dimensions would be needed.

In this representation, each dot represents a single unit, but some dots may be overlapping and appear as a single one. This is the case, for instance, of the dots representing the units *today, tomorrow, tonight* and *yesterday*; this means that these units are at a distance of zero, because they have the same grammatical properties. Figure 1 also shows adverbs colored according to the cluster they belong to, as determined by the agglomerative hierarchical clustering presented in §3.2:
- Cluster A includes most of the units of the list, notably all units in *-ly*;
- Cluster B is made up of 10 units: *early, far, fast, hard, late, little, long, much, soon* and *well*;
- Cluster C is composed of the four traditional *wh-* adverbs: *how, when, where* and *why*;
- Cluster D consists of traditional place adverbs and the unit *before*, most of which are also classified as prepositions when they have an NP complement.

Most of these adverbs were annotated according to their semantic category, using Mittwoch et al.'s (2002) typology. Represented below in Figure 2 are the most common categories: connective, degree, frequency, manner, modality, place and time adverbs.

Figure 2: Two-dimensional scaling of adverb units, colored by semantic category.

Figure 2 clearly shows that Cluster D, which was already morphosyntactically coherent, is also semantically coherent, as it is almost exclusively composed of traditional adverbs expressing location. Clusters A and B are semantically far more heterogeneous, but the rightmost elements of Cluster A are mainly units primarily expressing manner, as well as frequency and modality.

In multidimensional scaling, the first dimension of variation (represented by the abscissa) is the most relevant one. This means that within the traditional category of adverbs (as defined for instance in Quirk *et al.* 1985), place elements on the one hand and manner, frequency and modality elements on the other act as two attracting poles. Other adverbs are scattered along the continuum that lies between these two poles.

The fact that these categories constitute opposite poles is no coincidence, given the fact that they have very different morphosyntactic properties. As seen in the examples in (2), place elements (but not manner elements, for instance) mostly accept NPs as complements, can be modified by *right* or *straight* and can function as complements of *be*, *go* and *put*. Unlike place elements, on the other hand, manner, frequency and modality elements are mostly morphologically complex, are gradable (they can be modified by degree adverbs and can enter into the scalar equality comparative construction) and can modify verbs in all linear positions as well as adjectives, as can be seen in (5) below:

(5) a. I am talking to you as **frankly** ⟨*outside⟩ as I can. ⟨COCA 1993: NEWS⟩
    b. She **frankly** ⟨*outside⟩ confessed that all efforts to change his views were futile. ⟨COCA 2012: WEB⟩
    c. I can't believe what I'm hearing, **frankly** ⟨*outside⟩. ⟨COCA 1996: SPOK⟩
    d. I reminded him that for me to say such a thing in his presence would have been a **frankly** ⟨*outside⟩ stupid thing to do. ⟨COCA 2012: BLOG⟩

The plot also shows that degree elements are neither concentrated in one area nor clearly distinct from other adverbs. It therefore appears that Fries's and Biber *et al.*'s distinct class of "intensifiers" is not the most relevant one, despite their convincing arguments. This is most probably due to the fact that there are very few units that only express degree, like *quite*, *rather*, *too* or *very*. Most adverbs expressing degree can also express other semantic categories, mostly manner (e.g. *entirely*, *perfectly*, *roughly*, *strongly*); in that case, the semantic category is generally determined by the linear position of the adverb and the word it modifies. Yet, precisely because degree adverbs can have many linear positions, they do not have properties that distinguish them sharply from other units, and are therefore scattered across the plot.

The second dimension of variation (represented by the ordinate) is less significant but is still important. The plot shows that most traditional adverbs lie around the center of the vertical axis. More interesting are the topmost dot and the scattered group of dots at the bottom forming Cluster B.

The topmost dot represents the unit *how*, which indeed has special properties compared with most other adverbs: as a *wh-* word, it will be mostly restricted to front position (except for *in-situ* questions) and will always trigger subject-auxiliary inversion; as a potential manner element it can replace the complements of *behave* and *treat*; and as a degree element that modifies an adjective within an NP, it will impose a predeterminer position for the adjective phrase (e.g. *how bad a situation is it?*). More generally, the fact that *wh-* words form a distinct cluster shows that they might constitute a micro-class of units that is distinct from the adverb word class. Note, however, that in Figure 1 the unit *where* is not far from

Cluster D, presumably because it can function as a complement to the same verbs as place adverbs.

The units in Cluster B are few and semantically different; these are *early, far, fast, hard, late, little, long, much, soon* and *well*. Despite their semantic diversity, they still bear a few similarities: all of them are monomorphemic,[12] all of them have an inflectional comparative form (sometimes an irregular one) and most of them can also be analyzed as adjectives or determinatives, which would make them adjective-adverb hybrids (*early, far, fast, hard, late, long, well*) or determinative-adverb hybrids (*little, much*). Semantic categories do therefore influence how traditional adverbs can be divided into subclasses, but purely morphosyntactic properties are still the main criterion.

4.2 Adverbs and other word classes

If the analysis carried out so far established that there are clear subclasses of traditional adverbs, it did not establish whether this traditional class is relevant in the description of English. That is, one of these apparent subclasses might well belong with another word class. The second and final step of the analysis is therefore to compare traditional adverbs with other units and to see whether one or several of the subclasses that were established rather belongs with another word class.

To do so, the most frequent units traditionally classified as adjectives, (subordinating) conjunctions and prepositions in the COCA were selected:

Table 3: Units from other traditional word classes.

Adjectives		Conjunctions	Prepositions	
able	large	because	across	in case
alive	national	although	after	in front
American	new	if	against	into
bad	old	in order	among	like
big	other	lest	as	near
black	political	unless	at	of
different	public	whereas	between	since
good	real	whether	beyond	toward
great	small	while	despite	until
happy	social		during	with
high	sure		for	without
important	young		from	

---

12 *Early* is diachronically analyzable as *ere* + *·ly*, but it is not in synchrony, notably because it is not pronounced /ɛɹli/.

Some of the units in Table 3 exhibit a few properties that are not among the original 39 presented in §3. Five criteria therefore had to be added to go on with the analysis:
- The unit can have no complement;[13]
- The unit can be complemented by PPs headed by the specified prepositions *about*, *at* and *than*;
- The unit can be complemented by a subjunctive bare content clause.

The same statistical analysis was run as the one described in §3.2. A new two-dimensional representation of the distance between all those units is given below in Figure 3:

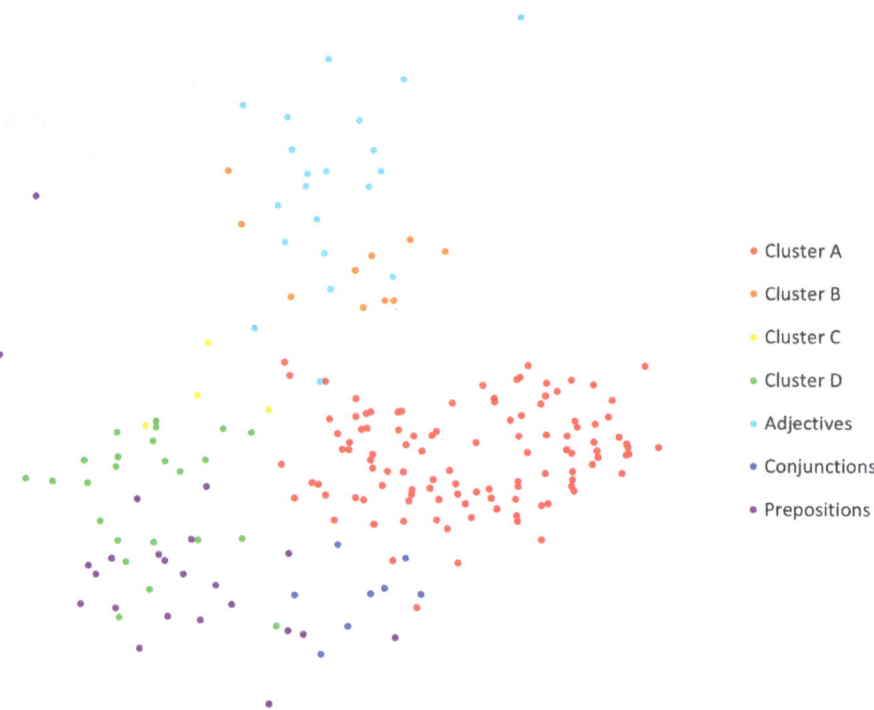

Figure 3: Two-dimensional representation of adverbs, prepositions, conjunctions and adjectives.

---

13 This property was not distinctive with traditional adverbs, as all of them can occur without a complement.

Several conclusions can be drawn from this new representation.

If prepositions are to be considered a distinct word class, which is what almost all linguists seem to believe, then most units traditionally called "place adverbs" (cluster D) should be part of that word class as well. Indeed, the plot shows that these two groups are almost blended, which indicates a large set of common grammatical properties. These results seem to confirm Huddleston & Pullum's (2002) analysis of prepositions and adverbs presented in §1, according to which all place elements (and some time elements) should be reassigned to the preposition class, whether they have a complement or not. Units such as *here, there, abroad, ahead, home, downstairs* or *forward* should therefore move from the class of adverbs to that of prepositions.

My analysis, however, failed to show that *now* and *then* should be grouped with prepositions, unlike what Pullum & Huddleston (2002: 615–616) assume. Although they are indeed the temporal equivalents of *here* and *there* and although they can be modified by *right*, they cannot appear in the same complement slots as prepositions and they can modify verbs in central position (*the show has **now** begun*). Compounds in ·*where* are not clearly part of the preposition class either; Payne & Huddleston (2002: 423) rather analyze them as compound determinatives.

Another case of class blending arises with so-called "flat adverbs" (most of cluster B), i.e. adverbs that have the same form as an adjective (*early, far, fast, hard, late, long*). The representation indicates that these units should rather be grouped with units such as *big, important, large* or *old*. This would suggest that "flat adverbs" are actually full adjectives (hence their comparative form) that can occur in adjunct function without the need to be derived into adverbs. A surprising fact is that *soon* can also be considered part of this group, due to its simple form and its inflectional comparative. All this will have to be confirmed by another study that takes into account a larger set of properties and a larger set of adjectives, notably non-prototypical ones, like non-gradable adjectives or adjectives limited to the attributive or predicative position.

Some units traditionally described as subordinating conjunctions, like *after, before, since* or *until*, should probably be analyzed as prepositions (see Delhem 2018). If those units are reassigned to the category of prepositions, the remaining conjunctions form a small group. Since they seem to have similar properties, especially in terms of complementation, they might be considered a micro-class. If they were to be grouped with another class, agglomerative hierarchical clustering suggests that they should be fused with adverbs rather than prepositions. This is probably due to the fact that, like most adverbs, subordinating conjunctions do not have many positive properties: they can be described as being UNable to enter into a certain number of syntactic contexts.

From the traditional class of adverbs, one can therefore establish at least three distinct word classes, two of which belong with other established classes: adverbs, intransitive prepositions and "adverbial" adjectives. Most traditional adverbs can be assigned to one of these classes, even as peripheral members, except for two cases:
- The units *like*, and less importantly *near*, seem to be at best adjective-preposition hybrids, exhibiting grammatical properties of these two classes, or even isolated units that should not be assigned to any class (especially *like*);
- *Wh·* units (*where*, *when*, *why*, *how*) seem to constitute a micro-class of units with common syntactic and semantic features, although they also exhibit strong individual behaviors, especially *where* and *how*.

However, in accordance with what Lee (1998: 135) found, the multidimensional scaling analysis showed that there is no sharp distinction between adverbs and prepositions. Some elements (*now* and *then*, compounds in *·where*) lie in the middle, somewhere between these two poles. It would therefore seem either that prepositions and adverbs exhibit intersective gradience (Aarts 2007: 124), i.e. that some elements have properties of both categories, or that adverbs (Cluster A) exhibit heavy subsective gradience (Aarts 2007: 97), i.e. that the adverb class constitutes a gradient between core and peripheral members.

5 Conclusion

The fact that traditional adverbs are considered a residual category is mainly due to classification problems rather than to the nature of adverbs itself. A statistical analysis that took into account a large number of criteria showed that adverbs could be subdivided into three major groups, which should preferably be considered three distinct classes. More precisely, it would probably be better to consider the group of "place adverbs" as intransitive prepositions, and the group of "flat adverbs" as full-fledged adjectives that can have the same syntactic functions as most adverbs.

This does not solve the heterogeneity of the remaining adverb class: its members still express manner, frequency, time, modality, degree and other smaller semantic categories. Yet this mainly results from the fact that many adverbs can have several interpretations (and hence belong to several semantic categories) depending on their linear position in the sentence or the verb they depend on. Greater coherence is brought by the fact that adverbs either are formed by the suffixation of *-ly* to an existing adjective, or have the same function as such units.

The resulting adverb class was not made more homogeneous, however. Another study that would take more units into account may yield different results, as less frequent lexemes tend to be less polysemous (Pawley 2006). Moreover, no criterion was given more weight than the others; refining this study will therefore involve adding criteria of distinction. A greater number of properties and units might therefore shine a new light on this analysis.

References

Aarts, Bas. 2007. *Syntactic gradience: The nature of grammatical indeterminacy*. Oxford: Oxford University Press.
Berko, Jean. 1958. The child's learning of English morphology. *WORD* 14(2–3). 150–177.
Biber, Douglas, Susan Conrad & Geoffrey Leech. 2002. *Longman student grammar of spoken and written English*. Harlow: Pearson Education Limited.
Blank, Andreas. 2003. Polysemy in lexicon and discourse. In Brigitte Nerlich, Zazie Todd, Vimala Herman & David D. Clarke (eds.), *Polysemy: Flexible patterns of meaning in mind and language*, 267–293. New York: Mouton de Gruyter.
Burton-Roberts, Noel. 1991. Prepositions, adverbs and adverbials. In Ingrid Tieken-Boon van Ostade & John Frankis (eds.), *Language, usage and description*, 159–172. Amsterdam: Rodopi.
Creissels, Denis. 2006. *Syntaxe générale, une introduction typologique. Volume 1: Catégories et constructions*. Paris: Hermès.
Crystal, David. 1967. English. *Lingua* 17. 24–56.
Davidson, Thomas. 1874. *The grammar of Dionysios Thrax*. Saint Louis: Studley. [Translation of Τέχνη Γραμματική, attributed to Dionysius Thrax.]
Delhem, Romain. 2018. Prépositions, adverbes et conjonctions en anglais: pour une redéfinition des classes lexicales. *Anglophonia* 26. [online] https://journals.openedition.org/anglophonia/1821 (last accessed 18.11.2021)
Eastwood, John. 2002. *Oxford guide to English grammar*. 7th edition. Oxford: Oxford University Press.
Fries, Charles C. 1952. *The structure of English*. New York: Harcourt & Brace.
Goldberg, Adele. 2006. *Constructions at work: The nature of generalization in language*. Oxford: Oxford University Press.
Haspelmath, Martin. 2001. Word classes and parts of speech. In Neil J. Smelser & Paul B. Baltes (eds.), *International encyclopedia of the social and behavioral sciences*, 16538–16545. Oxford: Pergamon.
Huddleston, Rodney & Geoffrey Pullum. 2002. *The Cambridge grammar of the English language*. Cambridge: Cambridge University Press.
Iordanskaja, Lidija & Igor Mel'čuk. 2009. Establishing an inventory of surface-syntactic relations: Valence-controlled surface-syntactic dependents of the verb in French. In Alain Polguère & Igor Mel'čuk, *Dependency in linguistic description*, 151–234. Amsterdam: John Benjamins.
Jespersen, Otto. 1924. *The philosophy of grammar*. London: Allen & Unwin.

Kolln, Martha & Robert Funk. 2012. *Understanding English grammar*. 9th edition. Upper Saddle River: Pearson.

Langacker, Ronald. 2008. *Cognitive grammar: A basic introduction*. Oxford: Oxford University Press.

Lee, David. 1998. Intransitive prepositions: are they viable? In Peter Collins & David Lee, *The Clause in English*, 133–148. Amsterdam: John Benjamins.

Mittwoch, Anna, Rodney Huddleston & Peter Collins. 2002. The clause: adjuncts. In Rodney Huddleston & Geoffrey Pullum, *The Cambridge grammar of the English language*, 663–784. Cambridge: Cambridge University Press.

Pawley, Andrew. 2006. Where have all the verbs gone? Remarks on the organisation of language with small, closed verb classes. Paper presented at the 11th Biennial Rice University Linguistics Symposium, Austin (TX), 16–18 March 2006.

Payne, John & Rodney Huddleston. Nouns and noun phrases. 2002. In Rodney Huddleston & Geoffrey Pullum, *The Cambridge grammar of the English language*, 323–523. Cambridge: Cambridge University Press.

Pullum, Geoffrey & Rodney Huddleston. 2002. Prepositions and preposition phrases. In Rodney Huddleston & Geoffrey Pullum, *The Cambridge grammar of the English language*, 597–661. Cambridge: Cambridge University Press.

Quirk, Randolph, Sidney Greenbaum, Geoffrey Leech & Jan Svartvik. 1985. *A comprehensive grammar of the English language*. London: Longman.

R Core Team. 2015. R: A Language and Environment for Statistical Computing. R Foundation for Statistical Computing, Vienna. http://r-project.org/ (last accessed 18.11.2021)

Christina Sanchez-Stockhammer & Antony Unwin
The subcategorization of English adverbs: A feature-based clustering approach

Abstract: The category of the adverb in the English language is notoriously heterogeneous, and Crystal (1995: 211) even considers it a "dustbin category" which combines such disparate members as the manner adverb *happily*, the intensifier *very*, the comparative *more* and the postmodifier *indeed*. In order to determine the most appropriate subclassification of the category of the adverb in English, the present contribution presents original research based on a dataset of the 2500 most frequent words in the *British National Corpus* (Sanchez 2008). The 206 adverbs in this high-frequency sample were coded with regard to their decomposability into semantic components, word-family integration, language of origin, age, underlying word formation process , suffix type used and semantic class. Using a tree plot, we first investigated whether the adverbs in our dataset are more similar to the lexical or the grammatical parts of speech, but with no conclusive evidence. We then used a recent clustering approach (consensus clustering; cf. Chiu 2018) and an innovative visualization in the form of an adaptation of parallel coordinate plots for multivariate categorical data to determine whether cluster analyses can be used to automatically subcategorize words assigned to the traditional category of the adverb into meaningful subcategories. We did indeed find a linguistically meaningful categorization into three clusters that are distinguished with regard to the word formation type characteristic of the group members, namely simplex adverbs (e.g. *next*), *-ly* suffixations (e.g. *regularly*) and other complex word formations (e.g. *meanwhile*). Our results indicate that the presence or absence of an adjectival base is a much better criterion for the subcategorization of English adverbs than the property of permitting inflection.

Keywords: adverb, subcategorization, consensus clustering, tree plot, multidimensional scaling, parallel coordinate plot

---

Christina Sanchez-Stockhammer, Universität Chemnitz, christina.sanchez@phil.tu-chemnitz.de
Antony Unwin, Universität Augsburg, unwin@math.uni-augsburg.de

https://doi.org/10.1515/9783110767971-003

1 Introduction: The problem of the adverb

The category of the adverb in the English language is notoriously heterogeneous (cf. e.g. Nakamura 1997: 247; Huddleston & Pullum 2002: 563; Pittner, Elsner & Barteld 2015: 1 with a whole collection of similar statements from the literature). In line with prototype theory (cf. Rosch 1975), however, the category of the adverb can be described as consisting of a core and a periphery (cf. also Ramat & Ricca 1994). As the etymology of its name suggests (cf. e.g. OED s.v. *adverb*), the adverb has the grammatical function of modifying verbs, and this function stands out as particularly central: thus Huddleston & Pullum (2002: 563) refer to it as the prototypical function of adverbs, and Hallonsten Halling (2017: 40), in her typological comparison of adverbs in 41 languages, boils down the category to its core and defines the adverb as "a lexeme that denotes a descriptive property and can be used to narrow the predication of a verb". A famous pedagogical part-of-speech poem by Tower and Tweed (1853) also lists this function in the first place for adverbs:

> *How* things are done the ADVERBS tell;
> As, *slowly*, *quickly*, *ill*, or *well*.

Adding, in the next verses:

> They also tell us *where* and *when*;
> As, *here*, and *there*, and *now*, and *then*.

This semantic description of the members of the adverb category as providing information on the spatial and temporal context of a sentence or utterance contrasts with the very commonly found distributional accounts which lead Huddleston & Pullum (2002: 612) to state that "Adverbs are traditionally defined as words that modify verbs, adjectives, and other adverbs." However, it does not stop there, and Vermeire (1984: 2) notes that "adverbs can modify almost any element in the clause", including the clause itself. As Huddleston & Pullum (2002: 563) note, however, this does not include nouns, so that they define the adverb category by exclusion, stating that "Adverbs characteristically modify verbs and other categories except nouns, especially adjectives and adverbs". In view of the large number of items with high token frequency that are no manner adverbs (e.g. the above-mentioned *here*, *there*, *now* and *then*), Ramat & Ricca (1994: 316) recognize a "heterogeneous core-group" in their prototype account of the structure of the adverb category.

The traditional category of the adverb as described by a vast number of grammars (e.g. grammar books used in the school context) combines such disparate members as the manner adverb *happily*, which modifies verbs, the intensifier *very* and the comparative *more*, which both premodify adjectives and adverbs, and *indeed*, which functions as a postmodifier (cf. Quirk et al. 1985: 63, 66). Since this part of speech assembles those words that do "not fit the definitions for other word classes" (Quirk et al. 1985: 438), Huddleston & Pullum (2002: 563) characterize the adverb as a "miscellaneous or residual category", and Crystal (1995: 211) even refers to it by the derogatory term "dustbin category". Its variety of grammatical functions leads Quirk et al. (1985: 438) to conclude that "the adverb class is the most nebulous and puzzling of the traditional word classes", and Herbst and Schüller (2008: 59) state that "Adverbs are one of the most problematic word classes". They criticize the comprehensive traditional category of the adverb, since it comprises words whose distribution has nothing in common, e.g. *very* and *here* (Herbst & Schüller 2008: 60–61). In their re-evaluation of the traditional English part-of-speech categories, Herbst and Schüller (2008: 59) propose as an alternative "to define the class of adverbs in a more restrictive way than is done traditionally and subsume a number of words that are traditionally classified as adverbs under other word classes". The most influential grammar using such an approach "to make the adverb a more coherent category" is Huddleston & Pullum's *Cambridge Grammar of the English Language* (2002: 564).[1] For instance, Huddleston & Pullum (2002: 614) re-categorize some spatial items that are traditionally classified as adverbs (and which are therefore labelled as adverbs in the list of lexeme types used in the present analyses) as prepositions, because they occur as complements of the verb (rather than in the adjunct function of prototypical adverbs), e.g. *together* (as in *They are together*) and only differ from traditional prepositions such as *on* in that they cannot (always) take an NP complement. Huddleston & Pullum also exclude several other traditional adverbs with multiple class membership from their restricted adverb category – e.g. *yesterday*, which can also function as a noun, or *much*, which can also function as an adjective (Huddleston & Pullum 2002: 564–565) or determiner in Quirk et al.'s (1985) terminology when followed by a noun, e.g. *much milk*.[2]

To conclude, in spite of attempts to clarify and redraw its boundaries, the category of English adverbs remains puzzling (Rauh 2015: 19), and its heterogeneity raises a variety of questions. For instance, it is unclear whether adverbs (many of

---

[1] This discussion of drawing the boundary of the category of the adverb seems to be restricted to linguistic grammars. Grammars with a more practical focus, such as Swan (2005), Foley and Hall (2003) or Hewings (2005), restrict themselves to explaining the form and function of numerous subtypes without any critical comments about the heterogeneous character of the category.

[2] This approach has the disadvantage that items with different distribution and thus multiple class membership are no longer recognized as adverbs, in spite of the fact that grammatical homonymy or polysemy is a relatively frequent phenomenon in the English language, which can e.g. be observed for many nouns and verbs (e.g. *an approach/to approach, a ship/to ship*) that would still be classified as two separate parts of speech.

which are derived from adjectives by means of the suffix -*ly*) are more similar to the lexical parts of speech (noun, verb, adjective) or rather resemble grammatical words (like pronouns or prepositions). Furthermore, it would be interesting to see if it is possible to find an objective way of arranging those words that are conventionally classified as adverbs into groups in such a way that they provide a meaningful subcategorization. The present paper attempts to answer both of these questions by using statistical methods, namely tree models and clustering.

2 Empirical study: Aims and method

As we have seen so far, most critical treatments of adverbs in English limit themselves to stating the problem of the heterogeneity of the adverb category (e.g. Krapp 1928 only discusses a small number of examples) and provide suggestions for alternative drawing of boundaries either for the category of the adverb as a whole or for its potential subcategories from a theoretical, mainly distribution-based perspective. Other treatments tend to focus on the contrast between adverbs and other parts of speech, such as adjectives (e.g. McNally & Kennedy 2008) or prepositions and conjunctions (Delhem 2018), or they focus on one particular type of adverb (e.g. preverbal adverbs in Jacobson 1978, focus adverbs in Hoeksema & Zwarts 1991, or evaluative adverbs in Liu 2012). Many accounts provide descriptions with examples (e.g. Vermeire 1984), but there are only few attempts that approach this issue from a large-scale quantitative empirical perspective (as Hoye 1997 does for the restricted topic of collocations between modal verbs and adverbs). No statistical clustering approaches seem to have been applied to English adverbs so far – but that the time has come to apply new methods to a long-standing problem can be deduced from the fact that the only comparable statistical perspective on English adverbs to the one presented here can be found in another contribution to this very volume (cf. Delhem, this volume). In line with the aims of our overarching topic of the problem of the adverb, we thus apply a new approach to the category of the adverb and attempt to determine whether the application of a feature-based clustering approach (cf. Hennig et al. 2016) to the traditional part of speech can contribute to a consistent (sub)categorization of the words that are traditionally subsumed by this part of speech. We identify adverbs based on the extension of the category (cf. Rauh 2015: 24) provided by a pre-classified sample based on an established set of items in earlier grammars: In order to analyse a relevant and representative sample of English adverbs, we selected the 2500 most frequent lemma types from Kilgarriff's lemmatized corpus-based frequency list lemma.num, which is based on the balanced 100-million-word *British*

National Corpus.[3] The part-of-speech codes for all items were taken over unedited from Kilgarriff. This means that the part-of-speech categorization of the items in the dataset draws on traditional models of part-of-speech categorisation and is based on the items' occurrence in authentic syntactic context (so that a distinction is made e.g. between *up* as a preposition and *up* as an adverb). Some of the adverbs in our list may thus be formally identical with functionally or semantically differing words: cf. e.g. the multiple class membership of *round* as an adverb in *the plane circled round* in contrast to its prepositional use in *round the corner*. The sample contains a total of 206 adverb types. All analyses were carried out using the software R (R Core Team 2020).

Most recent linguistic research on adverbs focuses on syntactic distribution as the criterion for the delimitation of the category, whereas more traditional grammars tend to use semantic and morphological criteria for part-of-speech classification (cf. Rauh 2015: 29–34). The present study thus complements the existing quantitative research with a new perspective, since it uses features that are inherent in the adverbs themselves, and some of which have not been used yet in the discussion of subcategorization, such as

1) the adverbs' word-family integration in terms of
   a) their morpho-semantic compositionality and
   b) their ability to serve as the base for longer word formations and
2) the adverbs' historical origin in terms of their language of origin and their age.

The features listed in Table 1 were coded for the items in the sample according to the principles and coding criteria which are outlined in detail in Sanchez (2008: 86–127) and summarized in the following:

Table 1: Codes assigned to the items in the database for the empirical study.

Code	Content	Possible values		Examples
POS_lg	lexical (lex) or grammatical (gr) part of speech; adverbs are marked as adv	lex	adj, n, v	*great, thing, feel*
		gr	conj, det, infinitive-marker, interjection, modal, prep, pron	*and, the, to, yes, will, of, it*
		adv		*only*
Motiv.	decomposability of the target word into semantic components	MO	fully motivatable	*slowly*
		MP	partially motivatable	*gently; today*
		U	unmotivatable	*more*

---

[3] URL: http://www.kilgarriff.co.uk/BNClists/lemma.num, 31.10.2006 (last retrieved Sept. 23rd, 2021); cf. Kilgarriff 1997 for the compilation method.

Table 1 (continued)

Code	Content	Possible values		Examples
Word family	word-family integration of the target word = 1) motivatability (= decomposability into morpho-semantic components) and/or 2) expandability (= existence of longer word formed on the basis of the target word)	M	only motivatable, but not expandable	*unfortunately*
		E	only expandable, but not motivatable	*now* (> *nowadays*)
		B	both motivatable and expandable	*fully* (> *fully fledged*)
		N	neither motivatable nor expandable	*however*
Etym_language	etymological origin: language of origin (simplified codes)	g	Germanic	*here*
		r	Romance	*very*
		b	Germanic-and-Romance	*certainly*
		o	other	
Etym_age	age of the target word (simplified codes)	o	Old English	*when*
		m	Middle English	*easy*
		l	later	*okay*

The **part-of-speech** codes from Kilgarriff's list were semi-automatically categorized into three groups: 1) lexical parts of speech (adjectives, nouns and verbs), 2) grammatical parts of speech (e.g. prepositions and pronouns), and 3) adverbs as the test category whose closeness to the other categories was to be tested.

Motivatability was defined as the decomposability of the target word into meaningful semantic components by a competent speaker of present-day English. A word is therefore *motivatable* if it can be related to other words and/or affixes of the same language, which are both formally and semantically related to the complex word. Thus the adverb *slowly* is motivatable because it is related to the adjective *slow* and the adverb-forming suffix *-ly*. Words that are not found to be related to any other words are called *unmotivatable*, e.g. *more* or *quite*. Various kinds of obstacle may occur in the analysis of motivatability – e.g. a difference in form between *gentle* + *-ly* and resulting *gently*, or the semantically problematic initial *to* in *today*. This results in so-called *partial motivatability*. A very detailed coding system was used to document combined difficulties in various domains by joining labels for different types of obstacle to the analysis (Sanchez-Stockhammer 2008: 87–95). For instance, *alright* (which can be related to the constituents *all* + *right*) was coded as MPFW#, which means that the word is motivatable (M) partially (P) with a formal obstacle (F) concerning only the written modality (W – namely the second <l> in *all*, which is not present in the complex word *alright*) and a semantic obstacle (#), as the meaning of the combined constituents (i.e. 'everything correct') does not correspond completely to the established meaning of the complex word (which would rather be paraphrased as 'suitable, but not perfect'). For the purpose of the present study, however, all instances of partial motivatability were considered jointly, regardless of the form and number of obstacles to the analysis.

The adverbs in the sample could be integrated into contemporary English **word families** either by means of their motivatability and/or because of the existence of morpho-semantically related complex words in which the search word is contained: for example, the adverb *now* can be expanded into longer *nowadays*. Such *expansions* were sought in the latest editions of monolingual English dictionaries and corpora of increasing size, namely the learner's dictionary *Oxford Advanced Learner's Dictionary*, the medium-sized general dictionary *Shorter Oxford English Dictionary*, the large reference work *Oxford English Dictionary* as well as the *British National Corpus*. Some adverbs, like *fully*, are related to other items in the lexicon both through motivatability and expandability, whereas *however* cannot be expanded and is only superficially (but not semantically) related to shorter lexical items.

Furthermore, two types of **historical information** were coded based on the entries in the *Shorter Oxford English Dictionary*: the language of origin (i.e. Germanic, Romance, both at the same time or neither of the two)[4] of the full word or (if not retrievable) its constituents and the age of the target word based on the period of first attestation (Old English, Middle English or later). These codes once again represent a simplification of the more detailed system of classification found in Sanchez (2008: 117–127), which includes the more detailed language-of-origin codes *u* for unknown or undocumented origin, *n* for eponymic origin involving a proper name and *e* for words that were excluded because of a more exotic origin not covered by the other categories, as well as additional codes to mark e.g. a specifically French (*f*), Latin (*l*) or Greek (*k*) origin. The more detailed original codes for period of first attestation also include the code *x* for words with no documented period of first attestation, or the additional code *h*, which marks homonyms with differing etymologies (as is the case of the noun *ball*, whose toy meaning is of Germanic origin, whereas the social event meaning is a Romance loan word).

---

4 The category *o* (other) is not relevant for the adverbs in the dataset, but it is still included in Table 1 because of its relevance for the words with other part of speech represented in node 1 of Figure 1.

3 Adverbs vs. lexical and grammatical parts of speech

We first attempted to answer the question whether the adverbs in our dataset are more similar to the lexical or the grammatical parts of speech. To this end, we computed a tree plot using conditional inference trees (Hothorn 2006) based on the variables LANGUAGE OF ORIGIN (Etym_language), AGE OF THE WORD (Etym_age),[5] MORPHO-SEMANTIC COMPOSITIONALITY (Motiv.) and WORD-FAMILY INTEGRATION (Word_family) (cf. Figure 1). All statistical analyses were carried out using the R *partykit* package (Hothorn 2020).

The analysis pursued two aims: the first was to build a tree model using the four features Etym_language, Etym_age, Motiv. and Word_family to differentiate between the three categories of POS_lg (i.e. *adv*, *gr* and *lex*). The second and particularly important aim was to see whether the results imply that the adverb class is closer to the grammatical class or the lexical class.

Table 2 summarizes the absolute numbers and relative proportions of adverb types, lexical word types and grammatical word types in the final nodes at the bottom of Figure 1. Two relevant groups stand out with regard to our research question: Node 11, which is practically completely lexical (and in which the proportion of adverbs resembles that of grammatical words), and Node 4, which contains a mixture of adverbs and lexical items and thus suggests a closer similarity between these two groups (as opposed to the underrepresented grammatical words). Node 5 (n= 29) and Node 10 (n=19) are too small to allow any statistically valid conclusions. The final two nodes, Node 8 and Node 9, are fairly similar, comprising a large number of lexical words as well as roughly equal percentages of adverbs and grammatical words. They superficially suggest a stronger similarity of adverbs to grammatical words, but the results are inconclusive because of the large number of lexical words in those nodes. The results are thus skewed by the fact that there are far more lexical than grammatical words in the sample (cf. Table 3).

The conclusion could be that for the group in Node 4 (which represents both adverbs and lexical words but hardly any grammatical words), adverbs are like lexical words. By contrast, for the two large groups in nodes 8 and 9, there is no strong evidence for saying that adverbs are more or less like grammaticals or lexicals.

---

[5] Note that the age of the word does not appear in Figure 1, because it correlates with the other features and is automatically ignored by the statistical algorithm. It was, however, necessary to include it among the features in order to determine whether this makes any difference.

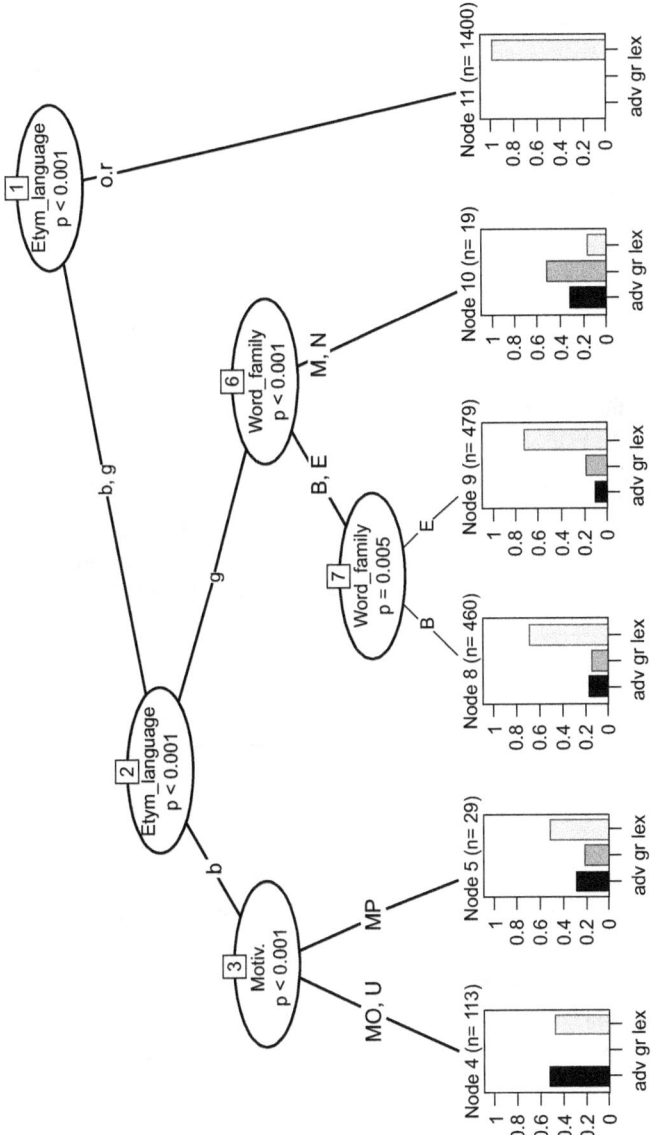

Figure 1: Tree plot of the 2500 most frequent lexemes from the *British National Corpus*: adverbs vs. lexical words vs. grammatical words based on the variables LANGUAGE OF ORIGIN (Etym_language), MORPHO-SEMANTIC COMPOSITIONALITY (Motiv.) and WORD-FAMILY INTEGRATION (Word_family).[6]

---

6 While it may seem unintuitive at first sight to contrast the completely motivatable words (MO) and the completely unmotivatable words on the one side of Node 3 in Figure 1 with the partially

Table 2: Absolute number and relative proportion of adverb types, lexical word types and grammatical word types in the final nodes of Figure 1.

Node	Total words	Adverbs	Lexical words	Grammatical words	adv (%)	lex (%)	gr (%)
4	113	59	53	1	52.2	46.9	0.9
5	29	8	15	6	27.6	51.7	20.7
8	460	78	314	68	17.0	68.3	14.8
9	479	45	345	89	9.4	72.0	18.6
10	19	6	3	10	31.6	15.8	52.6
11	1400	10	1378	12	0.7	98.4	0.9

Table 3: Word-family integration in adverbs/lexical words/grammatical words for nodes 8 and 9 from Figure 1.

	Node 8: item can be 1) segmented into morpho-semantic constituents and 2) used as the basis for longer word formations (B)	Node 9: item cannot be segmented into morpho-semantic constituents but can be used as the basis for longer word formations (E)
adverbs	78	45
grammatical words	68	89
lexical words	314	345

However, one further argument that could be advanced is that there are only 10 Romance adverbs (*just, very, quite, round, apart, ahead, close, easy, sure* and *across*) in Node 11. That makes the adverb column hard to discern, and this node irrelevant for the discussion of the adverbs. As a consequence, the first split at Node 1 in Figure 1 indicates that almost all adverbs in the sample are either purely Germanic (g) or consist of a combination of Germanic and Romance constituents (b = both). This would suggest a stronger affinity of the group of adverbs in the sample to grammatical words, which are typically of Germanic origin.

To sum up, the conclusion to draw from all this is that the adverbs in the dataset cannot be said to behave more like lexical or grammatical words – which confirms their unclear status in the literature. A different frequency cut-off point or other types of feature (e.g. ordinal features such as word length) might also yield different results. For instance, if one were to limit the sample to the ten

---

motivated words (MP) on the other side, this is actually the best result in statistical terms. While it is theoretically also possible to examine other types of split, the purely statistical approach adopted here arrives at the conclusion that there is no more appropriate split.

most frequent adverbs in the *British National Corpus* (i.e. *not, out, up, so, then, more, now, just, also, well*), the conclusion would be very different from that for our whole 2500-word sample or for the ten least frequent adverbs in our sample (*specifically, deeply, subsequently, gradually, essentially, aside, precisely, across, successfully, greatly*). This is because none of the 15 most frequent adverbs is of the type derived with *-ly* (Sanchez 2008: 133), which is considered to be so characteristic for the category as a whole (see the introduction to this article). Adverbs in the top frequency band are thus more similar to grammatical words, whereas adverbs in the lower frequency band are more similar to lexical words.

This can also be demonstrated graphically: as Figures 2 and 3 show very nicely, "the roughly 250 most frequent words are not representative of the English language as a whole as far as part of speech is concerned" (Sanchez 2008: 134). The proportion of grammatical part-of-speech types (i.e. prepositions, determiners, pronouns and conjunctions) is very large in the high-frequency band corresponding to the ranks on the left of the figures and then decreases exponentially (see the characteristic curve for grammatical parts of speech in the bottom part of Figure 3). This contrasts with the distribution of the lexical parts of speech – particularly nouns and adjectives –, which are less common in the highest frequency band, but whose number of types increases logarithmically in the lower frequency ranks. The verbs have a few high-frequency outliers but otherwise show the same curve pattern as the other lexical parts of speech (see the first three graphs in the top line of Figure 3). The curve of the adverbs (4th graph in Figure 3) is noteworthy because its shape constitutes a mixture between the usual curves for lexical and grammatical words. This reflects the heterogeneity of the adverb category with a preponderance of adverb types that are more similar to the grammatical word classes (e.g. *up* or *now*) in the high-frequency range and a large number of adverb types that rather resemble the lexical word classes (e.g. *precisely* and *successfully*) in the lower frequency ranges.

4 Subcategorization of English adverbs by means of cluster analysis

Another question that we attempted to answer with our study is whether cluster analyses can be used to subcategorize adverbs into meaningful categories. Cluster analysis is an exploratory tool for studying whether there might be groups in multivariate data. The method can be used to generate interesting hypotheses, which then need to be checked in other ways. This means that the results are not conclusive on their own, but that they need to be assessed in context. Since there is an unlimited number of clustering options, one can never determine results

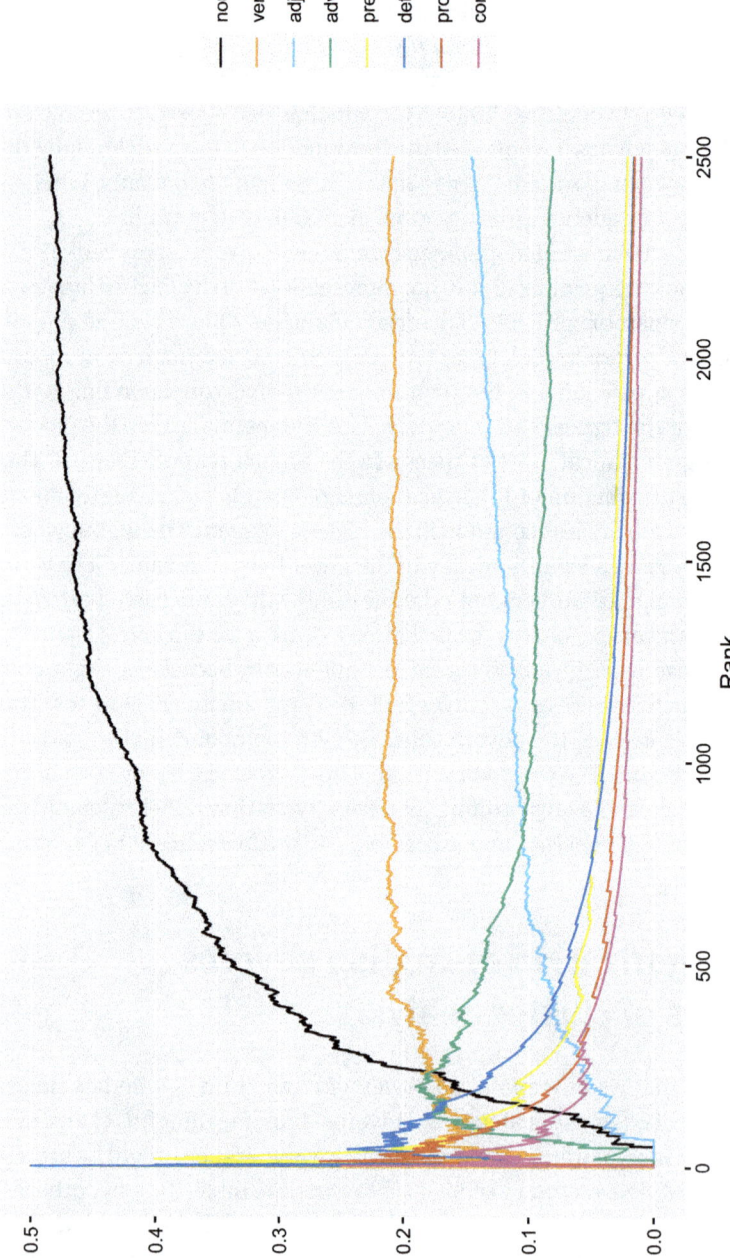

Figure 2: Part of speech and rank of the 2500 most frequent lemmas in the *British National Corpus* (combined graphs).

The subcategorization of English adverbs: A feature-based clustering approach

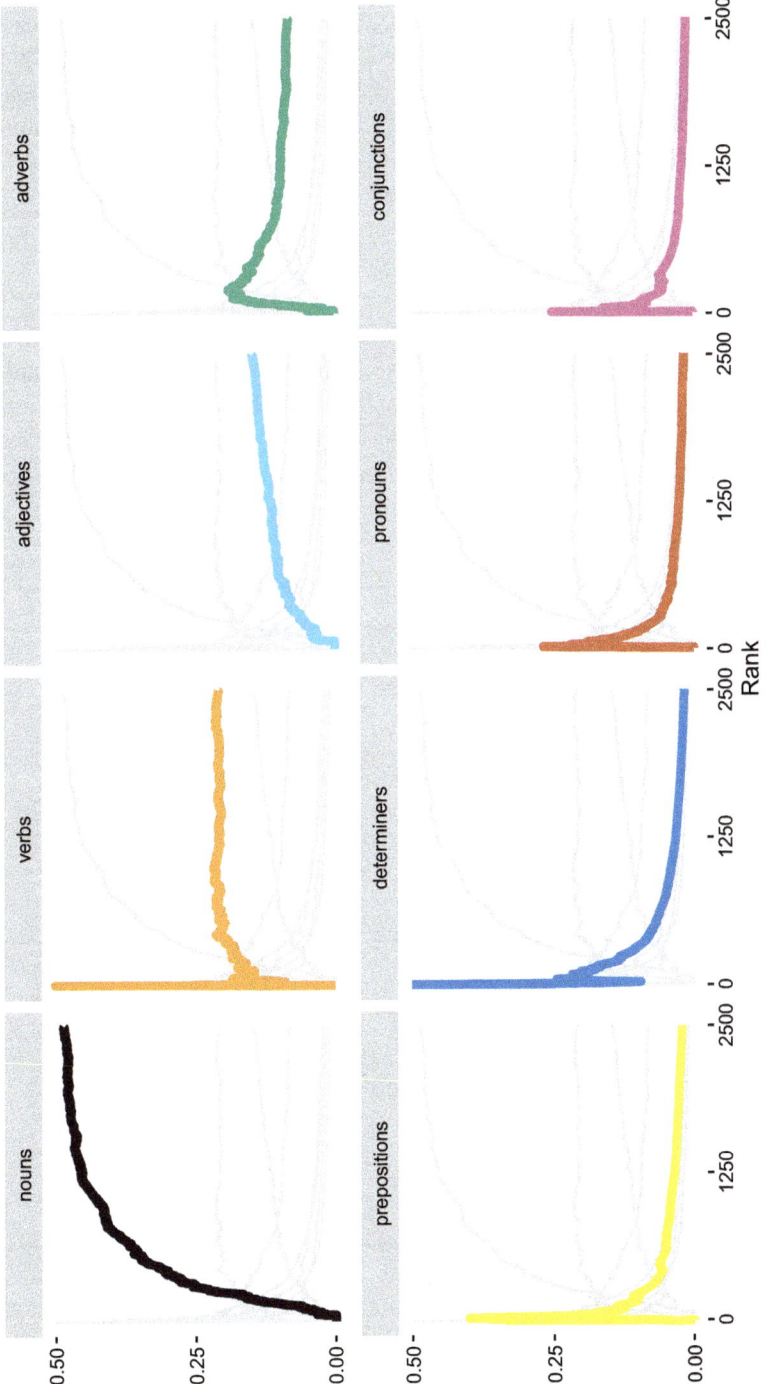

Figure 3: Part of speech and rank of the 2500 most frequent lemmas in the *British National Corpus* (individual graphs).

with certainty using cluster analysis alone. Options include the sample of cases studied, the individual case features measured, the distance function, the cluster analysis method, how the number of clusters is determined, and what is done about possible outliers. In the present study, the clustering is based on the morpho-semantic and historical features of the adverbs under consideration.

4.1 Method

We carried out cluster analyses on the adverb dataset described above (n=206 adverbs) based on seven features: four features which were already used in the analyses above (Etym_language, Etym_age, Motiv., Word_family) as well as three new features that code adverb-related information (Adv_word_formation, Adv_suffixes and Adv_semantics), and which are explained in Table 4 and below.

Table 4: Codes for adverb-related information.

Code	Content	Possible values
Adv_word_formation	word formation type of the target word based on the *Oxford English Dictionary*	simple compound derivation other
Adv_suffixes	more specific information regarding the suffix types	suffix types: LY SIDE WARD WARDS WISE
Adv_semantics	subcategorization into semantic classes	connective (*however, therefore*) degree (*very, completely*) place (*there*) OR direction (*out*) distance (*far, widely*) frequency (*always, once*) manner (*beautifully, hard*) modality (*probably, not*) reason (*why*) relation (*either, instead*) time (*then, ago*)

The feature **word formation type** codes the mechanisms of word formation underlying the creation of the individual items in the dataset. It distinguishes the categories *simple* (for items that are not formed using word formation), *compound* (for items involving the combination of at least two freely occurring bases with no derivation on the highest level),[7] *derivation* (for items containing a prefix or suffix on the highest level of analysis) and *other*.

Within the category of derivation, suffixations were further analyzed and coded with regard to the **suffix** used. The derivations in the dataset contain the five suffixes *-ly, -side, -ward, -wards* and *-wise*.

Finally, the **semantic class** of each adverb was determined and coded in the spreadsheet with the data. Semantic categorization was largely based on Quirk et al. (1985: 479) and supported by dictionary checks of the adverbs' definitions in Oxford University Press' online dictionary www.lexico.com. Each adverb was classified into the categories listed in bold print below based on whether the adverb could be used to provide an answer to the corresponding test question:

- **PLACE:** Where did you do it? – *There.*
  was combined with
  DIRECTION: Where did you send it? – *Out.*
- **TIME:** When did you do it? – *Then.*
- **FREQUENCY:** How often did you do it? – *Always.*
- **MANNER:** How did you do it? – *Beautifully.*
- **DEGREE:** How large is it? – *Very* (large).
- **MODALITY:** How likely did you do it? – *Probably.*

Where this method yielded no results, the adverb in question was assigned to the following categories based on their meaning and (in some cases) based on the syntactic functions of their members:
- **REASON** has the unique member *why*
- **DISTANCE** comprises adverbs that refer to the amount of space between two entities (*far, apart, close, widely, closely, short, to* 'nearly closed')
- **CONNECTIVE** comprises adverbs that link clauses and readily occur in clause-initial position (*anyway, nevertheless, moreover, thus, though, however, therefore, hence*)
- **RELATION** comprises adverbs that also link entities (but not necessarily clauses) and that typically occur in positions other than sentence-initially (*also, too, together, else, both, either, instead, otherwise, neither*).

With regard to the choice of statistical methods for the subcategorization of English adverbs, there are two general approaches to hierarchical cluster analysis: agglomerative clustering and divisive clustering (see Figure 4). Agglomerative clustering is a

---

[7] See Sanchez-Stockhammer (2018: 57) for a more detailed definition of the compound concept.

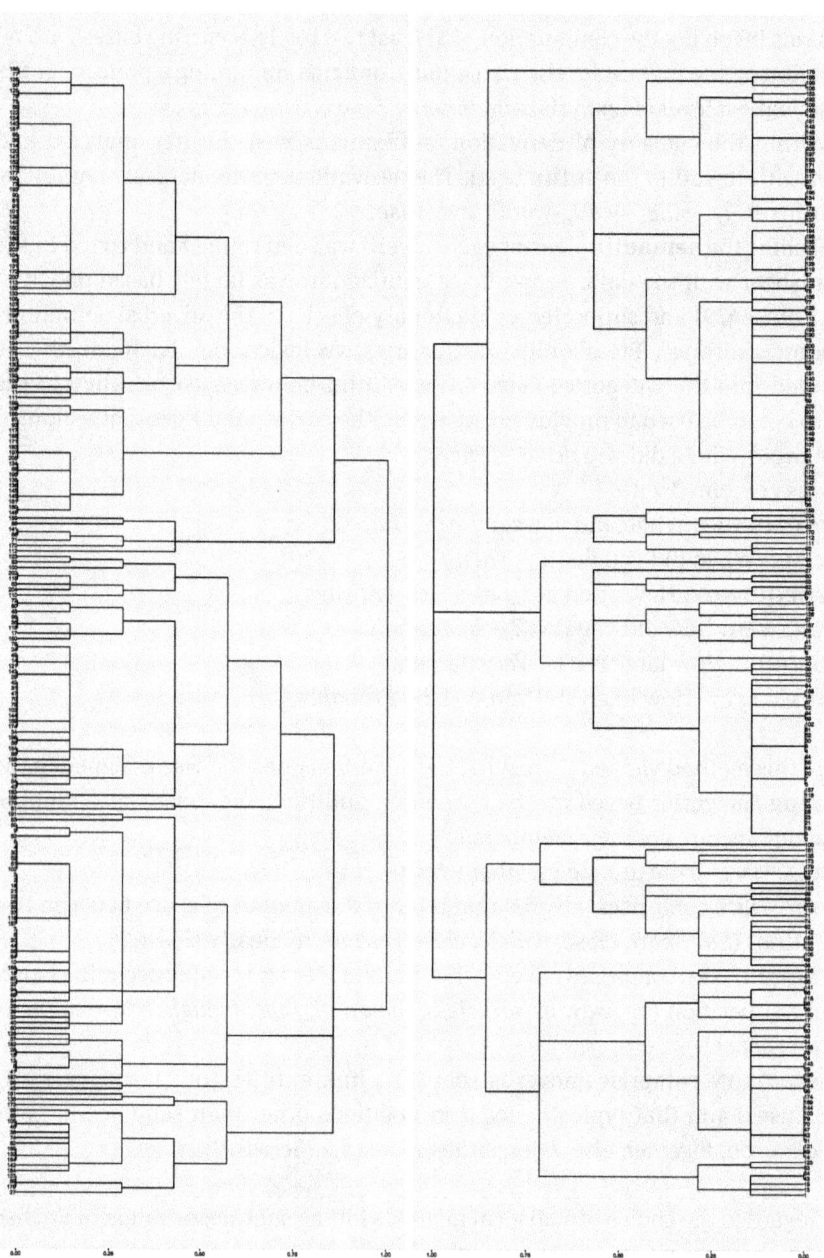

Figure 4: Agglomerative clustering of the adverbs data on the left and divisive clustering of the same data on the right based on the features Etym_language, Etym_age, Motiv., Word_family, Adv_word_formation, Adv_suffixes and Adv_semantics. Figure 4 is available in full size and high resolution at https://www.degruyter.com/document/isbn/9783110767971/html

stepwise bottom-up approach in which items are combined into clusters of growing size. In this approach, the individual adverbs from our sample were combined into ever larger groups. Divisive clustering, by contrast, is a top-down approach which starts out with a single group and keeps splitting it until only individuals are left.

Figure 4 shows that the results from the two clustering approaches suggest different structures, and it is also necessary to choose a suitable level of granularity for the process. We therefore used three separate methods and combined the results, so as to select the number of clusters with the largest amount of agreement (i.e. the proportion of cases assigned to the same cluster by all three methods). We used Gower's distance function in our consensus clustering (Chiu 2018) with the R package *diceR* (Chiu 2020), because it is particularly suitable for categorical variables like ours (cf. Giordani et al 2020). The methods employed were
- agglomerative hierarchical clustering using Ward's method
- divisive hierarchical clustering using the *diana* algorithm
- clustering around medoids using the *pam* algorithm (a robust version of *kmeans*).

R's *hclust* function was used for hierarachical clustering (R Core Team 2020). The *diana* and *pam* algorithms (Kaufman 1990) are in the *cluster* package (Maechler et 2019). An overview of clustering methods and R can be found in Giordani et al. (2020).

For each of the three methods, we found clusterings for 2, 3, 4 and 5 clusters (i.e. 12 clusterings altogether). Table 5 shows the comparison between the three methods for each number of clusters (2, 3, 4, 5). The agreement is by far the best with 3 clusters, since all three methods agree for 197 of the 206 adverbs. In the following, cases that are in the same clusters for each method are assigned to that cluster and bordering cases are put in an "other" group. The three groups of adverbs that all three methods agree on are marked as (A), (B) and (C) in the following. A fourth group is defined negatively as containing the remaining adverbs that cannot be consistently assigned to a single one of the three consensual categories. These cases do not form a homogeneous group but arise along the borders between clusters.

Table 5: Agreement on clusters using hierarchical clustering, divisive clustering and partition around medoids.

Number of clusters	Cases agreed on	Cases not agreed on
2	145	61
3	197	9
4	176	30
5	171	35

4.2 Visualization of the clusters

We visualized our results using a Multidimensional Scaling (MDS) plot and a parallel coordinate plot specially adapted for categorical variables. Multidimensional Scaling is an exploratory method which attempts to model the p-dimensional similarities/differences between cases in two dimensions. The Multidimensional Scaling was carried out with the *smacof* package (Mair et al. 2020; de Leeuw et al. 2009). Since seven dimensions are rendered on a two-dimensional plane, it can only represent an approximation. The dots represent the 100 different feature combinations amongst the 206 adverbs. The visualization in Figure 5 is consistent with having 3 separated clusters (in orange, black and blue). The green dots represent the cases which cannot be clearly assigned to one group.

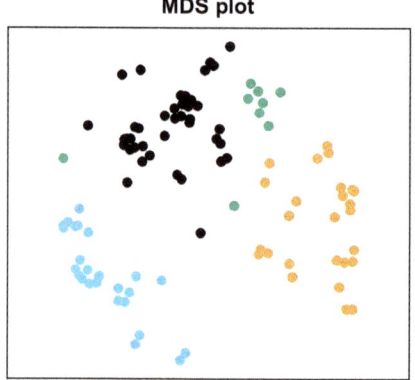

Figure 5: Multidimensional Scaling plot of the consensual clusters based on the features Etym_language, Etym_age, Motiv., Word_family, Adv_word_formation, Adv_suffixes and Adv_semantics, with Cluster 1 in black, Cluster 2 in orange, Cluster 3 in blue and the bordering cases in green. The isolated green dot in the middle is *only*, and the isolated green point on the right is *however*. The black point at the centre is *later*.

The second visualization of the clusters is represented by Parallel Coordinate Plots for displaying multivariate continuous data. These have been used more and more over the past thirty years, ever since they were introduced by Inselberg (1985). Parallel Coordinate Plots offer an intriguing way of viewing many dimensions simultaneously. Recent research has shown how the plots can be used for multivariate categorical data as well, and this approach has been applied to visualize the identified clusters of adverbs. A Parallel Coordinate Plot (as in Figure 6) has one vertical axis for each variable. With categorical variables, as in this application, the axes are divided into boxes whose height is proportional to the number of cases within that category. Each case in the plot is represented by a polyline, a set of connected lines linking the category values of the case on each successive axis. In this dataset, there are 206 cases and 7 variables, so that there are 206 polylines each made up of 6 straight lines. If cases have the same values on two successive axes, they are still drawn as separate lines, so that all 206 cases are individually represented in a Parallel Coordinate Plot. (This is not true of the Multidimensional Scaling plot, in which cases with the same values on all axes are drawn at the same point and are not distinguishable.)

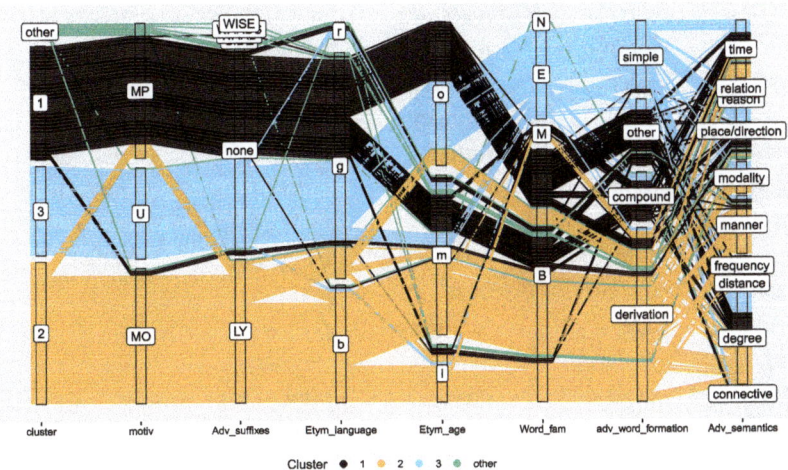

Figure 6: Parallel coordinate plot of the clusters based on the features Etym_language, Etym_age, Motiv., Word_family, Adv_word_formation, Adv_suffixes and Adv_semantics. Figure 6 is available in full size and high resolution at https://www.degruyter.com/document/isbn/9783110767971/html

The Parallel Coordinate Plot in Figure 6 (which was drawn using Ge & Hofmann 2020) indicates which variables separate the clusters. The ordering of the axes and the orderings of the categories on each axis were chosen to group clusters together. By reading down an axis, it is possible to see whether the members of a particular cluster (in the colour indicated at the bottom) can be determined by a particular part of the axis. By following a cluster in one particular colour across, one can determine the features that describe the cluster. For instance, the upper part of the vertical axis Word_fam shows that the members of the blue cluster differ from the members of the other clusters in that they exclusively have the feature E (= the word can only be expanded into a longer word, but it cannot be analysed into morpho-semantically meaningful parts). The orange cluster, by contrast, is distinguished on the Adv_suffixes axis as containing all adverbs ending in *-ly* except for *only*.

4.3 Linguistic analysis of the clusters

In the following, we present the full lists of words contained in the three consensual clusters followed by a discussion of each cluster's respective characteristics. The ordering of the adverbs is by decreasing frequency. The colours referred to in the headers correspond to those in Figure 6.

(1) **Cluster 1** (= black; 65 adverbs)

not	least	better	close	somewhat
how	almost	instead	nevertheless	inside
when	long	round	somewhere	deep
there	later	forward	tonight	somehow
back	once	anyway	before	that
where	far	hard	alone	moreover
never	today	above	twice	anywhere
most	early	maybe	high	short
why	sometimes	apart	elsewhere	aside
away	further	best	fast	
always	ago	tomorrow	pretty	
right	yesterday	below	neither	
often	indeed	along	meanwhile	
already	home	late	alright	

Table 6 provides an overview of the word formation types in the clusters and confirms Huddleston & Pullum's (2002: 565) observation about adverbs that "the great majority of them are morphologically complex". Nonetheless, important differences can be found: the comparison of the adverbs in Cluster 1 reveals a relatively large group of compounds like *anyway*, *somewhat* or *moreover* (23 out of 28). Even larger (with 31 out of 38) is the group of "other word formations", which includes zero-derivations (like *home*; from the noun), prefixations (like *along*) or extended variants of synonyms (e.g. *often* from *oft*; cf. the *Oxford English Dictionary*). While the result may at first sight seem almost as heterogeneous as the traditional adverb class, the difference to the traditional categorization is that most of the members of the category are actually linked by a common property: if we compare Cluster 1 to the other clusters, it emerges that Cluster 1 overwhelmingly contains complex words (i.e. word formations) that are predominantly partially motivatable. In addition, a very large proportion of the items in this cluster cannot take inflection – with the exception of those adverbs whose listed form already represents a comparative or superlative, namely *further*, *later*, *better*, *best*, *least* and *most*. While this is not unique to Cluster 1 (as Cluster 3 contains the comparatives *more* and *less*), all of the listed comparatives/superlatives in Cluster 1 end in -*er* or -*est* and are thus more readily recognizable as complex linguistic items – a quality that emerges as characteristic of Cluster 1.

Table 6: Word formation type by clusters.

Word formation type	Cluster 1	Cluster 2	Cluster 3	Bordering cases	Total
simple adverb	2	0	39	0	41
derivation	9	81	2	7	99
compound	23	0	4	1	28
other word formation	31	0	6	1	38

(2) **Cluster 2** (= orange; 81 adverbs)

really	easily	mainly	closely	occasionally
probably	immediately	currently	effectively	mostly
actually	eventually	entirely	unfortunately	regularly
particularly	highly	previously	strongly	shortly
usually	fully	extremely	rapidly	initially
certainly	slightly	fairly	similarly	specifically
simply	hardly	increasingly	originally	deeply
especially	directly	equally	perfectly	subsequently
clearly	completely	surely	virtually	gradually
finally	normally	totally	badly	essentially
quickly	slowly	frequently	rarely	precisely
recently	relatively	absolutely	significantly	successfully
suddenly	apparently	partly	naturally	greatly
generally	merely	seriously	quietly	
nearly	largely	necessarily	heavily	
obviously	possibly	properly	gently	
exactly	carefully	widely	firmly	

It immediately strikes the eye that the adverbs in Cluster 2 exclusively end in -*ly*, and Table 7 shows that all -*ly* adverbs are also exclusively contained in Cluster 2. This underlines the importance of this suffix as a marker of Cluster 2 as one highly characteristic and well-defined subclass of prototypical adverbs.[8] The decisive

---

[8] Only one word in Cluster 1, namely *early*, ends in -*ly*, but this is a special case, since the initial *ear* is merely a superficially transparent pseudo-constituent. Note that the status of the suffix -*ly* is disputed: Quirk et al. (1985: 1556) state that the suffix -*ly* "can be very generally added to an

criterion for this subcategory of adverbs can be expressed in different ways: as the presence of a suffix (as in our database), as the presence of an adjectival basis (as in Quirk et al.'s 1985 criterion for open-class adverbs) or as the presence of the specific suffix -*ly*.[9] The clustering approach adopted here can thus provide statistical support for one of the traditional subgroups of adverb classification. In addition, most of the adverbs with -*ly* can take a comparative or superlative (e.g. *more/most seriously*), though not all (e.g. **more/most mostly* does not occur in the *British National Corpus*). As Table 7 shows, suffixation is not exclusive to Cluster 2, but the only suffixed adverb in another cluster is *forward* in Cluster 1 with its mix of "other word formations".

Furthermore, 73 of the 81 adverbs in Cluster 2 are fully morpho-semantically motivatable (MO), and there are only 8 (e.g. *especially* or *hardly*) with partial motivatability (cf. Table 9).

Table 7: Suffixes by clusters.

Suffix	Cluster 1	Cluster 2	Cluster 3	Bordering cases
No Suffix	64	0	51	5
-*ly*	0	81	0	1
-*side*	0	0	0	1
-*ward*	1	0	0	0
-*wards*	0	0	0	1
-*wise*	0	0	0	1

Finally, let us consider the contribution of the adverbs' semantic categories to the subcategorization into clusters. Table 8 shows that all semantic categories with more than ten members (and thus with a sufficiently large number to derive more general patterns) occur in all three clusters, so that it is not possible to use semantic categorization to discriminate clearly between the clusters. Nonetheless, we

---

adjective in a grammatical environment requiring an adverb (gradable if the adjective concerned is gradable), so that it could almost be regarded as inflectional". This is how Fill (1980: 50–52) and Wolff (1969: 37) treat -*ly* adverbs in their quantitative analyses.

9 Note Huddleston & Pullum's (2002: 566) observation about "morphological constraints: -*ly* does not attach to adjectives beginning with the prefix *a*- [authors' note: actually, -*ly* does attach to adjectives with the negative prefix *a*-, as is exemplified by *atypically* or *asexually*] or, in general, ending with the Latin comparative suffix ·*or*, or to adjectives that themselves end in -*ly* (whether or not this represents the adjective-forming suffix -*ly*)" and semantic constraints, namely that the "-*ly* suffix does not attach to adjectives derived from place-names, nor in general to those denoting colours".

can discern a tendency for Cluster 2 to contain adverbs of degree, manner and modality and we observe an underrepresentation with regard to adverbs of place or direction, which are more characteristic of Cluster 1 and Cluster 3.

Table 8: Semantic classes by cluster.

Semantic class	Cluster 1	Cluster 2	Cluster 3	Bordering cases	Total (n)
connective (*however, therefore*)	3	0	4	1	8
degree (*very, completely*)	13	27	12	1	53
place (*there*)/direction (*out*)	15	1	13	4	33
distance (*far, widely*)	4	2	1	0	7
frequency (*always, once*)	5	5	1	0	11
manner (*beautifully, hard*)	5	25	2	1	33
modality (*probably, not*)	3	10	5	0	18
reason (*why*)	1	0	0	0	1
relation (*either, instead*)	2	0	6	1	9
time (*then, ago*)	14	11	7	1	33

(3) **Cluster 3** (= blue; 51 adverbs)

out	even	in	no	through
up	down	off	enough	straight
so	still	next	therefore	under
then	here	rather	soon	hence
more	too	quite	else	sure
now	on	yet	thus	like
just	over	perhaps	either	abroad
also	much	together	to	
well	again	less	though	
very	all	both	okay	
as	about	ever	little	

Most of the adverbs in Cluster 3 are grammatical words and cannot take inflection. However, there are also several lexical adverbs that can be graded, e.g. *much, soon* or *down*. Numerous items in Cluster 3 are formally identical with prepositions (e.g. *up* or *on*),[10] but in line with Sanchez (2008), these are not classified as zero-derivations, because only lexical words are considered as bases for this

---

[10] Huddleston & Pullum (2002: 614) would classify such items which are considered adverbs in the present approach as prepositions.

type of "other" word formation (due to the difficulty of establishing directionality between related grammatical parts of speech). Table 9 shows that Cluster 3 exclusively consists of unmotivatable adverbs (which cannot be decomposed into morpho-semantic constituents), and at the same time Cluster 3 is the only cluster containing unmotivatable adverbs. Morpho-semantic non-compositionality therefore emerges as a highly distinctive criterion for Cluster 3. Note that this variable also correlates with word-family integration, since only words that are either fully or partially motivatable have the opportunity to reach the status B for both motivatable and expandable items.

Table 9: Morpho-semantic compositionality in the clusters.

Motivatability	Cluster 1	Cluster 2	Cluster 3	Bordering cases
fully motivatable (MO)	3	73	0	1
partially motivatable (MP)	62	8	0	7
unmotivatable (U)	0	0	51	1

(4) **Bordering cases** (= green; 9 adverbs)
    only   *ahead*   *afterwards*
    however   *otherwise*   *easy*
    around   *outside*   *across*

There are 9 adverbs which the three methods do not classify in the same way, and which therefore do not fit neatly into any of the previous categories. The majority of these are prefixations or suffixations – so that even the negatively defined group shares some commonality.

To sum up, our cluster analyses manage to subdivide the heterogeneous mass of adverbs into three subcategories which share meaningful features from a linguistic perspective. Still, it should be noted that this method may yield different results for a different sample (e.g. the 1,000 most frequent words), different features (e.g. those used by Delhem, this volume) or a different clustering algorithm. Cluster analysis is no constant, universally applicable method supplying ready-made linguistic categorization, but should rather be viewed as a potential generator of ideas or as a technique for generating hypotheses. Its output depends crucially on the input and it needs to be validated by assessing the meaningfulness of the suggested groupings through the search for shared patterns within groups that are not present in the other groups. For the study of English adverbs in this paper, the selected clustering approach proved to work very well.

Finally, we also investigated to what extent the clustering of the adverbs in our dataset is better described in terms of
a) Quirk et al.'s (1985) suggested distinction between the class of open adverbs (with an adjectival base) and the class of closed adverbs (comprising all other adverbs)[11] or
b) in terms of the potential presence or absence of inflection (also including analytical comparatives and superlatives with *more* and *most*), which can be used to subcategorize adverbs into a lexical class (that can take inflection) and a grammatical class (that cannot).

To this end, we analysed the agreement between our clustering and the two categories Adv_CGEL (cf. Table 11) and Adv_lg (cf. Table 12).

Table 10: Codes for open/closed vs. lexical/grammatical distinction.

Code	Content	Possible values
Adv_CGEL	open adverbs (= with an adjectival base) vs. closed adverbs (= all other adverbs) following Quirk et al. (1985: 73)	open (*clearly*) closed (*soon*)
Adv_lg	subcategorization into lexical and grammatical adverbs based on the morphological criterion of inflection	lex can take inflection (*hard*) gr cannot take inflection (*then*)

For the coding of these categories, it was determined whether the adverbs in the dataset contain an adjectival base (Adv_CGEL) – which is the case for 82 out of 206 adverbs – and whether they can take inflection (Adv_lg). The morphological criterion of inflection was understood in a wide sense here and does not only comprise the addition of an inflectional suffix to form the comparative or superlative (e.g. *to work hard – harder – hardest*), but also includes comparatives and superlatives formed with periphrastic *more* and *most*, which is a common pattern in polysyllabic English adverbs (e.g. *obviously – more obviously – most obviously*). Altogether, this is the case of 122 out of 206 adverbs.

The results in Tables 11 and 12 suggest that the presence or absence of an adjectival base (i.e. Quirk et al.'s distinction) is a much stronger criterion for the

---

11 Quirk et al. (1985: 73) suggest that "the class of adverbs [...] may be separated into an open class consisting of adverbs with an adjectival base (especially those, like *completely*, which have an *-ly* suffix), and a closed class including adverbs such as *here, there, now*, etc." and also state that "Morphologically, we can distinguish three types of adverb, of which two are closed classes (simple and compound), and one is an open class (derivational)" (Quirk et al. 1985: 438).

subcategorization of English adverbs than the property of permitting inflection (or not). The CGEL system of using adjectival bases achieves clear agreement with our Cluster 2, no agreement at all with Cluster 1 and Cluster 3 and almost no agreement in the category of bordering cases (where *otherwise* is the only exception to an otherwise clear-cut picture). The criterion of inflection, by contrast, fails to distinguish clearly between the clusters and produces considerable overlap.

Table 11: Agreement between our clustering and the distinction between open and closed adverbs following Quirk et al.'s (1985) *Comprehensive Grammar of the English Language* (CGEL).

Cluster	CGEL open	CGEL closed
1	0	65
2	81	0
3	0	51
Bordering cases	1	8

Table 12: Agreement between our clustering and the presence or absence of inflection in the dataset.

Cluster	Inflection	No inflection
1	51	14
2	19	62
3	45	6
Bordering cases	7	2

5 Summary and conclusion

In our study, we analysed the 206 most frequent adverbs from the *British National Corpus* with state-of-the-art statistical methods. The aim was not to look at individual cases, but to generate ideas about more general structures of the category of English adverbs. Provided that a dataset with comparable features is available, the same method can in theory also be applied to other languages.

The combination of three different clustering approaches suggests three clusters (and a small group of bordering cases) within the category of the English adverb. These clusters are characterized by the following prevalent word formation types:

- Cluster 1 contains complex words (i.e. word formations) that are predominantly partially motivatable and no suffixations (e.g. *anywhere*).
- Cluster 2 contains only suffixations with *-ly* (e.g. *previously*).
- Cluster 3 exclusively consists of unmotivatable adverbs – and thus of morphologically simple words (e.g. *next*).

Our study thus shows that word formation type can serve as a criterion for the subcategorization of high-frequency English adverbs. Previous approaches have tended to emphasize the important status of *-ly* adverbs (which is corroborated by our statistical approach), but morpho-semantic (non-)compositionality as its higher-level abstraction emerges as yet another possible feature for adverb subcategorization.

It should be noted that there is some overlap between our clusters and Huddleston & Pullum's (2002: 565–570) discussion of the morphological form of adverbs: they distinguish the three subcategories of (a) de-adjectival adverbs in ·*ly* like *really*, (b) other morphologically complex adverb lexemes like *maybe*, and (c) adverbs that are homonymous with adjectives like *hard*. Furthermore, they discuss "Other lexically simple adverb lexemes" (Huddleston & Pullum 2002: 570) that are not homonymous with adjectives, such as *way* (in *way too big*). As a consequence, only our Cluster 2 provides a perfect match with their category (a), whereas their categories (b) and (c) only partially overlap with our clusters, since homonymy with other linguistic items does not play a role in our approach. As Huddleston & Pullum's classification always requires awareness of other contexts in which a word form to be classified can be potentially used, a morphologically simple item can only be assigned to subcategory (c) if the analyst is aware of alternative uses of the word form with the distribution that is typical of adjectives. This makes a purely context-based classification like that in e.g. Quirk et al. (1985) impossible and presupposes that the analyst following Huddleston & Pullum's classification system always manages to think of all conceivable options. While our analysis focuses on data at the word level (morpho-semantics and historical development), other empirical studies, such as Delhem (this volume), place more emphasis on distributional syntactic criteria. An interesting avenue of research might therefore lie in the combination of both types of information to yield the basis for an even more comprehensive clustering approach. Since Clusters A and B are still heterogeneous to a certain extent, such a combined approach might hold the potential for further subdifferentiation. At the same time, however, it must be noted that it is precisely the restriction to a small number of features that allows us to define our clusters in a very tight fashion corresponding to plausible linguistic categories – and this can in turn be considered an advantage of the present approach.

References

Chiu, Derek & Aline Talhouk. 2018. DiceR: An R package for class discovery using an ensemble driven approach. *BMC Bioinformatics* 19(11). 1–4.
Chiu, Derek, Aline Talhouk & Johnson Liu. 2020. *DiceR*. https://CRAN.R-project.org/package=diceR.
Crystal, David. 1995. *The Cambridge encyclopedia of the English language*. Cambridge: Cambridge University Press.
Delhem, Romain. 2018. Prépositions, adverbes et conjonctions en anglais: Pour une redéfinition des classes lexicales. *Anglophonia: French Journal of English Linguistics* 26. DOI: https://doi.org/10.4000/anglophonia.1821. (last accessed 16 June, 2021.)
Fill, Alwin. 1980. *Wortdurchsichtigkeit im Englischen: Eine nicht-generative Studie morphosemantischer Strukturen: Mit einer kontrastiven Untersuchung der Rolle durchsichtiger Wörter im Englischen und Deutschen der Gegenwart*. Innsbruck: Innsbrucker Beiträge zur Sprachwissenschaft.
Foley, Mark & Diane Hall. 2003. *Longman Advanced learners' grammar: A self-study reference & practice book with answers*. Harlow: Longman.
Ge, Yawei & Heike Hofmann. 2020. *ggpcp: Extension to 'ggplot2'*. https://github.com/yaweige/ggpcp.
Giordani, Paolo, Maria Ferraro & Francesca Martella. 2020. *An introduction to clustering with R*. Singapore: Springer.
Hallonsten Halling, Pernilla. 2017. Prototypical adverbs: from comparative concept to typological prototype. *Acta Linguistica Hafniensia* 49(1). 37–52.
Hengeveld, Kees & Marieke Valstar. 2010. Parts-of-speech systems and lexical subclasses. *Linguistics in Amsterdam* 3(1). 2–25.
Hennig, Christian, Marian Meila, Fionn Murtagh & Roberto Rocci. 2016. *Handbook of cluster analysis*. Boca Raton, Florida: CRC Press.
Herbst, Thomas & Susen Schüller. 2008. *Introduction to syntactic analysis: A valency approach*. Tübingen: Narr.
Hewings, Martin. 2005. *Advanced grammar in use. A self-study reference and practice book for advanced learners of English with answers*. 2nd edn. Cambridge: Cambridge University Press.
Hoeksema, Jack & Frans Zwarts. 1991. Some remarks on focus adverbs. *Journal of Semantics* 8(1–2). 51–70.
Hothorn, Torsten. 2020. Most likely transformations: The mlt package. *Journal of Statistical Software* 92(1). 1–68.
Hothorn, Torsten, Kurt Hornik & Achim Zeileis. 2006. Unbiased recursive partitioning: A conditional inference framework. *Journal of Computational and Graphical Statistics* 15(3). 651–674.
Hoye, Leo. 1997. *Adverbs and modality in English*. London: Longman.
Huddleston, Rodney & Geoffrey K. Pullum. 2002. *The Cambridge grammar of the English language*. Cambridge: Cambridge University Press.
Inselberg, Alfred. 1985. The plane with parallel coordinates. *The Visual Computer* 1. 69–91.
Jacobson, Sven. 1978. *On the use, meaning, and syntax of English preverbal adverbs*. Stockholm: Almqvist & Wiksell.
Kaufman, Leonard & Peter Rousseeuw. 1990. *Finding groups in data: An introduction to cluster analysis*. New York: Wiley.

Kilgarriff, Adam. 1997. Putting frequencies in the dictionary. *International Journal of Lexicography* 10. 135–155.
Krapp, George Philip. 1928. Troublesome adverbs. *The English Journal* 17(1). 31–33.
Leeuw, Jan de & Patrick Mair. 2009. Multidimensional scaling using majorization: SMACOF in R. *Journal of Statistical Software* 31(3). 1–30. https://www.jstatsoft.org/v31/i03/.
Liu, Mingya. 2012. *Multidimensional semantics of evaluative adverbs*. Leiden: Brill.
Maechler, Martin, Peter Rousseeuw, Anja Struyf & Mia Hubert. 2019. *Cluster*. https://CRAN.R-project.org/package=cluster.
Maienborn, Claudia & Schäfer, Martin. 2019. Adverbs and adverbials. Maienborn, Claudia, Heusinger, Klaus von & Portner, Paul (eds.), *Semantics – Lexical structures and adjectives*, 477–514. Berlin: De Gruyter.
Mair, Patrick, Jan de Leeuw & Patrick Groenen. 2020. *Smacof*. https://CRAN.R-project.org/package=smacof.
McNall, Louise E. & Chris Kennedy. 2008. Introduction. In Louise E. Louise McNally & Chris Kennedy (eds.), *Adverbs and adjectives: Syntax, semantics, and discourse*, 1–15. Oxford: Oxford University Press.
Nakamura, Wataru. 1997. A cognitive approach to English adverbs. *Linguistics* 35. 247–287.
Oxford English Dictionary. 2020. Oxford: Oxford University Press. www.oed.com.
Pittner, Karin, Daniela Elsner & Fabian Barteld. 2015. Introduction. In Karin Pittner, Daniela Elsner & Fabian Barteld (eds.), *Adverbs: Functional and diachronic aspects*, 1–17. Amsterdam: John Benjamins.
Quirk, Randolph, Sidney Greenbaum, Geoffrey Leech & Jan Svartvik. 1985. *A comprehensive grammar of the English language*. London: Longman.
R Core Team. 2020. *R: A language and environment for statistical computing*. Vienna, Austria: R Foundation for Statistical Computing. http://www.R-project.org/.
Ramat, Paolo & Davide Ricca. 1994. Prototypical adverbs: On the scalarity/radiality of the notion ADVERB. *Rivista di Linguistica* 6. 289–326.
Rauh, Gisa. 2015. Adverbs as a linguistic category (?). In Karin Pittner, Daniela Elsner & Fabian Barteld (eds.), *Adverbs: Functional and diachronic aspects*, 19–45. Amsterdam: John Benjamins.
Rosch, Eleanor. 1975. Cognitive representations of semantic categories. *Journal of Experimental Psychology, General* 104. 193–233.
Sanchez, Christina. 2008. *Consociation and dissociation: An empirical study of word-family integration in English and German*. Tübingen: Narr.
Sanchez-Stockhamer, Christina. 2018. *English compounds and their spelling*. Cambridge: Cambridge University Press.
Swan, Michael. *Practical English usage*. 3rd edn. Oxford: Oxford University Press.
Tower, David B. & Benjamin F. Tweed. 1853. *First lessons in language, or, Elements of English grammar*. Part-of-speech poem reprinted in Princeton Review Staff 2018, *Cracking the CSET California Subject Examinations for Teachers*, 22. 2nd edn. New York: Penguin Random House,
Vermeire, A. 1984. *Adverb phrases and adverbs. Pedagogical English grammar* 4. Trier: L.A.U.T.
Wolff, Dieter. 1969. *Statistische Untersuchungen zum Wortschatz englischer Zeitungen*. Universität des Saarlandes: Doctoral thesis.

2 Margins of the class

Ignazio Mauro Mirto
Proteus: Adverbial multi-word expressions in Italian and their cognate counterparts in *–mente*

> What is essential, Lewis, is
> usually invisible to the outward eye.
> Colin Dexter, *The Remorseful Day*

Abstract: This contribution focuses on Italian adverbs ending in *-mente* (e.g. *lussuosamente* 'luxuriously') with an analytic counterpart (a multi-word expression, MWE) which is etymologically related and capable of equally performing the adverbial function (e.g. *di lusso*). Two sentences diverging only in this regard have the same truth values and they entail each other. Morphologically, such adverbial MWEs are formed by a preposition which is followed by a noun/adjective sharing the content morpheme of the *-mente* adverb. However, in some contexts the cognate *-mente* adverb cannot replace its MWE. For instance, only MWE can be used as predicate in copular constructions (*La festa è di lusso*, 'the party is lavish'). For this research, more than a hundred pairs have been collected and classified. In this lexicographic enterprise, syntax happens to play a central role: one of the groups in the taxonomy (e.g. *vigliaccamente/da vigliacco*, 'like a coward'), has a revelatory property: the noun/adjective in the adverbial MWE inflects in gender and number. This suggests that these adverbial MWEs are predicates. It is argued that, due to the above-mentioned entailment relationships, *-mente* adverbs, even if invariable, function as predicates as well, and with identical argument structures. This leads to a reassessment of the joint role of syntax and suffixation in the lexical and grammatical construction of some semantic properties of adverbs and adverbials, leaving in the background traditional parts-of-speech distinctions.

Keywords: Subject-oriented adverb(ial)s, (multi-word) adjectives, morphemic invariance, inflectional requirements, entailments, object raising

Ignazio Mauro Mirto, Università di Palermo, ignazio.mirto@libero.it

1 Introduction

With a considerable number of Italian adverbs ending in *–mente*,[1] for example *lussuosamente* 'lavishly/luxuriously', an analytic counterpart can be identified, e.g. *di lusso*, which: (i) shares the content morpheme of the *–mente* adverb; (ii) is equally capable of performing the adverbial function, and (iii) can replace the *–mente* adverb without causing changes in meaning. The sentences below provide an example of such pairs:

(1) È andata lussuosamente.
     'It went very well.'

(2) È andata di lusso
     'It went very well.'

The adverb *lussuosamente* in (1) is replaced in (2) by the adverbial multi-word expression *di lusso* (*lussuosamente* and *lusso* 'luxury' share the content morpheme *luss-*). As the translations suggest, this paradigmatic operation "hold[s] meaning constant" (Harris 1981: 203).[2] Occasionally, a number of analytic counterparts can be identified, as is the case with *meravigliosamente* 'marvellously/wonderfully', which can be replaced either by the noun phrase (NP) *una meraviglia* 'a wonder' (*Mi sento una meraviglia* 'I feel very well') or by the prepositional phrase (PP) *a meraviglia* 'literally: to/at wonder' and the *that*-clause *che è una meraviglia* (*Funziona meravigliosamente/a meraviglia/che è una meraviglia* 'It works wonderfully'). The adverb *improvvisamente* 'suddenly' also has many counterparts: the etymologically-related *d'improvviso* and *all'improvviso*, in addition to the following suppletive adverbials (with differences in register) *di punto in bianco*, *di botto*, *di colpo*, *(tutto) d'un tratto*, *(tutto) d'un colpo*.

In my view, there are at least two good reasons for focusing on the relationship between e.g. *lussuosamente* and *di lusso*. The first regards the number of such pairs in Italian.[3] For this research, approximately 110 pairs were collected and

---

[1] I would like to extend my thanks to the colleagues who commented upon a previous version of this paper. Needless to say, any errors or shortcomings are the author's.
[2] Regarding sentences formally related by morphemic invariance and semantic equivalence, see Harris (1981: v, 6, 293–351, 377–391).
[3] To the best of my knowledge, there is no systematic collection or treatment of these pairs in the literature, and the exact number is therefore unknown. Adverbials are investigated in e.g. Elia (1995), classifying 3,086 of them, in De Gioia (2001), listing 6,000 "compound adverbs", and in the synopsis offered by Voghera in Grossmann & Rainer (2004: 67). A few, scattered etymolog-

classified (two of them exemplify productive patterns, see the Appendix and fn. 10) and the size of the phenomenon produces a taxonomy which many would consider useful in the field of lexicography. The second relates to syntax, because, in this taxonomy, one type of analytic adverbs inflects by gender and number (e.g. *Lei*[F.SG] *reagisce da vigliacca*[F.SG] 'She reacts like a coward'), a fact of paramount importance because, on the one hand, it casts doubt on one of the most well-known and widespread criteria characterizing adverbs and adverbials, i.e. their alleged invariability,[4] and, on the other hand, it sheds light on the nature of the relationship between adverbs and nouns/adjectives.

Regarding the structure of this paper, Section 2 is dedicated to morphological and terminological clarifications. Section 3 draws attention to adverbial inflection, whilst Section 4 provides a sample of cognate pairs. Section 5 illustrates forms which can be deployed either as adjectives or adverb(ial)s and Section 6 focuses on the well-known heterogeneity of the adverbial function. Section 7 draws conclusions.

2 Morphology and terminology

From a morphological viewpoint, the adverbials investigated in this paper are formed by a preposition and followed either by a noun or an adjective, as Table 1 illustrates:

Table 1: Prepositional Phrases with adverbial value.[5]

PREP	(DEF ART)	NOUN/ADJECTIVE	MW-ADV	–*MENTE* ADVERB
in	il	complesso	*nel complesso* 'overall'	*complessivamente*
a	–	lungo	*a lungo* 'long/at length'	*lungamente*
di	–	istinto	*d'istinto* 'instinctively'	*istintivamente*

---

ically-related adverbials such as *di lusso* are also found in the aforementioned works. De Gioia (2001) and Elia (1995) employ Maurice Gross's Lexicon-Grammar methodology (see Gross 1990).
4 See e.g. Crystal (1987: 2), Auwera (1999: 8–11), Haser & Kortmann (2006: 66–69), De Cesare (2019: 18–19 and *passim*). This criterion is so widespread and pervasive that in most writings (e.g. Schwarze 2009: 185, Sensini 1997: 340, Serianni 1989: 487) it is declared at the outset and taken for granted throughout the work.
5 In Italian, the preposition and the definite article coalesce (e.g. *in* + *il*, 'in + the' > *nel*). The brackets indicate optional items.

At this juncture, it can be considered opportune to raise a couple of terminological issues. First, the pattern shown in Table 1 is one of those discussed in the relevant literature regarding Italian, in which analytic adverbs are referred to with labels such as the following: the pretheoretical and widespread *locuzioni avverbiali* 'adverbial phrases' (see e.g. Serianni 1989: 491–492), *avverbi composti* 'compound adverbs' (De Gioia 2001), *polirematiche avverbiali* 'multi-word adverbials' and *avverbi sintagmatici* 'phrasal adverbs' (see Voghera, in Grossmann & Rainer 2004: 67).

Second, the label *multi-word adverbs* (henceforth, MW-Adv/s) will be adopted to describe adverbials. Furthermore, since the word occurring in an MW-Adv and the corresponding *–mente* adverb have the same content morpheme, as happens in English with e.g. *in particular/particularly, in person/personally, of importance/importantly, on impulse/impulsively, on instinct/instinctively, on purpose/purposefully*, such MW-Advs will be referred to with the term *cognate*.[6]

3 Inflecting MW-Advs

The sentences in (3) below illustrate a case of overt agreement. They deploy the MW-Adv *sano e salvo* 'safe and sound', formed by the conjunction of the adjectives *sano* 'healthy' and *salvo* 'safe'. The morphemes in bold are inflectional:

(3) a. Lui è tornat**o** san**o** e salv**o**
 he is come back healthy and safe
 'He came back safe and sound.'
 b. Lei è tornat**a** san**a** e salv**a**
 'She came back safe and sound.'

Given the agreement in number and gender between the subject of (3b) and *tornata*, i.e. the past participle of *tornare* 'come back', no one would doubt that this past participle is a predicate and that the subject *lei* 'she' is its argument. If this analysis is agreed upon, and considering that the same agreement occurs with *sano e salvo*, why should one doubt that this MW-Adv also functions as a predicate and that the (notional) subject is its argument?

Additional examples of inflecting MW-Advs derive from the sentences in (4) and those in (5). Both feature non-cognate adverbials: the former, i.e. *di tasca*

---

6 The word *cognate* is here employed as researchers do either in diachronic linguistics (e.g. Latin MŬSCA 'fly' and Sicilian *musca* 'fly' are cognate words, i.e. they are etymologically related) or with the so-called *cognate objects*, also known as *figura etymologica*.

sua/nostra, etc., is formed by the preposition *di* 'of', the mandatorily bare noun *tasca* 'pocket', and a possessive adjective, whilst the MW-Adv which occurs in the latter is *di testa sua/nostra* 'literally: of head his-her/our':

(4) a. Lei pagò di tasca sua
   'She paid out of her (own) pocket.'
   b. Noi pagammo di tasca nostra
   'We paid out of our (own) pocket.'

(5) a. Lei fa di testa sua
   'She acts without consulting anyone.'
   b. Noi facciamo di testa nostra
   'We act without consulting anyone.'

In parallel with (3), the above examples illustrate how the possessive adjective which is located within the MW-Adv agrees in person and number with the subject of the sentence. In (4a) and (5a) the subject pronoun *lei* 'she' is 3rd person and singular, and so is *sua* 'her'. In (4b) and (5b), the subject pronoun *noi* 'we' is 1st person and plural, just like the adjective *nostra* 'our'.[7] In other words, the controller of the MW-Advs *di tasca sua/nostra* and *di testa sua/nostra* is the subject. Of importance, other MW-Advs also including a possessive adjective do not show the same behaviour. Consider, for example, *a nostra insaputa* 'unbeknown' (*Lui lo fece a nostra insaputa* 'He did it without our knowing'), and *a nostre spese* 'at our expense' (*C'è andato a nostre spese* 'He went there at our expense').

Numerous tests have consistently demonstrated that MW-Advs such as those in (2), (3), (4), and (5) above do function as adverbs.[8] For example, just as with *–mente* manner adverbs, the related interrogative pronoun is *come* 'how' (additional evidence, e.g. from selectional restrictions, can be found in Mirto 2018):

(6) Q. Come è andata? [cf. (2)]
   A. Di lusso
   'How did it go? Very well.'

---

[7] The rightmost morpheme *–a* of the possessive adjectives *sua* and *nostra* is inflectional. In (4), it agrees with the feminine and singular noun *tasca* 'pocket', whilst in (5) it agrees with the feminine and singular noun *testa* 'head'.
[8] Anna Maria Thornton (in Basile *et al.* 2010: 218) reports that the GRADIT dictionary (*Grande Dizionario Italiano dell'uso*, De Mauro 1999) records 65,000 *polirematiche*, i.e. multi-word entries. According to Miriam Voghera (in Grossmann & Rainer 2004: 67), approximately 32% of all adverbial entries are multi-word units (see also Grossmann & Rainer 2004: 57, 472–473).

(7) Q. Lei come pagò? [cfr. (4)]
    A. Di tasca sua
       'How did she pay? Out of her own pocket.'

The mere existence of inflecting MW-Advs such as those above should lead researchers to question the invariability of adverb(ial)s, that is, one of the cornerstones of existing research. However, there are other reasons to doubt the validity of this defining criterion and develop an interest in MW-Advs: of the cognate pairs of adverb(ial)s compiled for this research, there is one type with which, as is the case in (3), (4), and (5) above, inflection is overt, a fact which also sheds light on cognate –*mente* adverbs.

4 Cognate adverbial pairs

A sample of etymologically-related pairs such as those in (1) and (2) above is provided below (the shared content morpheme is in bold):[9]

The majority of the MW-Advs in Table 2 have no internal structure and are therefore invariable. However, of these MW-Advs, the type whose preposition is *da* (which in English can be translated in a number of ways, e.g. 'at', 'by', 'from', 'since', 'to') has the revelatory property already observed in (3), (4) and (5): the MW-Adv comprises a noun/adjective,[10] inflecting by gender and number (Corbett 1991 and Stump 2001 mention a number of languages with inflecting adverb(ial)s):

---

9 The replacement of one form with another may be limited to certain contexts or even to a single context (see the comments in Serianni 1989: 492). The sharing of the content morpheme may also take place with –*oni* adverbs: *ginocchioni*/*in ginocchio* 'on one's knees'. Lines i, iv, xix, and xx show allomorphic roots.
10 There are reasons to believe that in e.g. (8) *vigliacco* combines with the preposition *da* as a noun. One comes from the Italian word *bruto* 'brute' (or *bullo* 'bully'), which can be either an adjective or a noun. In the former case, the word inflects for gender and number, and the adjective has therefore four forms (*bruto*, *bruta*, *bruti*, and *brute*). As a noun, however, it can only be masculine. When the preposition *da* combines with *bruto*, the feminine forms are hardly found (*da bruto*/*da bruti*, ?*da bruta*/?*da brute*). Thus, this word seems to enter the combination as a bare noun. Further corroboration originates from the contrast between *da vigliacco* and e.g. the unlikely *da carino* (*carino* = 'cute'). Again, the difference appears to be due to word classes, duly recorded in dictionaries: *vigliacco* is recorded as either a noun or an adjective (*Max è (un) vigliacco* 'Max is a coward'), whilst *carino* is only classified as an adjective (?*Max è un carino*).

Table 2: –*mente* adverbs and their analytic counterparts.[11]

i	**apparent**emente	in **apparenz**a	apparently
ii	**automatic**amente	in **automatico**	automatically
iii	**compless**ivamente	nel **complesso**	overall
iv	**conseguent**emente	di **conseguenza**	consequently
v	**contemp**oraneamente	al **contempo**	simultaneously
vi	**continu**amente	di **continuo**	continuously
vii	**dettagli**atamente	in **dettaglio**	in detail
viii	**foll**emente	alla **follia**	madly
ix	**frequent**emente	di **frequente**	frequently
x	**garb**atamente	con **garbo**	politely
xi	in**dubbi**amente	senza **dubbio**	undoubtedly
xii	**infinit**amente	all'**infinito**	infinitely
xiii	**nascost**amente	di **nascosto**	secretly
xiv	**necess**ariamente	di **necessità**	necessarily
xv	**pappagall**escamente	a **pappagallo**	parrot-like
xvi	**perpendicol**armente	in **perpendicolare**	perpendicularly
xvii	**person**almente	di **persona**	personally
xviii	**precauzion**almente	per **precauzione**	as a precaution
xix	**rar**amente	di **rado**	rarely
xx	**sorprend**entemente	a **sorpresa**	surprisingly
xxi	**sostanzi**almente	in **sostanza**	basically
xxii	**telefon**icamente	al **telefono**	on the phone
xxiii	**teoric**amente	in **teoria**	in theory
xxiv	**vicend**evolmente	a **vicenda**	each other
xxv	**vigliacc**amente	da **vigliacco**	like a coward

(8) Lui reagì da vigliacco.
'He reacted like a coward[M.SG].'

---

[11] The pair in line x of Table 2, i.e. *garbatamente/con garbo*, exemplifies a rather productive subclass, parallel to the English *easily/with ease*, from Schachter (1985: 21–22), *enthusiastically/ with enthusiasm*, from Nilsen (1972: 74), *spectroscopically/with a spectroscope*, from Huddleston (1988: 123), including e.g. *abilmente/con abilità* 'skilfully', *disinvoltamente/con disinvoltura* 'casually', *fiduciosamente/con fiducia* 'confidently', *tranquillamente/con tranquillità* 'quietly'. Additional pairs obtain with the antonym *senza* 'without', e.g. *sgarbatamente/senza garbo* 'rudely', *svogliatamente/senza voglia* 'listlessly'. Another productive correspondence is that between gerunds and MW-Advs, e.g. *ottemperando a* 'complying with'/*in ottemperanza a* 'in compliance with', '*trottando* 'trotting'/*al trotto* 'at a trot'.

(9) Lei reagì da vigliacca.
    'She reacted like a coward[F.SG].'

Below, the poorly-formed sentences in (10) and (11) demonstrate that agreement in gender and number between the MW-Adv and the subject is mandatory:

(10)* Lui reagì da vigliacca.
    intended: 'He reacted like a coward[F.SG].'

(11)* Lei reagì da vigliacco.
    intended: 'She reacted like a coward[M.SG].'

Furthermore, as with (1) and (2), the pairs of sentences (8)-(12) and (9)-(13) mutually entail each other:

(12) Lui reagì vigliaccamente.
    'He reacted like a coward.'

(13) Lei reagì vigliaccamente.
    'She reacted like a coward.'

I contend that MW-Advs such as *da vigliacco* provide evidence that inflection is observable in various adverbial phrases (for additional cases, see Mirto 2018). That is, not all adverbials are invariable, at least in Italian, a fact which prompts us to reconsider this foundation of the current research on adverbs. In my opinion, the importance of such evidence cannot be underestimated, and for the following reasons:

- in an MW-Adv, the inflectional morpheme of the inner noun/adjective reveals which sentence constituent controls agreement;
- the agreement phenomenon proves that a predicative relationship exists between the controller and the MW-Adv; such MW-Advs thus function as predicates and this raises an issue concerning their argument structure, which should therefore be investigated; and
- given the entailment relationship in pairs (1)-(2), (8)-(12) and (9)-(13), there are grounds to maintain that *–mente* adverbs also function as predicates, even if this predication remains covert, in that it does not determine morphological correlates.

The members of pairs (8)-(12) and (9)-(13) are related in at least two ways: formally, because the sentences share all their content morphemes, and semantically, because they have identical truth values. The effect of these relations appears comparable to that which on a cold day our breath has on the surrounding air: it becomes temporarily visible. That is, such relations allow us to 'see' properties of –*mente* adverbs which would otherwise remain imperceptible. In addition, they shed light on the hypothesis which sees pairs (8)-(12) and (9)-(13) as related in a third way, i.e. structurally: do they express the same set of predicate-argument structures?

5 MW-Advs and adjectives: One form, two parts of speech

The Italian word-formation process illustrated in Table 1 also applies to adjectives, as e.g. with *all'oscuro* 'literally: at the dark, i.e. unaware': *Mario è all'oscuro dei cambiamenti* 'Mario is unaware of the changes'. Table 3 shows a number of contextualized one-word adjectives together with their cognate multi-word counterparts:

Table 3: One-word adjectives and their cognate multi-word counterparts.[12]

i	uno specialista	**fam**oso	di **fama**	a famous specialist
ii	un vetro	**frantum**ato	in **frantumi**	a shattered glass
iii	una nottata	**infern**ale	d'**inferno**	a hell of a night
iv	un uomo	in**ginocchi**ato	in **ginocchio**	a man on his knees

---

[12] Unlike in Table 2, no adjectives follow the preposition in Table 3, which includes past and present participles with adjectival values. Similar to the pairs in Table 2, the replacement of one form with another may be constrained. For example, *valoroso* and *di valore* differ in selectional restrictions: the modification of [- Animate] nouns such as *libro* 'book' is unlikely with the former: ??*un libro valoroso*. Moreover, the word order of analytic adjectives is constrained: unlike most simple Italian adjectives, which can generally be pre- and post-nominal, they *must* follow the noun, as happens with invariable adjectives (e.g. *la stanza blu* 'the blue room', *la blu stanza; *una vista mozzafiato* 'a breathtaking view', **una mozzafiato vista*). To the best of my knowledge, this constraint on attributive adjectives (i.e. no inflection, no pre-nominal position) has passed unnoticed in the literature. Word order is also relevant in relation to adverbs in –*mente* and their cognate MW-Advs. Whilst the former can modify adverbs (*È andata meravigliosamente bene* 'It went wonderfully well'), the latter cannot (?**È andata a meraviglia bene*).

Table 3 (continued)

v	il fischio	**inizi**ale	d'**inizio**	the initial whistle
vi	complimenti	**obblig**atori	d'**obbligo**	obligatory compliments
vii	una misura	**pes**ante	di **peso**	a heavy measure
viii	un libro	**prestigi**oso	di **prestigio**	a prestigious book
ix	un anello	**prezi**oso	di **pregio**	a precious ring
x	una giornata	**primaveri**le	di **primavera**	a spring day
xi	una domanda	**rit**uale	di **rito**	a ritual question
xii	una questione	**rilev**ante	di **rilievo**	a relevant issue
xiii	un'analisi	**routin**aria	di **routine**	a routine analysis
xiv	un tipo	**talent**uoso	di **talento**	a talented guy
xv	un uomo	**valor**oso	di **valore**	a brave man
xvi	una strada	**zigzag**ante	a **zigzag**	a zigzagging road

The double use of the pattern illustrated in Table 1 thus gives rise to an interesting phenomenon: the very same prepositional phrase originating from this pattern can function either as a multi-word adverbial or a multi-word adjective. For example, the PP *di lusso* in (2) above modifies a verb phrase and is thus an adverbial, but it can also function as an attributive adjective, as shown in (14a), or a predicative adjective, as in (14b):

(14) a. Siamo stati a una festa di lusso.
 'We went to a lavish party.'
 b. La festa è di lusso.
 'The party is lavish.'

The above examples demonstrate that the multi-word expression *di lusso* 'lavish/luxuriously' can also be employed as an adjective, either predicatively or attributively. Table 4 below shows the three possible uses for the PP *di lusso* as exemplified in (2), (14a), and (14b):

Table 4: Uses of the PP *di lusso*.

ADVERBIAL	ATTRIBUTIVE ADJECTIVE	PREDICATIVE ADJECTIVE
+	+	+

Worthy of note is the fact that one-word adjectives, e.g. *strange*, can also be used as shown in Table 4. This is illustrated in Table 5 and exemplified in (15) to (17).[13] The use of one-word adjectives such as that in (15) has been termed 'enallage':[14]

Table 5: Uses of the adjective *strange*.

ADVERBIAL	ATTRIBUTIVE ADJECTIVE	PREDICATIVE ADJECTIVE
+	+	+

(15)   They are acting strange.   (Joni Mitchell, *Both sides now*, cf. *They are acting strangely*)

(16)   This is a strange place.

(17)   This place is strange.

For reasons still to be investigated, the unrestricted use of adverbial PPs illustrated in Table 4 is in contrast with the restricted case of MW-Advs such as *da vigliacco* 'as a coward', shown in Table 6 (these values also hold for *–mente* adverbs), as (18a, b) demonstrate:

Table 6: Uses of the PP *da vigliacco* modifying a [+ Human] noun.

ADVERBIAL	ATTRIBUTIVE ADJECTIVE	PREDICATIVE ADJECTIVE
+	–	–

---

13 Adjectives and adverbs, at least in English and Italian, are not in complementary distribution, insofar as in some contexts the former can replace the latter. This substitution can either give rise to distinct meanings, as e.g. with *John fell silently* and *John fell silent* (a minimal pair, discussed in Mirto 2018) or leave the meaning unvaried, as in the following case of free variation in Italian: *L'uomo si aggirava furtivamente* and *L'uomo si aggirava furtivo*, both translatable as 'The man was prowling around'.

14 Defined as "the use of one grammatical form in place of another" (*Collins English Dictionary*), *enallage* is a barely-discussed figure of speech in the literature (the word never occurs in Grossmann & Rainer 2004; Mirto 2018 discusses a few cases in Italian). Researchers working in the Italian and English traditions connote it differently. Unlike the former, the latter place greater emphasis on the component relating to its incorrect usage (solecism), in e.g. tense, form, or person. Regarding the related term *hypallage*, see Pullum & Huddleston (2002: 558–559).

(18) a. *un uomo da vigliacco
 'a man who is a coward'
 b. *Leo è da vigliacco.
 intended: 'Leo is a coward.'

6 Heterogeneity

Another cornerstone of current research on adverb(ial)s is their heterogeneity (see e.g. Huddleston 1988: 121). In Table 7 below, the first three lines report the types of adverb(ial)s examined above. When such cases are considered together with the one-word and multi-word adverbial patterns illustrated in the remaining lines of the table, the outcome provides us with an approximate idea of the large variety of forms with which the adverbial function can manifest itself in Italian:

Table 7: Some manifestations of the adverbial function.

EXAMPLE	TYPE	ADVERB(IAL)
(1)	One-word adverbs (with an internal structure)	*lussuosamente* 'lavishly'
(2)	Prepositional phrases	*di lusso* 'lavishly'
(19)	That-clause (sentential)	*che è una meraviglia* 'marvellously'
(20)	Adjectives (enallage)	*rapido* 'fast'
(21)	Noun phrases (with an indefinite article)	*una favola* 'a fairy tale'
(22)	Noun phrases (mandatorily bare)	*(da) eroe* '(as a) hero'
(23)	One-word adverbs (without internal structure)	*ieri* 'yesterday'
(24)	Compounds	*nottetempo* 'overnight'
(25)	Prepositions[15]	*contro* 'against'
(26)	Gerunds	*barcollando* 'staggering'

(19) Funziona che è una meraviglia.
 functions that is a wonder
 'It works wonderfully.'

---

15 Prepositions such as *contro* 'against' are generally named *improprie* 'improper'. See Jansen 2011 (online), Schwarze (2009: 212–213).

(20) Lei chiamò rapida   il medico responsabile.
    she called fast[F.SG] the doctor responsible
    'She rapidly called the doctor in charge.'

(21) Sto una favola.
    stay a fairy tale
    'I feel real(ly) good.'

(22) Il colonnello morì (da) eroe.[16]
    the colonel died (from) hero
    'The colonel died a hero.'

(23) Leo è arrivato ieri.
    Leo is arrived yesterday
    'Leo arrived yesterday.'

(24) Leo è arrivato nottetempo.
    Leo is arrived overnight
    'Leo arrived during the night.'

(25) Q. Come ha votato? A. Contro.
    how has voted against
    Q. 'How did s/he vote?' A. Against.

(26) Leo cammina barcollando.
    Leo walks staggering
    'Leo staggers.'

For taxonomic reasons, morphologists have expended considerable effort in attempting to identify all possible sequences which an MW-Adv can take (see e.g. the references in fn. 3). However, this effort, might prove to be of limited interest, as Serianni (1989: 492) appears to suggest in his description of *locuzioni avverbiali* 'adverbial phrases': "Si tratta di una categoria dilatabile quasi all'infinito" 'It is a category which can almost be endlessly expanded' (author's translation). A similar remark is made by Maienborn & Schäfer: "adverbs differ from nouns,

---

16 In Italian, the verb *morire* 'die' is unaccusative. Of great interest is the contrasting case with the unergative *parlare*, which does not permit this kind of adverbial modification: **Il colonnello parlò eroe* 'The colonel spoke [like] a hero' (cf. *Il colonnello parlò da eroe* 'The colonel spoke as a hero').

adjectives, and verbs in that they often do not possess clear markers for category membership" (Maienborn & Schäfer 2011: 1392). The polymorphic adverbial function brings to mind Proteus, the mythological god, who was known for his ability to assume whatever shape he liked. This truly protean function can obviously be realized with adverbial phrases; however, Table 7 demonstrates that the function can also take the shape of noun phrases, adjectival phrases, prepositional phrases, verb phrases, and sentential phrases (this list only concerns phrases, which by no means exhaust all the possibilities; for additional patterns, see Mirto 2018: 179). No other category seems to permit such wide-ranging phrase types. The cognate MW-Advs discussed above constitute just one subset of the PP type.

7 Conclusion

An encyclopedic entry regarding Noam Chomsky (Walmsley 2006: 382–384) includes the following assessment by the late John Lyons (1989: 167): "in *Aspects* [...] Chomsky was [...] content to operate, uncritically, with the categories and subcategories of traditional grammar". Considering the reactions to Chomsky's ideas on e.g. morphology and syntax, Walmsley (*ibidem*) maintains that "Underlying almost all these theories [...] are frequently untested assumptions about the fundamental categories of language – word classes, attributes, and their values [...] These categories have hardly been questioned by the big commercial grammars, either". Lyons' critique of traditional parts of speech is well-known.[17] Other scholars have warned of the dangers inherent in theories based on such traditional partitions. For example, according to Nunzio La Fauci, categories such as noun, verb, etc. are "nozioni tutt'altro che affidabili" 'far from reliable notions' (La Fauci 2011: 30), and syntax should *not* be conceived of as "un algoritmo combinatorio di enti che gli preesistono" 'a combinatorial algorithm of pre-existing entities' (La Fauci 2011: 26, author's translations).[18]

---

[17] See also paragraph 4.3 in Lyons (1981). According to Pullum (1999: 66), however, in his early career Lyons had a different view: "some linguists have continued to argue for some semantic basis to the theory of major word classes: Lyons (1966) is one example".
[18] La Fauci expresses his views in a volume mainly concerning the legacy of Saussure. He calls into question the principle of compositionality, often interpreted as if each of the combining elements carried a pre-existing meaning and the outcome of the combination were the sum of such meanings (as does e.g. Kemp 2018: 11–12; see also Ajdukiewicz 1973: 345). The author demonstrates that the ontological foundation of this interpretation is not in keeping with Saussure's ideas. Culler (1986: 147, 148) also does justice to the Genevan scholar: "[...] ontological primacy

If the aforementioned critique of traditional categories is embraced, how can adverbs be alternatively viewed? A suggestion comes from the pairs proposed below, in which *–mente* adverbs can be observed in their relationship with cognate adjectives. The pairs in (27) and (28) permit a rigorous examination and more in-depth understanding of the nature of the relationship between adverbs and adjectives *by leaving their parts of speech in the background*:

(27) a. La Rai è orgogliosa di presentarlo.
    'The Rai is proud to present it.'
  b. La Rai lo presenta orgogliosamente.
    'The Rai proudly presents it.'

(28) a. Il Papa slavo non era facile a commuoversi.
    'The Slavic Pope was not easy to be moved.'
  b. Il Papa slavo non si commuoveva facilmente.
    'The Slavic Pope would not be moved easily.'

In each of the above pairs (additional pairs are discussed in Mirto 2018), an adjective and a cognate adverb occur, thus the adjective and the adverb share the same content morpheme. Semantically, these pairs behave as the sentences in (1) and (2), in which the substitution of the *–mente* adverb with an MW-Adv occurs without changes in truth values. That is, (27a) and (27b) entail each other and one is a paraphrase of the other. The same holds true for (28a) and (28b).[19]

Against this background, the following questions arise: which syntactic relations can guarantee these entailments? And, given that one member of the pair contains an adjective and the other contains an adverb, how can it be the case that truth values are preserved? The sentences in (27) lend themselves to the following type of analysis: in both, the content morpheme *orgogli-* 'pride' takes the derivational morpheme *–os* (its closest counterpart in English is probably *–ful*, as with *rispettoso* 'respectful'), which, however, is among those affixes unable to 'seal' a word, i.e. make it 'ready' to occur in an utterance. The outcome of this suffixation process therefore requires at least one additional morpheme, one which must be capable of producing a full-fledged word. In this view, the 'destiny' of

---

to objects gives way [. . .] to a theory based on the primacy of relations. [. . .] It is relationships that create and define objects, not the other way around".
19 It goes without saying that, unlike in pair (1)-(2), the (a) sentences of (27)-(28) differ from their (b) counterparts in the packaging of information.

orgoglios- depends on this sealing morpheme, which can only be of two types, mutually exclusive, as (29) illustrates:[20]

(29) a. An inflectional morpheme, agreeing in number and gender (four forms);
     b. The derivational morpheme *–mente* (invariable).

The outcome of (29a) is the lemma *orgoglioso*, which is deployable either as a predicative adjective (*Il Paese è orgoglioso di loro* 'The country is proud of them') or an attributive adjective (*genitori orgogliosi* 'proud parents'). The former option is selected in the copulative (27a), where *orgoglioso* functions as a two-place predicate capable of 'initiating' the structure:[21] it licenses the final subject *la Rai* (see Mirto 2008) and an optional oblique, which is invariably introduced by the preposition *di*. In (27a), this oblique is an infinitive.

The outcome of (29b) is the adverb *orgogliosamente* 'proudly', which, unlike *orgoglioso*, is unable to initiate[22] a copulative clause (**Il Paese è orgogliosamente* '*The country is proudly').[23] As a manner adverb, *orgogliosamente* can only combine with a main clause initiated *by another predicate*, which in (27b) is the verb *presentare* 'present', the same as the infinitive in (27a). That which characterizes *orgogliosamente* in (27b) is the fact that it is a subject-oriented adverb, thus metonymically referring to *la Rai*, the NP to which it assigns the meaning >the one who is proud< (a semantic role expressing membership in a set). The same line of analysis can be applied to pair (28). However, (28a) is more complex than (27a). This is easy to ascertain because whilst (27a) conveys the meaning *The Rai is proud*, sentence (28a), i.e. a case of object raising, does not convey the meaning *The Slavic Pope is easy*.[24] In other words, in (28a) *facile* is not a subject-oriented adjective (that is, *il Papa slavo* is not its argument). Rather, its scope appears to be the subordinate predicate *commuoversi* (together with the argument it licenses),

---

[20] Superlatives such as *orgogliosissimo* 'very proud' are ignored here.
[21] Italian adjectives do not inflect for the feature [person] and consequently do not provide the inflection required to 'seal' a finite clause. As is well-known, this sealing requires a verb.
[22] In parallel to certain attributive-only adjectives, as in English with e.g. *drunken* (**a sailor who was drunken*), *damn* (**That noise is damn*), *frigging, principal, putative* (these examples are from Huddleston & Pullum (2002: 553), who provide a long list). A formalization of predicates (in)capable of giving origin to a proposition is proposed in La Fauci & Mirto 2003.
[23] Unlike the adjective *orgoglioso* 'proud', the adverb *orgogliosamente* 'proudly' cannot license an additional argument.
[24] Regarding (28a), the English counterpart of *facile*, i.e. *easy*, should be considered. This adjective permits the so-called 'object raising', as in *John is easy to please*, a well-known example by Chomsky. On the other hand, the adjective *orgoglioso* 'proud' functions like *eager* in *John is eager to please*, the contrasting example provided by Chomsky (see Clark 2006: 231).

the same scope which *facilmente* has in (28b), a fact which paves the way for an account of the mutual entailments between these sentences.

To summarize: (27a) includes the meaning *La Rai è orgogliosa* 'The Rai is proud', whilst, if sentence polarity is ignored, (28a) includes the meaning *È facile (per il Papa slavo) commuoversi* 'It is easy (for the Slavic Pope) to be moved'. Under the foregoing analysis, such meanings originate from syntactic relations: that between the predicate *orgogliosa* and its argument *la Rai*, and that between the predicate *facile* and the infinitive *commuoversi*. The fact that (27a) and (27b) entail each other, as do (28a) and (28b), should be interpreted as if the aforementioned syntactic relationships in the (a) sentences also occur in the (b) counterparts, i.e. those with a *–mente* adverb. This hypothesis raises at least two questions regarding the (b) sentences: in (27b), which syntactic relation originates the meaning *La Rai è orgogliosa*? And, in (28b) which syntactic relation gives rise to the meaning *È facile (per il Papa slavo) commuoversi* 'It is easy (for the Slavic Pope) to be moved'?

Traditionally, the relationship between adjectives and *–mente* adverbs has been confined to the area of derivational morphology: such adverbs obtain by adding the suffix *–mente* to an adjective. I would like to propose extending this relationship to syntax. From this perspective, the uncontroversial starting point is that adjectives are predicates. The hypothesis under examination is whether adverb(ial)s can also function as predicates, a view defended by some scholars (see Gross 1981, Harris 1981). Pairs of sentences with cognate adverbs and adverbials are revelatory because they suggest that also *–mente* adverbs, although invariable, enter the combination as predicates. With *da vigliacco/ vigliaccamente* 'like a coward', I believe that evidence of this predicative nature originates from the mutual entailment between the sentences in pairs such as (8)-(12) and (9)-(13). These entailments guarantee that certain truth values are preserved in each pair. Given the identity of *all* content morphemes, it seems reasonable to conclude that the meaning which *da vigliacco/a* conveys in (8) and (9) must be the same as that which *vigliaccamente* conveys in (12) and (13) respectively. Referring to the viewpoint taken in this paper, the content morpheme *vigliacc–* fulfills a predicative role. This morpheme can surface either as an adjective (*È vigliacco* 'He is a coward') or as an adverb (*Agisce vigliaccamente/da vigliacco* 'He acts in a cowardly way'). Its lexical category, in turn, will determine which inflectional sealing the clause will take.

The same revelatory nature appears to hold true in (27) and (28), where the relationship is between a *–mente* adverb and a cognate *adjective*. In the sentences in (27), it is the content morpheme *orgogli–* which functions as a predicate: the suffixes it takes determine whether the observed real sentence will be (27a), with an adjective, or (27b), with an adverb. In pair (28), the predicative content morpheme is *facil–*, which may surface either as an adjective, in (28a), or as an adverb, in (28b). Therefore, pairs (27) and (28) are distinct for two reasons: first, (28a) is characterized by object raising; second, in (28b) *facilmente* is not a subject-oriented adverb.

Final remarks revert to *Il Paese è orgogliosamente*, an ill-formed sentence which can be considered of some relevance for 'the problem of the adverb'. As with *Leo è vigliaccamente/da vigliacco*, the sentence does contain those constituents which are indispensable for a –*mente* adverb to occur, i.e. a subject NP (*orgogliosamente* being subject-oriented) and a verb phrase. However, copulative verbs such as *essere* 'to be' do not license their subject and they too are unable to initiate a clause structure.[25] To the best of my knowledge, (a) contrasts in grammaticality such as the well-formed *Nevica pesantemente* 'It snows heavily' vs. the ill-formed **È pesantemente* '*It is heavily' have been overlooked in the literature; (b) no mention is made of developmental errors of this nature in language acquisition studies concerning Italian and English. Should it be true that children acquiring Italian or English do not produce these ill-formed sentences, then something in the grammar component must block such errors. As pointed out above, the two morphological paths described in (29) are *mutually exclusive*. It follows that, within the hypothesis advanced in this paper, there is no need to account for combinations of this sort because the very word-formation process prevents them from occurring.

---

[25] Radford (1997: 33) dedicates a few words to this matter: "[...] adjectives (but not adverbs) can serve as the complement of the verb *be* (i.e. can be used after *be*) [...]". Given the stance defended in this paper, as well as the view (hopefully uncontroversial among syntacticians, nowadays) that in sentences such as (27a) *essere* and *be* function as auxiliaries —more precisely, as zero-valent support verbs—, I obviously do not share the author's standpoint on predicative adjectives as complements of the copula (see Mirto 2008).

Appendix

Other –*mente* adverbs and their analytic counterparts

	–*mente* adverb	analytic counterpart	English equivalent
1	abbondantemente	in abbondanza	plentifully
2	abitualmente	d'abitudine	usually
3	allegramente	in allegria	cheerfully
4	approfonditamente	in profondità	deeply
5	artatamente	ad arte	craftily
6	brevemente	in breve	briefly
7	casualmente	a caso	accidentally
8	casualmente	per caso	by chance
9	certamente	di certo	certainly
10	ciclicamente	a cicli	cyclically
11	circolarmente	in circolo	circularly
12	conformemente a	in conformità a	according to
13	continuamente	in continuazione	continuously
14	cretinamente	da cretino	stupidly
15	diagonalmente	in diagonale	diagonally
16	differentemente da	a differenza di	differently from
17	divinamente	da dio	excellently
18	effettivamente	in effetti	actually
19	eroicamente	da eroe	heroically
20	erroneamente	per errore	by mistake
21	esternamente	all'esterno	externally
22	etnicamente	per etnia	ethnically
23	(del tutto) evidentemente	in tutta evidenza	evidently
24	fortunatamente	per fortuna	luckily
25	forzatamente	per forza	forcedly
26	francamente	in tutta franchezza	frankly
27	frettolosamente	in fretta	hastily
28	frettolosamente	di fretta	hastily
29	generalmente	in generale	generally
30	genericamente	in genere	generically
31	gradualmente	per gradi	gradually
32	immotivatamente	senza motivo	in an unjustified way
33	improvvisamente	d'improvviso	suddenly
34	improvvisamente	all'improvviso	suddenly
35	inizialmente	all'inizio	initially
36	intuitivamente	a intuito	intuitively
37	istantaneamente	all'istante	instantly
38	istintivamente	d'istinto	by instinct
39	lentamente	a rilento	slowly
40	letteralmente	alla lettera	literally
41	lungamente	a lungo	at length
42	lussuosamente	di lusso	in a sumptuous way
43	magicamente	per magia	by magic

44	mediamente	in media	on the average
45	meravigliosamente	a meraviglia	in a marvellous way
46	momentaneamente	al momento	temporarily
47	mortalmente	a morte	mortally
48	necessariamente	in tutta necessità	necessarily
49	normalmente	di norma	normally
50	numericamente	per numero	numerically
51	nuovamente	di nuovo	again
52	originariamente	in origine	originally
53	parallelamente	in parallelo	in parallel
54	particolarmente	in particolare	particularly
55	parzialmente	in parte	partially
56	perfettamente	alla perfezione	perfectly
57	perfettamente	a perfezione	perfectly
58	pienamente	in pieno	fully
59	potenzialmente	in potenza	potentially
60	praticamente	in pratica	practically
61	precedentemente	in precedenza	previously
62	precisamente	di preciso	precisely
63	preferibilmente	di preferenza	preferably
64	prevalentemente	in prevalenza	mostly
65	privatamente	in privato	privately
66	profondamente	in profondità	deeply
67	pubblicamente	in pubblico	publicly
68	recentemente	di recente	recently
69	relativamente a	in relazione a	as regards
70	scioccamente	da sciocco	foolishly
71	segretamente	in segreto	secretly
72	seriamente	sul serio	seriously
73	sicuramente	di sicuro	certainly
74	sincronicamente	in sincronia	synchronically
75	sinteticamente	in sintesi	succinctly
76	solitamente	di solito	usually
77	soventemente	di sovente	frequently
78	stentatamente	a stento	with difficulty
79	strutturalmente	in struttura	structurally
80	strutturalmente	per struttura	structurally
81	stupidamente	da stupido	stupidly
82	sufficientemente	a sufficienza	enough
83	superficialmente	in superficie	superficially
84	sveltamente	alla svelta	rapidly
85	teoricamente	in linea teorica	in theory
86	veramente	in verità	truly
87	verticalmente	in verticale	vertically

References

Ajdukiewicz, Kazimierz. 1973. La connessità sintattica. In Andrea Bonomi (ed.), *La struttura logica del linguaggio*, 345–372. Milano: Bompiani. (original version: *Die syntaktische Konnexität*, in *Studia Philosophica* 1. 1935. 1–27).
Auwera, Johan van der. 1999. Adverbs and adverbials. In Keith Brown & Jim Miller (eds.), *Concise Encyclopedia of Grammatical Categories*, 8–11. Oxford: Elsevier.
Basile, Grazia, Federica Casadei, Luca Lorenzetti, Giancarlo Schirru & Anna-Maria Thornton. 2010. *Linguistica generale*. Roma: Carocci.
Clark, Billy. 2006. Linguistics as a science. In Keith Brown (ed.), *Encyclopedia of Language and Linguistics*. Vol. 7, 227–234. Boston: Elsevier.
Crystal, David. 1987. *The Cambridge Encyclopedia of Language*. Oxford: Oxford University Press.
Corbett, Grevile G. 2001. Morphology and agreement. In Andrew Spencer & Arnold M. Zwicky (eds.), *The Handbook of Morphology*, 191–205. Hoboken, NJ: Wiley.
Culler, Jonathan. 1986. *Ferdinand de Saussure*. Revised edition. Ithaca, NY: Cornell University Press.
De Cesare, Anna-Maria. 2019. *Le parti invariabili del discorso*. Roma: Carocci.
De Gioia, Michele. 2001. *Avverbi idiomatici dell'italiano*. Torino: L'Harmattan Italia.
De Mauro, Tullio. 1999. *Grande Dizionario Italiano dell'uso*. Torino: Utet.
Elia, Annibale. 1995. Per filo e per segno: la struttura degli avverbi composti. In Emilio d'Agostino (ed.), *Tra sintassi e semantica: descrizioni e metodi di elaborazione della lingua d'uso*, 167–263. Napoli: Edizioni scientifiche italiane.
Gross, Maurice. 1981. Les bases empiriques de la notion de prédicat sémantique. *Langages* 63. 7–52.
Gross, Maurice. 1990. *Grammaire transformationnelle du français, vol. 3: Syntaxe de l'adverbe*. Paris: ASSTRIL.
Grossmann, Maria & Franz Rainer. 2004. *La formazione delle parole in italiano*. Tübingen: Max Niemeyer Verlag.
Harris, Zellig S. 1981. *Papers on syntax*. Dordrecht/Boston/London: Reidel.
Haser, Verena & Bernd Kortmann. 2006. Adverbs. In Keith Brown (ed.), *Encyclopedia of Language and Linguistics, vol. 1*, 66–69. Boston: Elsevier.
Huddleston, Rodney. 1988. *English Grammar: an outline*. Cambridge: Cambridge University Press.
Jansen, H. 2011. Preposizioni. *Enciclopedia dell'italiano*. Online. Roma: Treccani. https://www.treccani.it/enciclopedia/preposizioni_(Enciclopedia-dell'Italiano)
Kemp, Gary. 2018. *What is this thing called Philosophy of Language?* New York: Routledge.
La Fauci, Nunzio. 2011. *Relazioni e differenze. Questioni di linguistica razionale*. Palermo: Sellerio.
La Fauci, Nunzio & Ignazio Mauro Mirto. 2003. *Fare. Elementi di sintassi*. Pisa: ETS.
Lyons, John. 1966. Towards a notional theory of the parts of speech. *Journal of Linguistics* 2(2). 209–236.
Lyons, John. 1981. *Language and Linguistics*. Cambridge: Cambridge University Press.
Lyons, John. 1989. Semantic ascent: a neglected aspect of syntactic typology. In Doug Arnold, Martin Atkinson, Jacques Durand, Claire Grover & Louisa Sadler (eds.), *Essays on Grammatical Theory and Universal Grammar*, 153–186. Oxford: Clarendon Press.

Maienborn, Claudia & Martin Schäfer. 2011. Adverbs and adverbials. In Claudia Maienborn, Klaus von Heusinger & Paul Portner (eds.), *Semantics: An International Handbook of Natural Language Meaning*, 1390–1419. Berlin/Boston: Walter de Gruyter.

Mirto, Ignazio Mauro. 2008. Aggettivi e valenza in italiano. *Écho des Études Romanes* 4(2). 5–21.

Mirto, Ignazio Mauro. 2018. The hidden side of adverbs. *Linguistik Online* 92 (5/18). 173–191.

Nilsen, Don Lee Fred. 1972. *English Adverbials*. The Hague/Paris: Mouton.

Pullum, G. K. 1999. Linguistic categories. In Keith Brown & Jim Miller (eds.), *Concise Encyclopedia of Grammatical Categories*, 66–70. Oxford: Elsevier.

Pullum, Geoffrey Keith & Rodney Huddleston. 2002. Adjectives and adverbs. In Rodney Huddleston & Geoffrey Keith Pullum (eds.), *The Cambridge Grammar of the English Language*, 525–596. Cambridge: Cambridge University Press.

Radford, Andrew. 1997. *Syntax. A minimalist introduction*. Cambridge/New York: Cambridge University Press.

Schachter, Paul & Timothy Shopen. 2007. Parts-of-speech systems. In Timothy Shopen (ed.), *Language Typology and Syntactic Description, vol. 1: Clause structure*, 3–60. Cambridge/New York/Melbourne: Cambridge University Press.

Schwarze, Christoph. 2009. *Grammatica della lingua italiana*. Roma: Carocci.

Sensini, Marcello. 1997. *La grammatica della lingua italiana*. Milano: Arnoldo Mondadori.

Serianni, Luca. 1989. *Grammatica italiana. Italiano comune e lingua letteraria*. Torino: Utet.

Stump, Gregory T. 2001. Inflection. In Andrew Spencer & Arnold M. Zwicky (eds.), *The Handbook of Morphology*, 13–43. Hoboken, NJ: Wiley.

Voghera, Miriam. 2004. Polirematiche. In Maria Grossmann & Franz Rainer, *La formazione delle parole in italiano*, 56–68. Tübingen: Max Niemeyer Verlag.

Walmsley, John B. 2006. Noam Chomsky. In Keith Brown (main ed.), *Encyclopedia of Language and Linguistics, vol. 2*, 382–384. Boston: Elsevier.

Marius Albers
Prenominal adverbs in German? The cases of *auf* and *zu*

Abstract: In German, the lexemes *auf* 'open' and *zu* 'closed' are traditionally considered to be adverbs and/or verb particles derived from adverbs. Therefore, their prenominal and inflected use in constructions like *die aufe/zue Tür* 'the open/ closed door', which can be found especially in colloquial and spoken language, is rejected by normative grammarians. Regardless of such grammaticality judgments, this contribution attempts to provide an explanation of how the units *auf* and *zu* can advance to the prenominal position. The solution presented here assumes that the historically based semantic independence of the units from their base verbs makes it possible to connect them with semantically empty copula verbs. This predicative use acts as a bridge into attributive use, where by the constraint of declension then takes effect. Because of their semantic and grammatical properties, *auf* 'open' and *zu* 'closed' should therefore be regarded as adjectives, not as inflected adverbs.

Keywords: German, Parts of Speech, Adverb, Adjective, Preposition, Resultative Construction, Verb Particle, Inflection, Secondary Predicate

1 Introduction

The attributive position between a determiner and a noun is the classical touchstone for determining adjectives in German[1]. What can occur in this position (and is usually inflected then) is an adjective (see e.g. Thieroff and Vogel 2009: 54; Eichinger 2007: 144). However, in the literature (mostly on grammatical cases of doubt), one might come across examples like the following in (1):

---

[1] I owe thanks to many colleagues for their comments on earlier versions of this contribution, namely Olivier Duplâtre, Linda Hilkenbach, Clemens Knobloch, Ignazio Mauro Mirto, Pierre-Yves Modicom, and also two anonymous reviewers. And of course, I would like to thank all the participants of the (unfortunately only virtual) conference *The Problem of the Adverb* (1–2 October 2020) for their comments.

Marius Albers, Universität Siegen, albers@germanistik.uni-siegen.de

https://doi.org/10.1515/9783110767971-005

(1) a. eine   auf-e   Flasche
       an   open-NOM.SG   bottle
       'an open bottle'
       (Dittmann, Thieroff, and Adolphs 2003: 443)
    b. das   zu-(n)-e   Fenster
       the   closed-n^2-NOM.SG   window
       'the closed window'
       (Dittmann, Thieroff, and Adolphs 2003: 443)

Now the lexemes in question here, namely *auf* 'open' and *zu* 'closed', appear in the prototypical position for adjectives. Nevertheless, they are usually not classified as adjectives. Following for example Dittmann, Thieroff & Adolphs (2003: 443), Hentschel (2005: 287), and Duden (2016b), these units are classified as adverbs. At this point, a classification problem becomes obvious: The classification of these units as adverbs is only plausible if the examples in (1) are either omitted or rejected. The latter is done by the authors mentioned above. They adhere to the traditional characterization of adverbs as non-inflectable lexemes and consider their inflected use to be ungrammatical or incorrect. However, if such cases like those in (1) are considered, one would probably have to speak of adjectives – according to the definition presented at the beginning.

I will come back to the problem of classification later (section 4). Before doing so, the empirically tangible dimensions of this phenomenon will first be briefly explored (section 2). Subsequently, the semantic and morphosyntactic prerequisites for the emergence of these constructions[3] will be explained (section 3). This leads to the conclusion that the lexemes in (1) should be classified as adjectives, following Lüdeling (1999: 18) and Knobloch (2009: 548), which can also prevent the assumption of inflected adverbs.

---

[2] The epenthetic *n*, which is inserted for phonological reasons, namely the ending on a vowel, is analogous to certain (partly classified as inflexible) color adjectives like *rosa* 'pink' or *lila* 'purple': *die rosa(ne) Hose* 'the pink trousers', *der lila(ne) Pullover* 'the purple pullover' (cf. Duden 2016a: 348). In addition, inflected forms of the adjective /offen/ [italics] 'open' such as /offene/ could also serve as a model for the epenthetic *n*.
[3] I use the term 'construction' in a pre-theoretical way, not in a paradigm of Construction Grammar.

2 On the (empirically measurable) dimensions of this phenomenon

Before we come to the theoretical considerations, I would like to say a little about the dimensions of the phenomenon. Examples like in (1) are generally assigned to (spoken) colloquial language and explicitly not to written standard German (see e.g. Duden 2016a: 754, 2016b; Dittmann, Thieroff, & Adolphs 2003: 443; Hentschel 2005: 277; Engel 1970: 74). Sometimes they are moreover located in certain dialect regions only,[4] especially in northern German dialects (Lüdeling 1999: 18), but they are also documented in Bavarian (Merkle 1975: 176).[5] This is also reflected in two corpus queries. For this purpose, I used the lexemes in question in different variants (with and without an epenthetic *n*) as search queries. Using the placeholder '*', all possible inflection forms could be considered (see Table 1).

In the biggest archive of the German reference corpus *DeReKo* (Deutsches Referenzkorpus), W-öffentlich,[6] only 52 examples can be found. Another query in the much smaller spoken-language database *DGD* (Datenbank für gesprochenes Deutsch)[7] provides only four hits for variants of inflected *zu* 'closed', and none for *auf* 'open' (see Table 1).

Table 1: Number of authentic examples for prenominal *auf* 'open' and *zu* 'closed' in DeReKo and DGD.

	aufe*	*aufene**	*zue**	*zuene**	*zune**
DeReKo	4	0	38	8	2
DGD	0	0	2	0	2

Based on the little evidence from the corpora, one could now ask the question whether this is a relevant phenomenon at all. It is indeed difficult to estimate the

---

4 It would be interesting to take a closer look at this phenomenon in German dialects. The examples from the corpus research described below sometimes show a dialectal character of these constructions, as the spelling of *jeht* 'goes' (standard: *geht*) and *uff* 'open' (standard: *auf*) in the following example indicates: *Die zue Tür jeht plötzlich uff!* 'The closed door suddenly opens' (Berliner Morgenpost, 24.04.2017 | COSMAS II, w-öffentlich).
5 Thanks to Linnéa C. Weitkamp, who gave me the hint about the *Bairische Grammatik*.
6 This archive contains about 34 thousand texts with nearly 10 billion words (https://www.ids-mannheim.de/cosmas2/projekt/referenz/archive-alt/archive-umfang.html; accessed 25 September 2020).
7 The DGD currently comprises a total of 12.7 million transcribed tokens (Joachim Gasch, p.m., 28 September 2020).

dimensions outside the corpora. Nevertheless, there seems to be at least an (indirect) hint of the relevance of these constructions, namely the ongoing thematization in the literature as well as in the (public) discourse of language cultivation. Early mentions can be found in Hermann Wunderlich's *Umgangssprache* (Wunderlich 1894: 229), in the classic dictionary of Paul (1897: 571) and the *DWB* (1954), and in many linguistic publications, for example Engel (1970: 75–76), Vogel (1997: 420), Schmöe (2002: 11–12), Hentschel (2005: 277), Dürscheid (2010: 77), Menzel (2010: 10), Braun (2011: 47–48), and Harden (2014: 214), this list is not exhaustive. The author Bastian Sick has dealt with this topic in his very popular (but linguistically sometimes questionable) column *Zwiebelfisch* (Sick 2007), which can be regarded as an indication of its relevance also for non-linguists. This is also shown by the results of the query in *DeReKo*: In about 60 percent of the 52 examples, the constructions are clearly thematized in a somehow metalinguistic way, reflecting on their grammaticality or their overall use like in the following example in (2):

(2) In der Tat hält es die Grammatik für „nicht korrekt", Adverbien attributiv zu verwenden, und stützt das auch mit Beispielen wie „der aufe Laden" oder „der nicht lang genuge Rock".
[In fact, grammar considers it 'incorrect' to use adverbs attributively, and also supports this with examples such as 'the open store' or 'the not long enough skirt'.]
(Süddeutsche Zeitung, 08.08.2009 | COSMAS II, W-öffentlich)

This uninterrupted preoccupation with the subject in linguistics as well as in the public can be interpreted either as the hunt for a phantom, or as a reflex of an actual phenomenon in the German language, which, I have to admit, is rather shy and hardly shows up in corpora so far. Because I am no ghostbuster, I agree with Hentschel (2005: 277), who states that these constructions are well established in colloquial language and cannot be regarded as temporal or regional peculiarities (see section 3.1).[8] Hentschel (2005: 277) also emphasizes that such substandard phenomena are valid indicators for ongoing language change.[9] This position is also held by Harden (2014: 214), who claims that these structures are not too rare

---

[8] It would be interesting to ask speakers about the acceptability and prevalence of constructions of this type. However, this must be reserved for later investigations.

[9] Menzel (2010: 10) brings another factor into play, namely language acquisition. He claims that constructions like *die zune Tür* 'the closed door' might be the result of linguistic overgeneralization and therefore an index of (still) evolving language competence. But Knobloch (2002) already shows that the link of language acquisition and language change is not that straightforward. Knobloch further adds that social factors play an important role in language change. This is

and should therefore be taken into account by the grammatical description of German. This has hardly happened as far as I can see, mostly the references in the literature serve to attest to the colloquial or ungrammatical character of these constructions without any deeper linguistic analysis. Therefore, some further considerations on this topic shall now be presented.

3 Semantic and morphosyntactic prerequisites

3.1 Semantic properties of *auf* 'open' and *zu* 'closed'

The units *auf* and *zu* have a broad variety of different meanings and functions in contemporary German, for example as prepositions (*auf den Berg* 'up the mountain', *zu der Kirche* 'to the church') or verb particles (*aufgeben* 'to give up', *zuhören* 'to listen'). I do not want to talk further about the prepositions here for they form a well-definable group, which is not further relevant here. With regard to the use as verb particles, it should be said that both units are characterized by a great deal of polyfunctionality (see e.g. Fleischer & Barz 2012: 404–406; 416). For the purpose of this study, however, I will limit myself to only two clearly delineated meanings, namely *auf* 'open' and *zu* 'closed'. In all authentic examples of the attributive use from the corpora, only these meanings occur:

(3) a. eine auf-e   Tür
       an   open-NOM.SG   door
       'an open door'
       (http://de.wikipedia.org/wiki/Diskussion:SIX_Swiss_Exchange: Wikipedia, 2009 | COSMAS II, W-öffentlich)
    b. mit   zu-en   Augen
       with closed-DAT.PL eyes
       'with [my] eyes closed'
       (die tageszeitung, 10.06.2000 | COSMAS II, W-öffentlich)

With these meanings, *auf* and *zu* regularly appear as verb particles in contemporary German, for example in formations like *aufreißen* 'to tear open' and *zuschlagen* 'to slam sth. shut' (see also (4)). In the extensive study of Kühnhold, the meaning 'to open' accounts for 15.1% of the total number of particle verb forma-

---

shown in the present case by the fact that these formations are often declared wrong like in (2) and thus external forces act on the process of language change.

tions with *auf-* (Kühnhold 1973: 145), the meaning 'to close' for 29.4% of particle verb formations with *zu* (Kühnhold 1973: 154). The description of their meaning with processual 'to open/close' brings the word formation product, i.e. a complex verb, into focus. The units *auf* and *zu* alone rather express states and the action aspect is only brought in by the connection with a verb. *auf* and *zu* each express the goal, while the verbs bring in the manner of action (cf. Schneider 2013: 200, 206–207).[10] Now these specific meanings did not arise primarily, but only in the course of language history from originally spatial meanings of adverbs. Let us therefore take a short look at their etymology.

While *auf* originally existed as a directional adverb with the meaning 'up' and was grammaticalized into a preposition only later, the etymology of this word shows an interesting junction, namely the meaning 'open' (Paul 1897: 32). This is to be seen as a metonymical transfer of the directional 'up' in contexts where for example a lid is opened upwards (Paul 1897: 32; see also *DWB* 1854). In this process, the dynamic directional reading changed in to a stative one. From here, it is only a small step to horizontality to also describe for example the opening of doors and windows. It is precisely for this meaning that Paul (1897: 32) already shows examples of predicative use of *auf*.

An important aspect is the relation to the adjective *offen* 'open'. Originally, these two words had slightly different meanings: While *auf* rather focused on the process of opening, *offen* was used for the state description. Therefore, *auf* is primarily used with action verbs (*aufgehen* 'to open', *aufplatzen* 'to burst (open)'), while *offen* is primarily used with stative verbs (*offen stehen* 'to stand open', *offen lassen* 'to leave open'). However, this distinction has largely been abandoned over time, especially in colloquial language (Duden 2016b; see already Paul 1897: 32). The above-mentioned semantic shifts result in a further approximation of the two already very closely related concepts. The relationship to *offen* thus serves on the one hand as a model for the use of *auf* as an adjective, but on the other hand as an obstacle, since this systemic position is already occupied by a lexeme.

zu is a particularly interesting case etymologically (which is already shown by the length of the entry in *DWB* (1954), which contains over 100 pages). In principle – as with *auf* – a transfer of the spatial meaning applies here. *zu* as a directional adverb originally meant 'in the direction of'. The important addition here is a type of ending point, so it becomes 'approach, so that a connection is

---

[10] However, elliptical constructions in which the action verb is absent are also conceivable: *Auf das Tor!* 'Open the door!'. For these constructions, which occur mainly in spoken language, Dabóczi (2017: 123) suggests the term "imperative Bewegungspartikeln" [imperative particles of motion].

made' (Paul 1897: 571). This again can be seen as a metonymic shift towards a stative reading. Also in this case the predicative use is already mentioned early on by Paul (1897: 571). The *DWB* (1954) further notes that the predicative use resulted from shortening the past participle of particle verbs like *zugemacht* 'closed'. It is assumed for these constructions that *zu* dominates the overall meaning of the complex verbs like *zuotoun* 'to close sth. up' and that this factor in the first place enabled the connection with the copula verbs *sein* 'to be', and *bleiben* 'to stay'. I will come back to this in section 3.2. According to the *DWB* (1954), these constructions came into general use towards the end of the Middle Ages and have been used ever since.

Another interesting aspect is that, already in these older dictionaries, the transition of *zu* to the attributive position is reported: Paul (1897: 571) mentions it as a phenomenon of folksy language use and in the *DWB* (1954) it is described as a phenomenon that is widespread throughout the linguistic area of German (of course not without language-critical remarks, because it is characterized as a non-standard phenomenon). So we see that Hentschel's (2005: 277) assessment, that this is not a temporally and areally limited phenomenon is supported by the classic dictionaries.

A difference to *auf* is that there is no synonymous adjective for *zu* 'closed', so that we can potentially speak of filling a lexical gap here. In this context, only the participle *geschlossen* 'closed' is otherwise usable. Language-economic reasons could be decisive here (one syllable in *zu* vs. three syllables in combination with morphological complexity in *geschlossen*). This may also explain why there are significantly more cases for attributive *zu* than for attributive *auf* (see Table 1).

In summary it can be said, that the meanings 'open' and 'closed', which *auf* and *zu* take over in (1), are only secondarily derived from the directional meaning of the underlying adverbs. This leads to the question of whether the shift in meaning has also created new lexemes in addition to the original adverbs, or whether these are merely cases of polysemy. According to Löbner (2013: 54, 59), differentiation is a meaning shift that leads to polysemy. This is what can be observed in the presented cases. However, it can also be seen that the meaning shifts have led to the development of new morphosyntactic properties: The attributive use represented by Paul and the *DWB* cannot be found for the directional meaning of *auf* and *zu*, it is strictly limited to the stative readings 'open' and 'closed'. Therefore, a field of tension arises here between the undoubtedly related meanings which are typical of polysemic lexemes on the one hand and different grammatical properties of these carriers of meaning on the other. The latter could be used as a fundamental argument for an independent lexeme, as Löbner (2013: 42) points out: "In general the same word in different grammatical categories constitutes as many different lexemes." The question remains whether these differences are "substantial" (Löbner 2013: 44) enough to justify different lexemes. One might also assume heterosemy here, "where two or more meanings or functions that are historically related, in the sense of deriving from the same ultimate source, are borne by reflexes of the common source element that belong in different morphosyntactic categories." (Lichtenberk 1991: 476).

3.2 Particle verbs, resultative constructions, (co-)predicates

In addition to the semantic aspects, morphosyntactic properties also play an important role in the development of the prenominal use of *auf* and *zu* as in (1) and (3). Some of these aspects have been touched upon briefly in section 3.1, but now these will be discussed in more detail. As already mentioned above, *auf* 'open' and *zu* 'closed' appear in contemporary German primarily as verb particles and thereby often in antonymous couples like in (4):

(4) X dreht die Flasche auf/zu
     X turns the bottle   open/closed
     'X twists open/closed the bottle.'

In these formations the verb particles can be interpreted as secondary predicates that describe the result of the action:

(5) X dreht die Flasche auf/zu.   → Die Flasche ist auf/zu.
     'X twists off the bottle cap.'   'X twists the bottle closed.'

This illustrates the frequently observed similarity of (morphological?) particle verbs and (syntactic) resultative constructions (see e.g. Chang 2007; Knobloch 2009, 2018; Haider 2018[11]). Lüdeling (1999: 9) provides a short definition of resultative constructions: "Resultative secondary predicates, together with certain verbs, form resultative constructions in which the verb expresses an action and the resultative secondary predicate specifies the result of the action." At this point

---

11 Interestingly, Haider (2018: 186) "reverses" the analogy from resultative constructions acting on particle verbs shown in this article with regard to the basic organizational principles of language: He argues that languages with particle verbs also allow constructions with resultative adjectives. It should be noted, however, that the genesis of attributive adjectives from resultative verb particles described here does not (and should not) say anything about whether resultative constructions or particle verbs are primary in a language.

I skip a more detailed discussion of the resultative constructions (cf. e.g. Lüdeling 1999: Chapter 6; Chang 2007). A typical example can be found in (6a). Here, the adjective *kaputt* 'broken' functions as a secondary predicate (object predicate) to the object *die Tür* 'the door': The result of *schlagen* 'to slam' is that *die Tür* 'the door' is *kaputt* 'broken'.[12] Let us now look at some variants of the construction in (6b-e):

(6) a. X   schlägt   die   Tür   kaputt
        X   slams   the   door   broken
        'X breaks the door'
    b. weil   X   die   Tür   kaputtschlägt
        because   X   the   door   broken.slams
        'because X slams the door'
    c. (?)Kaputt schlägt   X   die   Tür
        broken   slams   X   the   door
        'X breaks the door.'
    d. Die   Tür   ist   ganz   kaputt
        the   door   is   all   broken
        'The door is (all) broken.'
    e. die   kaputte   Tür   muss   repariert   werden
        the   broken   door must   repaired   get
        'The broken door needs to be repaired.'

Next to (6), we now place the two particle verbs *aufreißen* 'rip open' and *zuschlagen* 'slam' and take a look their possible syntactic variants:[13]

(7) a. X   reißt   die   Tür   auf
        X   tears   the   door   open
        'X tears open the door'
    b. weil   X   die   Tür   aufreißt
        because   X   the   door   open.tears
        'because X tears the door open'

---

[12] Depictive copredicates of the type *X trinkt den Kaffee schwarz* 'X drinks the coffee black' are to be distinguished from this. They don't describe the result of the action but a property of the object *during* the process. Depictive copredicates cannot be (re-)analyzed as particle verbs, too: *X trinkt den Kaffee schwarz* 'X drinks the coffee black' → **schwarztrinken* 'blackdrink'. Therefore, depictive predicates cannot be regarded as products of word formation (Duden 2016a: 715).
[13] For the sake of clarity, I have made the constructions in (6–8) uniform. Authentic examples for the arguable constructions in (6–8c, e) can be found in (3) and (10).

c. ?Auf reißt X die Tür
   open tears X the door
   'X tears the door open.'
d. Die Tür ist ganz auf
   the door is all open
   'The door is (fully) open.'
e. die ?auf-e Tür muss repariert werden
   the open-NOM.SG door must repaired get
   'The open door needs to be repaired.'

(8) a. X schlägt die Tür zu
       X slams the door closed
       'X slams the door'
   b. weil X die Tür zuschlägt
      because X the door closed.slams
      'because X slams the door'
   c. ?Zu schlägt X die Tür
      closed slams X the door
      'X tears the door open.'
   d. Die Tür ist ganz zu
      the door is all closed
      'The door is (fully) closed.'
   e. die ?zu-e Tür muss repariert werden
      the closed-NOM.SG door must repaired get
      'The closed door needs to be repaired.'

If one compares the examples in (7–8) with those in (6), a noticeable parallelism can be attested. Not least for this reason, various attempts have been made to distinguish "real" resultative constructions like in (6) from similar particle verb constructions (some authors, like e.g. Lüdeling (1999), do not distinguish these constructions at all). Chang (2007: 87–88) mentions three criteria for distinguishing verb particles and resultative predicates: In contrast to the former, the latter can be fronted, combined with a copula verb and modified with *ganz* 'completely'. While these criteria can in fact be used for differentiation sometimes (see Chang 2007: 88), *auf* and *zu* in the meanings discussed here behave in a very analogous manner to resultative adjectives, as we can see in (6–8). Chang (2007: 89) notes in this context that there are overlapping ranges of verb particles and resultative predicates. We are in exactly such a transitional area here: *auf* and *zu* are typical verb particles, but they can be interpreted as properties of an object which are caused by a verbal action. In these cases, they adopt an adjective-like reading and function as secondary predicates.

At this point the different variants from (6–8) shall be discussed briefly. (6–8a) show the simple declarative sentence. An important property of the semantic relations of constructions like these should be pointed out here: While the resultative adjective in (6) is syntactically connected to the verb (*schlagen* 'to slam'), it is semantically a predication over the object (*Tür* 'door') (Knobloch 2018: 3). The same applies here for (7–8a). This semantic reference to the object is decisive for the differentiation of resultative adjectives from adverbial adjectives or adverbials (Vogel 1997: 406, 410) and an important requirement for the (co-)predicative use.

In the subordinate clause in (6b), the verb and the resultative predicate appear adjacent in the right bracket. For *kaputtschlagen* 'to smash', this leads to the (notorious) question of whether they are written as one word or separately, which is closely related to whether one assumes a syntactic or a morphological construction (see e.g. Eisenberg 2017: 74). However, this cannot and need not to be discussed further here. Now for the subordinate clauses in (7–8b), there is little doubt as to whether these constructions are written as one word or separated: Here, writing as one word seems to be the usual thing. This can be attributed to the high degree of lexicalization of particle verbs with these particles. They represent the prototypical core of verb particles (cf. Duden 2016a: 709).

In principle, it is possible to front the resultative adjective *kaputt* 'broken' like in (6c). Depending on the adjective used, the acceptability of such constructions is doubted sometimes (Lüdeling 1999: 141). But such examples with *kaputt* 'broken' can actually be found:

(9) Kaputt habe ich aber nichts gemacht.
    broken have I but nothing made
    'But I did not break anything.'
    (Nordkurier, 18.01.2000 | COSMAS II, W-öffentlich)

The fronting of verb particles like in (7–8c) is admittedly disputable: The possibility of fronting verb particles is often generally neglected (cf. the overview in Müller 2002: 121; Lüdeling 1999: 48–51). From an empirical point of view, however, this is questioned, especially as a categoric statement. As a rule of thumb, Müller formulates: "The frontability seems to depend on the semantic content of the particle and the content of the verb. The more content a particle has, the better the fronting is." (Müller 2002: 127). Stiebels (1996: 161) mentions yet another criterion for fronting, namely a contrasting meaning with a contrary particle like in (4).[14] In this respect, *auf* and *zu* show the pairing that is also characteristic of a central group of adjectives (e.g. *groß – klein* 'large – small'; cf. Eichinger 2007: 146).

For *auf* and *zu*, these two criteria can be well attested. Therefore, it is not surprising that both also occur fronted:

(10) a. Auf reißt der Himmel
    open rips the sky
    'The sky opens up.'
    (Frankfurter Rundschau, 12.06.1998 | COSMAS II, W-öffentlich)
 b. Zu hat ebenfalls das Burg Stargard Museum
    closed has also the Burg Stargard Museum
    in dieser Zeit
    in this time
    'The Burg Stargrad Museum is also closed during this time.'
    (Nordkurier, 18.12.2002 | COSMAS II, W-öffentlich)

But not only the semantics of the verb particle, also that of the verb itself plays an important role here. Stiebels (1996: 161) points out that the independence of a verb particle is especially given in combination with semantically "empty" verbs like *machen* 'make', which only introduces a moment of action. This is possible with the predicates in (7–8), as shown in (11):

(11) X macht die Tür kaputt/auf/zu
    X makes the door broken/open/closed
    'X smashes/opens/closes the door'

With such semantically "empty" verbs, the particle carries the main meaning, which stands out even more with copula verbs (cf. Vogel 1997: 404). This shows the general characteristics of German as a "satellite-framed language", where the verb particles as satellites make a crucial contribution to the meaning of the whole expression (cf. Talmy 2019: 25–26). The opposing "verb-framed" character of English can be observed in many translations throughout this chapter.

---

14 In addition to grammatical and semantic aspects, pragmatics also play a role in fronting. Recently, Trotzke and Wittenberg (2017) investigate the conditions of particle fronting in the context of expressivity of particle verbs. Their results show that verb particles tend to be better fronted in expressive formations like *rausschmeißen* 'to bounce sb.' rather than in non-expressive ones like *rausbringen* 'to take out [the trash]'.

This leads directly to the predicative use in (6–8d). All three predicates show the ability to form the predicate of the sentence with a linking verb without any problems; the semantics of a "lexical" verb is no longer required for this.[15] Thereby, a modification of the adjective with *ganz* 'all' is also possible (6–8d, cf. Lüdeling 1999: 52–54; Chang 2007). This ability to form predicates is, again, closely related to fronting in the sense that a frontable particle must also be permitted in a predicative phrase with the copula (Stiebels 1996: 161).

Finally, when the copredicative construction in (6a) is re-used in another sentence, the adjective can also move to the position in front of the noun and thus function as an attribute (6e). While this is undoubtedly the case with (6e), the acceptability of the attributive use in front of a noun in (7–8e) is questionable. The problem here is obvious: While *kaputt* is (meanwhile, it must be said) a prototypical adjective that can be inflected and used in attributive position, the other units in (7–8) are mainly known as prepositions and verb particles in contemporary German. These are not inflectable and cannot appear between article and noun. However, this attributive position can be "initiated" through predicative use, and this is possible as shown in (7–8d). In this respect, predicative use represents a "gateway" for attributive (and thus typically adjectival) use (Eichinger 2007: 159; see also Eisenberg 2013: 246).[16] However, lexical units now sometimes need a longer time to "get used" to a new syntactic environment (or to get the speakers and language purists used to them) when moving into another category without explicit derivation. Eichinger (2000: 30) describes this for the prenominal and uninflected use of denominal units like *klasse* 'marvelous' and *spitze* 'great': Words like these sometimes do not reach all grammatical possibilities of the target word class (immediately). This applies to the verb particles in the same way, i.e. they slowly develop their prenominal use and inflection.

This prenominal use is – as outlined in the beginning – frequently rejected, especially by normative grammarians, with the explanation that adverbs cannot

---

15 Predicative use, however, is already given by the copredicative use: An adjective that can be used as a copredicate can also be used predicatively (Plank 1985: 173).

16 From a diachronic point of view, the prototypical adjective itself has only grown in this position: In Middle High German the adjective attribute could appear both pre-nominally and post-nominally, and in both positions both inflected and uninflected, while in contemporary German the prenominal and inflected use is prototypical (Altmann & Hofmann 2004: 163). Furthermore, Knobloch (2018: 1, following Hengeveld) justifiably points out that the attributive use, which is claimed to be prototypical for adjectives in German, requires the greatest morphological effort compared to the adverbial and predicative use, while usually the simplest uses are considered prototypical. Without wanting to go into detail, it should be noted here that it is perhaps precisely this particularity that makes the adaptation of new adjectives difficult and makes new units appear strange.

occur in an attributive position, because they are not inflectable. Of course, this is no binding rule for the language community which is making use of it (and thus, ironically, calls the language purists into action). And once arrived in the attributive position, the principally non-inflectable lexemes now come under a strong systemic compulsion to declension (Thieroff & Vogel 2009: 59), they thus follow the usual pattern.[17] Schmöe (2002: 11) justifiably points out, that inflection is obligatory: A construction such as *die zu Tür 'the closed door' would therefore be absolutely ungrammatical. Thus, the "abnormal" prenominal units actually seem to behave in accordance with the norm – one is tempted to say that they behave like adjectives.

As seen in this section, semantic shifts were the basic prerequisites for the formation of these constructions. On the grammatical side, in analogy to resultative constructions, they first developed predicative use, which is the basis for upcoming attributive usage. However, the new function makes it difficult to classify these units. In the literature, these units are generally classified in different ways, what will be considered now.

4 Approaches to synchronic classification

If one understands *auf* and *zu* as verb particles, the problem of categorization is not in focus at first sight. Verb particles are often regarded as parts of the verb, i.e. they are not autonomous syntactic units (cf. e.g. Schmöe 2002: 23). The common co-occurrence of verb particle and base verb is undoubtedly prototypical, and therefore the part-of-speech status is usually rarely discussed. It is probably not least for this reason that Dabóczi (2017: 182) attests a lack of attention to the part-of-speech-status of verb particles. However, this field is not completely raw: Lüdeling (1999) discusses three different approaches from the literature: a) preverbs can belong to any major word class, b) preverbs are intransitive prepositions, or c) preverbs are homophonous elements to adverbs, prepositions, adjectives etc. But

---

[17] An interesting idea that arises here is the question of the extent to which inflectability can be understood as a characteristic of lexemes or as a morphosyntactic "compulsion" within the syntactic constituent structure. Perhaps lexemes as such are not inflectable or not, but are initially category neutral (cf. Bergenholtz & Mugdan 1979). Only their use in a particular syntactic slot results in the necessity for inflection (i.e. an external compulsion, not an inherent property of the lexeme). That there are different degrees of familiarity with certain inflected variants can be traced back to the distinction between system, norm and speech (Coseriu 1975). But for the time being this is no more than a digressive thought.

she rejects all of these approaches and ultimately comes to only a negative conclusion in the form that "the preverb is not of category N or V" (Lüdeling 1999: 19).

In the cases at hand in (1) and (3), however, the corresponding verb is missing, the verb particle has become "independent" to a certain extent and is now a standalone constituent in the predicate or within the NP. Thus, the (former) verb particle is in principle in need of categorization. Various classifications can be found in the literature, which oscillate between preposition, adverb, and (deadverbal) adjective. These are now to be discussed.

4.1 Preposition

Schmöe (2002: 11) discusses the analogous example *der abbe Knopf* 'the loose button' and calls such units "prepositions", without explaining this in detail. The same is done by Dürscheid (2010: 77), and Harden (2014: 214). There is no doubt that there are homonymous units that have to be regarded as prototypical representatives of the word class preposition (cf. Hentschel 2005: 269). However, this classification does not seem particularly valid for the units in question, and this for three reasons: On the one hand, prepositions usually do not form the predicate together with the copula (Hentschel 2005: 270), which is an important property of the constructions considered here. Knobloch (2009: 552) also notes that a preposition without any governed nominal argument is no longer a preposition (see also Eisenberg 2013: 214).[18] Finally, one can also mention the semantics of the units considered here: It differs (more or less) clearly from the semantics of the (formally) parallel preposition, which becomes immediately apparent when you compare a sentence like *Die Tür geht auf* 'The door opens' with the examples in (12) (cf. Stiebels 1996: 160–161; Henzen 1969: 274):

(12) a. X   geht   auf   den   Berg
        X   goes   up.DIR   the   mountain
        'X goes up the mountain.'
    b. X   steht   auf   dem   Berg
        X   stands   on.LOC   the   mountain
        'Y stands on the mountain.'
    c. X   wartet   auf   Y
        X   waits   for.GOV.PREP   Y
        'X waits for Y.'

---

[18] In some theoretical frameworks, some adverbs and preverbs are classified as prepositions without an argument ("intransitive prepositions"). See for a critical discussion Lüdeling (1999: 17–19).

Having shown that the classification as prepositions seems rather unsustainable, the attempts at classification as adverbs or (deadverbal) adjectives are now to be first presented and then compared.

4.2 Adverb and adverb-adjective conversion

As already mentioned in the beginning, Dittmann, Thieroff, and Adolphs (2003: 443) speak of adverbs, likewise Duden (2016b). These language guides do not (understandably, because of the target group they are aimed at) problematize the classification of these units, but simply present them. Hentschel (2005: 287) on the other hand operates with a diachronic approach. As seen above, the relevant meanings of *auf* and *zu* have developed from spatial adverbs. Hentschel now claims that these adverbs have "survived" besides the grammaticalized prepositions. Altmann (2011: 153) also speaks of parallel adverbs for the verb particles in question, although claiming the adverbial meaning is only preserved in lexicalized constructions, as which he also considers predicative constructions (*etw. ist ab/an/auf/aus/los/zu* 'sth. is loose/on/open/off/closed'). However, both authors only focus on predicative use, which can also be taken regularly by adverbs. If now *auf* and *zu* would appear in predicative constructions only, this would be a valid explanation, but as seen in (1) and (3), attributive use does also occur. Hentschel (2005: 277) at least states the attributive use, but does not take it into account in the classification due to its non-standard character. So this position does not cover cases like in (1).

Next, an analysis with conversion from adverb to adjective is also represented, although the markedness of these constructions is emphasized (Duden 2016a: 754; Donalies 2005: 130). Eisenberg (2013: 222) speaks in the case of attributive – and thus inflected – use of modal adverbs (*die zweifellose Annäherung* 'the unquestionable approximation', *eine vermutliche Einigung* 'a presumed agreement'[19]) of the last stronghold of the traditional adverb concept, namely inflectability. If this falls, which Eisenberg tries to prevent by assuming conversion, then the (morphological) distinction between adverb and adjective is possibly invalid. In principle, Eisenberg's analysis could also be applied to the cases focused on here, if they are assigned to the basic category of adverb. However, this position is worthy of discussion, because on the one hand there are no other examples for conversion

---

19 However, these units cannot be used predicatively: **die Annäherung ist zweifellos* 'the approximation is unquestionable', **die Einigung ist vermutlich* 'the agreement is presumable'. Therefore, the converted units do not represent typical adjectives.

from adverb to adjective (cf. Fleischer & Barz 2012: 358).[20] On the other hand, it is claimed that transposed lexemes gain the morphosyntactic properties of the "target word class" (see e.g. Fleischer & Barz 2012: 89). This, however, is questioned for the items under investigation, which can be interpreted as an argument against the assumption of conversion. Even Eisenberg himself has been critical of this position and described it as an unsatisfactory solution (Eisenberg 2002: 74).

The two approaches presented so far start from adverbs. In the following, the grammatical behavior of these units will be looked at again, this time by focusing on some characteristics of adjectives and adverbs. Adjectives as well as adverbs share the function of categorial modifiers, which establish their "appropriate" references depending on the syntactic-semantic environment. They stand in the continuum of lexical classes between the maximally time-stable and subject-related nouns and the minimally time-stable and event-describing verbs (Lehmann 1992: 158) and act as their modifiers. In principle, only the scope is distinguished: "In fact Advs differ from Adjs only in their distribution: adjectives are nominal modifiers, adverbs are verbal modifiers; there are no adverbs in prenominal position." (Alexiadou 2002: 31; see also Gunkel & Schlotthauer 2012: 273). The boundary in the modifying field is thus by no means sharply drawn, so that one can in principle also conclude that adjectives and adverbs actually represent a single word class (general modifier), which can be differentiated in each case by the (realized) reference to other units of the chain of speech (for discussion see also Duplâtre & Modicom (this volume)).

Now adjectives and adverbs in German can, in principle and with some exceptions, have the same morphosyntactic positions: They can be used in predicative (13a), adverbial (13b), and attributive position (13c).

(13)   a.   X   ist   schön   X   ist   heute
            X   is   nice   X   is   today
            'X is nice.'   'X is today'
       b.   X   singt   schön   X   singt   heute
            X   sings   nicely   X   sings   today
            'X sings nicely'   'X sings today'

---

20 But what they call, however, is the conversion of participles. Looking back on the etymological remarks in section 3.1, one could say here that the conversion was "transferred", so to speak: First the participle of the particle verb was transposed to an adjective, then the base verb was dropped (*DWB* 1954). Hentschel (2005: 272–274) discusses whether the predicative use of prepositional units can be described as elliptical constructions with a dropped base verb. She comes to the conclusion that in many cases it is not possible to bring back the base verb which makes this approach problematic as a general explanation of this phenomenon.

c. die schöne Sitzung   die Sitzung heute
   the nice meeting   the meeting today
   'the nice meeting'   'today's meeting'

As long as the predicative and adverbial function is concerned, no difference can be seen, at least on the morphosyntactic level: The inflectable adjective appears uninflected in these uses, whereas the non-inflectable adverb has no inflectional endings anyway. In this context, the non-marked adverbial use of adjectives (13b) is discussed as a notorious problem case in German, with some authors calling these adverbs in principle, others considering them uninflected uses of adjectives (see recently Dabóczi 2018).

For our purposes, however, the possibility of lexemes to be used attributively with a noun like in (13c) is crucial.[21] Here, too, there are basically different options, namely prenominal and inflected or postnominal and uninflected. The attributive function is not completely exceptional for adverbs, although it is rather rare and subject to certain restrictions (cf. Eisenberg 2013: 217). Gunkel & Schlotthauer (2012: 278–282) describe in detail the attributive use of temporal and local adverbs in German and discuss the morphosyntactic conditions that allow the adverb to be connected to the noun grammatically: They can occur postnominally (14a), with a formal junction (14b) or by way of adjectivization (14c):

(14) a. die Sitzung heute
        'the meeting today'
     b. die Sitzung von heute
        'the meeting of today'
     c. die heutige Sitzung
        'today's meeting'

A few brief comments on these procedures in contrast to adjectives: As already mentioned, under certain circumstances, adjectives can also be postponed, which then also remain uninflected (*Whisky pur* 'pure Whisky'; cf. Vogel 1997). The formal connection via prepositions is not possible for adjectives, but also not necessary. The adjectivization of adverbs by suffixes such as *-ig* does usually not involve any semantic modification (as is often the case with suffixes, cf. Fleischer & Barz 2012: 339), but merely a syntactic recategorization, i.e. making the lexeme usable for new syntactic slots. However, simple conversion is not possible (**die*

---

21 For an analysis of the postnominal use of adverbs in English and German cf. Schäfer (2015).

heute Sitzung 'the today meeting'), which makes the above-mentioned thesis of conversion problematic once again.

It is now noticeable that the units *auf* and *zu* cannot fulfil exactly these three options:

(15) a. *die Tür auf/zu[22]
'the door open/closed'
b. *die Tür von auf/zu
'the door of open/closed'
c. *die zu-/auf-ig-e Tür
'the open/closed door'

This shows that these possibilities of connecting adverbs to nouns – which Gunkel & Schlotthauer (2012: 275) also emphasize – apply to local and temporal adverbs largely. These situate an event, but they do not modify a referent as *auf* and *zu* do. This functional difference between situating an event and describing a referent could be regarded as one reason for the different morphosyntactic behavior. It is also very interesting that *auf* and *zu* cannot be combined with the suffix -*ig*, which, as mentioned above, only is in charge of syntactic recategorization and does not change the meaning of its base. Surely, lexemes derived with -*ig* need to be semantically compatible with the use as nominal modifiers, but *auf* and *zu* fulfill this criterion, as they can also occur as object predicatives (cf. section 3.2). This gives rise to the assumption that these are no real adverbs and hence do not need to be adjectivized.

4.3 Adjective

There is another position that clearly names these units as adjectives already in their function as verb particles and does not assume an underlying adverb:

> There is some structural evidence that the preverbs *auf, ab, an,* and *zu* have adjectival readings. Adjectives can be positioned attributively or predicatively. Since the category adjective cannot be inferred without a doubt from the predicative position (adverbs might also be in this position), it is interesting to see whether the elements in question can be used attributively. Some speakers of German (especially speakers with northern German dia-

---

[22] This example is grammatical, if you interpret it as an order in which the basic verb is deleted: (*Mach*) *die Tür auf/zu* 'Open/Close the door!'. Here, following Dabóczi (2017: 183), one could admittedly not speak of "imperative particles of movement", but nevertheless of "imperative particles of action".

lects) accept *an, auf, ab*, and *zu* as attributive adjectives, although they are not [yet; M.A.] accepted in Standard German. [...] It might be argued that in constructions like *zuschließen*, close+lock, 'to lock', or *abrasieren*, off+shave, 'to shave off' the preverb is used in its adjectival reading. (Lüdeling 1999: 18).

In line with Lüdeling, Knobloch (2009: 548) refers to *auf* with the meaning 'open' as an adjective, and Braun (2011: 47–48) claims that for *zu* in *die zue Tür* 'the closed door' the classification as adjective would be valid.

The central morphosyntactic criterion for this position is the prenominal attributive use, which is – as already seen above – of crucial importance for the classification of word classes: It is regarded as necessary and sufficient for the classification of adjectives (Eisenberg 2002: 74). It is precisely into this attributive position that the units under consideration here advance. Thus, they clearly fulfil a central condition for their classification as an adjective. The fact that these units often appear as verb particles is no problem for this classification, since adjectives can also act as verb particles (*festfrieren* 'to freeze on'; Fleischer & Barz 2012: 424) and, as Lüdeling (1999: 19) notes, a preverb can belong to any part of speech except for nouns and verbs.

If classified as adjectives, however, one might raise the question whether these units also develop other adjectival properties, for example the characteristic comparison or prefixation with the negation prefix *un-* 'non'. In *DeReKo*, only three examples for the comparative degree of *zu* 'closed' like in (16) can be found:

(16) noch   zu-er
 even   closed-COMP
 'even more closed'
 (Süddeutsche Zeitung, 09.12.1995 | COSMAS II, w-öffentlich)

There is no such example of comparison for *auf* 'open', and for both units no prefixation with *un-* can be detected. However, this might not only be due to the non-prototypicality of these words as adjectives, but also to the semantics. As seen above, *auf* and *zu* form a pair of opposites. Therefore, the systematic negation by *un-* is not necessary here, just as with prototypical paired adjectives (*groß* 'big' – *klein* 'small', **un-groß* 'not big' – **un-klein* 'not small'). Moreover, *auf* and *zu* can be described as tendentially absolute properties, which makes the comparison unusual (see e.g. adjectives as *tot* 'dead' or *schwanger* 'pregnant', to which no meaningful comparative can be formed either).

At the end I want to widen the view a bit to the units *auf* and *zu* also outside the meanings considered here. They show a remarkable polyfunctionality as verb particles, prepositions, and adjectives. This polyfunctionality is caused by phenomena such as grammaticalization (see the prepositional use of *auf* and *zu*) or meaning shifts like those described in section 3.1. On the one hand, polyfunctionality is a characteristic of "the natural economic tendency of language" (Löbner 2013: 46; see also Plank 1985: 158). On the other hand, this shows the difficulties of clearly classifying such units. Generally, it is problematic to classify lexemes into "rigid" classes with fixed criteria: On the one hand, language reality sometimes "resists" a clear classification, on the other hand, a looser assignment of lexical units and syntactic classes could also expand the expressive possibilities of a certain language. As Knobloch & Schaeder (2005: IX) point out, a system with a very strict assignment of lexical meanings to syntactic categories would be stiff and sometimes hard to use. The question remains how to deal with the fact that sometimes the same unit can be classified differently, depending on the synchronic syntactic environment: If I say *X reißt die Tür auf* 'X rips open the door', then *auf* 'open' is to be considered as the preverb of *aufreißen* 'to rip open', but this is not common with *die Tür ist auf* 'the door is open',[23] and seems very problematic with *die aufe Tür* 'the open door', where there is no verb at all.

In addition to these different ways of using a unit, the numerous groups of meaning of verb particles in general have also been pointed out many times (cf. for an overview Fleischer & Barz 2012: 369). Thus, a number of different meanings are evident for *auf* and *zu*. The fact that, despite the ambiguity and polyfunctionality, there is nevertheless smooth communication can be traced back to the context: Verb and particle influence each other and finally receive their exact definition in the sentence (Kempcke 1965/66: 393 in Knobloch 2009: 546). These disambiguating contexts also exist when the particle occurs without a verb.

5 Conclusion

Finally, it should be noted that the verb particles *auf* 'open' and *zu* 'closed' can be classified as adjectives. These units developed from spatial adverbs by way of meaning shifts. Since *auf* and *zu* in the readings discussed here have relatively clearly defined and independent semantics (cf. Henzen 1969: 275), they can also detach themselves from the base verbs and, on the one hand, be coupled with a verb like *machen* 'make', which is semantically reduced to the aspect of 'action',

---

23 Hentschel (2005: 274–276) discusses the ability of the linking verb *sein* 'to be' to take a preverb but neglects this solution primarily because *sein* cannot take a verbal prefix and therefore seems unlikely as a word formations basis.

but also with the completely grammaticalized copula verbs and form predicates with these. This predicative use is regarded as the "gateway" for new adjectives (Eichinger 2007: 159). It is in a certain sense the preliminary stage of attributive use. Therefore, over time, an attributive use develops from these predicative structures – for the time being largely limited to spoken language (and certain dialectal areas) – which could, however, be extended. The way into the prenominal slot is made more difficult by various factors, firstly, the fundamental non-inflectability of verb particles in general, secondly, other ways of using the same verb particles that cannot be used predicatively, and thirdly, the related non-inflectable prepositions. On the other hand, there are "competitors" like *offen* 'open', *geöffnet* 'open', *geschlossen* 'closed'. Here one could try to work out similarities and differences in use by means of corpus-based analyses, which must remain a desideratum at this point.

Moreover, these considerations can be extended. In the literature, the following verb particles are often mentioned in the context of "irregular" attributive use: *ab-* 'off', *an-* 'on', *auf-* 'open', *aus-* 'off', and *zu-* 'closed' (Stiebels 1996: 160; Lüdeling 1999: 18). It would be interesting to take a closer look at the development of these other cases.

To return to the question that inspired the title of this chapter: Prenominal adverbs in German are – at least with regard to the units considered here – not an issue. By classifying *auf* and *zu* as adjectives, their independence is taken into account and at the same time the problem of inflectable adverbs, which Eisenberg (2002: 74) addresses, is avoided. Thus, the solution presented here appears on the one hand to be in line with the general tendency towards polyfunctionality for certain lexical units, and on the other hand, one of the "last strongholds" of the traditional concept of adverb (Eisenberg 2013: 222), i.e. non-inflectability, can be defended (for the time being).

References

Alexiadou, Artemis. 2002. On the status of Adverb in a grammar without a lexicon. In Friederike Schmöe (ed.), *Das Adverb. Zentrum und Peripherie einer Wortklasse*, 25–42. Wien: Praesens.
Altmann, Hans. 2011. *Prüfungswissen Wortbildung*. Göttingen: Vandenhoeck & Ruprecht.
Altmann, Hans & Ute Hofmann. 2004. *Topologie fürs Examen*. Wiesbaden: VS.
Bergenholtz, Henning & Joachim Mugdan. 1979. Ist Liebe primär? – Über Ableitung und Wortarten. In Peter Braun (ed.), *Deutsche Gegenwartssprache. Entwicklungen, Entwürfe, Diskussionen*, 339–354. München: Fink.

Braun, Christian. 2011. Grammatik (nicht) verstehen – Knackpunkte des Scheiterns. In Klaus-Michael Köpcke & Arne Ziegler (eds.), *Grammatik – Lehren, Lernen, Verstehen. Zugänge zur Grammatik des Gegenwartsdeutschen*, 34–50. Berlin & Boston: de Gruyter.
Chang, Lingling. 2007. Resultative Prädikate und Verbpartikeln. *Deutsch als Fremdsprache* 44(2). 81–89.
Coseriu, Eugenio. 1975. System, Norm und ‚Rede'. In Uwe Petersen (ed.), *Sprache. Strukturen und Funktionen*, 53–72. Tübingen: Tübinger Beiträge zur Linguistik.
Dabóczi, Viktória. 2017. *Wort und Wortarten aus Sicht der gesprochenen Sprache*. Frankfurt/M.: Lang.
Dabóczi, Viktória. 2018. Am Rande der Wortarten: Zum Problem der Klassifikation von Randphänomenen am Beispiel des unflektierten Adjektivs. In Carolin Baumann, Viktória Dabóczi & Sarah Hartlmaier (eds.), *Adjektive. Grammatik, Pragmatik, Erwerb*, 152–176. Berlin & Boston: de Gruyter.
Dittmann, Jürgen, Rolf Thieroff & Ulrich Adolphs. 2003. *Wahrig. Fehlerfreies und gutes Deutsch*. Gütersloh: Wissen-Media.
Donalies, Elke. 2005. *Die Wortbildung des Deutschen. Ein Überblick*. 2nd edn. Tübingen: Narr.
Duden. 2016a. *Die Grammatik*. 9th edn. Berlin: Dudenverlag.
Dürscheid, Christa. 2010. *Syntax. Grundlagen und Theorien*. 5th edn. Göttingen: Vandenhoeck & Ruprecht.
Eichinger, Ludwig M. 2000. *Deutsche Wortbildung. Eine Einführung*. Tübingen: Narr.
Eichinger, Ludwig M. 2007. Adjektiv (und Adkopula). In Ludger Hoffmann (ed.), *Handbuch der deutschen Wortarten*, 143–188. Berlin & Boston: de Gruyter.
Eisenberg, Peter. 2002. Morphologie und Distribution – Zur Morphosyntax von Adjektiv und Adverb im Deutschen. In Friederike Schmöe (ed.), *Das Adverb. Zentrum und Peripherie einer Wortklasse*, 61–76. Wien: Praesens.
Eisenberg, Peter. 2013. *Grundriss der deutschen Grammatik. Der Satz*. 4th edn. Stuttgart: Metzler.
Eisenberg, Peter. 2017. *Deutsche Orthografie, Regelwerk und Kommentar*. Berlin & Boston: de Gruyter.
Engel, Ulrich. 1970. *Regeln zur Wortstellung*. Mannheim: Institut für deutsche Sprache.
Fleischer, Wolfgang & Irmhild Barz. 2012. *Wortbildung der deutschen Gegenwartssprache*. 4th edn. Berlin & Boston: de Gruyter.
Gunkel, Lutz & Susan Schlotthauer. 2012. Adnominale Adverbien im europäischen Vergleich. In Lutz Gunkel & Gisela Zifonun (eds.), *Deutsch im Sprachvergleich. Grammatische Kontraste und Konvergenzen*, 273–300. Berlin & Boston: de Gruyter.
Haider, Hubert. 2018. Sprachen mit ‚resultativ' interpretierbaren Adjektiven – vorhersagbar? In Elisabeth Leiss & Sonja Zeman (eds.), *Die Zukunft von Grammatik – Die Grammatik der Zukunft. Festschrift für Werner Abraham anlässlich seines 80. Geburtstags*, 165–189. Tübingen: Stauffenburg.
Harden, Theo. 2014. Ein PS für die Fans formaler Systeme: Syntaxmodelle. In Theo Harden & Elke Hentschel, *Einführung in die germanistische Linguistik*, 213–232. Bern: Lang.
Hentschel, Elke. 2005. Die Frist ist um. Prädikativer Gebrauch von Präpositionen. *Zeitschrift für germanistische Linguistik* 33. 268–288.
Henzen, Walter. 1969. *Die Bezeichnung von Richtung und Gegenrichtung im Deutschen*. Tübingen: Niemeyer.
Knobloch, Clemens. 2002. Spracherwerb und Sprachwandel: Zweckehe oder gefährliche Liebschaft? In Kennosuke Ezawa, Wilfried Kürschner, Karl H. Rensch & Manfred Ringmacher (eds.), *Linguistik jenseits des Strukturalismus. Akten des II. Ost-West-Kolloquiums Berlin 1998*, 105–124. Tübingen: Narr.

Knobloch, Clemens. 2009. Noch einmal: Partikelverbkonstruktionen. *Zeitschrift für germanistische Linguistik* 37. 544–564.
Knobloch, Clemens. 2018. Adjektive – koreferentiell, kokonzeptuell, koprädikativ. Paper presented at University of Kassel, 15 January 2018.
Knobloch, Clemens & Burkhard Schaeder. 2005. Wortarten und Grammatikalisierung: ein Vorwort. In Clemens Knobloch & Burkhard Schaeder (eds.), *Wortarten und Grammatikalisierung. Perspektiven in System und Erwerb*, V–XV. Berlin & New York: de Gruyter.
Kühnhold, Ingeburg. 1973. Präfixverben. In Hans Wellmann & Ingeburg Kühnhold, *Deutsche Wortbildung. Typen und Tendenzen in der Gegenwartssprache. Erster Hauptteil: Das Verb*, 141–362. Düsseldorf: Schwann.
Lehmann, Christian. 1992. Deutsche Prädikatsklassen in typologischer Sicht. In Ludger Hoffmann (ed.), *Deutsche Syntax. Ansichten und Aussichten*, 155–185. Berlin & New York: de Gruyter.
Lichtenberk, Frantisek. 1991. Semantic Change and Heterosemy in Grammaticalization. *Language* 67. 475–509.
Löbner, Sebastian. 2013. *Understanding Semantics*. 2nd edn. London & New York: Routledge.
Lüdeling, Anke. 1999. *On Particle Verbs and similar constructions in German*. Stuttgart: Universität.
Menzel, Wolfgang. 2010. *Grammatik-Werkstatt. Theorie und Praxis eines prozessorientierten Grammatikunterrichts für die Primar- und Sekundarstufe*. 4th edn. Seelze: Klett-Kallmeyer.
Merkle, Ludwig. 1975. *Bairische Grammatik*. München: Heimeran.
Müller, Stefan. 2002. Syntax or morphology: German particle-verbs revisited. In Nicole Dehé, Ray Jackendoff, Andrew McIntyre & Silke Urban (eds.), *Verb-particle explorations*, 119–140. Berlin & New York: de Gruyter.
Paul, Hermann. 1897. *Deutsches Wörterbuch*. Halle/Saale: Niemeyer.
Plank, Frans. 1985. Prädikativ und koprädikativ. *Zeitschrift für germanistische Linguistik* 13. 154–185.
Schäfer, Martin. 2015. Adverbs in unusual places. In Karin Pittner, Daniela Elsner & Fabian Barteld (eds.), *Adverbs. Functional and diachronic perspectives*, 239–272. Amsterdam/Philadelphia: Benjamins.
Schmöe, Friederike. 2002. *Die deutschen Adverbien als Wortklasse*. Bamberg: University of Bamberg habilitation dissertation.
Schneider, Ricarda. 2013. Zwei Fliegen mit einer Klappe schlagen: Biprädikative Partikelverben im Deutschen aus typologischer und kontrastiver Sicht. In Irmtraud Behr & Zofia Berdychowska (eds.), *Prädikative Strukturen in Theorien und Text(en)*, 197–211. Frankfurt/M.: Lang.
Stiebels, Barbara. 1996. *Lexikalische Argumente und Adjunkte*. Berlin: Akademie.
Talmy, Leonard. 2019. Cognitive Semantics: An overview. In Claudia Maienborn, Klaus von Heusinger & Paul Portner (eds.), *Semantics. Theories*, 1–28. Berlin & Boston: de Gruyter.
Thieroff, Rolf & Petra M. Vogel. 2009. *Flexion*. Heidelberg: Winter.
Trotzke, Andreas & Eva Wittenberg. 2017. Expressive particle verbs and conditions of particle fronting. *Linguistics* 53. 407–435.
Vogel, Petra M. 1997. Unflektierte Adjektive im Deutschen: Zum Verhältnis von semantischer Struktur und syntaktischer Funktion und ein Vergleich mit flektierten Adjektiven. *Sprachwissenschaft* 22. 403–432.
Wunderlich, Hermann. 1894. *Unsere Umgangssprache in der Eigenart ihrer Satzfügung*. Weimar & Berlin: Felber.

Online resources

DeReKo = *Deutsches Referenzkorpus.* https://www.ids-mannheim.de/cosmas2/. (accessed 30 September 2020).
DGD = Datenbank für gesprochenes Deutsch. https://dgd.ids-mannheim.de. (accessed 30 September 2020).
Duden. 2016b. Auszug aus Munzinger Online/Duden – Das Wörterbuch der sprachlichen Zweifelsfälle; 8., vollständig überarbeitete und erweiterte Auflage, Bibliographisches Institut GmbH, Berlin, 2016. (accessed via Universitätsbibliothek Siegen 26 February 2020).
DWB (1854) = *"auf" In: Deutsches Wörterbuch von Jacob Grimm und Wilhelm Grimm, Erstbearbeitung (1854–1960). Digitalisierte Version im Digitalen Wörterbuch der deutschen Sprache,* https://www.dwds.de/wb/dwb/auf. *(accessed 08 April 2020).*
DWB (1954): *"zu" In: Deutsches Wörterbuch von Jacob Grimm und Wilhelm Grimm, Erstbearbeitung (1854–1960). Digitalisierte Version im Digitalen Wörterbuch der deutschen Sprache,* https://www.dwds.de/wb/dwb/zu. *(accessed 16 April 2020).*
Sick, Bastian. 2007. Bei zuen Gardinen und ausem Licht. https://bastiansick.de/kolumnen/zwiebelfisch/bei-zuen-gardinen-und-ausem-licht/, (accessed 25 September 2020).

II Classificational approaches

3 **Adverbial scope: beyond the low / high dichotomy**

Aquiles Tescari Neto

'Sentence adverbs' don't exist!

Abstract: Different theoretical and typological approaches to adverbs uncontroversially acknowledge the existence of a subgroup of adverbs descriptively called "sentence adverbs" (SAs). Nonetheless, as Costa (2008) observes, one and the same sentence having a SA to the right of the main verb may be ambiguous in meaning in European Portuguese as the domain of modification of the adverb can either be the propositional content, or one of its constituents. In this paper, I argue against the existence of a (sub)class of adverbs which has been lumped together under the label "SAs". Instead of taking some classes of adverbs in English to be representatives of SAs cross-linguistically, I bring some syntactic diagnostics which allow one to distinguish (i) adverbs which can take under their scope the propositional content in some contexts and only sentential constituents in others from (ii) adverbs which do not take the propositional content under their scope. I present syntactic tests which can discriminate between "high" adverbs, which I take to be the best terminology to refer to the universal subclass of "SAs", i.e. those located in the highest portion of the structure in the spirit of Cinque (1999), and "low" adverbs, i.e. those occupying lower portions of the clause. The arguments put forward in this study point to the conclusion that the status of an adverb as a SA is only epiphenomenal. That is, those adverbs occupying higher positions in the hierarchy may coincidentally take the sentence under their scope in some cases but not in all the possible cases.

Keywords: adjuncts, cartography, focus, scope

1 Introduction

Many theoretical and typological approaches to adverbs[1] acknowledge the existence of a subgroup of adverbs descriptively called "sentence adverbs" (SAs) (Jackendoff

---

[1] I would like to thank the participants of the conference *The Problem of the Adverb*, which took place *on-line* on October 1st-2nd 2020. A previous version of the paper has received interesting contributions from Pierre-Yves Modicom, Olivier Duplâtre and from an anonymous reader who also attended the same conference. I am very grateful to their thoughtful remarks. I also would like to thank the interventions from the other colleagues attending the conference. After the confer-

---

Aquiles Tescari Neto, LaCaSa - Cartographic Syntax Laboratory, University of Campinas, tescari@unicamp.br

https://doi.org/10.1515/9783110767971-006

1972; Thomason & Stalnaker 1973; Bellert 1977; Ramat & Ricca 1998; Shu 2011 a.o.). These adverbs modify the content of the sentence in which they appear (Ramat & Ricca 1998: 189), being characterized (at least in formal approaches to semantics) as "functions taking propositions into propositions" (Thomason & Stalnaker 1973; Bellert 1977). A sentence like (1) would differ in meaning and truth value if compared to a sentence without the SA *probably* (2), in that they have different truth values. Besides that, the literature also reports that each specific class of SA convey a distinct semantic value (Bellert 1977; Casteleiro 1982; Ramat & Ricca 1998; Cinque 1999, a.o.). Hence, besides modifying the content of the sentence, they also add a specific semantic import to it (e.g. 'domain': *politically*; 'speech act': *sincerely*; 'evaluation': *unfortunately*; 'doubt': *probably*; etc.), as in (3):[2]

(1) Phillip has probably forgotten his credit card number

(2) Phillip has forgotten his credit card number

(3) Sincerely/Unfortunately/Evidently, the situation generated by covid-19 is very chaotic

Nonetheless, one and the same sentence having a SA to the right of the main verb may be ambiguous in meaning in Brazilian (BP) and also in European (EP) Portuguese (Tescari Neto 2013: 205–206, see ex. 4), as the domain of modification of the adverb can either be the propositional content (4'), or one of its constituents, such as the PP to the right of the adverb in paraphrase (4").

(4) A Maria   cantou   provavelmente para   o patrão.
    The Maria   sang   probably   for   the boss
    'Maria sang probably for her boss'
    (Costa 2008: 15; Tescari Neto 2013: 206)

---

ence, the paper has received important suggestions and insightful contributions from two anonymous reviewers from DeGruyter to whom I would like to express my gratitude. A previous draft of the paper has also been read and discussed by the members of my research group, *LaCaSa*, whom I also would like to thank. The paper has also been presented at the *Syntax Silk Road: meetings in Cartography*, organised by the Linguistics Department at the Beijing Language and Culture University, by the Università degli Studi di Padova and by the International Association of Syntactic Cartographic Studies (from Macao). Many thanks also go to the audience at that colloquia, specially to Giuseppe Samo, Luigi Rizzi and Adriana Belletti.
2 On the different semantic classes of sentence adverbs see, among many others, Bellert (1977); Dik et al. (1990); Lonzi (1993); Hengeveld (1997); Ramat & Ricca (1998); Cinque (1999); Tescari Neto (2013).

(4) is ambiguous between (4') and (4") in Brazilian Portuguese provided that the sentence is uttered with "flat intonation". Needless to say, the exclusive association of the adverb with the focus *para o patrão* 'for her boss' preferentially shows up if this PP is prosodically marked.

(4') It is probable that Maria sang for her boss.

(4") It is probably for her boss that Maria sang.

Regarding the scope of the "SA" in (4), it is reported that it has wide scope, i.e. scope over the propositional content (whose reading is given by the paraphrase in ex. 4'), or narrow focus, where the adverb does not modify the propositional content but the complement to its right, as suggested by the paraphrase in ex. 4" (Tescari Neto 2013: 205).[3] It is not an idiosyncrasy of Portuguese that "SAs" may be associated to the focus if placed between the V and its internal argument. Laenzlinger (1996) reports that the French adverb *probablement* 'probably' in (5) may also be ambiguous regarding its domain of modification, as it can take scope over the sentence, in one possible reading, or be associated with the focus, namely, the nominal complement in the other reading.

(5) Jean lira probablement tous les livres
    J. will-read probably all the books
    'J. will probably read all the books'
    (Laenzlinger 1996: 124, n.1)[4]

That the ambiguity of (5) is not due to the obligatory raising of the V(erb) in French is attested by (6), a sentence having both an auxiliary and the main verb to the left of *probablement*. Were the ambiguity of (5) due to V raising, one should not expect to find it again in (6). Yet, (6') and (6") are possible paraphrases for (6).

---

3 See, however, the discussions in Giorgi (2016); Schifano (2018).
4 Some speakers may reject the focusing reading in (4) which would be blocked by the quantification (Olivier Duplâtre, personal communication). Anyway, since the focusing reading is kept with the replacement of 'tous les' by 'ces', Laenzlinger's observation on the ambiguity of (5) is still valid. As Olivier Duplâtre observed, if one takes prosody into account, (5) would no longer be ambiguous. It would be the case that Laenzlinger's French behave as my (Brazilian) Portuguese, for which a sentence like (4) is ambiguous with flat intonation.

(6) *French* (Christopher Laenzlinger, p.c.)
Les étudiants ont vu probablement ce film[5]
The students have seen probably this film

(6') 'It is probable that the students have seen this film'[6]

(6") 'It is probably this film that the students have seen'

Hence, in the best of possible worlds, given the association of the epistemic adverb *provavelemente/probablement* 'probably' with the verb complement in (4–6), as respectively attested by the paraphrases in (4") and (6"), one would only descriptively use the term "SA" in reference to some subclasses of adverbs which can occasionally take the sentence under their scope in Romance.

The main goal of this paper is to argue that the domain of modification of an adverb (namely, its scope) cannot be directly associated to its "syntactic status" (if SA or predicate adverb/adverb of constituent/phrasal adverb). This is so because the adverbs we are used to calling "SA" are not always modifiers of the propositional content. As we have seen, they may be modifiers of sentential constituents. Putting that differently, the paper aims to argue against the direct connection often made in the literature according to which SAs should always take wide scope, contrary to facts, as we have seen in (4–6).[7] Hence, the paper will argue that

---

5 One of the two anonymous reviewers has kindly provided the example in (i), below, which also shows that the high adverb *probablement* 'probably' can occur to the left of the participle of *être*:

(i) Jean (n') a été probablement (qu') un joueur médiocre de tennis.
'John was probably (only) a poor tennis player.'

6 I am aware of the fact that the usual placement of *probablement* 'probably' in Standard French is between *ont* and *vu* whenever this adverb modifies the whole propositional content. Actually, French speakers do favour the interpretation in (6") for (6), as Pierre-Yves Modicom told me out. One of the two anonymous reviewers also agrees that the two readings, namely, (6') and (6"), are available to (6), though they also have a preference for (6"). (6') is still possible with the appropriate intonation. Yet, as the same reviewer has pointed out, these two possible readings (namely, a wide scope and a narrow scope interpretation) are even easier to catch in (i) below (their example):

(i) Les enfants sont allés probablement (tous) à la plage.
'The kids probably (all) went to the beach.'

All in all, what is important for our concerns here is that (6') is not excluded at all, at least for some speakers of French like Christopher Laenzlinger. Hence, in a theory of *I-language*, the wide scope reading for the adverb in (6), as suggested by the paraphrase in (6'), should not be discarded.
7 According to Giorgi (2016), the epistemic adverb of (i), from Italian, would only modify the direct object to its right in this case. Nonetheless, the very fact that in Giorgi's Italian a SA can

wide scope or narrow focus are not directly translated as the scope of a "SA" and scope of a predicate adverb/adverb of constituent/phrasal adverb, respectively.

Instead of taking some classes of adverbs in English (a language lacking "verb raising" (Pollock 1989), in terms of generative grammar) to be representatives of SAs cross-linguistically, I bring some syntactic diagnostics which allow one to distinguish (i) the adverbs which can either have wide scope or be associated with the focus of the sentence (see the examples in (4–6), above) from (ii) those which never have wide scope. At the end of the paper, it will be concluded that the classification of a given semantic class of adverb as a "SA" is, in the best of possible worlds, only epiphenomenal. This is so because some adverbs occupying higher positions in the layered structure of the clause which is usual in Cartographic representations (e.g. Cinque 1999) may coincidentally take the (whole) propositional content under their scope in some but not in all possible cases, at least in Romance, as we have seen in (4–6). Hence, a more correct description would rather make reference to the position of the adverb in the clausal hierarchy, which, on the basis of syntactic tests, can indeed be subdivided in two areas, namely a high zone and a low zone, not necessarily matching the semantic scope of the adverb.

To achieve that goal, the paper is organized as follows. First, it goes through some very general considerations on SAs, mainly from a syntactic point of view. Then, it critically reviews some tests often used in the literature as *bona fide* diagnostics for the syntactico-semantic status of an adverb, as SA or predicate/VP adverb. I will show that the correct interpretation of the results of those tests must take into consideration languages having more "flexible" positions for adjuncts other than English. The conclusion will be that the tests critically discussed in section 3 actually serve as good indicators of the height of the adverb in the structure of the sentence, once the properties explored by those tests exclusively depend on their position in the clausal hierarchy.

2 On the problematic status of "SAs"

In many papers within the current generative literature, SAs are simply called "high adverbs" (see, for instance, Cinque 1999; Tescari Neto 2013; Forero 2019, a.o.). Treating high adverbs and SAs as synonyms within Generative Grammar

---

only have narrow focus if placed to the right of the lexical verb is an interesting piece of evidence against considering *probabilmente* (and, eventually, all high adverbs) as a "SA":

(i)   Gianni ha mangiato probabilmente la torta.
      'Gianni ate probably the cake.' (Giorgi 2016: 100)

only makes sense in pre-Cartographic/non-Cartographic works, which assume a minimal clausal skeleton as in Chomsky (1986, 1995), having, besides the VP, at most three functional layers or projections, as represented in Figure 1.

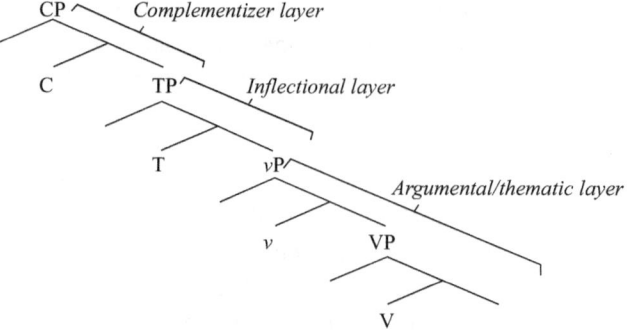

Figure 1: The functional structure of the clause in minimalist approaches.

The ordinary way to integrate SAs within approaches assuming representations like the one given in Figure 1 is by assuming that they normally adjoin to the TP. VP adverbs or "predicate adverbs" in other approaches (Thomason & Stalnaker 1974; Bellert 1977), on their turn, adjoin to the vP/VP, in line with Jackendoff's (1972) analysis. In the wake of Jackendoff, Costa (2004: 716) explicitly mentions the two fundamental domains for adverbs attachment through adjunction in the structure of the clause according to the most spread minimalist assumption, namely, the TP and the vP/VP (also see Ernst [2002]). Jackendoff's initial idea has stood the test of time and is still used in many generativist analyses. The existence of languages like English, which lacks verb raising (in Pollock's 1989 spirit),[8] matches very well with Jackendoff's adjunction loci system since the lexical V remain in the argumental/thematic layer. That may have eventually been the motivation for the (direct) connection often made in the literature which associates SAs to wide scope (i.e. to scope over the propositional content, as said before). There is much literature on SAs devoted to English, a language lacking V raising, as mentioned. For that reason, once the V does not leave the thematic field (of Figure 1) in the language, SAs always appear to the left of the V (see Figure 2).

---

8 As correctly pointed out to me by one of the two reviewers, the grammaticality of (i) below would suggest that the V can raise at least over its PP-complement:

(i)   John spoke recently to Mary.

For more examples of this type, see Johnson (1991).

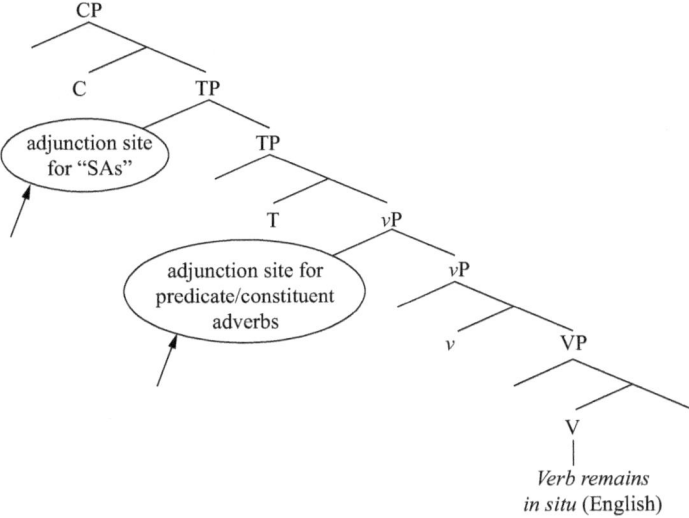

Figure 2: The two adjunction loci approach for adverbs.

The theory of free adjunction would have nothing to say on the precise adjunction site for adverbs of constituents. As one of the reviewers pointed out to me, an alternative would be to directly adjoin the modifier to its modifee (see, for instance, Zyman 2012). Thus, in the case of the narrow focus reading of *provavelmente* 'probably' in (4"), one could alternatively directly adjoin the epistemic adverb to the PP. For a critical review of such an analysis, see Tescari Neto (2013, chapter 5).

Nonetheless, the very fact that a sentence like (4), reproduced below for convenience, may be ambiguous in meaning would cast some doubts on the validity of this two-adjunction loci approach (summarized in Figure 2) for languages other than English. Thus, as noted in the Introduction, in the best of possible worlds, the ambiguity of (4) would make one agnostic not only on the validity of the two-adjunction loci approach for languages other than English but also on the existence of SAs.

(4) A Maria   cantou   provavelmente   para   o patrão.
     The Maria   sang   probably   for   the boss
     'Maria sang probably for her boss'

(4') It is probable that Maria sang for her boss.

(4") It is probably for her boss that Maria sang.

The domain of modification of the adverb can either be the sentence, an interpretation which easily comes up if one considers the paraphrase in (4'), or just one of its constituents (4"). The same is true of French, as discussed in the previous section. It is well known that a "SA" cannot intervene between a V and its object in English. In (7), the only ungrammatical sentence is (d) where the SA appears between the V and its internal argument:

(7) *English* (Sportiche 1988: 430)
    a. Probably, John left.
    b. John probably will leave.
    c. John will probably leave.
    d. *John will buy probably shoes.

Be as it may be, at first glance, the paradigm in (7) would suggest that the ungrammaticality of (7d) is due to the ban on V raising in English.[9] Hence, the traditional analysis for SAs is coincidentally descriptively accurate for English. If one turns to Romance (and Portuguese is probably the best example in this concern), the two-adjunction loci approach (of Figure 2) does not hold water, given the discussion of (4–6) in the previous section, a fact observed in Tescari Neto (2013).

With the development of the Principles and Parameters theory of Generative Grammar some authors have questioned (Ernst 2002: 467–468; Tescari Neto 2013, chapter 5; 2015) or at least remained agnostic on (Cinque 1999, chapter 1) the strict correlation between scope and "attachment site". Thomas Ernst, the exponent of one of the most prominent approaches for adverbs in Generative Grammar, explicitly states that

> the frequently invoked terms S(entential) adverb and VP adverb are no longer useful or accurate and, in fact, are quite misleading to the extent that they are meant to express a correlation between adjunction to S[entence]/VP and a type of meaning. (. . .) [T]he correlation between meaning and adjunction site has never been as close as the terms imply. This was so even before the development of the articulated Infl made up of many functional heads, since "VP adverbs" like shrewdly may occur before or after subjects (thus being under S (IP)), while "S adverbs" like perhaps sometimes show up after one or even two auxiliaries (under VP). With the proliferation of functional heads between subject and V, the inappropriateness of the terms is even more severe.   (Ernst 2002: 467–468)

Cinque (1999) seems to remain agnostic on the existence of "sentence adverbs". The author in fact uses the terms higher vs. lower adverbs to make reference to these two groups of adverbs sometimes (incorrectly) referred to as SAs vs. VP/predicate adverbs. Cinque (1999) proposes a Universal Hierarchy of adverbs which

---

9 An alternative analysis for the ungrammaticality of (7d) would be the adjacency constraint between the V and its complement.

matches the hierarchy of functional heads and can be divided in two "zones" on syntactic grounds as shown below:

[*frankly* MOOD$_{SpeechAct}$
 [*luckily* MOOD$_{Evaluative}$
  [*allegedly* MOOD$_{Evidential}$
   [*probably* MOD$_{Epistemic}$
    [*once* T$_{Past}$ "Higher adverbs"
     [*then* T$_{Future}$
      [*perhaps* MOOD$_{Irrealis}$
       [*necessarily* MOD$_{Necessity}$
        [*possibly* MOD$_{Possibility}$
         [*usually* ASP$_{Habitual}$
          [*finally* ASP$_{Delayed}$
           [*tendencially* ASP$_{Predispositional}$
            [*again* ASP$_{Repetitive(I)}$
             [*often* ASP$_{Frequentative(I)}$
              [*willingly* MOD$_{Volition}$
               [*quickly* ASP$_{Celerative(I)}$
                [*already* T$_{Anterior}$
                 [*no longer* ASP$_{Terminative}$
                  [*still* ASP$_{Continuative}$
                   [*always* ASP$_{Continuous}$
                    [*just* ASP$_{Retrospective}$
                     [*soon* ASP$_{Proximative}$
                      [*briefly* ASP$_{Durative}$ "Lower adverbs"
                       [(?) ASP$_{Generic/Progressive}$
                        [*almost* ASP$_{Prospective}$
                         [*suddenly* ASP$_{Inceptive}$
                          [*obligatorily* MOD$_{Obligation}$
                           [*in vain* ASP$_{Frustrative}$
                            [(?) ASP$_{Conative}$
                             [*completely* ASP$_{SgCompletive(I)}$
                              [*tutto* ASP$_{PlCompletive}$
                               [*well* VOICE
                                [*early* ASP$_{Celerative(II)}$
                                 [(?) ASP$_{Inceptive(II)}$
                                  [*again* ASP$_{Repetitive(II)}$
                                   [*often* ASP$_{Frequentative(II)}$
                                      Verb

(8) The Universal Hierarchy of Functional Projections (Cinque 1999:106, modified in Cinque 2006)[10,11]

In any case, the increasing of the number of functional categories assumed for the representation of the IP/Middlefield domain, which is very typical in the Cartographic versions of the Principles and Parameters Theory of Generative Grammar (Rizzi 1997, Cinque 1999 and subsequent work), made "obsolete" the use of the labels "SAs"/VP-adverbs etc. Hence, the "TP" of Figure 1 soon came to be seen as a complex "zone" made of almost thirty functional projections, as indicated by the (almost) thirty categories given by Cinque's (1999) Universal Hierarchy of adverbs and functional projections in (8). This observation would be valid in other theoretical frameworks as well. Functional theories turning to layered representations of the clause (Hengeveld 1989; Dik et al., 1990; Dik 1997; Ramat & Ricca 1998; Hengeveld & Mackenzie 2006) would also face the same problem if

---

10 This version, with this quite elaborated design, is quoted in a handout by David Pesetsky (2003): http://ocw.mit.edu/courses/linguistics-and-philosophy/24-902-language-and-its-structure-ii-syntax-fall-2003/lecture-notes/class_1_handout.pdf [Accessed April 19, 2020]
11 To arrive at this hierarchy, Cinque (1999) turns to *precedence and transitivity* tests, the most cartographic methodological expedient. Thus, he takes combinations of two adverbs of distinct (semantic) classes in Jackendoff's (1972) sense in the two possible relative orders, as illustrated in (*i-ii*) in the sequence, to give their position in the functional hierarchy.

(i)   a. $AdvP_A > AdvP_B$
       b. $*AdvP_B > AdvP_A$

(ii)   a. $AdvP_B > AdvP_C$
       b. $*AdvP_C > AdvP_B$

The combination of the *precedence* tests in (i) and (ii) gives, by transitivity, the (hierarchical) extract in (iii):

(iii) $AdvP_A > AdvP_B > AdvP_C$.

This *precedence* test is illustrated by (iv) below, whose results allowed Cinque to conclude that $Mood_{SpeechAct} > Mood_{Evaluative}$. He then turns to other combinations of two adverbs each time to arrive at the complete hierarchy given in (8) in the text.

(iv)   *Italian* (Cinque 1999: 12)
       a.   Francamente ho purtroppo una pessima opinione di voi.
            'Frankly I have unfortunately a very bad opinion of you.'
       b.   *Purtroppo ho francamente una pessima opinione di voi.
            'Unfortunately I have frankly a very bad opinion of you.'

they were applied to the analysis of Romance data like (4–6) from the Introduction. This is so because these theories assume that, in the underlying structure of the clause, adverbial-satellites would occupy different layers, depending on their semantic class.[12] Hence, acknowledging as "SAs" third and fourth level satellites (in Dik et al.'s 1990 sense) would not be the best choice, unless a "climbing down" mechanism across the layers of the clausal structure is assumed to guarantee that the corresponding adverbial-satellites have narrow scope in cases like (4–6).

Another complicating issue to the classification of some adverbs as "Sas" or, more precisely, to the acknowledgment that adverbs may be classified into two subgroups (SAs vs. constituent adverbs; TP adverbs vs. VP adverbs and the like), has to do to the fact that some low/VP adjuncts may come to occupy left peripheral positions (being placed at the beginning of the sentence), a fact also noted by the literature on Cartography (see Rizzi 2001b, 2004; Laenzlinger 2000, 2002, 2011; Cinque 2004). This is illustrated by the sentence in (9) from Italian.

(9) Rapidamente, i tecnici hanno risolto ___$_i$ il problema.
    'Rapidly, the technicians have resolved the problem.'   (Rizzi 2001: 102)

It is clear that the adverb in (9) does not take the propositional content/the sentence under its scope. Rather, its domain of modification is the V(P) as suggested by the subscripted index "i" to the left of the underscore, which indicates the default position of the adverb before its raising to the leftmost peripheral position.[13] Hence, empirically speaking, it is again very problematic to keep with those traditional approaches to adverbs which associate their scope to their adjunction site.

All things considered, there are empirical and theoretical arguments against the direct link often made between "SAs" and wide scope. If this is so, one should revisit the tests often used by linguists to recognize "SAs" and give those tests a sense in light of the facts discussed so far.

---

12 The layered structure of the clause according to Dik et al. 1990 (also see Hengeveld 1997) presupposes a hierarchy of four semantic levels, each level having an adverbial-satellite and an operator of the same semantic type. On the parallel between Dik's (1997) framework and the Cartographic version of Generative Syntax (Cinque 1999; Rizzi 1997), see Tescari Neto (2021).
13 The very fact that the placement of *rapidamente* 'quickly' in a left-peripheral position in (9) adds some information-structure-like flavour to the adverb (a [+modifier] feature, in Rizzi's (2001, 2004) sense) is beside the point here, once the adverb still continues to modify the participle *risolto* 'solved' in (9). Moreover, as pointed out to me by one of the anonymous reviewers, (9) is a good example to show that "there is no matching between surface position (second merge) and scope".

3 Syntactic tests to determine the height of the adverb in the sentence structure

The issues discussed in section 2 lead one to conclude that SAs do not exist or, to put it in a more elaborated way, that the direct link between the position occupied by an adverb in the clausal hierarchy (independently on the theory assumed) and its domain of modification does not hold water. Nonetheless, as I will show in this section, that does not mean that one should throw the tests away but give them a new interpretation. The tests actually point to a cluster of syntactic properties of a group of adverbs occupying specific positions in the clausal hierarchy. As we are going to see in this section, the tests can be used to indicate whether an adverb occupies a high or a low position within the clausal hierarchy.

Let us begin with Müller de Oliveira's (1993) study. Of the ten tests discussed by this author and often used by the literature as criteria to decide whether an adverb is a "SA" or not, he convincingly shows that five tests are *bona fide* diagnostics to indicate whether an adverb may take the sentence under its scope. Given the limited number of pages, I am only going through those five tests he considers "correct". For the time being, I am assuming Müller de Oliveira's (1993) conclusion on the "non-validity" of the other five tests to be correct. Of course, future investigation may test his "incorrect tests" again so as to make it sure that they are indeed "incorrect". Once, as shown, "SAs" can appear to the right of the main V in Portuguese and in other Romance languages like Italian and Spanish, one can turn to Müller de Oliveira's diagnostics to see whether they show different results in contexts where a high adverb/"SA" modifies the focus (as in the sentences (4–6) of the Introduction).[14] If so, that does not necessarily imply a failure in the (application of the) tests but a misinterpretation of the results. The same tests will be applied to "low" adverbs. The conclusion will show that Müller de Oliveira's tests actually do not indicate whether an adverb has wide scope or if it associated to focus. Rather, they are good indicators of the position the adverb occupies in the functional hierarchies.

To begin with, let us consider the sentence in (10) – where the adverb *provavelmente* 'probably' modifies the proposition (see paraphrase 10') and clearly is not associated to the DP-object *o bolo* 'the cake' – in order to verify the extension of Müller de Oliveira's conclusions on the five "correct" tests.

---

14 See Belletti (2001) for a low focus position in the low-IP area. As Quarezemin and Tescari Neto (2016) pointed out, in the narrow focus reading of (4) (see 4"), the focus position is the left peripheral one, nonetheless.

(10) O João   provavelmente comprou   o bolo
     The João probably   buy.3SG.PAST the cake
     'João probably bought the cake'

(10') It is probable that João bought the cake.

The paraphrase in (10') suggests that *provavelmente* in (10) has sentential scope. Müller de Oliveira's (i-v) "correct tests" given below would confirm that the adverb of (10) is a "SA". Each test will be also applied to an undoubtedly low adverb (i.e. one not having wide/sentential scope). The data are from Brazilian Portuguese:

(i) a SA cannot be denied:

(11) *O João   não provavelmente comprou   o bolo
     The João NEG probably   buy.3SG.PAST the cake
     'João didn't probably buy the cake'

Notice that a low adverb can be under the scope of negation:

(12) O João   não em vão   comprou   o bolo
     The João NEG in vain buy. 3SG.PAST the cake
     'João didn't buy the cake in vain'

Although it is not clear whether sentential negation would have a dedicated position in the clausal hierarchy of adverbs given in (8) (from Cinque 1999), it is very plausible that it should occupy a position below the lowest high adverb. That would explain the ill-formedness of (11).

(ii) a SA cannot be the focus of a cleft-sentence:[15]

(13) *Foi   provavelmente que o João   comprou   o bolo[15]
     It-was   probably   that the João buy. 3SG.PAST the cake
     'It was probably that João bought the cake'

While the adverb in (13) cannot be the focus of the cleft-sentence, a low adverb can (see ex. 14):

---

[15] As mentioned by one of the reviewers, the ungrammaticality of (13) can be accounted for in terms of Rizzi & Shlonsky's (2007) Criterial Freezing. In their own words, "the modal adverb cannot move to Foc, because its first-merge position is an IP-like position. In other words, the adverb is frozen in place."

(14) Foi em vão que o João comprou o bolo
It-was in vain that the João buy.3SG.PAST the cake
'It was in vain that João bought the cake'

(iii) a SA cannot be coordinated with the proposition:

(15) *O João comprou o bolo e provavelmente
The João buy.3SG.PAST the cake and probably
'João bought the cake and probably'

Low adverbs can:

(16) O João comprou o bolo e em vão
The João buy.3SG.PAST the cake and in vain
'João bought the cake and in vain'

(iv) SAs cannot be used as answers to questions introduced by wh-words (where, when, how, etc.). They are only compatible with yes/no questions.

(17) A: - Como/onde/quando o João comprou o bolo?
How/where/when the João buy.3SG.PAST the cake
'How/where/when did João buy the cake?'
B: *-Provavelmente.
- Probably.

Differently from high adverbs, low adverbs can be used as answers to wh-questions:

(18) A: - Como o João comprou o bolo?
How the João buy.3SG.PAST the cake
'How did João buy the cake?'
B: - Em vão.
- In vain.

(v) SAs cannot be the focus in a question:

(19) *Foi provavelmente que o João comeu o bolo?
ser.3SG.PAST probably that the João eat.3SG.PAST the cake
'It was probably that João ate the cake?'

Here, again, a possible explanation for the ungrammaticality of (19) is Rizzi & Shlonsky's "Criterial Freezing": the epistemic adverb is frozen in place; thus, no further raising would be allowed. Low adverbs, on the other hand, can be the focus in a question:

(20) Foi   em vão   que   o João   comeu   o bolo?
      ser.3SG.PAST in vain that the João eat.3SG.PAST the cake
      'It was in vain that João ate the cake?'

For the time being, the conclusion drawn on the basis of Müller de Oliveira's "correct" tests would be that these five criteria can discriminate between high and low adverbs, irrespective of their adjunction site. Nonetheless, if one considers the association of the adverb with the focus in (21), for which is given the paraphrase in (21'), they will realize that the epistemic adverb will retain the same properties generally associated with "SAs", irrespective of its scope in that sentence. That is enough to suggest that this set of five properties are not associated with "scope over the sentence", as the name "SA" would imply. Rather, they are tied to the height the adverb occupies in the clausal hierarchy (given in (8) in the previous section). Below the reader will find the application of the five criteria already seen to the epistemic *provavelmente* 'probably' of (21), this time in its narrow focus use, as suggested by the paraphrase in (21').

(21)   O João   comprou   provavelmente   o bolo[16]
       The João   buy.3SG.PAST probably   the cake
       'João bought probably the cake'

(21') It was probably the cake that João bought.

By applying the five tests to (21) (see items i' to v'), one arrives at the same results seen for this high adverb in its uncontroversial wide scope reading (namely, that shown in ex. 10):

(i')   a SA cannot be denied and neither can the adverb *provavelmente* 'probably' of (21) in its narrow focus use (21'):

---

[16] On the derivation of the narrow focus reading of (21), see Tescari Neto (2013, Chapter 5; 2020, as well as Figure 3 below and related text). It virtually follows the same steps proposed to derive (39a).

(22) */??O João   não   comprou   provavelmente   o bolo
     The João   NEG   buy. 3SG.PAST   probably   the cake
     'João did not probably buy the cake'

(ii') a SA cannot be the focus of a cleft-sentence; the adverb *provavelmente*, when directly modifying only single constituents from the sentence, e.g. in (21), cannot be the focus either:

(23) *Foi   provavelmente que   o João   comprou   o bolo
     It-was   probably   that the João   buy. 3SG.PAST   the cake
     'It was probably that João bought the cake'

(iii') a SA cannot be coordinated with the proposition; neither can the adverb *provavelmente* in contexts like (21):

(24) *O João   comprou   o bolo   e provavelmente
     The João   buy.3SG.PAST   the cake   and probably
     'João bought the cake and probably'

(iv') SAs cannot be used as answers to questions introduced by *wh*-words (where, when, how, etc.); the same observation can be extended to the *provavelmente* of (21):

(25) A: – Como/onde/quando   o João   comprou   o bolo
         How/where/when   the João   buy. 3SG.PAST   the cake?
         'How/where/when did João buy the cake?'
     B: *-Provavelmente.
         - Probably.

(v') SAs cannot be the focus in a question; neither can the *provavelmente* of (21):

(26) *Foi   provavelmente que   o João   comprou   o bolo?
     ser. 3SG.PAST probably   that the João   buy. 3SG.PAST   the cake
     'It was probably that João bought the cake'

Were high adverbs always SAs, irrespective of their scope, one should expect the sentences in (22–26), where *provavelmente* uncontroversially has narrow focus, to show different results from those in (11, 13, 15, 17, 19) where epistemic *provavelmente* 'probably' uncontroversially has wide scope. The results should be the same of those shown for (12, 14, 16, 18, 20), contrary to facts. Everything being equal, what Müller de Oliveira's tests actually show is that there is a group of adverbs, called "SAs" by the general literature and 'high adverbs' here, which can be characterized by a cluster of syntactic properties. These properties do not depend on the syntactic status of the adverb, namely, if they take under their scope a constituent or the sentence. Hence, when a high adverb has narrow focus, the tests are still valid, suggesting that the relevant information is the position of the adverb in the clausal hierarchy instead of the domain of modification by the adverb (whether a sentence or a constituent). This is so because "sentence adverbs don't exist!". Thus, a given high adverb, in both the wide scope and in the narrow focus readings, is always occupying the same syntactic position in the higher portion of the inflectional domain.

As we are going to see in the sequence, besides Müller de Oliveira's tests other syntactic expedients can be used to indicate whether an adverb is low or high.

The following four properties are due to Casteleiro's (1982) study whose criteria are mainly based on Bellert's (1977) work. Although, Casteleiro used these tests as criteria to indicate if an adverb is a sentence adverb or not, the same observations made for Müller de Oliveira's criteria can be done here. Where indicated, Casteleiro's data is from European Portuguese. The same judgments are valid for Brazilian Portuguese (BP). The data added (on low adverbs) are from BP.

(vi) high adverbs are subject to a wide mobility in the sentence (at least in Romance):

(27) *Brazilian Portuguese*
 (Provavelmente,)   o João (provavelmente)   comprou (provavelmente)
 (Probably,)   the João (probably)   bought (probably)
 o bolo (, provavelmente)
 the cake (, probably)

Low adverbs, either change their meaning or give rise to ill-formedness if they appear in different syntactic positions:

(28) *Brazilian Portuguese*
 (Cuidadosamente,)   o João (cuidadosamente)   comprou (cuidadosamente)
 (Carefully,)   the João (carefully)   buy.3SG.PAST (carefully)
 o bolo (cuidadosamente)
 the cake (carefully)

The adverb *cuidadosamente* 'carefully' is subject-oriented when placed to the immediate right of the subject in (28), and a manner adverb if placed after the V in that sentence.[17] Cinque (1999: 19; 2006: 125) on these apparent cases of ambiguity explicitly acknowledges the existence of a "common core" between the different interpretations of the "ambiguous" adverbs. In the case of (28), for instance, the manner and the subject-oriented interpretations are conveyed by one and the same lexical item which is underspecified w.r.t. the two distinct positions (the subject-oriented and the manner ones) and consequently compatible with both. As for the sentence-initial position of the adverb, its scope is ambiguous: that position is "accessible" for both manner and subject-oriented adverbs, as attested by (28a), where the subject-oriented adverb *cuidadosamente* 'carefully' co-occurs with the manner adverb *bem* 'well' in the order *cuidadosamente > bem*, as expected under relativised minimality considerations (see the ungrammaticality of (28b), where the adverb *bem*, which is uncontroversially a manner adverb in BP, cannot appear before *cuidadosamente*):

(28) a. *Brazilian Portuguese*
Cuidadosamente, bem, o João comprou o bolo
Carefully, well, the João buy.3SG.PAST the cake
'Carefully, well, João bought the cake'

(28) b. *Brazilian Portuguese*
??Bem, cuidadosamente, o João comprou o bolo.

(vii) high adverbs serve as answers to yes/no questions (Casteleiro 1982: 100):

(29) *European Portuguese*
– Então o sismo não provocou estragos?
('So the earthquake did not cause damage?')
– Felizmente.
('Fortunately') (Casteleiro 1982: 100)

(30) *European Portuguese*
– Então o colóquio vai ser adiado?
('So the colloquium will be postponed?')
Provavelmente.
('Probably') (Casteleiro 1982: 100)

---

17 These different meanings generated by the placement of *cuidadosamente* 'carefully' in (28) can be illustrated by the paraphrases below: (i), subject-oriented reading; (ii), manner reading:

(i) It was careful of João to have bought the cake.
(ii) John bought the cake in a careful way.

Low adverbs, on the other hand, cannot be used as answers to yes/no questions:

(31) - Então o terremoto não provocou estragos?
('So the earthquake did not cause damage?')
*-Bem/mal/catastroficamente/já/frequentemente/sempre/em vão
Well/bad/catastrofically/already/frequently/Always/in vain

(viii) they cannot be the focus of emphatic constructions marked by the phrase é que 'is that':

(32) *Felizmente é que o sismo não provocou estragos.
'Fortunately is that the earthquake did not cause damage.'

(33) * Provavelmente é que o colóquio vai ser adiado.
'Probably is that the colloquium will be postponed.

Low adverbs can:

(34) Completamente/Frequentemente/tremendamente/de novo/do nada/em vão/. . . é que o terremoto não provocou/a estragos.
'Completely/frequently/terribly/again/out of nowhere/in vain/ . . . is that the earthquake did not cause damage'

(ix) these adverbs cannot be the focus of a negative sentence marked with the restrictor senão 'except':

(35) *European Portuguese*
*O sismo não provocou estragos senão felizmente.
The earthquake did not wreaked havoc but fortunately. (Casteleiro 1982: 101)

(36) *O colóquio não vai ser adiado senão provavelmente.
The colloquium will not be postponed but probably

Low adverbs can:

(37) O terremoto não provocou estragos senão imediatamente/rapidamente/ bem/cedo/já/de novo/do nada/completamente/frequentemente/em vão
The earthquake did not wreaked havoc but immediately/quickly/well/early/already/out of nowhere/completely/frequently/in vain.

(38) O colóquio não vai ser adiado senão imediatamente/rapidamente/bem/
cedo/já/de novo/do nada/completamente/frequentemente/em vão.
The colloquium will not be postponed but immediately/quickly/well/early/
already/out of nowhere/completely/frequently/in vain.

So far, we have nine diagnostics which help linguists to distinguish low adverbs from high adverbs. Applied to Portuguese, these tests convincingly show that any attempt to associate "SAs" with wide scope is very problematic. There is a tenth diagnostic, adapted from Cinque (1999: 4; chapter 2). This author takes the raising of the active past participle in Italian as the deciding factor to put high adverbs in one side and low adverbs in the other. According to him, active past participle movement would be limited to the (functional) heads found to the right of the lowest 'higher' adverb, namely, *solitamente* 'usually' (habitual adverb). In this view, high adverbs would resist active past participle movement over them. Nonetheless, the contention that high adverbs cannot be crossed-over by the active past participle could be apparently denied on the basis of (39) from Nilsen (2004: 842):

(39) *Italian*
a. Due incendi   che non hanno   avuto   fortunatamente   conseguenze
   Two fires   that not have   had   fortunately   consequences
   rilevanti...
   relevant...
   'Two fires that haven't fortunately had relevant consequences...'
b. le analisi   hanno   dato   fortunatamente   esito   negativo.
   The analyses have-3PL had   fortunately   output   negative
   'The analyses have fortunately had negative output'

As Nilsen points out, it should be the case that the past-participle would have raised over relatively higher adverbs. Yet, the correct approach to (39) would not involve the raising of the past participle over the high adverb. As Tescari Neto (2013, chapter 5) argues, it would first actually involve attraction of the constituent surfacing to the right of the high adverb, i.e. the constituent directly modified by the high adverb, namely, *conseguenze rilevanti*, in (39a) (see "step (1)" of Figure 3 in the sequence); and *esito negativo*, in (39b). In the sequence, the high adverb would enter the derivation, in accordance with Cinque's hierarchy, followed by the raising of the remnant past it, namely, the raising of... *non hanno avuto*, in (39a) (see "step (2)" in the same figure) and of *le analisi hanno dato*, in (39b), along the lines of a modified

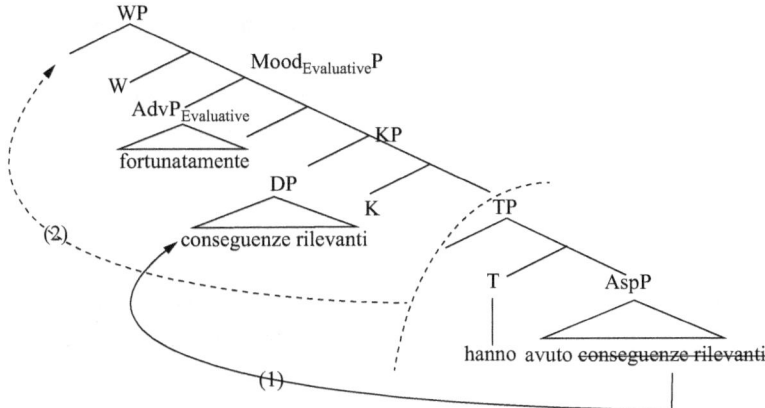

Figure 3: On deriving the narrow focus reading of (39a).

version of Kayne (1998). Since the remnant contains the active past participle, it gives us the impression that the participle has (head-)moved past the high adverb.[18]

---

[18] According to Cinque (1999), French lacks active past participle raising, as the data in (i) below show. Thus, the participle *compris* 'understood' cannot raise over *bien* 'well' one of the lowest adverbs of Cinque's hierarchy:

(i) *French* (Cinque 1999: 46)
a. *Il en a bien compris à peine la moitié.*
   'He has of it well understood hardly half.'
b. **Il en a compris bien à peine la moitié.*
   'He has of it understood well hardly half.'

Nonetheless, as in the Italian example (in ex. 39), high adverbs can appear to the right of the participle (see the example (6) above and the related footnotes; also see (ii), below, provided by the reviewer):

(ii) Il   a   eu   heureusement/probablement le prix du jury.
     He   has   won   fortunately/probably the prize of jury.
     'Fortunately/probably he won the jury prize'.

Thus, as in (39), (ii) would not involve the raising of the participle over the DP-object *le prix du jury*, as there is no active past participle raising in French (see ex. (i)b in this footnote). Its derivation would rather involve the raising of the object over the participle, the merge of the adverb and a further raising of the remnant (along the lines of the derivation suggested in Figure 3). All things being equal, the data in (39) and in (i-ii) would strongly disfavour an analysis whereby the modifier is directly merged with its modifee in the «narrow scope/narrow focus» reading of the adverb.

One way to get around this problem, and this is the tenth test, is by taking an unergative active past participle in the application of the test. (40a,b), from BP, illustrate that. High adverbs (ex. 40b), as opposed to low adverbs (ex. 40a), cannot appear sentence-finally, if the sentence is uttered with flat intonation:

(40) a. João tinha mentido com frequência/de novo/do nada/cedo/bem/rapidamente/etc.
J. had told-lies often/again/out of nowhere/early/well/quickly/etc.
'John had told lies often/again/out of nowhere/early well/quickly/etc.'
b. *João tinha mentido provavelmente/evidentemente/infelizmente/sinceramente/etc.
J. had told-lies *probably/evidently/unfortunately/sincerely/etc.
'J. had told lies probably/evidently/unfortunately/sincerely/etc.'

Last but not least, the eleventh tool to discriminate high and low adverbs is given by languages having VP-ellipsis but with a limited raising of the main V to the inflectional domain. Some (varieties of) Portuguese are good examples of such languages. Brazilian and Mozambican Portuguese both have V-to-I with finite verbs but this V cannot raise in both varieties past *já* 'already', a medial adverb. Hence, the prediction made by the theory of V raising for these two varieties is that high adverbs cannot be recovered by the gap in the second member of the coordination in VP-ellipsis structures like the one in (41).

(41) O Eduardo limpa ADVERB a casa e a Mara também limpa [-]
The Eduardo clean.3SG.PRES ADVERB the house and the Mara also clean.3SG.PRES
'Eduardo cleans ADVERB the house and so does Mary'

Considering that "adverb" in (41) may be substituted by any adverb from the hierarchy in (8) of section 2, there is evidence that only adverbs lower than *já* 'already' can be recovered by the gap in the second element of the coordination both in Brazilian and European Portuguese. High adverbs can never be recovered by the gap and the only possible interpretation for the gap is the one associated to the null object construction (Tescari Neto 2013).

An experiment has been conducted with speakers of Mozambican Portuguese, in Maputo, Mozambique. They were asked to give an interpretation for the gap "[-]" in structures like (41), where the word ADVERB was filled by one of the adverbs of the following table each time. For each sentence, they were asked to mark one or even both interpretations available for the gap, as exemplified below in (42):

(42) O Eduardo limpa frequentemente a casa e a Mara
      The Eduardo cleans often the house and the Mara
      também limpa [-]:
      too cleans
      'Eduardo often cleans the house and so does Mara'
   a. ( ) frequentemente a casa
          often the house
   b. ( ) a casa
          the house

The results are reproduced below in the table.

Table 1: V raising and VP-ellipsis: is the adverb recovered within the gap in Mozambican Portuguese?

Lexical item	Class	VP-ellipsis		Null object	
		n	%	n	%
evidentemente	Mood$_{Evidential}$	5/23	21,7	20/23	87
provavelmente	Mood$_{Epistemic}$	5/23	21,7	21/23	91,3
sempre (VOA)	Asp$_{Continuous}$	4/23	17,4	22/23	95,7
sempre (VAO)	Asp$_{Continuous}$	9/23	39,1	15/23	65,2
obrigatoriamente	Mood$_{Obligation}$	11/23	47,8	15/23	65,2
em vão / à toa	Asp$_{Frustrative}$	3/23	13	21/23	91,3
completamente	Asp$_{SgCompletive(I)}$	16/33	48,5	21/33	63,6
tudo	Asp$_{PlCompletive}$	17/33	51,5	20/33	60,6
bem	Voice	22/33	66,7	16/33	48,5
cedo	Asp$_{Celerative(I)}$	17/33	51,5	23/33	69,7
do nada	Asp$_{Inceptive(II)}$	13/33	39,4	27/33	81,8
de novo	Asp$_{Repetitive(II)}$	13/33	39,4	26/33	78,8
com frequência	Asp$_{Frequentative(II)}$	19/33	57,6	18/33	54,5

The table suggests that although speakers of Mozambican Portuguese tend to prefer the null object interpretation for the gap, the interpretation associated to the VP-ellipsis construction (where the adverb is recovered by the gap) is possible if the adverb is low: according to the hierarchy in (8), *obrigatoriamente* 'obligatorily' and all the adverbs below it in the table (which, in turn, follow it in the hierarchy) are more likely to be recovered by the gap than high adverbs, which, in fact, should not be recovered. Crucially, if a high adverb is present, the null object interpretation is more prone to be facilitated (87 and 91,3%) and the adverbs *evidentemente* 'evidently' and *provavelmente* 'probably' are not recovered. Thus, VP ellipsis would help one to decide whether an adverb is high or low since only low adverbs can be recovered by the gap, while high adverbs, if present, tend to induce a null-object interpretation for the gap.[19]

All things considered, on the basis of these eleven essentially syntactic diagnostics one can decide whether an adverb is high or low. As we have seen, the scope of an adverb cannot be directly associated to the position it occupies in the hierarchy (or with its specifier position/adjunction loci), as high adverbs can independently have wide scope or be associated with the focus.

4 In guise of conclusion

There are convincing syntactic arguments pointing to the conclusion that SAs do not exist or at least that scholars should take care when they use the term "SA". First, the assumption of enriched structural representations for the clause, which is very typical in the Cartographic versions of the Principles and Parameters Theory of Generative Grammar (Rizzi 1997, Cinque 1999 and subsequent work), casts doubts on the putative use of the labels "SAs"/VP-adverbs etc. The same conclusion may be arrived at by different grammatical theories provided that they acknowledge articulated structures for the clause, as we have seen. Secondly, the very fact that the appearance of the main verb to the left of a "SA" in Romance triggers a narrow focus interpretation for the adverb would again question the direct connection often established between the scope of an adverb and its syntactic status. Since high adverbs cannot be recovered by the elliptical VP in Mozambican Portuguese (see the eleventh test, its results reported in the Table in the previous section, and related discussion), there are no reasons to turn to a derivation whereby the high/modal adverb would be directly adjoined to its DP/PP-modifee. If the narrow scope reading was derived by means of the adjunction of the modifier to its modifee directly, one would expect the recovering of the adverb by the elliptical VP in Mozambican Portuguese, for instance, contrary to facts (see Tescari Neto (2013) for more arguments against the assumption of such a derivation). Third, given that low adverbs may be displaced to the left periphery of the clause (Rizzi 2001), any attempt to favour the aforementioned connec-

---

[19] One of the reviewers asked me whether there might be differences among the Portuguese varieties (namely, Brazilian, European and Mozambican Portuguese) pointing to a parametrization regarding the property described by this test. According to Tescari Neto (ms.) there is a parametrisation regarding the portion of the hierarchy that can be recovered by the elliptical-VP in African Portuguese (Angolan and Mozambican Portuguese). Hence, the answer is positive. On Brazilian and European Portuguese see Tescari Neto (2013, chapter 5).

tion between scope and the syntactic status of an adverb would be blurred by the effects carried by these displacements on information structure grounds. These three arguments point to the conclusion that the status of an adverb as a SA is only epiphenomenal. That is, those adverbs occupying higher positions in the hierarchy may coincidentally take the sentence under their scope in some cases but not in all the possible cases (as shown on the basis of ex. 4 to 6).

I have presented eleven syntactic tests which, instead of discriminating between "SAs" and "predicate"/VP adverbs, since these notions are misleading for the reasons given in the previous paragraphs, illustrate a cluster of syntactic properties which characterize high adverbs, i.e. the adjuncts occupying the highest positions within the hierarchy in (8). All things considered, these eleven syntactic properties characterizing high adverbs are a direct effect of their position in the functional hierarchy of the clause which is a very important conclusion for every cartographic approach.

References

Bellert, Irena. 1977. On Semantic and Distributional Properties of Sentential Adverbs. *Linguistic Inquiry* 8(2). 337–351.
Belletti, Adriana. 2001. Inversion as Focalization. In Aafke Hulk & Jean-Yves Pollock (eds.), *Inversion in Romance and the Theory of Universal Grammar*, 60–90. New York/Oxford: Oxford University Press.
Casteleiro, João-Malaca. 1982. Análise gramatical dos advérbios de frase [Grammatical analysis of sentence adverbs]. Coimbra: Biblos. 99–109.
Chomsky, Noam. 1986. *Barriers*. Massachusetts: MIT Press.
Chomsky, Noam. 1995. *The Minimalist Program*. Massachusetts: MIT Press.
Cinque, Guglielmo. 1999. *Adverbs and Functional Heads: a Cross-linguistic Perspective*. New York & Oxford: Oxford University Press.
Cinque, Guglielmo. 2004. Issues in adverbial syntax. *Lingua* 114. 683–710.
Cinque, Guglielmo. 2006. *Restructuring and Functional Heads. The Cartography of Syntactic Structures, vol. 4*. New York and Oxford: Oxford University Press.
Costa, João. 2004. A multifactorial approach to adverb placement: assumptions, facts, and problems. *Lingua* 114. 711–753.
Costa, João. 2008. Adverbs and the Syntax-Semantics Interplay. *Estudos Linguísticos* 2. 13–25.
Dik, Simon C. 1997. *The Theory of Functional Grammar. Part I: The Structure of the Clause*. Berlin: Mouton de Gruyter.
Dik, Simon C., Kees Hengeveld, Elseline Vester & Co Vet. 1990. The hierarchical structure of the clause and the typology of adverbial satellites. In Jan Nuyts, A. Machtelt Bolkestein & Co Vet (eds.), *Layers and Levels of Representation in Language Theory: A functional view*, 25–70. Amsterdam: John Benjamins.
Ernst, Thomas. 2002. *The Syntax of Adjuncts*. Cambridge: Cambridge University Press.

Forero Pataquiva, Francisco de Paula. 2019. Valência verbal e tempo verbal no espanhol colombiano: uma análise cartográfica da subida do verbo [Verb valency and verb tense in Colombian Spanish: a Cartographic Analysis]. *Cadernos de Squibs: Temas em estudos formais da linguagem* 5(2). 28-38.

Giorgi, Alessandra. 2016. Epistemic adverbs, the prosody-syntax interface, and the theory of phases. In Christina Tortora, Marcel den Dikken, Ignacio L. Montoya & Teresa O'Neill (eds.), *Romance Linguistics 2013: Selected papers from the 43rd Linguistic Symposium on Romance Languages* (LSRL), 99-118. Amsterdam: John Benjamins.

Hengeveld, Kees. 1989. Layers and Operators in Functional Grammar. *Journal of Linguistics* 25(1). 127-157.

Hengeveld, Kees. 1997. Adverbs in Functional Grammar. In Gerd Wotjak (ed.), *Toward a Functional Lexicology*, 121-136. Frankfurt am Main: Peter Lang.

Hengeveld, Kees & J. Lachlan Mackenzie. 2008. *Functional Discourse Grammar: a typologically-based theory of language structure*. New York & Oxford: Oxford University Press.

Jackendoff, Ray. 1972. *Semantic Interpretation in Generative Grammar*. Massachusetts: MIT Press.

Johnson, Kyle. 1991. Object Positions. *Natural Language and Linguistic Theory* 9. 577-636.

Kayne, Richard S. 1998. Overt vs. Covert Movements. *Syntax* 1. 128-191.

Laenzlinger, Christopher. 1996. Adverb Syntax and Phrase Structure. In Anna-Maria Di Sciullo (ed.), *Configurations: Essays on structure and interpretation*, 99-127. Sommerville: Cascadilla Press.

Laenzlinger, Christopher. 2000. More on Adverb Syntax. In Artemis Alexiadou & Peter Svenonius (eds.), *Linguistics in Potsdam* 6, 103-32. Postdam: Universität Potsdam.

Laenzlinger, Christopher. 2002. A Feature-based Theory of Adverb Syntax. *GG@G (Generative Grammar in Geneva)* 3. 67-105.

Laenzlinger, Christopher. 2011. *Elements of Comparative Generative Grammar: a Cartographic Approach*. Padova: Unipress.

Lonzi, Lidia. 1991. Il sintagma avverbiale. [The Adverbial Phrase] In Lorenzo Renzi & Gianpaolo Salvi (eds.), *Grande grammatica italiana di consultazione*. Vol. 2, 341-412. Bologna: Il Mulino.

Müller de Oliveira, Gilvan. 1993. Os advérbios sentenciais e os testes sintáticos [Sentence Adverbs and the Syntactic Tests]. *Letras (Santa Maria)* 5. 101-120.

Nilsen, Øystein. 2004. Domains for Adverbs. *Lingua* 114. 809-847.

Pollock, Jean-Yves. 1989. Verb Movement, Universal Grammar, and the Structure of IP. *Linguistic Inquiry* 20(3). 365-474.

Quarezemin, Sandra & Aquiles Tescari Neto. 2015. Da sintatização dos focos contrastivo e exaustivo em CP e das estratégias de marcação de foco. *ReVEL* 10. 42-77.

Ramat, Paolo & Davide Ricca. 1998. Sentence Adverbs in the Languages of Europe. In Johan van der Auwera (ed.), *Adverbial Constructions in the Languages of Europe*, 187-275. Berlin: Mouton de Gruyter.

Rizzi, Luigi. 1997. The Fine Structure of Left Periphery. In Liliane Haegman (ed.), *Elements of Grammar*, 281-337. Dordrecht: Kluwer Academic Publisher.

Rizzi, Luigi. 2001. Relativized Minimality Effects. In Mark Baltin & Chris Collins (eds.), *The Handbook of Contemporary Syntactic Theory*, 89-110. Oxford: Blackwell.

Rizzi, L. 2004. Locality and Left Periphery. In Adriana Belletti (ed.), *Structures and Beyond: The Cartography of Syntactic Structures, vol.3*, 223-241. New York & Oxford: Oxford University Press.

Rizzi, Luigi & Ur Shlonsky. 2007. Strategies of subject extraction. In Hans Martin Gärtner & Uli Sauerland (eds.), *Interfaces + recursion = language? Chomsky's minimalism and the view from syntax-semantics*, 115-160. Berlin: Mouton de Gruyter.

Schifano, Norma. 2018. *Verb Movement in Romance: a comparative study*. Oxford: Oxford University Press.

Shu, Chih-hsiang. 2011. *Sentence Adverbs in the Kingdom of Agree*. Stony Brook University dissertation.

Sportiche, Dominique. 1988. A Theory of Floating Quantifiers and Its Corollaries for Constituent Structure. *Linguistic Inquiry* 19(3). 425-449.

Tescari Neto, Aquiles. 2013. *On Verb Movement in Brazilian Portuguese: a Cartographic Study*. Venice, Italy: Università Ca'Foscari di Venezia. Dissertation.

Tescari Neto, Aquiles. 2020. Diagnosing verb raising: the view from cartography. In Roberta Pires de Oliveira, Ina Emmel & Sandra Quarezemin (eds.), *Brazilian Portuguese, Syntax and Semantics: 20 years of Núcleo de Estudos Gramaticais*, 168-190. Amsterdam: John Benjamins.

Tescari Neto, Aquiles. 2021. Paralelos entre a Cartografia Sintática da Gramática Gerativa e a Gramática Funcional holandesa. In Edson Rosa Francisco de Souza, Joceli Catarina Stassi-Sé, Norma Barbosa Novaes Marques & Talita Storti Garcia (eds.), *Linguística Funcional: retrospectivas, atuações e diálogos – uma homenagem à profa. Erotilde Goreti Pezatti*, 286-305. Campinas: Pontes Editores.

Tescari Neto, Aquiles. (unpublished). On the Raising of the Finite Main Verb in Angolan Portuguese and in Mozambican Portuguese: Cartographic Hierarchies, Micro-variation and the Use of Adverbs as Diagnostics for Movements. Manuscript, University of Campinas, UNICAMP.

Thomason, Richmond H. & Robert C. Stalnaker. 1973. A Semantic Theory of Adverbs. *Linguistic Inquiry* 4(2). 195-220.

Zyman, Erik. 2012. *Two Investigations of Adverbs and Clause Structure in English*. Princeton, New Jersey: Princeton University Senior Thesis.

Fryni Kakoyianni-Doa
Formal and functional features of modal adverbs in French and Modern Greek

Abstract: The purpose of this article is to present a study of modal adverbs and adverbials in French and Modern Greek and to examine their formal and functional properties using, in addition to resources from the specialized literature, a bilingual French-Greek online parallel corpus. The adverbs' formal and semantic characteristics are compared and discussed, intralinguistically and interlinguistically. This allows us to highlight similarities and divergences between French and Modern Greek. Special attention is paid to word-formation and morphological classes, and to syntactic tests. While the morphological properties of modal adverbs in French and in Modern Greek differ considerably, the syntactic tests used to characterize them in French are shown to be highly relevant in Modern Greek as well, where they deliver similar results, corroborating the cross-linguistic relevance of the notion of modal adverb, and the suitability of syntactic distribution tests for comparative investigations.

Keywords: adverbs, adverbials, modality, bilingual corpus, French, Modern Greek

1 Introduction

The class of adverbs has been and continues to be a topic of considerable discussion among linguists, because it covers a vast domain which embraces various categories organized, as a general rule, "according to the nature of the communicative function they fulfil" (Rossari 2002: 41). Moreover, adverbs are often grouped under the same hyperonym, though they can be differentiated on the basis of both their internal structure and their behaviour in context. An elaborate description of this part of speech seems therefore to be necessary according to Nølke (1990a: 3), who, as proof of the complexity of the class of adverbs, evokes (1990b: 117–127) the numerous works devoted to the study of the different members of the class: those of traditional grammarians such as Grevisse (Grevisse & Goosse 2008); those of linguists aware of the need to establish criteria to isolate the specific aspects of the class (Vet 1994, Ernst 2007, Blumenthal 1990, Grellson 1981); those of linguists who attempt to classify adverbs on the basis

Fryni Kakoyianni-Doa, University of Cyprus, frynidoa@ucy.ac.cy

of tests (Chomsky 1965, Greenbaum 1969, Jackendoff 1972, Martin 1974, Mørdrup 1976, Sabourin & Chandioux 1977, Schlyter 1974, Bartsch 1972, Schwarz 1980, Ducrot 1998, Melis 1983, Molinier 1984, Molinier & Lévrier 2000, Gross 1990, Bonami, Godard & Kampers-Manhe 2004, among others). This procedure mainly uses a battery of tests to establish various groupings of adverbs and identify more precisely defined classes of adverbs: for instance, sentence adverbs, which are not integrated syntactically into the sentence, i.e. not attached to the verb of the clause, and affect, or provide additional information on, the meaning of the whole sentence; adverbs integrated into the clause, i.e. attached to the verb or to any other constituent of the clause; and many other subclasses designated by different names depending on the approach of the scholars who study them. Adverbs such as *franchement* 'frankly' or *sincèrement* 'sincerely' for example, have received various names: "speaker-oriented adverbs" (Martin 1974), "relational adverbs" (Schlyter 1974), "pragmatic adverbs" (Bellert 1977), "style disjuncts" (Greenbaum 1969, Mørdrup 1976, Molinier & Lévrier 2000), "enunciative comment adverbs" (Riegel, Pellat & Rioul 2003), "illocutive adverbs" (Guimier 1996). As a consequence of this extensive scholarly work, new designations for types of adverbs have found their way into French linguistic terminology.

In this contribution, I discuss a subclass of French and Greek sentence adverbs, such as *apparemment – φαινομενικά (fenomenika,* 'apparently'), *assurément – ενδεχομένως (endechomenos,* 'certainly'), *certainement – φυσικά (fisika,* 'naturally') and *effectivement, όντως (ontos,* 'indeed'), called *modals ("modaux")* (Molinier & Lévrier 2000: 91) or *adverbs modalizing the assertion ("modalisateurs de l'assertion")* (Borillo 1976: 77). They are also known as *assertive* adverbs (*"assertifs"*) (Borillo 1976: 77). The present study will show that, although their behaviour is generally similar in French and Greek, these adverbs display important differences which would partially confirm Gleason's remark that an adverbial class corresponds to "a set of elements that have very little, if anything, in common" when they belong to different linguistic systems (1965: 129). As already mentioned above, they have been studied under different names but I have chosen here the term "modal" adverbs because of their relationship with the concept of epistemic modality in logic (see Aristotle 1974, Kneale & Kneale 1962, Blanché 1970, Gardies 1979, Le Querler 2004, etc.), which is dealt with in the next section.

In this article, I (re)examine the properties of French and Greek modal adverbs, using data from a bilingual French-Greek corpus. These adverbs were investigated in a somewhat intuitive manner by Molinier, for French, in his *Grammaire des adverbes* (Molinier & Lévrier 2000) and by Kakoyianni-Doa, for Greek, in *Étude contrastive des adverbes français et grecs* (2008). I first review their properties within the linguistic systems of French and Greek. Then, I examine and compare their morphological, syntactic and pragmatic/semantic features, both intralinguistically and interlinguistically, which allows us to highlight similarities and differences.

2 Adverbs and modality

At the syntactic level, modal adverbs are external to the propositional content, and at the pragmatic level, they give "hints on truth evaluation" as does the verb form *je crois*, 'I believe' (Rossari 2002: 4). They indicate as well "the speaker's different degrees of certainty about the validity of the propositional content" (Vybíhalová 2015: 265): they modalize the assertion and correspond quite clearly to the epistemic modalities of logic. Thus, modal adverbs have the particularity of relating to the whole of the sentence in which they are used because they affect the content of the utterance and give it a truth value of certainty, on a necessarily positive scale. For instance, a modal adverb may convey that something is likely, desirable, or permissible, just like forms such as the auxiliary *should* or the adjective *possible*. Given its relationship with modality, this subset of adverbs therefore has a special status in the linguistic system.

Modality has been studied from a variety of perspectives and interpreted in different ways in the framework of new linguistic approaches and with the help of new tools (see Flaux & Lagae 2014). However, as Le Querler notes (2004: 643), the definition of modality remains "nebulous" because it is not always easy to determine what the notion covers in a precise way in all languages. According to Aristotelian logic that is recalled here following Le Querler's account, modality includes the following domains: 1) alethic/ontic modalities including the necessary, the possible and the impossible; 2) epistemic modalities (*he may come*); 3) temporal modalities (*It just so happens that Peter came*); 4) axiological modalities (*It would be good if Peter came*); 5) boulic modalities (*Paul demands that Peter come*); and 6) erothetic modalities (*it is asked, it is questioned, is Peter coming?*) (2004: 645). Le Querler adds that "the main difficulty in investigating modalities in French comes from the fact that French implements the three notions of modality, temporality and aspect in a very interrelated way" (2004: 645). As far as Greek is concerned, the situation is similar: how does one distinguish between the three notions of "modality (mood), temporality and aspect" given the language's inflectional morphology? Various inflectional/derivational and periphrastic elements (prefixes, suffixes and particles such as the future marker θα (*tha*)), can indicate tense or modality (Staraki 2017: 17). Tsangalidis adds that "the exact value of any modalized utterance in Greek is often not clear and has to be calculated taking into account a number of factors. In other words, the interpretation cannot rely on any single meaning; thus, the Greek modals are 'polyfonctional' [. . .] and comparable with their counterparts in many other European languages" (2009: 143). Meunier had already said that "to speak about modalities, without being more precise, is to risk being gravely misunderstood" because "the term is, in fact, saturated with interpretations that [. . .] refer to very diverse linguistic realities [. . .]: grammatical moods; tenses; aspects; 'modal' auxiliaries (*can, must*); negation; sentence types: affirmation, interrogation, command; 'modal' verbs (*to know, to want*); 'modal' adverbs (*certainly, perhaps*, etc)" (1974: 8). Finally, both Le Querler (2004) and Riegel, Pellat and Rioul (2003) attempt to give a simple general definition of the concept of modality. For them "modality is the expression of the speaker's attitude towards the propositional content of his statement. This definition excludes simple assertions, which do not contain any indication of the speaker's attitude" (Le Querler 2004: 646). On the basis of this definition, the classification of modalities can be organized into broader domains such as epistemic, intersubjective, or implicative modalities (Le Querler 2004: 646). It is epistemic modality that interests us here, of the type that expresses the speakers' degree of certainty about the propositional content of their utterances. I come back to this question in the contrastive analysis of French and Greek modal adverbs.

3 Methodology and data collection

For the initial indexing of modal adverbs in French, I rely on the work of Molinier & Lévrier (2000) and Borillo (1976). For Greek, I used the work of Voyatzi (2006) and Kakoyianni-Doa (2008). I completed the classification by collecting samples from everyday use in today's language (native speaker's intuitions) and the *Internet* via *Google*. However, as Granger says "intuitions can be misleading and [. . .] striking differences can lead to dangerous over-generalisations" (2003: 18). Nowadays, research can rely on structured data (corpora), usually contained in computer databases: this began in the 1960s, albeit timidly, with the well-known *Brown Corpus* (Kennedy 1998: 23). In the following decades the concept was developed (see Leech 1991, Biber, Conrad & Reppen 1994) and electronic corpora became extremely popular for quantitative and comparative analysis among researchers. These corpora offer the opportunity to study the uses of language in different situations, to see how words are used in context in order to focus on particular aspects of language in its authentic version and actual usages. For contrastive research, bilingual corpora (translated texts) emerged with Baker's investigations "to light a number of potential 'translation universals' in the early 1990s" (Granger 2003: 19). Such parallel corpora, presenting original texts aligned with their corresponding translations, make it possible to reach a higher level of descriptive adequacy of different properties across languages, and to verify, confirm and improve data. Therefore, researchers in contrastive linguistics rely more and more on parallel corpora for studies that previously had little or no empirical support.

For French there is an adequate number of digitized monolingual texts and research resources that are freely available (e.g. *Frantext*, for exclusively literary texts) and of bilingual digitized resources belonging to various genres. For Greek, there are also monolingual corpora, such as the *Treasure of the Greek Language* (Εθνικός Θησαυρός Ελληνικής Γλώσσας (ΕΘΕΓ), the *Corpus of Greek Texts* (Σώμα Ελληνικών Κειμένων, ΣΕΚ), the *Corpus of 20th Century Greek Texts* by Goutsos, as well as Dimitroulia's bilingual parallel corpus of exclusively literary *French-Greek texts* (FREL). What has been produced for French-Greek comparison purposes is limited to literary texts or to posts on the worldwide Internet network (*Glosbe* and *Linguee*). This led to the creation of a specific bilingual Greek ↔ French online and open-access corpus, thanks to which it has been possible to enrich our list of modal adverbs and identify authentic examples in both languages. This bilingual French-Greek parallel corpus (*Source Corpus*) (Kakoyianni-Doa, Antaris & Tziafa 2013) is made up of texts belonging to various genres (political, literary, scientific, educational and movie subtitles). The translation inputs are based on human understanding of textual relations. The *Source Corpus* so far includes 760,282 aligned sentences. It is on the basis of this data that I made the second indexing and analysis of the modal adverbs in each language. The examples used in the present chapter are taken from various sources: a) from native speakers' productions; b) when they are simple sentences with limited context, from the authors quoted above (e.g. Molinier & Lévrier 2000, Molinier 2001), based on Maurice Gross-type analyses (1934–2001)[1]; c) from the *Source Corpus* when there is an extended context.

4 Formal and functional features of French modals

4.1 General properties

For French about thirty adverbs ending in *-ment* are considered to be modal adverbs, e.g. *apparemment* 'apparently', *assurément* 'certainly', *certainement* 'certainly', *évidemment* 'obviously', *effectivement* 'indeed', *fatalement* 'fatally', *forcément* 'inevitably', etc. As regards morphology, these adverbs are mainly

---

[1] Maurice Gross' analyses are based on simple sentences with minimal syntactic and semantic contexts. This is considered to be a formalization and description method suitable for any language.

based on corresponding adjectives which do not necessarily mean the same thing as in example (1); I further discuss this issue in 4.2. For example:

(1) Évidemment, il ne veut pas faire ses devoirs.
'Obviously, he doesn't want to do his homework.' (native speaker)
≈ Il est évident qu'il ne veut pas faire ses devoirs.
≈ ' It is obvious that he doesn't want to do his homework.'

There are also in French a few modal adverbs formed from adjectives prefixed by *in-* (a negative prefix having the function of reversing the orientation of the base-adjective): *indiscutablement* 'indisputably', *inévitablement* 'inevitably', *indubitablement* 'undoubtedly', *indéniablement* 'undeniably', *incontestablement* 'unquestionably', etc. (see Molinier 2001: 260–261). French also displays complex adverbs (called here "adverbials") such as: *à coup sûr* 'definitely', *bien entendu* 'of course', *bien sûr* 'for sure', *peut-être* 'perhaps', 'maybe', *sans doute* 'undoubtedly'. These forms are formally and semantically fixed and are made up of inseparable elements (see Gross 1990: 40). For Gross, another necessary condition to be able to speak of *figement* ('frozen status' or 'fixedness') is to have "a sequence of several words and, possibly, at least one separator, and that these words have an autonomous existence" (Tolone & Voyatzi 2011: 56). As separators, I consider blank spaces and apostrophes (indicating elision), like in the Greek adverb κατ'ανάγκην (*kat'anagin*, 'mandatorily').

According to Molinier, the function of modal adverbs "is to assess the degree of certainty, on a necessarily positive scale, of the proposition they are used with: they, therefore, modalize the assertion" (2001: 260). Moreover, these adverbs "positively assert the statement they occur with" thanks to their adjectival bases, all of which have "necessarily a positive semantic orientation" (see Borillo 1976: 75–76, Molinier 2001: 259). Thus, it is possible to make semantic groupings of the modal adverbs on the basis of the adjectives which they are derived, considering the type of modality the adjectives express. Molinier (2001: 270) sorts modal adverbs into five groups. The first one includes adverbs based on adjectives which express necessity: *fatal* 'fatal', *forcé* 'forced', *immanquable* 'unmistakable', *inéluctable* 'unavoidable', *inévitable* 'inevitable', *infaillible* 'infallible', *nécessaire* 'necessary', *obligatoire* 'compulsory'. Adverbs in this class do not express an absolute truth but a requirement or a necessity (in Aristotelian logic: what cannot not be true). The second group includes adverbs formed from adjectives which convey the epistemic modality of certainty such as: *assuré* 'certain', *certain* 'certain', *indiscutable* 'undisputable', *sûr* 'sure'. The process corresponds to the expectation of an absolute truth for the speaker, who may put pressure on his interlocutor to recognize it, based on the fact that the content of the sentence is viewed as being beyond doubt. The third group consists of adverbs formed from adjectives that express possibility/probability, such as: *éventuel* 'possible', *plausible* 'plausible', *possible* 'possible', *probable* 'probable', *présumable* 'presumable', *supposé* 'assumed', *vraisemblable* 'likely'[2]. For this group one cannot know when the process will occur, or even if it will occur at all, but it is represented as being within the realm of possibility (*Il est possible/il est peu probable qu'il vienne ce soir*, 'It's possible/It's unlikely that he'll be coming tonight')[3]. The fourth group is comprised of adverbs derived from adjectives linked to the notion of visibility, such as: *apparent* 'apparent', *évident* 'obvious', *manifeste* 'manifest', *visible* 'visible'. It refers to what seems to be true according to appearances, if one judges on the basis of the way things appear to be. The fifth and last group includes two adverbs that convey the idea of "conformity to facts and conformity to the order of things": *effectivement* 'indeed' and *naturellement*[4] 'naturally', 'of course'. Both adverbs, as modals, confirm or underscore the reality of what has just happened/been done. They have a very strong argumentative flavour: *effectivement* is corroborative and provides a justification; *naturellement* makes a claim about the immediate accessibility of the propositional content.

Epistemic modality not only presents the speaker's knowledge in terms of positive certainty, but also takes on finer nuances concerning what is possible or impossible, necessary or contingent (that which may or may not occur). According to Vybíhalová, the level of certainty varies from total certainty to low certainty: 1) 100%, regardless of the source of the certainty or truth of the content: the speaker presents the information as certain (*je sais*, 'I know'); 2) high degree of certainty when the speaker is almost convinced of the validity or the invalidity of the content (*Je ne suis pas persuadé que/Je doute que*, 'I am not convinced that/I am doubtful'); 3) medium degree of certainty when the speaker may lean towards the validity or invalidity of the content (*Il est possible que*, 'It is possible that'); 4) low degree of certainty when the speaker's certainty fluctuates (*C'est peut-être*, 'It may be') (2015: 266–267). In sum, it can be said that, since modal

---

2 According to Pérennec (2002), the items of this group express a comment on the content, but do not contribute to the assertion of this content, as opposed to *certainement* 'certainly', *probablement* 'probably', *vraisemblablement* 'presumably', etc., which perform the assertion. Hence the impossibility of separating the modal from the content with which it occurs. See *Il viendra probablement* (one single assertion) ('He will probably come'); *Il viendra; c'est probable* (two assertions) ('He'll come; it's probable').
3 Note that what is *possible* and what is *probable* are both feasible, but the latter is higher than the former in terms of feasibility. In other words, something probable is more likely to happen than something possible.
4 The adverb *naturellement* can also be a manner adverb in other contexts (see "syntactic homonymy" in Molinier 2001: 264).

adverbs refer to the speaker (or 'utterer') and mark his/her attitude towards the content of the utterance, the level of certainty is gradable. It is even possible for the speaker to upgrade the level of certainty of the content of the utterance, but always on a positive scale, as is the case in the following example:

(2) Il va probablement pleuvoir aujourd'hui. Oui il va sûrement pleuvoir aujourd'hui.
'It's probably going to rain today. Yes, it's definitely going to rain today.'

Like all sentence adverbs, modal adverbs are characterized by five shared syntactic properties:
a. They can generally be used in initial position (i.e. "theme" position) in a positive or negative sentence, which makes it possible for them to take scope over the whole sentence (Molinier & Lévrier 2000: 45).

(3) Évidemment, Max a répondu à ma question.
'Obviously/Of course, Max did answer my question.'

(4) Évidemment, Max n'a pas répondu à ma question.
'Obviously/Of course, Max did not answer my question.'

b. Nevertheless, they enjoy great positional freedom (Molinier 2001: 263). They can be stressed (but not necessarily), followed by a pause, at the beginning of a sentence (see (3), (4) above), to the right of the subject, to the right of the verb, or in the final position, provided that they constitute a separate prosodic unit as in (5), (6) and (7):

(5) Éventuellement Paul arrivera en retard.
'Possibly Paul will arrive late.'

(6) Paul, éventuellement, arrivera en retard.
'Paul, possibly, will arrive late.'

(7) Paul arrivera, éventuellement, en retard.
'Paul will arrive, possibly, late.'

As noted by Guimier, when positioned to the right of the verb the adverb does not modify the verb but comments on the possibility of occurrence of the process. He adds that isolating the adverb via intonation has the effect of enhancing it and bringing the speaker to the foreground (1996: 117).

c. They are found in *c'est... que* cleft constructions with an extracted ("pied-piped") NP (subject, object, adverbial complement) which moves with them, in which case they are fully integrated into the semantic content of the proposition. For example:

(8) C'est apparemment Jean qui est venu hier soir.
'It was apparently Jean who came last night.' (subject)

(9) C'est certainement un livre que ton ami t'a apporté.
'It is certainly a book that your friend brought you.' (object) (native speaker)

For this reason, I consider that the adverb has a double scope: scope over the sentence (that fronts) and scope over the extracted NP (it establishes a close link with the extracted constituent). The sentences (8), (9) are semantically synonymous with (10), (11):

(10) Apparemment, c'est Jean qui est venu hier soir.
'Apparently, it was Jean who came last night.' (subject)

(11) Certainement, c'est un livre que ton ami t'a apporté.
'Certainly, it is a book that your friend brought you.' (object) (native speaker)

d. Moreover, modal adverbs can provide the answer to a polar question. For example:

(12) Est-ce que Paul est venu? Oui, (apparemment, certainement, sûrement).[5]
'Did Paul come?' 'Yes, (apparently, certainly, surely).'

e. They are compatible with all tenses and moods with the exception of the subjunctive, because the adverb used in a subjunctive subordinate clause would conflict with the main clause in the indicative: the indicative signifies an assertion while the subjunctive is a "signal of non-assertion" (Confais 1990: 333). Therefore, we cannot have: *Il faut que plausiblement tu viennes demain* (*'You must plausibly come tomorrow') or *Marie doute que Paul vienne certainement* (*'Mary doubts that Paul will certainly come').

---

[5] Example modelled on that of Molinier (2001: 259).

They are even found with the conditional and the semi-auxiliary modal *pouvoir*, which both convey the idea of possibility and are opposed to reality, as in (13) and (14):

(13)   Probablement, (il vient, il viendra, venait, est venu) de loin.
        'He probably (comes, will come, was coming, came) from far away.' (native speaker)

(14)   Éventuellement, je pourrais regretter ma décision.
        'Possibly/Maybe, I could come to regret my decision.' (native speaker)

4.2 Variable properties

The bilingual corpus provided additional information about the frequency of modal adverbs in current usage. Some adverbs and adverbials show a high frequency of use: for *peut-être, nécessairement, naturellement* ('perhaps', 'necessarily', 'naturally') there are 5,082, 4,512 and 3,435 tokens respectively, compared to 99 for *visiblement* 'visibly', 78 for *fatalement* 'fatally', 67 for *à coup sûr* 'definitely', 59 for *vraisemblablement* 'presumably', 44 for *sans nul doute* 'undoubtedly' and 33 for *indiscutablement* 'indisputably'. There are also absentees, such as *présumablement* 'presumably', *plausiblement* 'plausibly', *possiblement* 'possibly', *irréfutablement* 'irrefutably'. Their absence from the corpus may be explained by the fact that they are long, polysyllabic -*ment* adverbs, often judged cumbersome and not stylistically elegant[6].

Furthermore, as Molinier says (1990: 33), modal adverbs are not syntactically homogeneous, a feature which has led to specific studies on some of them (see Guimier 1996, Rossari 2002, Anscombre 2013, Giannakidou & Mari 2016, Dendale & Kreutz 2019, etc.). For example, only the following modal adverbs are often accepted in negative sentences even to the right of the negator *pas* 'not' without a break in intonation:

> *forcément* 'inevitably', *nécessairement* 'necessarily', *obligatoirement* 'obligatorily', *apparemment* 'apparently', *assurément* 'certainly', *certainement* 'certainly', *évidemment* 'obviously', *naturellement* 'naturally', *probablement* 'probably', *sûrement* 'surely', *vraisemblablement* 'plausibly', *certes* 'certainly', *peut-être* 'perhaps', 'maybe', *sans doute* 'undoubtedly'

---

[6] For *irréfutablement*, for example, *Google Books Ngram Viewer* which displays a graph showing how a lexical item has occurred in a corpus of books (e.g. "British English", "English Fiction", "French"), indicates lower frequency of use during the current decade.

For example:

(15) Paul n'est pas nécessairement / pas obligatoirement coupable.
'Paul is not necessarily guilty.'

Moreover, only the modal adverbs *forcément, fatalement, nécessairement* and *obligatoirement* ('inevitably', 'fatally', 'necessarily' and 'compulsorily') can provide an answer to a polar question preceded by *pas* (Molinier & Lévrier 2000: 99):

(16) Paul est-il coupable? Pas forcément / Pas nécessairement / Pas obligatoirement.
'Is Paul guilty?' 'Not necessarily.'

This is probably due to the fact that adverbs in this group do not express an absolute truth but a requirement or a necessity. The negative particle *pas*, which precedes the adverb, indicates a kind of hesitation or doubt. But in the *Source Corpus*, the adverbs *certainement* 'certainly', *apparemment* 'apparently' and *sûrement* 'surely' are found in contexts where they provide an answer to a polar question followed by *pas* with or without an intonation break (i.e. no comma in the text):

(17) Nous sommes appelés à voter pour ou contre le procès-verbal? Certainement pas.
'Are we called to vote for or against the minutes?' 'Certainly not.'
(Source Corpus)

Probablement pas does not act as an adverb but as an adverbial (or fixed expression) with a more general semantic content. Grevisse classifies this category of adverbs among what he calls "word phrases" (mots-phrases), as "they play a role of incidental elements in the sentence but they can also be used as sentences on their own." Here the adverb associated with negation in answer to a question seems to reinforce the certainty expressed by the speaker: *certainement pas* ('certainly not') conveys a stronger pragmatic/semantic value than a simple negation.

Furthermore, paraphrased structures that highlight the scope and role of modals adverbs are also variable. As stated by Borillo (1976) and Molinier (2001), paraphrased synonymous constructions based on the corresponding adjectives are only possible for some modal adverbs. For example, *Que P est Adj* ('That P is Adj') and *Il est Adj que P* ('It is Adj that P') are attested for the following adverbs:

> *incontestablement* 'unquestionably', *indiscutablement* 'indisputably', *inévitablement* 'inevitably', *probablement* 'probably', *visiblement* 'apparently', *vraisemblablement* 'presumably'.

We can have:

(18) Probablement Paul n'a pas travaillé.
= Que Paul n'ait pas travaillé est probable.
= Il est probable que Paul n'a pas travaillé.
'Probably Paul did not work.'
= That Paul did not work is likely.
= It is likely that Paul did not work. (native speaker)

However, a few adverbs are not attested in this construction:

certainement 'certainly', *assurément* 'certainly', *forcément* 'inevitably', *apparemment* 'apparently', *naturellement* 'naturally'.

(19a) and (19b) below appear to contradict what was just said, as the adverbs *certainement* ('certainly') and *évidemment* ('obviously') can be paraphrased by the corresponding adjective but in a slightly different sense. It seems that in the adverbial construction, the propositional content no longer belongs to the realm of what is certain, but is rather regarded as plausible, whereas in the adjectival paraphrase, it is still certain and accepted as true. Molinier and Dendale speak here of a weakening of meaning (Molinier 2001, Dendale & Kreutz 2019: 3[7]).

(19) a. Certainement Paul a raison./Il est certain que Paul a raison.
'Paul is certainly right.'/'It is certain that Paul is right.' (Molinier 2001: 261)
b. Vous aurez certainement toutes ces informations rapidement. / Il est certain que vous aurez toutes ces informations rapidement.
'You will certainly get all this information quickly.' / 'It is certain that you will certainly get all this information quickly'. (Source Corpus)

According to *Treasury of the French Language (TLFi)*, *to be certain* is *to be sure* or *assured*, whereas the adverb *certainly* expresses or reinforces an affirmation. What is *certain* or *évident* must be probable and what is probable may be possible.

Finally, the paraphrased structure followed by a complement clause introduced by *que (Adv Que P)* without an intonation break is acceptable for *certainement* 'certainly', *probablement* 'probably', *sûrement* 'surely', *peut-être* 'perhaps', 'maybe', *sans doute* 'undoubtedly' and for *bien sûr* 'for sure' with an intonation break and an exclamative prosody, as in examples (20) and (21):

---

7 For *certainement* see Dendale and Kreutz 2019.

(20) a. Certainement Paul n'a pas travaillé[8].
 'Certainly, Paul did not work.' (native speaker)
 b. Certainement que Paul n'a pas travaillé!
 * 'Certainly that Paul did not work' (constructed)

(21) a. Probablement on n'atteindra pas cet objectif [...]
 'Probably this goal will not be achieved.' (Source Corpus)
 b. Probablement que l'on n'atteindra pas cet objectif!
 * 'Probably that this goal will not be achieved.' (constructed)

Furthermore, only some modal adverbs can cooccur with degree modifiers such as *très, fort* and *bien*. For example, *très* associates with *certainement, sûrement, probablement, vraisemblablement* ('certainly', 'surely', 'probably', 'presumably'), but is incompatible with adverbs expressing necessity *fatalement, forcément, immanquablement* ('fatally', 'inevitably', 'unmistakably') (Molinier & Lévrier 2000: 104). Obviously, a distinction based on the degree of necessity cannot be made with forms which express what is inevitable, obligatory, constraining (see Patty 2013). The adverb *fort* is often combined with *probablement* 'probably' and *bien* is often associated with *évidemment* 'obviously' in an assertive sentence, but also in response to a polar question. For example:

(22) Paul viendra-t-il? Fort probablement/Bien évidemment.
 'Will Paul come?' 'Most probably/Of course'. (native speaker)

We have seen that for French members of the group of modal adverbs have both homogeneous and variable properties. If formal and to some extent semantic homogeneity is dominant, this does not guarantee the scope and role of the adverb. The syntactic functioning of these adverbs seems then to depend rather on the internal semantic dynamics of these adverbs than on their derivational properties. This is probably a grammaticalization effect whereby closed categories (here modal adverbs) evolve from open categories (here adjectives), acquiring in the process more specific, restricted or abstract semantico-pragmatic values/uses. The question which now arises is the following: Are these properties of the French modal adverbs that I have discussed in the previous section comparable

---

[8] Example modelled on that of Molinier 2001: 262.

to those of the corresponding forms in Greek? In order to answer this question, I now present the formal, syntactic, and semantic features of modals in Modern Greek.

5 Formal, syntactic, semantic features of modals in Modern Greek

5.1 General properties

For Greek, monolexical adverbs with several types of suffixes are considered as modal adverbs. They can be divided into four groups:
a) a first group includes adverbs ending in (-α + -ά) and (-ως + -ώς). They are listed in Table 1 below:

Table 1: adverbs ending either in -α or in –ως.

Greek form	Transliteration	English translation
αναγκαστικά	anagastika	indispensably
αναγκαστικώς	anagastikos	mandatorily
απαραίτητα	aparetita	necessarily
απαραιτήτως	aparetitos	necessarily
βέβαια	vevea	certainly
βεβαίως	veveos	certainly

b) a second group consists of adverbs ending only either in (-α + -ά) or (-ως + -ώς). For example, the following adverbs (Table 2) only take the suffix (-α + -ά):

Table 2: adverbs always ending in –α.

Greek form	Transliteration	English translation
ορατά	orata	obviously
σίγουρα	sigoura	surely
φαινομενικά	fenomenika	apparently
φυσικά	fisika	naturally

Conversely, the following adverbs (Table 3) only accept the suffix *(ως + -ώς)*:

Table 3: adverbs always ending in –ως.

Greek form	Transliteration	English translation
εμφανώς	emfanos	obviously
ενδεχομένως	endechomenos	certainly
ίσως	isos	perhaps
πιθανώς	pithanos	probably
προφανώς	profanos	apparently

The search in *Source* also revealed a Greek modal adverb not previously listed in the specialized literature, i.e. *πρόδηλα* (*prodila*, 'clearly'):

(23) Πρόδηλα,   αυτό   αποτελεί   διακριτική   μεταχείριση
     ADV   afto   apotelei   diakritiki   metaxirisi
     Clearly   this   consists   discriminating   treatment
     'Clearly, this is a discrimination'   (Source Corpus)

c) a third group is composed of adverbs prefixed in *ανα-, αδια-* such as *αναμφισβήτητα* or *αδιαμφισβήτητα* (*anamfisvitita* or *adiamfisvitita*, 'undeniably'), *αναποφεύκτα* (*anapofeukta*, 'inevitably'), corresponding to French *in-* (see section 4.1), whose role is to reverse the negative orientation of the stem.
d) a fourth group includes forms ending in various suffixes and archaic forms (Table 4):

Table 4: mixed suffixes and archaic forms.

Greek form	Transliteration	English translation
ασυζητητί	asizititi	unquestionably
μάλλον	mallon	possibly
οπωσδήποτε	oposdipote	absolutely
πιθανόν	pithanon	probably
όντως	ontos	indeed

The adverb *όντως*, which expresses certainty, comes from the Ancient Greek present participle *ὤν-οὖσα-ὄν* (*on-ousa-on*) (nominative, neuter, plural: *όντα-onta*) of the verb *εἰμί* (*imi*, 'to be'). Despite its archaic form, *όντως* is still widely used in the spoken language. The ancient adverb *ασυζητητί* (*asizititi*, 'unquestionably') is also very common nowadays. *Μάλλον* (*mallon*, 'possibly') as a modal adverb expressing possibility, is perhaps a derived form of *μάλα* (*mala*), an adverb of quantity meaning *a lot* (*melior* in Latin, *meilleur* in French) (Babiniotis 2002: 1042–1043). *Οπωσδήποτε* (*oposdipote*, 'absolutely'), comes from the conjunction *όπως* (*opos*, 'as') followed by the indefinite compound morpheme *-δήποτε* (*-dipote*), *-δη* (*di*) and *-ποτέ* (*pote*), *δη* (*di*) in ancient Greek meaning *certainly* and *ποτέ* (*pote*) 'ever' (Babiniotis 2002: 1267).

Modal adverbs may also have a polylexical form (Table 5, adverbials):

Table 5: polylexical modal adverbials.

Greek form	Transliteration	English
στα σίγουρα	sta sigoura	for sure
δίχως άλλο	dichos allo	inevitably
χωρίς αμφιβολία	choris amfivolia	without a doubt
πέραν πάσας αμφιβολίας	peran pasas amfivolias	undoubtedly
χωρίς καμία αμφιβολία	choris kamia amfivolia	without any doubt

These forms include the combination of three elements divided by separators (a preposition, followed by a determiner (optional) and a noun, with case endings) and they are not modifiable. (See section 4.1, concerning adverbials).

Discussing the two variants (adverbs with the *-α* suffix and the *-ώς* suffix) in groups a) and b), Clairis and Babiniotis (2001: 179) point out that the *-α* suffix seems to be more characteristic of current Modern Greek, while the *-ως* suffix is exclusively a learned form. This could explain the fact that the frequency of these two types of adverbs is unequal in the data from the corpus, due to the types of texts included in the *Source Corpus* (see section 3 above). It should be noted that some very common adverbs take both suffixes, but with a semantic difference. Compare, for example, the manner adverb *ευχάριστα* ('pleasantly') with the evaluative adverb *ευχαρίστως* ('with pleasure', 'gladly') (see Boulogiorgos 2003: 139). The only exception to the low frequency of the *-ως* modal adverb in the corpus is the archaic *όντως* (*ontos*, 'indeed') encountered 614 times, possibly because of its brevity. As for *ασυζητητί* (*asizititi*, 'unquestionably') and *τω όντι* (*to onti*, 'indeed'), they appear only once in the corpus.

Semantically, as example (24) illustrates, Greek modal adverbs are part of the content of the sentence they are associated with and are conducive to contesting and challenging the content of that sentence, always on a positive scale.

(24) *Μάλλον θα χιονίσει στον Όλυμπο.*
    ADV   tha   chionisi ston Olibo
    Probably FUT snow   on the Olympus
    'It will probably snow on Mount Olympus.'

Όχι	μάλλον	σίγουρα	θα	χιονίσει	στον	Όλυμπο
ADV		sigoura	tha	chionisi	ston	Olibo
not	probably	surely	FUT	snow	on the	Olympus

'Probably not! It will surely snow on Mount Olympus.'

(Greek native speakers)

Greek modal adverbs can be characterized by five shared syntactic properties, just like French modal adverbs:

a) Like all Greek sentence adverbs, they can appear in the initial position in a positive or a negative sentence, as in (25):

(25)
Βεβαίως,	δεν	μπορούμε	να	παρακολουθούμε	άπραγοι
ADV	den	boroume	na	parakolouthoume	apragi
of course	NEG	we can	SBJV	we watch	idle

το	καταφύγιο.
to	katafigio
the	retreat

'Of course, we cannot stand idly by and watch the retreat area.'

(Source Corpus)

b) They can also be the focus in a cleft sentence, in the είναι...που (ine...pou, 'it is...that') construction, if they are accompanied by an extracted major NP/PP (subject, object, complement). For example:

(26)
Είναι	μάλλον	το	σύστημα	Nike	που	γνωρίζετε
Ine	ADV	to	sistima	Nike	pou	gnorizete
is	probably	the	system	Nike	that	you know

'It is probably the Nike system which you are familiar with.' (Source Corpus)

c) They may constitute all by themselves an answer to a polar question and may be preceded by the proform ναι/όχι 'yes'. For example:

(27)
Χιόνισε	στον	Όλυμπο;	Ναι/όχι	Βέβαια.
chionise	ston	Olimbo?	nai/ohi	ADV
snowed	on the	Olympos?	AFF/NEG	Certainly.

'Did it snow on Olympus? Yes, certainly/Not certainly'.   (Source Corpus)

d) Moreover, modal adverbs are compatible with all tenses and moods, even with the subjunctive (which is excluded for all French modals, as we have seen above). The subjunctive mood is common in Greek since the modern language doesn't have an infinitive[9] (see 25).

(28) Πάω   να   δω   τα   παιδιά   μου
     Pao   na   do   ta   pedia   mou
     go   SBJV I see the   children mine
     'I am going to see my children.'

According to Sampanis, "complements with *na* are widely used in MG [Modern Greek], since this language has no infinitival complementation and therefore finite complements occur even in environments in which (West) Romance or Germanic languages, for instance, make use of infinitives, e.g. after modal [...] or aspectual [...] verbs that obligatorily control the subject of the embedded predicate such as Πρέπει (*Prepi*, 'Must')" (2012: 66). We can therefore find modal adverbs associated with subjunctive clauses, both main, as in (29a), and subordinate, as in (29b).

(29) a. Τούτο   ίσως   να   αποτελεί Ιδιαιτερότητα [...]
        Touto   ADV   na   apoteli   idieterotita
        this   maybe   SBJV   is   particularity
        'it may be a particularity,' (Source Corpus)
     b. Δεν   χρειάζεται απαραιτήτως να   πάνε   στην   εργασία τους [...]
        Den   chriazete   ADV   na   pane   stin   ergasia tous
        not   need   necessarily SBJV go   to the work   them
        'They don't necessarily have to go to work.'   (Source Corpus)

They enjoy positional freedom but are found mostly at the beginning of a sentence and to the right of the verb (30 and 31). They can also appear at the end of a sentence with an intonation break in speech or a comma in written texts (example 32):

(30) Φυσικά   θα1   ήθελα   να   επιστρέψω   στη   Ρεάλ
     ADV   tha   ithela   na   epistrepso   sti   Real
     Naturally COND   I liked SBJV to come back to.the Real
     'Naturally I would like to come back to Real.'

---

[9] Note that in Modern Greek, the indicative and the subjunctive moods do not have different morphological endings. The only difference is indicated by the preverbal particle *na*.

(31) Θα   ήθελα   φυσικά   να   επιστρέψω   στη   Ρεάλ
     Tha   ithela ADV   na   epistepso   sti   Real
     COND   I liked naturally SBJV to come back sti   Real
     'I would like naturally to come back to Real'

(32) Θα   ήθελα   να   επιστρέψω   στη   Ρεάλ,   φυσικά
     Tha   ithela na   epistrepso   sti   Real,   ADV
     COND   liked   SBJV to come back to the   Real,   naturally
     'I would like to come back to Real, naturally.'   (Greek native speaker)

5.2 Variable properties

According to the corpus, the adverbs *φυσικά* (*fisika*, 'naturally'), *ασφαλώς* (*asfalos*, 'certainly'), *προφανώς* (*profanos*, 'apparently'), *βέβαια* (*vevea*, 'certainly') are the most frequent. The number of tokens for each form is listed in Table 6 below

The majority of forms in *(-ως + -ώς)* do not appear at all in the corpus (e.g. *υποχρεωτικώς* (*ipochreotikos*, 'obligatorily'), *αναγκαστικώς* (*anagastikos*, 'mandatorily'), *αναμφιβόλως* (*anamfivolos*, 'undoubtedly'), *απαραιτήτως* (*aparetitos*, 'necessarily'). One exception is the archaic *όντως* (*ontos*, 'indeed') encountered 614 times in the corpus (see 5.1 above). As for *ασυζητητί* (*asizititi*, 'unquestionably') and *τω όντι* (*to onti*, 'indeed'), they are found only once in the corpus.

Table 6: number of occurrences for the most common Greek modal adverbs and adverbials (Source Corpus).

Greek form	Transliteration	English translation	Occurrences
φυσικά	fisika	naturally	4,239
ασφαλώς	asfalos	certainly	1,272
προφανώς	profanos	apparently	1,162
βέβαια	vevea	certainly	939
αναμφισβήτητα	anamfisvitita	undeniably	78
υποχρεωτικά	ipocherotika	compulsorily	76
αναμφίβολα	anamfivola	undoubtedly	48
χωρίς αμφιβολία	choris amfivolia	without doubt	29
ολοφάνερα	olofanera	manifestly	26
εμφανώς	emfanos	obviously	23
στα σίγουρα	sta sigoura	for sure	14

Further, in the case of the French adverb *apparemment* ('apparently'), it was not the Greek corresponding adverb φαινομενικά (*fenomenika*) that was given as a translation, but semantically close verb forms related to visibility such as φαίνεται (*fenete*, 'it appears/seems that'), φαντάζομαι (*fantazome*, 'I imagine/ envisage that'). These verbs express the degree of commitment of the speaker to the truth of the proposition associated with them (Vet 1994: 56–57). In (33), for instance, Greek prefers a comparative clause with a modal impersonal verb to a modal adverb:

(33) Όπως φαίνεται   αυτό   δεν   μπορεί   να   γίνει
     opos fenete   afto   den   bori   na   gini
     as is apparent   that   not   can   SBJV   be/happen
     'Apparently this is not possible.'   (Source Corpus)

French modal adverbs in the corpus were translated into Greek in a variety of ways, but not *vice versa*. For example, the adverbial *à coup sûr* ('definitely') was associated with ασφαλώς (*asfalos*, 'certainly'), its exact semantic equivalent in Greek, in 67 entries, and the other 7140 cases involved eight less exact equivalents:

στα σίγουρα (*sta sigoura*, 'for sure'), σίγουρα (*sigoura*, 'for sure'), σαφώς (*safos*, 'clearly'), φυσικά (*fisika*, 'naturally'), αναμφίβολα (*anamfivola*, 'undoubtedly'), οπωσδήποτε (*oposdipote*, 'absolutely'), βεβαίως (*veveos*, 'certainly'), είναι βέβαιο (*ine veveos*, 'it is certain')

The adverb *apparemment* ('apparently') had 585 "exact matches" (morphologically and semantically) with προφανώς (*profanos*, 'apparently') and 5,045 partial matches with ten different forms (adverbs, adverbials, copula + adjectives, impersonal modal verbs):

είναι προφανές (*ine profanes*, 'it is obvious'), είναι φανερό (*ine fanero*, 'it is obvious'), είναι πασιφανές (*ine pasifanes*, 'it is obvious'), φαινομενικά (*fenomenika*, 'apparently'), όπως φαίνεται (*opos fenete*, 'as illustrated'), φαίνεται (*fenete*, 'it seems'), φαντάζομαι (*fantazome*, 'I imagine'), εκ πρώτης όψεως (*ek protis opseos*, 'at first sight').

Finally, an important observation which applies to both Greek and French is that modal adverbs can co-exist with modal verbs within the same sentence. Moreover, this sort of association is found with almost all modal adverbs (see 34):

(34) Πρέπει   αναμφίβολα   να   δώσουμε   προσοχή
     Prepei   ADV   na   dosoume   prosochi
     must   certainly   SBJV   we give   attention

στις	παραδοσιακές	κουλτούρες
stis	paradosiakes	koultoures
to	traditional	cultures

'We certainly have to be concerned about the traditional cultures of these people'. (Source Corpus)

This has been argued to be "a modal spread and not a redundancy" by Giannakidou & Mari. Following Lyons (1977: 88), they hold that when modal verbs like *must* and *may* co-occur with modal adverbs like *probably/certainly/possibly*, "there is a kind of concord running through the clause, which results in the double realization of a single modality" (2016: 2).

As noted in 3.1, monolexical adverbs are not always morphologically based on adjectives. Furthermore, even when they are, in some cases the adjective and the derived adverb have developed quite different meanings: ασφαλής (*asfalis*) means 'safe', but ασφαλώς (*asfalos*) means 'certainly'; φαινονεμικός (*fenonemikos*) means 'superficial', but φαινομενικώς (*fenomenikos*) means 'likely', 'probably'. Consequently, it is not possible to produce adjectivally-based paraphrastic structures for a number of Greek adverbs. Example (35) illustrates the paraphrastic structures *(Το ότι S είναι Adj – Que S être – Adj-That S be Adj)* and *(Είναι Adj ότι P – Il est Adj que S – It is Adj that S)* which are attested for some adverbs.

(35)	Προφανώς	ο	Παύλος	δεν	διάβασε
	Profanos	o	Pavlos	den	diavase
	Apparently	the	Paul	not	worked

'Apparently, Paul hasn't been working.'

(35) is synonymous with the following paraphrases:

Το	ότι	ο	Παύλος	δεν	διάβασε	είναι	προφανές
To	oti	o	Pavlos	den	diavase	ine	profanes
the	that	the	Paul	NEG	worked	is	obvious

That/The fact that Paul did not work is apparent'

Είναι	προφανές	ότι	ο	Παύλος	δεν	διάβασε
Ine	profanes	oti	o	Pavlos	den	diavase
is	obvious	that	the	Paul	NEG	worked

'It's obvious that Paul didn't work.'

It is also important to note the frequent use of structures of the type *είναι Adj ότι S* ('*Iine* Adj *oti* S – 'il est Adj que S' – 'it is Adj that S') in the corpus. These structures contain adjectives which some of the modal adverbs are based on and which were translated into French by adverbs (see examples 33, 34). In particular we found the forms *είναι σαφές* (*ine safes*, 'it is manifest'), *είναι βέβαιο* (ine veveo, 'it is certain'), *είναι αυτονόητο* (*ine aftonoito*, 'it is self-evident'), *είναι σίγουρο* (*ine sigouro*, 'it is certain'), *είναι πασιφανές* (*ine pasifanes*, 'it is notorious'). For example:

(36) Είναι σίγουρο ότι η πράξη αυτή συνέβαλε
Ine sigouro oti i praksi afti sinevale
is sure that the action this contributed
στη σταθερότητα
sti statherotita
to.the stability
'Certainly, this has helped to maintain stability.' (Source Corpus)

(37) Είναι σαφές ότι αυτή θα εμπλέκει έναν αριθμό
Ine safes oti afti tha ebleki enan arithmo
is clear that this FUT involve a number
κρατών μελών
kraton melon
states members
'A range of Member States will, of course, be involved'. (Source Corpus)

In addition, the paraphrastic structure *Adj-ment que S – Adj-ment that S* (*certainement que tout se passera bien*, 'Certainly everything will go well'), which can be used with a number of French adverbs, has no equivalent in Greek syntax. But it seems that the conjunction *και* ('and'), with its emphatic value (cf. Babiniotis 2002: 806), can constitute a structure semantically close to the French "Adv + que" construction when it is used in sentence initial position followed by a modal adverb. For example:

(38) Και βέβαια δεν επεμβαίνουμε στις υποθέσεις σας
Ke ADV den epemvenoume stis ipothesis sas
and of.course no interfere to.the business yours
'Of course, we don't interfere in your business' (equivalent to French
'*Bien sûr que* nous n'intervenons pas dans vos affaires')

In Greek, as in French, some modal adverbs can be graded. The intensity modifier *πολύ* (*poli*, 'very') is found in the corpus only with the adverb *πιθανώς/πιθανόν* (*pithanos/pithanon*, 'probably').

(39) Πολύ   πιθανώς   το   μέλλον [..] της   Ένωσης   να
    Poli   ADV   to   mellon   tis   Enosis   na
    Very   probably   the   future   the   EU   SBJV
    μην   είναι   λαμπρό
    min   ine   labro
    no   is   brilliant
    'It is very likely that the future of the Union will not be bright'.
                                                              (Source Corpus)

But Greek has another grading strategy (a morphological one) to add an intensity value to the assertion expressed by the adverb: the superlative form (parallel to that of adjectives), but this form is applicable only to some modals based on adjectives. Examples of superlative adverbs are: *πιθανότατα* (*pithanotata*, 'very likely'), *σιγουρότατα* (*sigourotata*, 'very surely'), *βεβαιότατα* (*veneotata*, 'very certainly'), *ασφαλέστατα* (*asfalestata*, 'most certainly').

(40) *Πιθανότατα*   θα   χάσουμε   τις   ψηφοφορίες
    ADV   tha   chasoume   tis   psifofories
    Most probably   FUT   will lose   the   votes
    'We will probably miss the votes'   (Source Corpus)

Finally, according to the *Source Corpus*, some modal adverbs such as *απαραίτητα* (*aparetita*, 'necessarily'), *βέβαια* (*vevea*, 'certainly'), *σίγουρα* (*sigoura*, 'surely'), *φυσικά* (*fisika*, naturally'), *ασφαλώς* (*asfalos*, *a*, 'certainly'), etc., can be used to answer a polar question and can combine with double negatives *όχι* ('no') for more emphasis:

(41) *Θα*   *το*   *κάνει;*   *όχι*   *απαραίτητα,*   *όχι.*
    Tha   to   kani?   ochi   ADV   ochi.
    FUT   it   does   not   necessarily   no
    'Is he going to do it?' 'No, not necessarily'.   (Source Corpus)

We have seen that for Greek modal adverbs there is an important morphological variability, with different suffixes and different types of adverbial formation: we have also noted that when intensification is possible it is normally done via morphology (with the superlative), and not periphrastically (with an added quantity adverb). The syntactic behavior of Greek modals has many similarities with that of French modals, though some features (e.g. the initial *kai* construction or the possibility of associating modal adverbs with the subjunctive) are the result of idiosyncrasies of the two languages.

In the corpus, we observed a broad difference in the frequency of different adverbs, ranging from *hapax legomena* to hundreds of occurrences. This variety may stem from the fact that there seems to be a lot of freedom to use synonymic expressions carrying similar modality (e.g. impersonal adjectival constructions, impersonal modal verbs) instead of modal adverbs. This may also explain why there are usually more Greek translations for a single French adverb in the corpus than the other way round.

6 Conclusion

The contrastive study presented here has allowed us to update and deepen research on sentence adverbials that express modalized assertion in French and Greek. From a morphological point of view both languages have simple adverbs as well as adverbials. Simple adverbs are more homogeneous in French (often bearing the *-ment* suffix attached to an adjective). In Greek the suffixes are more diverse, and the adverbs much less often correlated with an adjective. Even when there is such a link between a certain suffix and a class of adjectives, the word-formation processes display a broader span of possibilities and differences in Greek. Thus, while it is possible to establish classes of adverbs on the basis of the type of modality expressed by the base-adjective (necessity, certainty, possibility, visibility/appearance, factual conformity) in French, this is more problematic in Greek. Another consequence of the morphological difference in derivation is that paraphrased synonymous constructions are more difficult to obtain in Greek than in French. Furthermore, in both languages, some modal adverbs are gradable, but the intensification and gradation strategies are different: while French uses adverbial modifiers (e.g. *fort, très*), Greek uses mostly derivational superlative forms parallel to the superlative of the base adjective.

From a syntactic discourse/pragmatic point of view, on the contrary, there are many similarities between the modal adverbs in French and Greek, possibly due to the fact that they belong to the same language family or that these are general/universal properties of modal adverbs: modal adverbs can be placed in thematic position at the beginning of positive or negative sentences; they can be focalized in cleft sentences in association with another constituent; in dialogic situations they can constitute an answer to a polar question all by themselves; in general they enjoy great positional freedom and are compatible with all tenses and moods (with the exception of the subjunctive in French). Hence, in the case of modal adverbs, it appears that syntax and semantics are a more reliable and more efficient way of relating languages than is morphology.

Sources

Main corpus

Source Corpus: Kakoyianni-Doa, Fryni, Stefanos Antaris & Eleni Tziafa. 2013. A Free Online Parallel Corpus Construction Tool for Language Teachers and Learners. *Procedia–Social and Behavioral Sciences* 95. 535–541.

Other corpora mentioned for French

Frantext: ATILF. 1998–2021. *Base textuelle Frantext*. ATILF-CNRS & Université de Lorraine. https://www.frantext.fr/
TLFi: ATILF. 1994–2021. Trésor de la langue Française informatisé. ATILF – CNRS & Université de Lorraine. http://www.atilf.fr/tlfi
Other corpora mentioned for Greek:
ΕΘΕΓ Institute for Language and Speech Processing/R.C. "Athena". 2019–2020. Εθνικός Θησαυρός Ελληνικής Γλώσσας (Hellenic National Corpus), version 2.6.2. http://hnc.ilsp.gr/
ΣΕΚ Centre for the Greek Language. 2006–2008. *Text corpora*. (Σώμα Ελληνικών Κειμένων)/ https://www.greek-language.gr/greekLang/modern_greek/tools/corpora/index.html
Other bilingual corpus mentioned:
FREL Τομέας Μετάφρασης & Μεταφρασεολογίας (Department of Translation Studies). 2015. *FREL-Parallel Literary Translations' Corpus (French to Greek)*. Aristotle University of Thessaloniky. http://corpora.frl.auth.gr/joomla/

References

Anscombre, Jean-Claude. 2013. À coup sûr et bien sûr et les fondements de la certitude. *Revue de sémantique et pragmatique* 33–34. 67–98.
Aristote. 1974. *Métaphysique* [transl. into French by Jean Tricot]. Paris: Vrin.
Babiniotis, Giorgos. 2002. *Lexiko tis neas ellinikis glossas,* tomos 2 [Dictionary of modern Greek, volume 2]. Athens: Centre of Lexicology.
Baker, Mona. 1993. Corpus Linguistics and Translation Studies. Implications and Applications. In Mona Baker, Gill Francis & Elena Tognini-Bonelli (eds), *Text and Technology,* 233–250. Amsterdam & Philadelphia: John Benjamins.
Bartsch, Renate. 1972. *Adverbialsemantik*. Frankfurt am Main: Athenäum Verlag.
Bellert, Irena. 1977. On semantic and distributional properties of sentential adverbs. *Linguistic Inquiry* 8. 337–351.
Biber, Douglas, Susan Conrad & Randi Reppen. 1994. Corpus-based Approaches to Issues in Applied Linguistics. *Applied Linguistics* 15(2). 169–189.
Blanché, Robert. 1968. *Introduction à la logique contemporaine*. Paris: Armand Colin.

Blumenthal, Peter. 1990. Classement des adverbes: Pas la couleur, rien que la nuance? *Langue française* 88. 41–59.
Bonami, Olivier, Danièle Godard & Brigitte Kampers-Manhe. 2004. Adverb Classification. In Francis Corblin & Henriëtte de Swart (eds.), *Handbook of French Semantics*, 143–184. Stanford: CSLI Publications.
Borillo, Andrée. 1976. Les adverbes et la modalisation de l'assertion. *Langue française* 30. 74–89.
Boulogiorgios, Achilleas. 2003. *Éducation langagière. Le juste et le faux dans notre langue*. Athènes: Ekdosis Grigoris.
Chomsky, Noam. 1965. *Aspects of the Theory of Syntax*. Cambridge, MA: MIT Press.
Clairis, Christos & Giorgos Babiniotis. 2001. *Grammatiki tis neas ellinikis* [Grammar of modern Greek]. Athens: Nea Grammata.
Confais, Jean-Paul. 1990. *Temps Mode Aspect. Les approches des morphèmes verbaux et leurs problèmes à l'exemple du français et de l'allemand*. 2nd ed. Toulouse: Presses Universitaires du Mirail.
Dendale, Patrick & Philippe Kreutz. 2019. 'Certainement': adverbe épistemico-modal ou évidentiel? *Le discours et la langue* [to be published].
Ducrot, Oswald. 1998. *Dire et ne pas dire*. Paris: Hermann.
Ernst, Thomas. 2007. On the role of semantics in a theory of adverb syntax. *Lingua* 117(6). 1008–1033.
Flaux, Nelly & Véronique Lagae. 2014. Syntaxe et sémantique des marqueurs modaux: présentation. *Langages* 193. 3–15.
Gardies, Jean-Louis. 1979. *Essai sur la logique des modalités*. Paris: PUF.
Giannakidou, Anastasia & Alda Mari. 2016. A two dimensional analysis of the future: Modal adverbs and speaker's bias. In Maria Aloni, Michael Franke & Flo Roelofsen (eds.), *Proceedings of the 19th Amsterdam Colloquium*, 115–122. Amsterdam: ILLC, University of Amsterdam.
Gleason, Henry Allan. 1965. *Linguistics and English grammar*. New York: Holt, Rinehart & Winston.
Granger, Sylviane. 2003. The corpus approach: a common way forward for Contrastive Linguistics and Translation Studies. In Sylviane Granger, Jacques Lerot & Stephanie Petch-Tyson (eds.), *Corpus-based Approaches to Contrastive Linguistics and Translation Studies*, 17–29. Amsterdam: Rodopi.
Greenbaum, Sidney. 1969. *Studies in English Adverbial Usage*. London: Longmans.
Grellson, Sigvard. 1981. *Les adverbes en -ment: Étude psychomécanique et psychosystématique*. Lund: C.W.K. Gleerup.
Grevisse, Maurice & André Goosse. 2008. *Le bon usage: grammaire française*. Paris: Duculot/Bruxelles: De Boeck & Larcier.
Gross, Maurice. 1990. La caractérisation des adverbes dans un lexique-grammaire. *Langue française* 86. 90–102.
Guimier, Claude. 1996. *Les adverbes du français: le cas des adverbes en -ment*. Paris: Orphys.
Hopper, Paul J. & Elizabeth Closs Traugott. 2003. *Grammaticalization*. 2nd edn. Cambridge: Cambridge University Press.
Jackendoff, Ray S. 1972. *Semantic Interpretation in Generative Grammar*. Cambridge, MA: MIT Press.
Kakoyianni-Doa, Fryni. 2008. *Adverbes de phrase français et grecs: étude contrastive et perspectives didactiques*. Toulouse: Université de Toulouse-le Mirail. Dissertation.
Kennedy, Greame D. 1998. *An Introduction to Corpus Linguistics*. London: Longman.
Kneale, William & Martha Kneale. 1962. *The development of logic*. Oxford: Clarendon Press.

Leech, Geoffrey. 1991. The state of the art in corpus linguistics. In Karin Aijmer & Bengt Altenberg (eds.), *English Corpus Linguistics: Studies in Honour of Jan Svartvik*, 8–29. London: Longman.
Le Querler, Nicole. 2004. Les modalités en français. *Revue belge de philologie et d'histoire* 82(3). 643–656.
Lyons, John. 1977. *Semantics*. Cambridge: Cambridge University Press.
Martin, Robert. 1974. La notion d'adverbe de phrase: essai d'interprétation en grammaire générative. In Christian Rohrer & Nicolas Ruwet (eds.), *Actes du Colloque franco-allemand de grammaire transformationnelle*, II. 66–75. Tübingen: Max Niemeyer Verlag.
Melis, Ludo. 1983. *Les circonstants et la phrase*. Leuven: Presses Universitaires de Louvain.
Meunier, André. 1974. Modalités et communication. *Langue française* 21. 8–25.
Molinier, Christian. 1984. *Étude syntaxique et sémantique des adverbes de manière en -ment*. Université Toulouse II-le Mirail. Dissertation.
Molinier, Christian. 1990. Une classification des adverbes en -ment. *Langue française* 88. 28–40.
Molinier, Christian. 2001. Les adverbes modaux du français. In Claude Buridant, Georges Kleiber & Jean-Christophe Pellat (eds.), *Par monts et par vaux: Itinéraires linguistiques et grammaticaux. Mélanges de linguistique offerts au Professeur Martin Riegel par ses collègues et amis*, 259–272. Leuven: Peeters.
Molinier, Christian & Françoise Lévrier. 2000. *Grammaire des adverbes: Description des formes en -ment*. Geneva: Librairie Droz.
Mørdrup, Ole. 1976. Une Analyse non-transformationnelle des adverbes en -ment. *Études romanes de l'Université de Copenhague* 11.
Nølke, Henning. 1900a. Présentation. *Langue française* 88. 3–4.
Nølke, Henning. 1990b. Recherches sur les adverbes: bref aperçu historique des travaux de classification. *Langue française* 88. 117–127.
Patty, Michel. 2013. Chapitre 11: Matière et nécessité dans la connaissance scientifique. In Marc Silberstein (ed.), *Matériaux philosophiques et scientifiques pour un matérialisme contemporain. Volume 1: Sciences, ontologie, épistémologie*, 367–397. Paris: Éditions Matériologiques.
Pérennec, Marcel. 2002. *Sur le texte: énonciation et mots du discours en allemand*. Lyon: Presses universitaires de Lyon.
Riegel, Martin, Jean-Christophe Pellat & René Rioul. 2003. *Grammaire méthodique du français*. Paris: PUF.
Rossari, Corinne. 2002. Les adverbes connecteurs: vers une identification de la classe et des sous-classes. *Cahiers de linguistique française* 24. 11–44.
Sabourin, Conrad & John Chandioux. 1977. *L'adverbe français: essai de catégorisation (Classification statistique des adverbes en -ment)*. Paris: Éditions Jean-Favard.
Sampanis, Konstantinos. 2012. Chapter 3: The Modern Greek Subjunctive Mood and its Semantic Features. In Georgia Fragaki, Thanasis Georgakopoulos & Charalambos Themistocleous (eds.), *Current Trends in Greek Linguistics*, 66–91. Newcastle upon Tyne: Cambridge Scholars Publishing.
Schlyter, Suzanne. 1974. Une hiérarchie d'adverbes et leurs distributions: par quelles transformations? In Christian Rohrer & Nicolas Ruwet (eds.), *Actes du Colloque franco-allemand de grammaire transformationnelle*, II. 76–86. Tübingen: Max Niemeyer Verlag.
Schwarz, Christoph. 1980. *Der nicht-nominale «ment»-Ausdruck im Französischen*. Romanica Monacensia 18. München: Wilhelm Fink Verlag.

Staraki, Eleni. 2017. *Modality in Modern Greek*. Newcastle upon Tyne: Cambridge Scholars Publishing.
Tolone, Elsa & Stavroula Voyatzi. 2011. Extending the adverbial coverage of a NLP oriented resource for French. In *Proceedings of the 5th International Joint Conference on Natural Language Processing (IJCNLP11)*, 1225–1233. Chiang Mai, Thailand, 8–13 November.
Tsangalidis, Anastasios. 2009. Modals in Greek. In Björn Hansen & Ferdinand de Haan (eds.), *Modals in the Languages of Europe: A Reference Work*, 139–163. Berlin: De Gruyter.
Vet, Co. 1994. Savoir et croire. *Langue française* 102. 56–68.
Voyatzi, Stavroula. 2006. *Description morphosyntaxique et sémantique des adverbes figés en vue d'un système d'analyse automatique des textes grecs*. Université de Marne-la-Vallée. Dissertation.
Vybíhalová, Michaela. 2015. Particules/adverbes exprimant la modalité épistémique: Vers la comparaison des systèmes des langues tchèque et française. *Svĕt Literatury/Le monde de la littérature* 12. 265–273.

Jian Courteaud Zhang

Different types of subject-oriented adverbials in French and in Mandarin Chinese: A contrastive study

Abstract: This paper is concerned with the comparison of French adverbs derived with the morpheme *-ment* and Mandarin Chinese adverbs derived with the morpheme *-di*. Both morphemes are used to build sentence-oriented adverbs, most of which are susceptible of being interpreted as agent-oriented manner adverbs. However, in each language, some of these adverbs may have to be interpreted as speaker-oriented rather than agent-oriented, raising the question if their scope is not larger than the mere verbal lexeme and if they should not be classified as sentence adverbs. The paper first recalls basic facts about Chinese adverbial syntax, especially the existence of a devoted slot for *di*-adverbs in the clause, which means that several tests used for the functional classification of adverbs Standard Average European, most prominently detachment, are not available in Chinese. The issue of finding a cross-linguistically valid grid of comparison is addressed in the next section thanks to a comparative review of the literature on speaker- vs. agent-oriented *ment-* and *di*-adverbs. The preliminary classification obtained for Chinese is then confronted with a series of tests and compared with the taxonomy of French speaker- and agent-oriented adverbials. I contrast subject-predicate oriented adverbials, scoping over the subject and the predicate; subject-sentence adverbials, scoping over the subject and the propositional content, and subject-oriented descriptive adverbials, scoping only over the subject. Most crucially, the second class is available only in French, and not in Mandarin Chinese. Further, I show that in Chinese, the agentive lexical meaning of the verb may still exert semantic pressure on the licensing of the adverb even when it is speaker-oriented. In the conclusion, I point at converging facts from other Chinese adverbs exterior to the *di*-class.

Keywords: Mandarin Chinese, sentence adverbs, speaker-oriented adverbs, manner adverbs

Jian Courteaud Zhang, Université Jean Moulin Lyon 3, jianzhzh@gmail.com

https://doi.org/10.1515/9783110767971-008

1 Introduction

French and Chinese differ by their morphological typology: while the morphology of French is extremely rich, Chinese only displays limited evidence of flectional and derivational morphemes. Overt lexical morphology allows French speakers to identify lexical and functional classes more easily. For example, words ending in -*ment* are classified indifferently in the category of "adverbs". However, items such as *heureusement* ('fortunately') and *soigneusement* ('carefully') are syntactically and semantically different.

In Chinese, the lack of morphological markers does not permit to identify the nature of words. For instance, *gongzuo* can either be interpreted as a noun ('work') or as a verb ('to work'). As for adverbs, a distinctive feature of their own is their placement in a specific slot called *zhuangyu* (adverbial adjunct), which is located between the *zhuyu* (subject) and the *weiyu* (predicate). In this position, polyfunctional words can be used as adverbials. They are distinguished from *buyu* (complement), which appears in post-verbal position. The following diagram shows the syntax of a basic sentence in Chinese:

zhuyu   *zhuangyu*   *weiyu*   *buyu*
(subject)   (adverbial)   predicate   complement

Example (1) illustrates this structure:

(1)   他竟然撞伤了一只兔子。
      ta   jingran   zhuang shang   le   yi   zhi   tuzi
      he   surprisingly   hit   wound   ASP[1] a   cl   rabbit
      'To my surprise, he hit and wounded a rabbit.'

In this sentence, *jingran* "to one's surprise" is the adverbial. It precedes the predicate *zhuang* 'hit'. *Shang*, in post-verbal position, is the complement that indicates the result of the action: the rabbit has been hit and it is wounded. Among the different adverbials, we can roughly distinguish three groups from a morphological point of view: the first one with the presence of the adverbial marker *di*,[2] the second without this marker; the last one can have *di* or not. In the first group, adverbials are often composed on the following pattern: "adjective/dif-

---

[1] Please refer to the list of abbreviations provided at the end of the paper.
[2] The character for *di* is 地, which has two pronunciations and two significations. The first one is *dì* (with the fourth tone), it means 'earth' or 'place'; the second one is *de* (neutral tone), an adverbial marker, whose main function is the description. We prefer the written form *di* in the pinyin

ferent types of phrase + *di*", where the presence of *di* is obligatory.[3] Adverbials of the second group often indicate space or time. They are never marked by *di*. In the last group, the presence of *di* is not necessary, some words with/without *di* can serve as adverbials.[4] It is interesting to note that the construction "adjective + *di*" looks like the one found in Romance "adjective + *ment(e)*" or in English: "adjective + *ly*". Taking this similarity as starting point, I carry out a contrastive study between French and Mandarin Chinese. I only consider comparable constructions, taking an adjective as derivation base. The pattern "different types of phrase + *di*" is left out of consideration in this study. Moreover, considering the heterogeneity of the adverbial class in *-ment*, I restrict the study to the Chinese and French subclasses of adverbs displaying a degree of orientation towards the subject, which raise specific theoretical issues.

In the following sections, I first present different classifications for French adverbs and Chinese adverbials in the literature (section 2). Then, based on these classifications, I carry out the proper contrastive study of subject-oriented adverbs, distinguishing three subclasses: subject-predicate adverbials (section 3), subject-oriented sentence adverbials, which show signs of speaker-orientedness, but still undergo selectional constraints on the subject (section 4), and finally, subject-oriented descriptive adverbials, which form a distinct subset (section 5). For each class, I compare the tests used in French (and sometimes in English) with

---

sentence in spite of its real pronunciation *de*, in order to avoid the confusion with the possession particle/determinant particle *de*.

3 We find *di* as an adverbial marker in the adverbial *gaoxingdi* 'happily', in which *gaoxing* 'happy' is an adjective: the addition of *di* transforms an adjective into an adverbial. Or else, *qianxinwankudi* 'with thousand pains', in which *qianxinwanku* 'thousand pains' is a noun: the marker *di* turns this nominal phrase into an adverbial. The same holds for *lianhongpupudi* 'with that the face is red', in which *lianhongpupu* 'the face is red' is a sentence or *teng de tongkuliuti di* 'have pain with tearing up and runny nose', in which *teng de tongkuliuti* is a complement phrase. Let us look at some of them in the following examples:

她千辛万苦地完成了这个工作。
Ta qianxinwanku   di wancheng le   zhe ge gongzuo.
she thousand pains   di finish ASP   this CL work
'She finished this work with thousand pains.'

她脸红扑扑地说...
Ta lian hongpupu di shuo. . .
she face red   *di* say
'She said with a red face. . .'

4 For more details about this adverbial group where the presence of *di* is not necessary, see Qian Nairong (1995), Aono Emi (2005) among others.

Chinese data, discussing the transferability of tests conceived for Standard Average European languages into East Asian Languages.

2 Previous studies on adverbs and adverbial classification

French linguists essentially use syntactic and semantic criteria to distinguish adverbial subclasses. As for Chinese linguists, syntactic criteria are hardly mentioned. My framework is based on the classifications proposed by different linguists for French adverbs; I specifically concentrate on the Chinese class equivalent to the class of subject-oriented adverbs in French.

2.1 In French

French speaker-oriented adverbs in *-ment* have been discussed extensively in the literature. This section is devoted to the presentation of four semantic and syntactic analyses that play a pivotal role in the analysis of these forms and are of particular relevance for the contrastive analysis. The modern standard series of tests used to distinguish between various subgroups of adverbials in French goes back to Mørdrup (1976):
1) The possibility to place the adverb before a negative sentence;
2) The possibility to place the adverb before the second morpheme of the French negation *pas*;
3) The possibility for the adverb to appear before a question;
4) The possibility to place the adverb before an imperative;
5) The possibility to place the adverb before the word *parlant* 'speaking', which has grammaticalised into a domain marker (*historiquement parlant*, 'historically speaking' = 'from a historical point of view');
6) The possibility for the adverb to be the focus of the negation;
7) The possibility for adverbs to be the focus of the interrogation;
8) The possibility for adverbs to be the focus in a cleft sentence;
9) The possibility for adverbs to modify the focus of a cleft sentence;
10) The possibility for adverbs to be the answer to a yes-no question;
11) The possibility for adverbs to be the answer to a question with *how*;
12) The possibility for adverbs to be the answer with *yes* to a yes-no question.

Criteria 1, 6, 7 and 8 are used to distinguish sentence adverbs (which do not fulfil these criteria) from manner adverbs. As for sentence adverbs, disjunctives (which encompass style disjuncts such as *franchement/'frankly'*, *sincèrement/'sincerely'* and attitudinal disjuncts such as *heureusement/'fortunately'*, *probablement/'probably'*) as well as conjunctives (*premièrement/'first of all'*; *également/'also'*; *inversement/'on the contrary'*, etc.) are differentiated by criterion 12. As for manner adverbs, two criteria are added, noted 1' and 13:

1') The possibility to place adverbs before a sentence that does not contain the negation;
13) The possibility for adverbs to modify the verb *faire* 'do' in a pseudo cleft construction.

According to these fourteen criteria, five sub-categories of manner adverbs can be distinguished: "subject-oriented sentence adverbs" (*adverbes de sujet-phrase*), "subject-oriented manner adverbs" (*adverbes de sujet-manière*), "verb-oriented manner adverbs" 1 and 2 (*adverbes de verbe-manière 1 et 2*), the last one being viewpoint adverbs. This repartition is in line with the proposal by Schlyter (1972), who divided the relevant adverbials in *-ment* into three groups with regard to their scope:
1) Subject-oriented sentence adverbs ('adverbes de sujet phrase'), as *intelligemment* 'intelligently';
2) subject-oriented manner adverbs ('adverbes de sujet manière'), as *attentivement* 'attentively';
3) verb-oriented manner adverbs ('adverbes de verbe manière'), as *étroitement* 'closely'.

A different path is followed by Guimier (1996), who takes a semantic point of view and opposes "endophrastic adverbs", which participate in the elaboration of the representational content of the utterance, to "exophrastic adverbs", which operate on this representational content from a higher level. Then, taking a syntactic viewpoint, he makes a difference between intra-predicative adverbs and extra-predicative adverbs and points out that a few adverbs can have two functions: they can be syntactically extra-predicative and semantically endophrastic. The following table shows his final classification of French adverbs in *ment*:

Intra-predicative				Extra-predicative		
Endophrastic				Exophrastic		
Incidence to the adjective	Incidence to the verb	Incidence to the relation subject-predicate	Incidence to the sentence	Incidence to the sentence or to a portion of the sentence		
scope on the adjective and/or on the (pro) noun	scope on the verb and/or on the subject and/or on the complement	scope on the subject and/or on the predicate	scope on the subject and/or on the sentence	scope on *le dit*, the propositional content – evaluative – assertive	scope on *le dire*, the procedural elaboration of what is said: – conjunctive – metalinguistic – paradigmatizing	scope on the aim of the discourse: frame – illocutionary

The present study is concerned with endophrastic adverbials that are incidental either to the verb and its subject, to the predicate and its subject and to the sentence and its subject. All these studies have in common their insistence on the fact that high adverbials or sentence adverbials may be subject-oriented and not necessarily speaker-oriented, which is manifested by Guimier's overlap between extra-predicativity and endophrasticity.

Molinier & Lévrier (2000), on the other hand, are less concerned with this overlap. They propose a transformational analysis for adverbs in –*ment*, based on two syntactic criteria:
1) The possibility to be placed at the beginning of the negative sentence with an intonative detachment;
2) The impossibility to be placed in the cleft construction *c'est. . . que* 'it's. . . that. . .'.

These adverbs are subdivided into two groups: sentence adverbs and adverbs integrated to the proposition. Sentence adverbs are divided into three subclasses: conjunctive adverbs, style disjunctive adverbs and attitude disjunctive adverbs. In the last one, we find four groups: habit adverbs, evaluative adverbs, modal adverbs and subject oriented attitude adverbs. Thus, even though they maintain a rather sharp distinction between constituent adverbials and sentence adverbials, Molinier & Lévrier (2000) are also led to admit that subject-orientation is a labile category questioning traditional dichotomies.

Overall, among the subclasses of subject-oriented adverbs identified in the literature, the most prominent is the one called "subject-oriented manner adverbs" by Molinier & Lévrier (2000). It is a subcategory of constituent adverbs, which apply to a segment of the sentence (as opposed to sentence adverbs, which apply to the whole sentence). They have the same semantic scope as Mørdrup's "subject-manner adverbs" (1976) and Guimier's "subject-predicate adverbs" (1996). According to them, these adverbs take scope not only over the subject, but also over the predicate. Mørdrup (1976:137) even writes that these adverbs still essentially modify the verbal phrase. Schlyter (1972) and Mørdrup (1976) also mention a class of "subject-sentence oriented adverbs", which are called "subject-oriented attitude adverbs" by Molinier & Lévrier (2000), whereas Nøjgaard (1995) identifies them as "circumstance-manner adverbials". This class of adverbs is also part of the present contrastive study.

2.2 In Chinese

In the following, I present the four main methods of adverbial classification used to subcategorize adverbials in Chinese. Zhu Dexi (1957, 1984) sketches an adverbial classification relying on parts of speech. He discerns eleven adverbial subclasses, opposing for instance adverbs used as adverbials, nouns used as adverbials, numbers used as adverbials. Since I am only concerned with one type, I move on to the other main methods of classification.

2.2.1 Agent adverbials vs. manner adverbials

In adverbial position, according to this author, adverbials can be classified into two categories, depending on the type of element they are associated with: non-descriptive adverbials and descriptive adverbials. Non-descriptive adverbials usually indicate time, place, purpose, etc. They have a restrictive function with respect to the sentence, the predicate and other elements, and are not relevant for us. On the contrary, the adverbials of the second group have a descriptive function and are usually marked by *di*. They can be divided into three subgroups, displaying important differences with respect to subject orientation: (i) adverbials describing the agent's expression, posture and mental state during the action; (ii) adverbials describing action and manner; (iii) adverbials describing the target of the action. Using semantic criteria, Qian Nairong (1995) establishes a list of seventeen adverbial subcategories which partly corroborate Liu Yuehua's classification: time adverbials, place adverbials, degree adverbials etc. Four subgroups are relevant for us: Agent and patient adverbials; manner adverbials, similarly to Liu Yuehua (1983); but also object adverbials, as well as purpose and cause adverbials, which are not lumped together as previously. Several linguists including Zheng Renshu (1997) or Zhao Boyuan (1999) have a similar classification.

2.2.2 Scope criteria

Another method to classify Chinese adverbials is based on their scopes. Zhang Lijun (1990), Li Ziyun (1993), Zheng Renshu (1997) and Zou Yanxia (2001) work on adverbials marked by *di* and propose categorising them this way. The following table summarizes the different scopes identified by each author. S is the subject, P the predicate and O the object, drawing on the traditional classification exposed in the introduction. Note the diverging views between the different scholars:

	S	O	P	S&P	P&O	S&O	S, P&O	Preposition & O.	Compl.	Exterior
Zhang (1990)	x	x	x	x						x
Li (1993)	x	x	x	x	x	x	x			
Zheng (1997)	x	x	x					x		x
Zou (2001)	x	x		x	x			x		

These first attempts were subsequently summarized and expanded by the Japanese linguist Aono Emi (2005). The result is a classification of "descriptive" *di*-adverbs into five subgroups defined by their scope:
1) Subject-describing descriptive adverbials;
2) Object-describing descriptive adverbials;
3) Predicate-describing descriptive adverbials;
4) Subject/predicate-describing descriptive adverbials;
5) Object/predicate-describing descriptive adverbials.

Summarizing these classifications, we can easily identify a group of subject-oriented adverbials. Liu Yuehua (1983) talks about the way some descriptive adverbials can describe the subject (his/her mental state, posture, etc.). This point of view is also shared by Aono Emi (2005): adverbials can either have a relation with the subject, or with the subject and the predicate. But nobody mentions subject-sentence adverbials.

2.2.3 Interim summary: French and Chinese classifications

In the rest of these papers, the different adverbials are to be examined in the following order: subject-predicate adverbials, subject-sentence adverbials and subject adverbials. The first class exists in both languages, the second one is only mentioned in French, and the last one belongs to the Chinese language. In the absence of syntactic studies about Chinese adverbials, this contribution also provides a first descriptive account of their syntactic distribution. I apply two syntactic tests implemented by Mørdrup (1976a) and Molinier & Lévrier (2000): the negation test and the cleft test, in order to determine the status of these adverbs among constituent adverbs, as opposed to sentence adverbs. The next step is a discussion of the semantic properties of Chinese subject-oriented adverbials, under specific consideration of their scope. The last issue is co-occurrence.

3 Subject-predicate adverbials

Subject-predicate adverbials are endophrastic and intra-predicative. They modify the predicate and the subject, and can be assimilated to Schlyter's "subject-oriented manner adverbials". In what follows, I summarize their main behavioral and semantic properties in French, before turning to the contrastive analysis with Chinese.

3.1 Properties of French subject-predicate adverbials

3.1.1 Syntactic properties

Soigneusement 'carefully' and *calmement* 'calmly' are akin to the subject-predicate adverbs defined for Chinese. They can be integrated within the core clause structure, but are also to be found at the end of the sentence and at the beginning of the sentence with an intonative detachment (indicated by the comma) as the following examples show:

(2) a. Il a fait soigneusement la lessive.
 'He carefully washed his clothes.'
 b. Il a fait la lessive soigneusement.
 'He washed his clothes carefully.'
 c. Soigneusement, il a fait la lessive.
 'He washed his clothes and showed great care in doing this' (lit. 'Carefully, he washed his clothes.')

(3) a. Il a accepté calmement cette réalité.
He accepted this reality calmly.'
b. Il a accepté cette réalité calmement.
'He accepted this reality calmly.'
c. Calmement, il a accepté cette réalité.
'He stayed calm and accepted this reality' (lit. 'Calmly, he accepted this reality.')

Compared to sentence adverbs, subject-predicate oriented adverbs are part of the predicate and apply to a constituent. First, adverbs of this type, cannot be placed at the beginning of a sentence that contains a negation, as shown in example (4); secondly, they can appear in a cleft construction, as shown in example (5):

(4) a. * Soigneusement, il n'a pas fait la lessive.
intended: 'Carefully, he didn't wash his clothes.'
b. * Calmement, il n'a pas accepté cette réalité.
intended: 'Calmly, he didn't accept this reality.'

(5) a. C'est soigneusement qu'il a fait la lessive.
'It's carefully that he washed his clothes.'
b. C'est calmement qu'il a accepté cette réalité.
'It's calmly that he accepted this reality.'

The contrary is true of sentence adverbs like *heureusement* 'fortunately': they can be located at the beginning of the negative sentence and cannot appear in cleft constructions.

(6) a. Heureusement, il n'a pas fait la lessive.
'Fortunately, he hasn't washed his clothes.'
b. * C'est heureusement qu'il a fait la lessive.
intended: 'It's fortunately that he washed his clothes.'

The different syntactic behaviors of sentence adverbs and constituent adverbs, according to Dik (1989, 1997), correspond respectively to the propositional level (*heureusement/fortunately*) and to the core predication[5] (*soigneusement* 'carefully' and *calmement* 'calmly').

---

[5] Dik (1989, 1997) proposes to describe the syntax, semantic and pragmatic of a sentence with five levels: the nuclear predication, which encompasses the predicate and its arguments; the

3.1.2 Semantic properties

Subject-predicate adverbs, as their name indicates, have a relation not only with the subject but also with the predicate. The paraphrase "subject is adj." allows us to show the relation between the adverb (*soigneusement* 'carefully'; *calmement* 'calmly') and the derived adjective (*soigneux* 'careful'; *calme* 'calm'):

(7) a. Il est soigneux.
'He is careful.'
b. Il est calme.
'He is calm.'

In examples (7a) and (7b), the subject is qualified by the adjective *soigneux* 'careful' and *calme* 'calm', which the adverbs *soigneusement* 'carefully' and *calmement* 'calmly' are derived from. This subject's property is only valid in its context as stated in Nilsson-Ehle (1941: 81) "*it (the adverb) qualifies the subject only in as much as it performs the action or as it is in the state indicated by the verb: it is not related to the quality, the "way of being" of the subject outside of this action or this state.*"

Soigneusement 'carefully' and *calmement* 'calmly' also apply to the verb. To illustrate this, we can use the paraphrase "in an *adj*. manner":

(8) a. Il a fait la lessive de manière soigneuse.
'He washed his clothes in a careful manner.'
b. Il a accepté cette réalité de manière calme.
'He accepted this reality in a calm manner.'

Both adverbs here indicate the manner to complete the process for the subject.

---

core predication, which indicates the aspect and contains manner adverbs/adverbials, spatial orientations of the SoA and additional participants; the extended predication, where circumstantial indications are expressed; the proposition, where the speaker's attitude is given, and the clause, in which the speaker comments on the speech act.

3.2 In Chinese

3.2.1 Syntactic properties

The traditional syntactic tests used in Standard Average European languages are jeopardized by the typological features of Chinese. I previously mentioned that in Chinese adverbials are located between the subject and the predicate, as shown in the examples below:

(9) a. 他仔细地洗了衣服。
 ta zixidi xi le yifu
 he careful-*di* wash ASP clothes
 'He washed the clothes carefully.'
 b. * 仔细地，他洗了衣服。
 zixidi ta xi le yifu
 careful-*di* he wash ASP clothes
 intended: 'Carefully, he washed the clothes.'
 c. * 他洗了衣服仔细地。
 ta xi le yifu zixidi
 he wash ASP clothes careful-*di*
 intended: 'He washed the clothes carefully.'

(10) a. 他平静地接受了这个事实。
 ta pingjingdi jieshou le zhe ge shishi
 he calm-*di* accept ASP this CL reality
 'He accepted this reality calmly.'
 b. * 平静地，他接受了这个事实。
 pingjingdi ta jieshou le zhe ge shishi
 calm-*di* he accept ASP this CL reality
 intended: 'Calmly, he accepted this reality.'
 c. * 他接受了这个事实平静地。
 ta jieshou le zhe ge shishi pingjingdi
 he accept ASP this CL reality calm-*di*
 intended: 'Calmly, he accepted this reality.'

The examples above show that *zixidi* 'carefully' and *pingjingdi* 'calmly' can only be placed between the subject and the predicate, as in (9a) and (10a); as shown in (9b) (10b) and (9c) (10c) respectively, intonative detachment as well as final position are excluded. The adverbials of this class do not apply to the whole sentence, they are part of the predicate and apply to a constituent. They are therefore under the scope of the negation:

(11) a. 他没有仔细地洗衣服。
 ta meiyou zixidi xi yifu
 he NEG careful-*di* wash clothes
 'He didn't wash the clothes carefully.'
 b. 他没有平静地接受这个事实。
 ta meiyou pingjingdi jieshou zhe ge shishi
 he NEG calm-*di* accept this CL reality
 'He didn't wash the clothes carefully.'

The cleft construction in Chinese consists in placing the focus-marking verb *shi* 'to be' before the focus constituents and the particle *de* at the end of the sentence.[6] Adverbials like *zixidi* 'carefully' and *pingjingdi* 'calmly' can be easily inserted in *shi*...*de*; in this case, they are obligatorily placed after the focus marker *shi* and receive the focus, as shown in example (12):

(12) a. 他是仔细地洗衣服的。
 ta shi zixidi xi yifu de
 he be careful-*di* wash clothes *de1*[3]
 'It's carefully that he washed the clothes.'
 b. 他是平静地接受这个事实的。
 ta shi pingjingdi jieshou zhe ge shishi de
 he be calm-*di*[7] accept this CL reality *de1*
 'It's calmly that he accepted this reality.'

This contrasts sharply with evaluative sentence adverbials such as *xinghao* 'fortunately'. Contrary to *zixidi* 'carefully' and *pingjingdi* 'calmly', evaluative sentence adverbials remain out of the scope of the negation. Neither can *xinghao* be moved into the cleft construction *shi*...*de* in order to receive contrast focus. Thus, example (13) is infelicitous:

---

6 Some studies, as Chiu (1993) and Shi (1994), consider that there is no difference between the construction *shi*...*de* and the construction *shi*...*∅*, but, in this paper, when I talk about the cleft construction, I only refer to *shi*...*de*.
7 Note than in the glosses, *de1* stands for the procession particle/determining particle; *de2* for the complement particle; *di* is the adverbial particle mentioned above.

(13) a. 他幸好没有接受这个事实。
    ta xinghao meiyou jieshou zhe ge shishi
    he fortunately NEG accept this CL reality
    'Fortunately, he accepted this reality.'
  b. *他是幸好接受了这个事实的。
    ta shi xinghao jieshou zhe ge shishi de
    he be fortunately accept this CL reality *de1*
    intended: 'Fortunately, he accepted this reality.'

Thus, in spite of traditional positional tests failing to assess the scope of Chinese adverbials, the (in)compatibility with negation and cleft constructions manifests the robustness of the syntactic distinction between predicate adverbials and sentence adverbials.

3.2.2 Semantic properties

As in French, the paraphrase method can show the relationship between the associated constituents and the corresponding adjectives. The adjectival form of the adverbials *zixidi* 'carefully' and *pingjingdi* 'calmly' can describe the subject in two ways. The first one is "Subject is adj.", as in example (14), and the second is illustrated by (15), where the adjective has a determining role:

(14) a. 他很仔细。   b. 他很平静。
    ta hen zixi   ta hen pingjing
    he very careful   he very calm
    'He is very careful.'   'He is very calm.'

(15) a. 仔细的他   b. 平静的他
    zixi de ta   pingjing de ta
    careful *de1* he   calm *de1* he
    'he who is careful'   'he who is calm'

In example (14), the adjectives *zixi* 'careful' and *pingjing* 'calm' assume the role of a predicate. They indicate the properties of the subject *ta* 'he'; in example (15), *zixi* 'careful' and *pingjing* 'calm', combined with the particle *de*, function as a determiner. They also attribute properties to the subject *ta* 'he'. These two paraphrases highlight the inseparable relation between the subject and the adjectives *zixi* 'careful' and *pingjing* 'calm', which the adverbials *zixidi* 'carefully' and *pingjingdi* 'calmly' are derived from. However, both adverbs can also modify the predicate, and not only the subject. This can be manifested using the same kind of paraphrase as in French, with *yi* adj. *de fangshi* 'in an *adj*. manner', as in example (16):

(16) a. * 以仔细的方式洗衣服
         yi   zixi   de   fangshi   xi   yifu
         with careful *de1* manner wash clothes
         intended: 'wash the clothes in a careful manner'
    b. 以平静的方式接受了这个事实
         yi   pingjing de   fangshi jieshou le   zhe   ge   shishi
         with calm   *de1* manner wash   ASP this CL reality
         'accept this reality in a calm manner'

In example (16b), *pingjingdi* 'calmly' can express the way to carry out the process, while *zixidi* 'carefully' in (16a) cannot: unlike what the English translation 'careful' or 'carefully' may suggest, the kind of 'carefulness' designated by *zixi*, *zixidi* applies to the subject or agent, but cannot see its scope restricted to the proper manner of the action, whereas the 'calm' of *pingjin*, *pingjindi* can be applied to the manner. Such incompatibility in example (16a) makes it necessary to look for into the relation of the adverb to the verbal predicate. In the following examples, I try to use the adjective form as predicate of the action verb:

(17) a. 洗衣服的动作很仔细。
         xi   yifu   de   dongzuo hen   zixi
         wash clothes *de1* action   very   careful
         'The action of washing the clothes is careful.'
    b. * 接受这个事实的动作很平静
         jieshou zhe ge shishi de   dondzuo hen   pingjing
         accept   this CL   reality *de1* action   very   calm
         intended: 'The action of accepting this reality is calm.'

In (17a), the adjectival form *zixi* 'careful' can be predicated onto the process of action *xiyifu* 'wash the clothes', whereas in (17b), *pingjing* 'calm' cannot describe *jieshou zhe ge shishi* 'accept this reality'.

The use of adjectives in examples (16) and (17), reveal different relation between the adverbials (*zixidi* 'carefully' and *pingjingdi* 'calmly') and the predicate: *zixidi* 'carefully' can only qualify the process as an event. On the other hand, *pingjingdi* 'calmly' can only modify the manner in which the action is carried out by the agent. This difference of scope is confirmed by the degree of accessibility to the position of the complement introduced by the particle *de*, as shown in example (18). The complement (*buyu* in Chinese) has the function of adjunct to the predicate, which refers to the properties of the agent performing the action and never expresses the manner to carry out the process. The complement also expresses the speaker's position about the process of the action.[8] The fact that (18a) is possible reveals that *zixi*, 'careful' is a subject-oriented adjunct to the predicate and cannot express the manner of action. On the contrary, the oddness of (18b) shows that *pingjing*, 'calm' expresses manner.

(18) a. 他衣服洗得很仔细。
 ta yifu xi de hen zixi
 he clothes wash *de2* very careful
 'He washed the clothes very carefully.'
 b. ?? 他这个事实接受得很平静。
 ta zhe ge shishi jieshou de hen pingjing
 he this CL reality accept *de2* very calm
 'He accepted this reality calmly.'

From the analysis above, we can distinguish two groups of subject-oriented adverbials, one represented by *zixidi* 'carefully' and the other by *pingjingdi* 'calmly'. The first one qualifies the subject and the process (as event). The second type also qualifies the subject, but at the same time it indicates the manner to carry out the action.

3.2.3 Cooccurrence

When these two types of subject-oriented adverbials occur in the same sentence, their order of appearance is not fixed:

(19) a. 他仔细地、平静地整理了父亲的手稿。
 ta zixidi pingjingdi zhengli le fuqin de shougao
 he careful-*di* calm-*di* arrange ASP father *de1* manuscript
 'He arranged his father's manuscript carefully and calmly.'
 b. 他平静地、仔细地整理了父亲的手稿。
 ta pingjingdi zixidi zhengli le fuqin de shougao
 he calm-*di* careful-*di* arrange ASP father *de1* manuscript
 'He arranged his father's manuscript carefully and calmly.'

---

[8] In addition to this evaluative value, Paris (1989:117) mentions "*a scalar quantity*" for *buyu* as "complement". She explains that the acceptability of the complement is "*linked to the functioning of comparative constructions and, specially, to the functioning of the measure expressions inside the comparative.*"

In example (19), *zixidi* 'carefully' and *pingjingdi* 'calmly' can be placed one after the other and the cooccurrence is acceptable without any condition of order. These two adverbials attribute properties to the subject and at the same time modify the predicate.

3.3 Interim findings

Subject-predicate adverbs are attested in both languages. From a syntactic viewpoint, these adverbs are in the scope of the negation and are compatible with cleft constructions. Both tests distinguish them from sentence adverbs. As to the syntactic distribution, note that Chinese adverbials can only appear between the subject and the predicate. At the semantic level, tests using the adjectival root of the adverb reveal differences in the relation of the adverbs to the subject and the verb. Four constructional patterns can be used as test:
1) "[subject] is [adjective]" (in French and in Chinese);
2) "[adjective] *de* [noun / pronoun]" (in Chinese), where the adjective is used as a defining property of the noun;
3) "in an [adjective] manner" as modifier or the verb (in French and in Chinese), showing whether the adjectival root can denote the manner of the action;
4) "The act of doing something is [adjective]" (in Chinese), showing whether the adjectival root can denote a property of the event denoted by the verb.

The first two paraphrases indicate the possibility for the subject to be modified by the adjective; and the last two show the relation between the verbal predicate and the property denoted by the root.

From the analysis above, we can conclude that subject-predicate adverbs in French and subject-predicate adverbials in Chinese, as indicated in their denomination, qualify the subject and the predicate, but also that two levels of semantic incidence ought to be distinguished in Chinese: one on the process as an action fulfilled in a certain manner, one on the process as an event.

4 Subject-oriented sentence adverbials

4.1 In French

Mørdrup (1976a) and Molinier & Lévrier (2000) use almost the same syntactic tests to show the properties of these adverbials, and they obtain converging results.

However, they do not classify these adverbs into the same adverbial classes. Mørdrup (1976a) places them among the constituent class, whereas Molinier & Lévrier hold that they belong to the larger group of sentence adverbs. Guimier (1996) analyzes them as being transferred from the realm of intra-predicativity to the realm of extra-predicativity (see above for the definition of these idiosyncratic concepts). Let us begin with the following sentences, where the adverbs at stake are detached to the left:

(20) a. Prudemment, Marie a répondu à cette question.
       'Cautiously, Mary answered this question.'
    b. Intelligemment, Marie a répondu à cette question.
       'Intelligently, Mary answered this question.'

The main tests (negation and cleft construction) are applied to (20a) and (20b):

(21) a. Prudemment, Marie n'a pas répondu à cette question.
       'Cautiously, Mary didn't answer the question.'
    b. Intelligemment, Marie n'a pas répondu à cette question.
       'Intelligently, Mary didn't answer the question.'

(22) a. *C'est prudemment que Marie a répondu à cette question.
       intended: 'It's cautiously that Mary answered this question.'
    b. *C'est intelligemment que Marie a répondu à cette question.
       intended: 'It's intelligently that Mary answered this question.'

Examples (21a) and (21b) show that the adverbs *prudemment* 'cautiously' and *intelligemment* 'intelligently' are not in the scope of the negation, which distinguish them from the same adverbs in the following sentences, where they are integrated to the VP and fall in the scope of the negation:

(23) a. Marie n'a pas répondu à cette question prudemment.
       'Mary didn't answer this question cautiously.'
    b. Marie n'a pas répondu à cette question intelligemment.
       'Mary didn't answer this question intelligently.'

Examples (22a) and (22b) are equally infelicitous: it is impossible to use a cleft construction unless the adverbs occur in the VP, in post-verbal position:

(24) a. Marie a répondu à cette question prudemment.
     'Mary answered this question cautiously.'
  b. Marie a répondu à cette question intelligemment.
     'Mary answered this question intelligently.'

(25) a. C'est prudemment que Marie a répondu à cette question.
     'It's cautiously that Mary answered this question.'
  b. C'est intelligemment que Marie a répondu à cette question.
     'It's intelligently that Mary answered this question.'

In (25), *prudemment* 'cautiously' and *intelligemment* 'intelligently' can be focused upon via a cleft construction, contrary to example (22). The result of the test depends on the detached vs. non-detached position in the original sentences. Their syntactic behavior shows that, intrinsically, neither *prudemment* 'cautiously' nor *intelligemment* 'intelligently' have only one function. In example (20), they have the properties of speaker-oriented sentence adverbs, as shown in (21) and (22); in example (24), they have the properties of subject-oriented constituent adverbs, like in (23) and (25). Molinier & Lévrier (2000) point out that *prudemment* 'cautiously' and *intelligemment* 'intelligently' can also have the properties of speaker-oriented sentence adverbs when they appear in the detached position on the right of the subject (example (26)) and in the detached final position (example (27)):

(26) a. Marie, prudemment, a répondu à cette question.
     'Marie, cautiously, answered this question.'
  b. Marie, intelligemment, a répondu à cette question.
     'Mary, intelligently, answered this question.'

(27) a. Marie a répondu à cette question, prudemment.
     'Mary answered this question, cautiously.'
  b. Marie a répondu à cette question, intelligemment."
     'Mary answered this question, intelligently.'

More precisely, when *prudemment* 'cautiously' and *intelligemment* 'intelligently' are constituent adverbs, they are subject-predicate adverbs, as shown by the paraphrases 'Subject is adjective' and 'in an adjective manner'. However, even when they are used as speaker-oriented sentence adverbials, these forms are sensitive to semantic properties of the subject. Mørdrup (1976a) distinguishes this adverbial class by the selective relation between subject and verb. In order for the sentence to be correct, the subject must be the agent of the sentence.[9] Normally, it has the + ANIMATE, + HUMAN features, as in (28):

(28) a. Prudemment, Marie surveillait les quais.
 'Cautiously, Mary scrutinized the docks.'
 b. *Prudemment, la caméra surveillait les quais.
 intended: 'Cautiously, the camera scrutinized the docks.'

In short, adverbs like *prudemment* 'cautiously' and *intelligemment* 'intelligently' have two different functions according to their position in the sentence: constituent adverbs and sentence adverbs. When they function as constituent adverbs, they have the syntactic and semantic behavior of subject-predicate adverbs. This confirms that speaker-orientation vs. subject-orientation are functional, not lexical features. However, it also appears that the lexical meaning of the adverb displays features of agent-orientedness that are independent from their construction in a certain function. In what follows, I discuss the extent to which the same may hold for Chinese.

4.2 In Chinese

As indicated above, this group of adverbs in French has two functions: it is their position in the sentence that determines the subject-sentence adverb function. This is my starting point to study the equivalents of this adverbial class in Chinese with *jinshendi* 'cautiously' and *congmingdi* 'intelligently'.

As shown in the following examples, adverbials *jinshendi* 'cautiously' and *congmingdi* 'intelligently' can be placed only between the subject and the predicate. The other places are not accessible to them:

(29) a. 玛丽谨慎地回答了这个问题。
 mali jinshendi huida le zhe ge wenti
 Mary cautious-*di* answer ASP this CL question
 'Mary answered this question cautiously.'
 b. *谨慎地，玛丽回答了这个问题。
 jinshendi mali huida le zhe ge wenti
 cautious-*di* Mary answer ASP this CL question
 intended: 'Cautiously, Mary answered this question.'

---

9 This relation is also mentioned by Guimier (1996) and Molinier & Lévrier (2000). Geuder (2000) also carries out a study on this adverbial group and calls them "agent adverbs".

(30) a. 玛丽聪明地回答了这个问题。
     mali   congmingdi   huida   le   zhe   ge   wenti
     Mary   intelligent-*di* answer ASP this   CL   question
     "Mary answered this question intelligently."
   b. *聪明地，玛丽回答了这个问题。
     congmingdi   mali   huida   le   zhe   ge   wenti
     intelligent-*di* Mary answer ASP this   CL   question
     intended: 'Intelligently, Mary answered this question.'

Only (29a) and (30a) are acceptable, where *jinshendi* 'cautiously' and *congmingdi* 'intelligently' display the subject-predicate adverbial function. But does it really mean that they cannot access the function of speaker-oriented sentence adverb?

In Chinese, roughly speaking, two ways to mark the evaluative value are available. The first is lexical: for example, *xinghao* 'fortunately', which expresses the speaker's attitude towards the speech. The second way of expressing evaluative meaning is syntactic: the speaker uses the 'complement' *buyu*, introduced by the particle *de*. Examples (31a) and (31b) illustrate this:

(31) a. 玛丽回答了这个问题的事情做得很谨慎。
     mali   huida   le   zhe   ge   wenti   de   shiqing   zuo
     Mary   answer ASP this CL   question *de1* fact   do
     de   hen   jinshen
     de2 very   cautious
     'The fact that Mary answered this question is very cautious.'
   b. 玛丽回答了这个问题的事情做得很聪明。
     mali   huida   le   zhe   ge   wenti   de   shiqing
     Mary   answer ASP this CL   question *de1* fact
     zuo   de   hen   congming
     do   *de2*   very   intelligent
     'The fact that Mary answered this question is very intelligent.'

In example (32), the adverbial *jinshendi* 'cautiously' disappears; the adjective radical *jinshen* 'cautious' and with the particle *hen* 'very', are placed after the particle *de*:

(32) *摄像头监视码头的事情做得很谨慎。
     shexiangtou   jianhi   matou   de   shiqing   zuo   de   hen
     camera   scrutinize   dock   *de1* fact   do   *de2* very
     jinshen
     cautious
     ?'The fact that the camera scrutinizes the docks is very cautious.'

All this constitutes the complement, which has an evaluative function. This evaluation applies to the verb *zuo* 'do', but it also qualifies the subject *Mali* 'Mary', as in (33):

(33) a. 玛丽很谨慎。 b. 玛丽很聪明。
          mali   hen   jinshen   mali   hen   congming
          Mary   very cautious   Mary   very intelligent
          'Mary is very cautious.'   'Mary is very intelligent.'

Even though the speaker-oriented sentence adverbial and the subject-oriented constituent adverbial are morphologically distinct, they are equally sensitive to the animacy of the agent, as was shown by example (32).

4.3 Results of the contrastive analysis

In this section, I examined the subject-sentence adverbs in French and in Chinese. In French, as observed earlier, this adverbial class has two functions depending on the position of the adverbs in the sentences. When they are in the detached position, they have the subject-sentence function, convey evaluative meaning and are speaker-oriented. However, they still qualify the subject, which must be the agent of the action and must be endowed with animacy. In Chinese, this adverbial class has no equivalent. This evaluative function is assumed by the predicative complement, introduced by the particle *de*, and not by the adverbial function. However, even in this construction, the secondary predicate retains its semantic association with animated subjects.

5 Subject-oriented descriptive adverbials

5.1 In Chinese

In the preceding sections, I investigated different adverbial classes in French and their equivalents in Chinese, such as the subject-predicate adverbial class and the subject-sentence adverbial class. Both classes take scope over the subject, the predicate or the sentence. These adverbs express the varied values to qualify the different contents. Meanwhile, in the following, I concentrate on adverbials taking scope only over the subject. These forms differ from the previous ones, which were oriented towards both the subject and the predicate or the sentence.

Liu Yuehua (1983), in her adverbial classification, points out that a class of adverbials has the describing function. It specifically describes the state, the expression, the posture, etc. of the animated being denoted by the subject constituent. Aono Emi (2005), among others, also analyzes these adverbials, with regard to their scope. She calls them "subject-describing descriptive" adverbials. Let us look at the following examples:

(34) a. 玛丽开心地拥抱了杰克。
    mali kaixindi yongbao le   jiecke
    Mary happy-*di* hug   ASP   Jack
    'Mary hugged Jack happily.'
  b. 玛丽愤怒地离开了教室。
    mali fennudi likai le   jiaoshi
    Mary angry-*di* leave ASP classroom
    'Mary left the classroom angrily.'

In what follows, I first take a look at their syntactic behavior before turning to their semantic properties. This adverbial class is a subset of constituent adverbials. They can stand in the scope of the negation (35) and can be focused upon via the cleft construction (37). They cannot be placed to the left of the negation (36) and cannot stand in the evaluative construction discussed above for speaker-oriented sentence-subject adverbials (38):

(35) a. 玛丽没有开心地拥抱杰克。
    mali meiyou kaixindi yongbao jiecke
    Mary NEG   happy-*di* hug   Jack
    'Mary didn't hug Jack happily.'
  b. 玛丽没有愤怒地离开教室。
    mali meiyou fennudi likai   jiaoshi
    Mary NEG   angry-*di* leave classroom
    'Mary didn't leave the classroom angrily.'

(36) a. *玛丽开心地没有拥抱杰克。
    mali kaixindi meiyou yongbao jiecke
    Mary happy-*di* NEG   hug   Jack
    intended: *'Happily, Mary didn't hug Jack.'
  b. *玛丽愤怒地没有离开教室。
    mali fennudi meiyou likai jiaoshi
    Mary angry-*di* NEG   leave classroom
    Intended: *'Angrily, Mary didn't leave the classroom.'

(37) a. 玛丽是开心地拥抱杰克的。
mali   shi   kaixindi   yongbao   jiecke   de
Mary   be   happy-*di* hug   Jack   *de1*
'It is with happiness that Mary hugged Jack.'
b. 玛丽是愤怒地离开教室的。
mali   shi   fennudi   likai   jiaoshi   de
Mary   be   angry-*di* leave   classroom *de1*
'It is with anger that Mary left the classroom.'

(38) a. *玛丽开心地是拥抱杰克的。
mali   kaixindi   shi   yongbao   jiecke   de
Mary   happy-*di* be   hug   Jack   *de1*
intended: 'What Mary did happily was to hug Jack.'
b. *玛丽愤怒地是离开教室的。
mali   fennudi   shi   likai   jiaoshi   de
Mary   angry-*di* be   leave   classroom *de1*
intended: 'What Mary did angrily was to leave the classroom.'

Examples (39) to (42) repeat the tests that were carried out above on the adjectival roots of subject-sentence adverbials. In (39a) and (39b), the subject appears in an attributive structure, where the corresponding adjective is the attribute; in (39c) and (39d), we see that the adjective can be used as NP modifier:

(39) a. 玛丽很开心。   b. 玛丽很愤怒。
     mali   hen   kaixin   mali   hen   fennu
     Mary   very happy   Mary   very angry
     'Mary is very happy.'   'Mary is very angry.'
   c. 开心的玛丽   d. 愤怒的玛丽
     kaixin de   mali   fennu de   mali
     happy   *de1* Mary   angry *de1* Mary
     'Mary, who is happy'   'Mary, who is angry'

(40) shows that the adjectival root is infelicitous as predicate of the action:

(40) a. *拥抱的动作很开心。
     yongbao   de   dongzuo   hen   kaixin
     hug   *de1* action   very   happy
     intended: 'The action of hugging is very happy.'

b. *离开教室的动作很愤怒。
likai jiaoshi de dongzuo hen fennu
leave classrooom *de1* action very angry
intended: 'The action of leaving the classroom is very angry'

(41) reveals that these adjectival roots cannot modify the noun *fangshi* 'manner' in what should be a standard way of expressing the way of carrying out an action:

(41) a. *以开心的方式拥抱了杰克
yi kaixin de fangshi yongbao le jieke
with happy *de1* manner hug ASP Jack
intended: 'to hug Jack in a happy manner"
b. *以愤怒的方式离开了教室
yi fennu de fangshi likai le jiaoshi
with angry *de1* manner leave ASP jiaoshi
intended: 'to leave the classroom in an angry manner'

Finally, (42) shows that these roots cannot get access to the position of complement:

(42) a. *拥抱杰克拥抱得很开心
yongbao Jieke yongbao de hen kaixin
hug Jack hug *de2* very happy
intended: 'to Hug Jack very happily'
b. *离开教室离开得很愤怒
likai jiaoshi likai de hen fennu
leave classroom leave *de2* very angry
intended: 'to leave the classroom very angrily'

Examples (39) to (42) indicate that adverbials *kaixindi* "happily" and *fennudi* "angrily" can only modify the subject; they describe neither the action, nor the manner to carry out the action. In line with the analysis in Lai Huiling (2017: 146), we can consider that "subject-oriented descriptive adverbials" (her terminology) "do not have a direct relationship with the predicate, they simply indicate when the subject or the individual carries out an action, his facial expressions or his mental state." This is confirmed by the possibility to paraphrase (34) as (43):

(43) a. 玛丽拥抱杰克的时候很开心。
mali yongbao Jieke de shihou hen kaixin
Mary hug Jack *de1* moment very happy
'When Mary hugged Jack, she was very happy.'

b. 玛丽离开教室的时候很愤怒。
   mali likai   jiaoshi   de   shihou   hen   fennu
   Mary leave classroom *de1* moment very angry
   'When Mary left the classroom, she was very angry.'

In example (43), Mali's mental state *kaixin* 'happy' or *fennu* 'angry' is indicated when she "hugs Jack" (*yongbao Jieke*) or "leaves the classroom" (*likai jiaoshi*). In other words, Mali's state of mind accompanies her action, but does not modify the action.

After showing the syntactic and semantic properties of subject-oriented descriptive adverbials, let us now have a look at their position, in case of cooccurrence with items from the subject-predicate adverbial class such as *zixidi* 'carefully' and *pingjingdi* 'calmly':

(44) a. 她伤心地、平静地离开了家。
     ta   shangxindi   pingjingdi   likai   le   jia
     she   sad-*di*   calm-*di*   leave   ASP   home
     'She left home sadly and calmly.'
   b. ?? 她平静地、伤心地离开了家。
     ta   pingjingdi   shangxindi   likai   le   jia
     she   calm-*di*   sad-*di*   leave   ASP   home
     intended: 'She left home calmly and sadly.'

(45) a. 他愤怒地、仔细地给她处理了伤口。
     ta   fennudi   zixidi   gei   ta   chuli   le   shangkou
     she   angry-*di* careful-*di* for   she   treat   ASP   injury
     'He treated her injury angrily and carefully.'
   b. ?? 他仔细地、愤怒地给她处理了伤口。
     ta   zixidi   fennudi   gei   ta   chuli   le   shangkou
     she   careful-*di* angry-*di* for   she   treat   ASP   injury
     intended: 'He treated her injury carefully and angrily.'

Examples (44) and (45) show that, when cooccurring, subject-oriented adverbials like *shangxindi* 'sadly' and *fennudi* 'angrily' are ideally placed to the left of subject-predicate adverbials such as *zixidi* 'carefully' and *pingjingdi* 'calmly', that their position is closer to the subject.[10]

---

10 The syntactic position of subject oriented adverbials is not always near to the subject. In the passive construction, sometimes, for semantic reasons, even if the adverbial immediately follows the patient, it is always oriented towards the agent. For more details, see Hashimoto (1971a).

Chinese subject-oriented descriptive adverbials describe the agent's state of mind when she carries out the action. Contrary to all other groups of content adverbs studied here, these adverbs do not modify the predicate. Yet, they respect the criteria of constituent adverbials: they can stand in the scope of the negation and take the focus position inside a cleft construction. In case of cooccurrence, the preferred order is where subject-oriented adverbials are placed closest to the subject, with subject-predicate adverbials placed to its right, which is near the predicate.

5.2 Cross-linguistic perspective

From a cross-linguistic point of view, this adverbial function has been dealt with in many works and under the varied denominations. The German linguist Geuder (2000) proposes the notion of transparent psychological adverbs, which differs from manner adverbs and depictive adjectives. For example:

(46) a. John shouted at them angrily. (manner)
 b. John angrily shouted at them. (transparent)
 c. John left angry. (depictive adjective) (Geuder 2000: 34)

Examples (46a) and (46b) differ with regard to the position of the adverb *angrily* in the sentence. When the adverb is placed after the verb, it is a manner adverb. When it is placed before the verb, it is a "transparent adverb". The author summarizes the main characteristics of transparent adverbs as such (2000: 191):
– *The paraphrase "in a... manner" cannot be applied;*
– *Transparent adverbs can show a preference for preverbal position while it is the opposite with manner adverbs. (Both types can in principle occur in either position, though);*
– *Most importantly, transparent adverbs assert the existence of a state of an individual; this state can even hold on after the event is over.*

In other words: Chinese subject-oriented descriptive adverbials are essentially similar to Geuder's English "transparent adverbs".

Geuder also examines the contrast between "transparent adverbs" and depictive adjectives. He discusses the difference between two minimal pairs of sentences: the first one contains a depictive adjective and the other one an adverb (Geuder 2000: 179):

(47) a. John left Mary sad. (depictive adjective)
     b. John left Mary sadly. (adverb)

In (47a), *sad* is a (subject) depictive adjective; it refers to a state of an individual. We can have the following reading: John was sad when he left Mary. In (47b), *sadly* is a transparent adverb. It resembles depictives. But contrary to depictives, which can be used independently of the event denoted by the verb, transparent adverbs are used when there is a relation between the state of an individual and the event denoted by the verb. Moreover, as Geuder points out, "transparent" or "subject-oriented descriptive" adverbs cannot be manner adverbs. He concludes that "the semantics of transparent adverbs differs from their adjectival base only by an additional clause that states a connection between the state and the event, in particular some sort of causal connection" (Geuder 2000: 210).

Ernst (2002) considers that adverbials such as *shangxindi* 'sadly' and *fennudi* 'angrily' belong to mental-attitude adverbs. With agent-oriented adverbs, such as 'cleverly' and 'rudely', they are two subclasses of subject-oriented adverbs in English.[11] His analysis suggests that mental-attitude adverbs, like agent-oriented adverbs – depending on their syntactic position – have two readings. 'Willingly' is a mental-attitude adverb and is placed in a different position in the following example. In (48a), it appears before the predicate and, in (48b), it is in the VP.

(48) a. Willingly, the sailors sang a few of the chanteys.
     b. The sailors sang a few of the chanteys willingly. (Ernst 2002: 63)

In (48a), we have the following reading: the sailors are willing when they sing. The adverb 'willingly' describes a mental state of the subject when the event occurs, and this mental state accompanies the whole event; in (48b), we have the manner reading, where 'willingly' indicates the manner of the action "sing".

Both scholars point out the importance of the position in the sentence of the adverbs that express the actor's emotion and psychological state. These adverbs, as well as the subject-sentence adverbs *prudemment* 'cautiously' or *intelligemment* 'intelligently' in French, have two functions depending on their syntactic position. The fact that an adverb has two statuses depending on its positions in the sentence has already been mentioned in the section of subject-sentence oriented adverbs in French. Conversely, in Chinese, the position between the subject and the predicate is the unique adverbial position. The scope of adverbials cannot be examined via positional tests, but only through paraphrases. However, semantic tests suggest that subject-oriented descriptive adverbials such as *fennudi* 'angrily' have nearly

---

11 See also Jackendoff (1972), McConnell-Ginet (1982).

the same scope as the "transparent adverbs" examined by Geuder (2000) or the "mental-attitude adverbs" discussed in Ernst (2002): They express the agent's state of mind, when the action takes place and the action itself is not affected.

6 Conclusion

In this paper, I undertook a first contrastive study of adverbs/adverbials that have a relation with the subject in French and Chinese. For that sake, I concentrated on three functions corresponding to different adverbial scopes and different kinds of orientation towards the subject: subject-predicate oriented adverbials, scoping over the subject and the predicate; subject-sentence adverbials, over the subject and the propositional content, and subject-oriented descriptive adverbials, scoping only over the subject.

From a morphological point of view, French adverbs are marked by the suffix *-ment*. In Chinese, we can observe a comparable morphological feature: the adverbial marker *di* transforms polyfunctional words into adverbs. I focused on the type "adjective + *di*" in order to draw a comparison with the adverbial pattern "adjective + *ment*". Then, I reviewed the classification of the adverbs/adverbials proposed by French and Chinese scholars. On the basis of these classifications, I considered all the adverbs/adverbials that have a relation with the subject and gathered them in the three aforementioned functional classes.

I began with subject-predicate adverbials. This class exists both in French and Chinese. I used two syntactic tests (negation and cleft construction) to differentiate them from sentence adverbs/adverbials. The classes in both languages are comparable: they modify the subject and at the same time describe the way of carrying out the action. This class should be defined as a strictly functional one, since it appears that the same lexemes may be recruited in the second class considered here, subject-oriented sentence adverbials. This second class of adverbs not only has scope over the subject, but also expresses an evaluation on the content of the sentence. Note, however, that their semantic licensing conditions are still indebted to parameters such as agent control and animacy, meaning that they are still semantically associated with the subject of active clauses. In French, subject-oriented sentence adverbials must stand in the initial detached position. The same lexical items can also be placed in other positions, for example at the end of the sentence, but their function changes: they become subject-predicate oriented adverbs of the kind described above. This is a very important contrast with Chinese, which does not display the same positional flexibility. In Chinese, the evaluative value is not expressed by the adverbial construction, but by the complement introduced by the particle *di*. Evaluative meaning is expressed via another construction involving the adjectival root.

Whereas *di*-phrases could be regarded as lexical adverbs under a broad definition of derivational morphology in Chinese, subject-oriented evaluative "adverbial" phrases are alien to the morphological kinship of *di*. This class of markers is set apart from standard adverbial constructions. Finally, subject-oriented descriptive adverbials are close to the formal prototype of "manner adverbs" in both languages. In Chinese, like subject-predicate adverbials, they are built with the morpheme *di* and placed in the canonical adverbial position. They take scope over the subject only. They describe the subject's mental state when she carries out the action; they do not modify the predicate, nor the manner to carry out the process. In case of co-occurrence, subject-oriented descriptive adverbials are ideally placed to the left of subject-predicate oriented adverbs, i. e. closer to the subject.

The persistence of lexical (selectional) biases in the use-conditions of adverbials irrespective of the functional class is an interesting finding from a theoretical perspective, and raises further questions as to other groups that had to be left aside of this study. In this chapter, I focused on the pattern "adjective + *di*" for the sake of comparison. Some adverbials of this class raise further interesting questions, especially those which are subject-oriented without expressing an interior state or a disposition and are thus freed from semantic constraints such as animacy. One example is *hongtongtongdi* 'with a bright red', which is derived from the adjective *hongtongtong* 'bright red'. It also takes scope only over the subject, as shown in the following example:

(49) 太阳红彤彤地升了起来。
     taiyang hongtongtongdi sheng le qilai
     sun red-bright-bright-*di* rise ASP up
     'The sun rises, bright red.'

In (49), the adverbial *hongtongtongdi* 'with a bright red' can express the state, more precisely, the color of the subject *taiyang* 'sun' as in paraphrases (50a) and (50b), but cannot indicate the manner the sun rises (paraphrase 50c):

(50) a. 太阳是红彤彤的。
        taiyang shi hongtongtong de
        sun be red-bright-bright *de1*
        'The sun is bright red.'

b. 红彤彤的太阳。
　　hongtongtong　　　de　　taiyang
　　red-bright-bright　　*de1*　sun
　　'bright red sun'
c. *以红彤彤的方式升了起来。
　　yi　　　hongtongtong　　　de　　fangshi　sheng　le　　qilai
　　with　　red-bright-bright　　*de1*　manner　rise　　ASP　up
　　'rise in a bright red manner'

It is very tempting to classify such an adverbial among the subject-oriented descriptive adverbials, thus establishing a functional class that is partly freed from semantic constraints weighing onto the subject, including the agency constraint. Thus, the investigation of the links between semantic (ontological) constraints and the limits of functional classes should stand in the foreground of future research on Chinese subject-oriented adverbials.

References

Aono, Emi. 2005. Xiandai hanyu miaoxiexing zhuangyu yanjiu [The study of descriptive adverbials in Modern Chinese]. Ph.D. dissertation. East China Normal University.

Chiu, Bonnie. 1993. The inflectional structure of Mandarin Chinese. UCLA, PhD Thesis.

Dik, Simon. 1989. *The theory of functional grammar. Part 1, The structure of the clause.* Dordrecht: Foris.

Dik, Simon. 1997. *The theory of functional grammar. Part 2, Complex and derived constructions.* Berlin, New York: Mouton de Gruyter.

Ernst, Thomas. 2002. *The syntax of adjuncts.* Cambridge: Cambridge University Press.

Geuder, Wilhelm. 2000. Oriented adverbs. Issues in the lexical semantics of event adverbs. Ph.D. dissertation. Universität Tübingen.

Guimier, Claude. 1996. *Les adverbes du français, le cas des adverbes en –ment.* Paris: Ophrys.

Hashimoto, Anne Yue. 1971a. Descriptive adverbials and the passive construction. *Unicorn 7.* 84–93.

Jackendoff, Ray. 1972. *Semantic interpretation in generative grammar.* Cambridge, Mass: MIT Press.

Lai, Huiling. 2017. *Xiandai hanyu zizhu zhuangyu yanjiu* [Study on the volitional adverbial modifier of the Modern Chinese]. China Social Science Press.

Li, Ziyun. 1993. Zhuangyu de yuyi zhixiang [Scope of the adverbials]. *Journal of Anhui Institute of Education* 3. 83–88.

Liu, Yuehua. 1983. Zhuangyu de fenlei he duoxiang zhuangyu de shunxu [The classes of adverbials and their relative order]. *Yufa yanjiu he tansuo* 1. 32–55.

McConell-Ginet, Sally. 1982. Adverbs and logical form: A linguistically realistic theory. *Language* 58(1). 144–184.

Molinier, Christian & Françoise Lévrier. 2000. *Grammaire des adverbes, description des formes en –ment.* Geneva: Droz.
Mørdrup, Ole. 1976. *Une analyse non-transformationnelle des adverbes en –ment.* Copenhagen: Akademisk Forlag.
Nilsson-Ehle, Hans. 1941. *Les adverbes en –ment compléments d'un verbe en français moderne: étude de classement syntaxique et sémantique.* Lund: Gleerup.
Nøjgaard, Morten. 1995. *Les adverbes français: essai de description fonctionnelle, III.* Copenhagen: Munksgaard.
Paris, Marie-Claude. 1989. Quelques aspects de la gradation en mandarin. In Marie-Claude Paris, *Linguistique générale et linguistique chinoise: quelques exemples d'argumentation*, 99–119. Paris: UFR-Linguistique, Université Paris 7.
Qian, Nairong. 1995. *Hanyu yuyanxue* [Chinese Linguistics]. Beijing: Language Institute Press.
Schlyter, Suzanne. 1972. Une hiérarchie d'adverbes en français. *Recherches Linguistiques* 1. 139–157.
Schlyter, Suzanne. 1977. La place des adverbes en -ment en français. Ph.D. dissertation. University of Konstanz, Germany.
Shi, Dingxu. 1994. The Nature of Chinese emphatic sentences. *Journal of East Asian Linguistics* 3(1). 81–100.
Zhao, Boyuan. 1999. *Hanri bijiao yufa* [A comparative grammar of Chinese and Japanese]. Nanjing: Jiangsu Education Publishing House.
Zhang, Lijun. 1990. Lun "NP1 + A + VP + NP2" geshi A zhong de yuyi zhixiang [Scope of A in "NP1+A+VP+NP2"]. *Journal of Yantai University* 3. 87–96.
Zheng, Renshu. 1997. Zhuangyu wenti yanjiu [Research on the adverbial issue]. Ph.D. dissertation. Shanghai Normal University.
Zhu, Dexi. 1957. *Dingyu he zhuangyu* [Determinant and adverbial]. Shanghai: New Affairs Press.
Zhu, Dexi. 1984. *Dingyu he zhuangyu* [Determinant and adverbial]. Shanghai: Shanghai Education Publishing House.
Zou, Yanxia. 2001. *Zhuangwei xingrongci de yuyi zhixiang* [Scope of the adjectival adverbial]. Capital Normal University.

4 The case of domain adverb(ial)s

Martina Werner & Nina C. Rastinger
Domain adverbials and morphology: The rivalry between -*mäßig* and -*technisch* in German

Abstract: This paper investigates the distribution of domain adverbials in present-day German. It will be shown that an inner-morphological perspective can lead to a deeper understanding of the distributional and semantic properties of domain adverbials. For this reason, we present a corpus study of domain adverbials derived by the morphemes -*mäßig* and -*technisch* in the "Falter" corpus of Austrian Standard German (in DeReKo). It will be shown that the two morphemes display different formal properties, which also has further consequences for semantics. More concretely, we demonstrate that -*technisch* is more widely distributed as regards the word class of the base involved (nouns, verbs). By contrast, the suffix -*mäßig* is formally more restricted in this regard and is strictly denominal. In addition, it is attestable with a non-frame-related, qualitative semantics, a semantic dimension, which, by contrast, cannot be attested for the inherently event-based -*technisch*-formations.

Keywords: domain adverbs, morphology, relational adjectives, suffix, word-formation

1 Point of departure

This article deals with the rivalry in the morphology of domain adverbials (DAs) derived by the morphemes -*mäßig* or -*technisch* in present-day German. So far, little research has been conducted on this topic in German (see De Cesare et al.

Acknowledgement: Martina Werner's and Nina C. Rastinger's research was supported by the stand-alone project P32415-G "Relational adjectives in the history of German", funded by the Austrian Science Fund FWF (PI: Martina Werner). Many thanks to Klaus Grübl, Anna-Maria De Cesare, Andrew McIntyre as well as to the editors of the volume for helpful comments on an earlier draft of this paper.

Martina Werner, Austrian Academy of Sciences & Universitiy of Vienna,
martina.werner@univie.ac.at
Nina C. Rastinger, University of Vienna, nina.rastinger@univie.ac.at

https://doi.org/10.1515/9783110767971-009

2020 for a first contrastive study together with English, French, Italian, and Spanish) as compared to other languages (cf. e.g. Diepeveen (2012) on Dutch *-gewijs, -matig* and *-technisch* as well as Marchand 1969: 358 and Lenker 2002 on English *-wise*, among others).

Syntactically, DAs are a specific type of sentential adverbials (Maienborn & Schäfer 2011: 8): the sentence modified by an extra-propositional DA is valid only for the domain denoted by the DA (1a-b), where it acts as the frame topic (Maienborn 2001, Krifka & Musan 2012, Salfner 2018), and it is in this regard obligatory (Frey & Pittner 1998). In other words, DAs "restrict the domain in which the proposition expressed by the rest of the sentence is claimed to hold true" (Maienborn & Schäfer 2011: 8), which means that the proposition is evaluated from the perspective of the DA and it is only true in its specific domain (1b, Maienborn & Schäfer 2011: 8, Schäfer 2013: 46). For this reason, *if*-sentences can serve as equivalents of DAs (Pittner 1999: 118) and metalinguistic phrases (Ruge 2004: 39) like *in terms of* (present-day German *gesehen/betrachtet* lit. 'seen') can be added to them without a change in meaning (1c).

(1) a. I knew before I started out that, **weatherwise**, the end of March is not the time to plan a journey to the Islands [. . .]. [example from Diepeveen 2012: 17; emphasis by the authors]
   b. **Einkaufsmäßig** steht Ljubljana Wien
      shopping-wise-DA stands Ljubljana-NOM Vienna-DAT
      in nichts nach.
      in nothing after
      'In terms of shopping, Ljubljana is in no way behind to Vienna.'
      -/-> *Ljubljana steht Wien in nichts nach.*
      'Ljubljana is in no way behind to Vienna.'
   c. *(Wenn man es)* **einkaufsmäßig** *betrachtet, steht Ljubljana Wien in nichts nach.*
      '(If it is) seen in terms of shopping, Ljubljana is in no way behind to Vienna.'

As opposed to other adverbs (cf. Schäfer 2013: 65ff for further details), domain adverb(ial)s possess specific properties in morphology and syntax (Ramaglia 2011: 26–28, Marchis Moreno 2010, 2015). Their adjectival counterparts are relational adjectives (RAs, also classifying or pseudo-adjectives) as a frequent phenomenon of many languages (such as Romance, cf. e.g. Ramaglia 2011), including German (Gunkel & Zifonun 2008, ten Hacken 2019). DAs and RAs share their non-qualitative (2a-b), non-scalable (2c), and non-polar (2d) character (Fábregas 2007: 4), which also entails the inability to combine with augmentative or diminutive morphology (Mravlag 2013). This can also be illustrated by (2e) with the German augmentative prefix *mega-*.

(2) a. (Die) ärztliche Praxis
'(the) medical practice'
b. *Die Praxis ist ärztlich.
'The practice is medical-RA.'
c. *(Die) ärztlichere Praxis
'(the) more medical practice'
d. *Die Praxis läuft (*un-)ärztlich.
'The practice runs (non-)medically-RA .'
e. *mega-schlaftechnisch etwas verabsäumen
'neglect a duty mega-sleepingwise'[1]

Just like RAs, DAs cannot be nominalized (as in 2f; cf. Holzer 1996, Frevel & Knobloch 2005, Zifonun 2011, Ganslmayer 2012: 138, among others). Hence, they are both in formal and semantic opposition to traditionally prototypical adjectives and adverbs (also called "adjectival adverbs") denoting qualities, most often termed as qualitative adjectives or adverbs (QAs). DAs or RAs respectively shift in their meaning towards a qualitative reading when being intensified (as in 2c-e), used as a predicative (as in 2b) or as a nominal (as in 2f).

f. *Die Ärztlichkeit der Praxis
lit. 'the medicality of the practice'

For present-day German, it was observed that relational adjectives (as in 3a, 3c) or DAs respectively (as 3b) are encoded via (semi-)suffixation[2] (1, 3a, 3b; see Dalton-Puffer & Plag 2000 on English *-wise*) or via pseudo-compounding (see 3c; cf. Hotzenköcherle 1968, Kann 1974, Inghult 1975, Ruge 2004). Although some formations with other suffixes (such as *-isch*) from former language stages have been synchronically attestable, DAs of present-day German are typically marked by two affixes, namely *-mäßig* and *-technisch* (see Ruge 2004, Salfner 2018, De Cesare et al. 2020).

---

[1] Note that the modification of the base (such as *Schlaf* (N) 'sleep' → *Megaschlaf*) is still possible so that a prefixed base is fine, but not a prefixation from the suffixations with *-technisch/-mäßig* (such as *[[mega][[schlaf]technisch]]). For this reason, the ungrammatical prefixation of the *-technisch*-suffixation in (2e) is glossed with a hyphen with the possible pattern [[[mega]schlaf]-technisch].
[2] Semi-suffixes are items which have an intermediate status between affixes and compound constituents. Semi-suffixation with a co-existing, independent lexeme including the possibility of linking elements is considered a subtype of suffixation here, following Decroos & Leuschner (2008: 22).

(3) a. Das Berliner Label "Live Demo" will **Party-technisches** Neuland betreten. 'The Berlin label "Live Demo" wants to break new party-RA ground.' [Berliner Zeitung 2003, see dwds.de]
  b. **Arbeitsmäßig** geht es ihm gut, aber **beziehungstechnisch** hat er nur Pech gehabt.
  'Work-wise he is doing well, but relationship-wise he only had bad luck.'
  c. **reinigungskraftgestütztes** Putzen
  'cleaning staff supported cleaning'

Morphologically, formations with -*technisch* or -*mäßig* have gained some attention (see e.g. Seibicke 1963, Inghult 1975, and Salfner 2018 on -*mäßig*, Ruge 2004 on -*technisch*). The strongest argument for assuming suffixation with -*technisch* and -*mäßig* is that the two morphemes productively form new word patterns. In this view, which is also followed up in this paper, the parallel existence of independent lexemes which are etymologically related is a matter of splitting (or "divergence"). For this reason, formations with full lexemes were excluded in our investigation and the two suffixes have undergone semantic bleaching and became productive for forming new lexemes (see Dalton-Puffer & Plag 2000). Spinning this view a bit further, the existence of pseudo-compounding can also be explained since it is characteristic for grammaticalization processes to display a rivalry between different grammaticalizing morphemes of which some are developed further to suffixes (such as -*technisch* as in 3a or -*mäßig* as in 3b) as opposed to others, which may still occur as heads of compounds (such as *gestützt* 'supported' as in 3c).

In present-day German, both -*technisch* and -*mäßig* act as suffixes which mark DAs (Ruge 2004, Salfner 2018, De Cesare et al. 2020). According to Ruge (2004), no other suffixes have been found to be synchronically productive in this function. However, the Duden grammar (1995: 532) mentions only -*mäßig* as a marker for DAs, whereas -*technisch* remains unmentioned. Furthermore, in the historical perspective of grammaticalization theory, this raises the question which of the two suffixes is grammaticalized further, or, put differently, if some restrictions in the pattern of one of the suffixes can synchronically be detected, which could speak for a beginning or ongoing increase in productivity and which is relevant for our study. Former studies have observed an increase in productivity for -*mäßig* (Inghult 1975) in New High German (1650 until 1950) and for -*technisch* (Ruge 2004: 39–40) during the 20th century, but the respective investigations lack comparable data for both morphemes.[3]

---

[3] Especially as regards -*technisch*, one may doubt if the point of departure of its productivity increase as stated before can be correct: a short investigation on the corpus "Deutsches Textarchiv"

One important aspect in investigating synchronic productivity is to look at the word class of the lexical base, an approach which has not been undertaken yet. The literature just briefly states that *-mäßig* is highly productive, but exclusively (Duden 2016: 768) or almost exclusively (Seibicke 1963: 41) tied to nominal bases. What we have seen from the examples so far is that *-technisch*, which has been neglected in the literature (see exemplarily Fleischer & Barz 2012 or Duden 2016), has also to be taken into consideration for a survey, a desideratum which is also expressed by Salfner 2018: 72). In addition, synchronically ambiguous cases such as *schlaftechnisch* (*Schlaf* (N) '(a) sleep' versus *schlaf-* (V) '(to) sleep') have not been part of the discussion so far. What has been observed previously is that *-mäßig* is a prominent suffix of present-day German for forming adjectives and adverbs from nouns without any formal restrictions (Duden 2016: 768).

Due to a lack of empirical data, this paper represents the first corpus-based investigation on DAs exclusively on present-day German encoded by the suffixes *-mäßig* and *-technisch* from a morphological perspective (on a comparative study, see De Cesare et al. 2020). Hereby, it pursues multiple goals: first, it aims to quantify the semantic distribution (frame-related vs. characterizing/qualitative) of the suffixes *-mäßig* and *-technisch*, especially with regard to the question of whether both suffixes can encode qualitative adverbs and DAs in an equal way or if one of the semantic types is prevalent only for one of the morphological patterns in question. Secondly, the study aims at identifying differences regarding the word class of the base, which is a first step in investigating the morphological structure of the formations more deeply. This is especially because both patterns were investigated with respect to underlying word formation patterns of the base (see De Cesare et al 2020), whereby the word class of the base remained neglected. Thirdly, we aim to investigate the role of language dynamics in synchrony, i.e. if there are any tendencies for one of the suffixes to show semantic peculiarities that the other one lacks.

(DTA) of historical German shows that first examples where *(-)technisch* is semantically bleached and acts as a productive (in the sense of serial) morpheme are attested in the end of the 19th century (see e.g. 1 and 2, from DTA):
(1) *Steuertechnisch spricht man dann gar nicht mehr von einer neuen Veranlagung* [. . .]' 'From a tax point of view, one no longer speaks of a new assessment [. . .]' [Mayer, Otto: *Deutsches Verwaltungsrecht*, 1895]
(2) *Erstens in der Art des Malens* [. . .] *und zweitens in der Wahl der Farben, welche reklametechnisch wirksam und doch wetterbeständig sein müssen.* 'Firstly in the way of painting [. . .] and secondly in the choice of colors, which must be effective advertising-wise [DA] and yet weatherproof.' [Kropeit, Richard: *Die Reklame-Schule*, 1906/1907]

2 Corpus-based investigation

The answers to the questions addressed in the end of the former section were sought with the help of a corpus-based investigation using the "Falterkorpus" (flt, 2000–2018), which contains newspaper articles in present-day Austrian Standard German of different text types (reports, reviews, interviews). This corpus belongs to the "Archive of Written Language" of "DeReKo-Cosmas II" and consists of 43.509.721 tokens (23/28/2019) from the Viennese newspaper "Falter". Since the corpus does not comprise any morpho-syntactic annotation, words with *-technisch* and *-mäßig* were identified through the search queries "*mäßig*" and "*technisch*" (survey duration 03/07-03/28/2019).

The results underwent a type/token-analysis which means that three instances of the same word were counted as three tokens, but one type. Hereby, orthographic variants (especially these with or without a hyphen) or morphological variants (with or without inflectional morphemes or interfixes such as *amateur(s)mäßig* 'amateur-related') were categorized as one type. In the sample, we found 975 types and 7399 tokens with **mäßig* and 392 types and 1503 tokens with **technisch* in the corpus. To get a representative data extract for the first time, we took a randomized sample of approximately 25% or at least 150 of all types, i.e. 250 types in the case of examples with **mäßig* and 150 types in the case of examples with **technisch*. This resulted in the data set of the study consisting of 344 tokens with **mäßig* and 361 tokens with **technisch*.

However, not all of these examples must necessarily be DAs since, for example, *technisch* and *mäßig* might also occur as lexical heads of compounds (see the word formation pattern in 4a)[4] or simplex lexemes (*technisch denken* 'to think technically'). For this reason, each example (token) was checked individually for each context. Since it was not possible in the corpus to filter the results any further, the list was controlled manually in a double-blind procedure by the authors using a keyword-in-context-view. Hereby, all cases in which the two morphemes in question were not attested as suffixes were excluded from the data set for the morphological analysis. The same was done for examples of derivations with *-mäßig* and *-technisch* which were part of adjuncts, as in (4b). These were excluded due to formal reasons because the current study focuses on extra-propositional DAs being related to the whole sentence, not a constituent (NP). Finally,

---

[4] Frequent examples in the data set include *gentechnisch* (80 tokens) and *tontechnisch* (8 tokens), which both are compounds and which are both derived from the noun *Gen-/Tontechnik*. Thus, they follow the same word formation pattern as in (4a).

examples without context (as in headlines or as part of subtitles of pictures) were also not taken up due to their dubious syntactic and semantic status.

(4) a. Stereo-technik > **stereotechn-isch**
'stereo-technique > stereo-technically'
b. Die **grilltechnisch** größten Sorgen bereiten den Förstern dabei zu nahe bei den Bäumen aufgestellte Brutzelanlagen.
'The greatest concerns of the foresters with respect to barbecuing cause the grillers [lit. sizzler-devices] being too close to the trees.' [flt, t, 63]

In a next step, DAs were identified by using the following context-sensitive tests: if examples appear as DAs, it should be feasible to add *betrachtet* or *gesehen* 'seen' to them (cf. Schäfer 2013: 65–67) in order to test whether the reading of a frame topic can be received. By contrast, if the formations are gradable or can be used as a predicative, they are adverbs with a qualitative semantics. The DAs being identified via those tests were then further analyzed in regard to the word class of their respective bases, if applicable. Only cases with a clearly morphological interpretability of the base were taken up in the sample. In some of the cases, we found ambiguous examples which formally do not allow a clear assignment to the word class of the base. An example would be *reimtechnisch* from *Reim* N 'rhyme' and *reimen* V 'to rhyme' or *fischmäßig* from *Fisch* N 'fish' and *fischen* V 'to fish'. Here, the context-sensitive analysis helped determine the original word class of the base. For instance, this was the case with *vorspieltechnisch*, which is formally ambiguous between a denominal formation (from N *Vorspiel* 'prelude, foreplay') and a deverbal formation (from V *vorspielen* 'to audition, to perform'). In this context, the interpretation in favor of a denominal formation was possible, see (4c), this is why the token was taken up in the sample.

(4) c. Dann nämlich liefert der Condomi Express Kondome frei Haus. [. . .] Innerhalb von 15 Minuten ist die Lieferung da, wird garantiert. [. . .] Und in dieser Zeit dürften eigentlich **vorspieltechnisch** noch nicht allzu viele Unsicherheiten passieren.
'Then the Condomi Express delivers condoms free of charge. [. . .] Delivery is guaranteed within 15 minutes. [. . .] And in this time, there shouldn't be too many uncertainties foreplay-wise.' [flt, t, 141]

Let us now move to the generalization which can be drawn from the results of the corpus-based investigation.

3 Results

3.1 Identifying domain adverbials by context

Within the data sample from the present-day German "Falterkorpus", the majority of the examples could be identified as DAs, namely 123 types (46%)[5] with *mäßig (5a) and 100 types (57%) with *technisch (5b).[6] These numbers speak for a high productivity of the investigated suffixes for encoding DAs.

(5) a. Vermutlich werde ich auf meine alten Tage schrullig, aber ich habe nicht das Gefühl,
diskursmäßig irgendetwas Neues oder gar Relevantes verpasst zu haben.
'I probably get cranky in my old days, but discourse-wise-DA I don't feel like I've missed anything new or even relevant.' [flt, m, 162]
b. **Liegestuhltechnisch** ist Wien nicht gerade unterversorgt, Vorreiter waren die Strandlokale am Donaukanal.
'Sunbed-wise-DA, Vienna is not exactly undersupplied, first institutions [with sunbeds] were the beach bars at the Danube canal.' [flt, t, 95]

Besides the large proportion of DAs within the data set, another index for measuring productivity of -*mäßig* and -*technisch* in encoding DAs is the type-token ratio: the more productive a pattern is, the more new forms are generated and the more different types associated with that pattern are empirically attested, whereas a small number of types, but a large number of tokens indicates that the attested types are highly lexicalized and, thus, represent a less productive word formation pattern (for more details see e.g. Müller 2005, Hahnfeld 2015, Hartmann 2016, among others). In our data, 71 of 100 DA-types (71%) with -*technisch* and 96 of 123 DA-types (78%) with -*mäßig* exhibit only a single token. Thus, the majority of DAs that were found can be considered hapax legomena or single examples. In terms of morphological productivity, this means a high productivity for the DA-pattern of both -*mäßig* and -*technisch* with the latter suffix being slightly more productive than the former. This tendency is be supported by the fact that the number of DAs

---

5 All percentages given in the paper were rounded to the nearest whole number, except for cases where the number lies between zero and one percent which were rounded to one decimal place.
6 While types can possibly fall into more than one of the used categories, tokens may belong to one group only. This is due to the fact that types were not split up if they were used as a DA in one context and as a QA in another context at the token-level since the syntactic context is not expected to directly influence the morphology (word-level; see section 5 for further discussion).

with -*technisch* (100 types) is almost equal to the one with -*mäßig* (123 types) in spite of the different sample size of the suffixes (150 vs. 250 types, see section 2).

In contrast to the examples identified as DAs, 183 tokens and 145 types with *mäßig as well as 194 tokens and 76 types with *technisch were categorized as other forms of adverbial forms due to their morphosyntactic or semantic characteristics. The overall distribution of the data set is shown in Table 1.

Table 1: Overall distribution of examples with *mäßig and *technisch.

	domain adverb	qualitative adverb	lexeme	part of an adjunct	missing context
*technish	100 types/167	0/0	25/123	45/65	6/6
*mäßig	123/160	43/55	0/0	93/118	6/11

As can be seen from Figure 1, we also found data types which are not directly related to sentence-related DAs: firstly, examples without a context (such as in headlines or subtitles of figures) which made it impossible to (un-)determine the status of a DA. Secondly, we found cases where DAs act as parts of adjuncts. These examples were not counted as DAs in the narrow sense here since they are not related to the whole sentence, but they modify the applicability of the adjunct of the nominal head (see e.g. Salfner 2018 for a detailed syntactic analysis).[7] This data type represents more than a quarter of the examples with *technisch (26%) and even more than one third of the examples with *mäßig (34%). An example is given in (4b) in section 2.

Furthermore, lexemes were attested through the search query *technisch and cover 14% of all results. In this category, 21 of its types, i.e. 12% of all types, were identified as compounds (subsumed under the lexeme category in Figure 1), which quantitatively confirms Ruge's (2004) findings on -*technisch*. By contrast, no compounds with -*mäßig* (? < N *Maß* 'measure(ment)') were detected within the data set although formations such as *gleichmäßig* 'equal, uniform' or *ebenmäßig* 'even, harmonious' are preserved as part of the present-day German vocabulary.

Semantically however, as can also be seen from Figure 1 and Table 1, the suffix -*mäßig* encodes not only DAs, but also qualitative adverbs (QA). Two examples are given in (6).

---

[7] Although it could also be illuminating to reconsider the syntactic position of the DA-tokens in question (as suggested by one reviewer), this should be part of a separate study since this paper takes a morphological perspective.

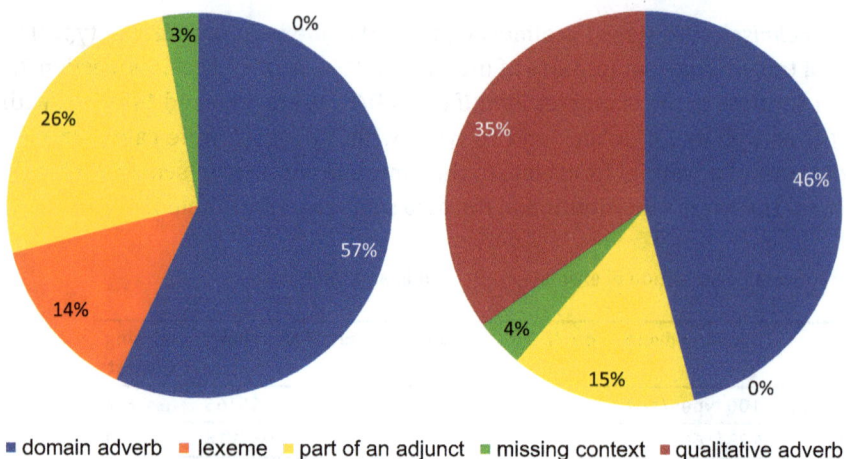

■ domain adverb ■ lexeme ■ part of an adjunct ■ missing context ■ qualitative adverb

Figure 1: Overall distribution of examples with **mäßig* and **technisch*.

(6) a. Nun sind italienische Produkte nicht einmal in Österreich sonderlich exotisch, aber hier werden sie ziemlich authentisch und **discontermäßig** angeboten.
'Nowadays, Italian products are not even exotic in Austria, but here they are offered in a rather authentic and discounter-like-QA way.' [flt, m, 161] [orthography according to the Austrian German original]
b. Da Hans-Peter Göbel Architekt ist, siehts entsprechend **"designermäßig"** aus.
'Since Hans-Peter Göbel is an architect, it looks accordingly "designer-like"-QA.' [flt, t, 156]

The adverbs *discontermäßig* and *designermäßig* in (6) carry the meaning 'like (at) a discounter/designer' and not the meaning 'in regard to discounters/designers'. So, the examples provide a qualitative meaning denoting properties instead of a frame topic meaning as in DAs. This kind of 'qualitative semantics' comprises 15% of all types attested with **mäßig* which means that it is characteristic for the suffix under investigation (see Figure 1). What makes this finding interesting is that no similar qualitative readings were attested with *-technisch*. In our data, the ability to encode qualitative adverbs seems to be restricted to the suffix *-mäßig*.

As a first result, we can see that extra-propositional DAs constitute the largest group within the data set for both -*technisch* and -*mäßig*. A difference between the two suffixes is, however, attested in regard to their productivity: with a higher proportion of DAs in its sample and a more balanced type-token ratio (see also Table 2 in the next section), -*technisch* is more productive in encoding DAs than -*mäßig*. This is also reflected in the semantics of the respective derivational patterns: qualitative readings have only been attested in the case of -*mäßig* (15%, e.g. *girlie-mäßig* 'girlie-like'), whereas no comparable examples were attested for -*technisch*. This is remarkable, given the former observations from the literature towards a priority of -*mäßig* (see section 1 and 2). Another aspect concerns the occurrence of lexemes which are synchronically homonymous to the two suffixes investigated: here, the corpus sample did not comprise any examples of formations containing the derivation *mäßig* (< N *Maß*). By contrast, about 14% of the examples with *technisch* (such as *gentechnisch* < N *Gentechnik* 'genetic engineering') were identified as lexemes, which confirms Ruge's (2004) findings. This result can be explained by the more recent nature of the latter morpheme and its fast development towards being a suffix as compared to other suffixes. Let us now take a closer look at the underlying word class of the base of the respective suffixal patterns.

3.2 Word class of the base

Regarding the word class of the bases combined with -*mäßig* and -*technisch* for forming DAs, a clear difference in the distribution of both suffixes is attestable, see Table 2.

Table 2: Word class of the bases combined with -mäßig and -technisch in Das.

	nominal base	verbal base
* *technish*	87 types/147 tokens	12 types/20 tokens
* *mäßig*	121 types/156 tokens	2 types/4 tokens

For both suffixes, nominal bases predominate with more than three quarters of the identified DAs being denominal, which is also illustrated in Figure 2.

In particular, -*mäßig* is almost exclusively denominal (98%, cf. 7a). It only includes 2 deverbal types, namely *fernsehmäßig* 'tv-watch-DA' (from *fernsehen* 'to watch tv', 3 tokens, cf. 7b) and *bademäßig* 'swim-DA' (from *baden* 'to swim, to bath', 1 token, cf. 7c):

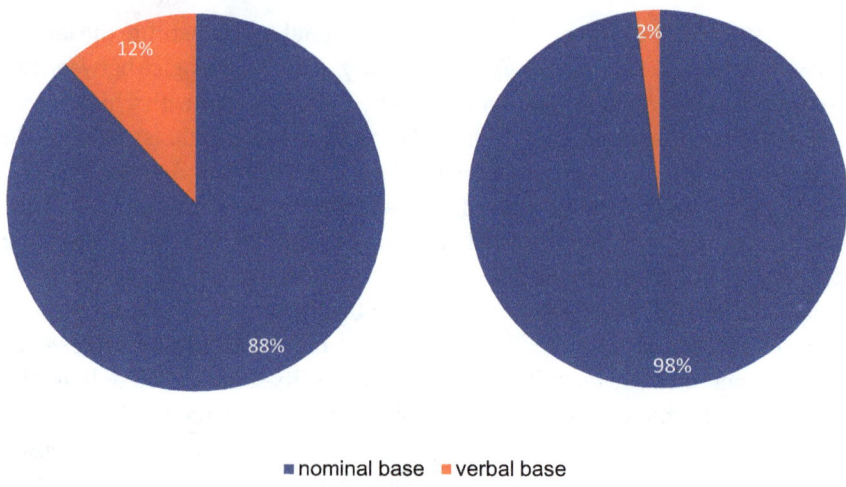

Figure 2: Word class of the bases combined with -*mäßig* and -*technisch* in DAs.

(7) a. Pita mit geschmorten Lammrippen ist **Füllbrot-mäßig** fast nicht zu toppen.
'Pita with braised lamb ribs is, bread-filling-N-wise-DA, almost unbeatable.' [flt, m, 240]
b. Fazit: das absolut Beste, was man sich derzeit in Wien **bademäßig** gönnen kann [. . .]
'Conclusion: the absolute best thing you can currently treat yourself to in Vienna, bathing-V-wise-DA [. . .]' [flt, m, 61]
c. Mir ist **fernsehmäßig** kaum was peinlich, auch nicht, dass ich wahrscheinlich der einzige Mensch über 30 bin, der die Jungmenschensoap "O.C., California" (Sa, 15.15 Uhr, Pro7) bei klarem Verstand konsumiert.
'Watching-TV-V-wise-DA, I'm hardly embarrassed about anything, not even that I'm probably the only person over 30 who consumes the young people's soap "O.C., California" (Sat, 15.15, Pro7) with a clear mind.' [flt, m, 207]

However, these two formations are highly doubtful: *fernsehmäßig* could in theory be derived from the verb *fernsehen* 'watch TV', itself backformed from *Fernseher* 'TV set' or *Fernsehen* 'television'. However, since we found hardly any other deverbal -*mäßig*-formations, it seems more likely that the first constituent is related to the noun *Fernsehen*, which refers to television in all senses other than that of the device. In compounds this noun quite regularly appears in the affixless form *fernseh-*, cf. e.g. *Fernsehprogramm* 'TV program', *Fernsehpersönlichkeit* 'TV personality', *fernsehsüchtig* 'addicted to TV'.

The second example *bad-e-mäßig* contains a linking element (*-e-*) with an unclear, but definitely historical motivation (Werner 2016), also because only denominal, but not deverbal derivations usually contain linking elements, as can be seen by the deverbal formations with *-technisch* (see e.g. 8b). So, both formations are, in our view, not representative examples for deverbal formations and both cases point to an originally (de)nominal origin. This may be reflected by the observation that deverbal formations with *-mäßig* are marginal and not the normal case, cf. **kochmäßig* (> *kochen* 'to cook, boil'), **essmäßig* (> *essen* 'to eat'), **schneimäßig* (> *schneien* 'to snow'). In this regard, Duden (2016: 768) seems to be correct by stating that *-mäßig* is associated with nominal bases. Other bases (such as adjectives) are not attested here.

By contrast, the suffix *-technisch* can be considered both denominal (see e.g. 8a) and deverbal (see e.g. 8b-c): out of the 100 types of DAs with *-technisch* found in the data sample, 88% involve a nominal base (147 tokens), while 12% contain a verbal base (20 tokens). In the light of the previous literature with a comparative view on both suffixes, this is a new finding. Furthermore, to our best knowledge, the existence of deverbal DAs has not been documented cross-linguistically.

(8) a. **Gesetzestechnisch** resultiert dieser Generalangriff auf den ORF aus einer Änderung des KommAustria-Gesetzes (KOG).
'Law-N-wise-DA, this general attack on the ORF [tv] resulted from an amendment to the KommAustria Act (KOG)' [flt, t, 62]

b. **Ausgehtechnisch** beginnt der europäische Südosten aber schon ein paar hundert Meter stadteinwärts, am Schwarzenbergplatz.
'With respect to going-out / Going-out-V-wise-DA, however, the European southeast begins a few hundred meters into the city, at Schwarzenbergplatz.' [flt, t, 21]

c. Das focht diesen freilich nicht an, denn abgesehen davon, dass er **aufstehtechnisch** ohnedies längst von der Eule zur Lerche mutiert ist, weiß er natürlich um das Motto der Birdwatcher: [...]
'This did not bother him, of course, because apart from the fact that, with respect to getting-up / getting-up-V-wise-DA, he has long since mutated from an owl to a lark, he knows the birdwatchers' motto: [...]' [flt, t, 16]

Taking a closer look at the semantics of the deverbal DA-formations (such as *ausgehtechnisch* as in 8b), we can see that they always denote an event.[8] Semantically, events are usually based on a nominal (cf. e.g. De Cesare et al. 2020: 43–44) but as we can see here also for the deverbal formations as regards the paraphrasis of the DAs in 8b-c ('with respect to going-out' in 8b e.g.) a nominal event-reading is reconstructable (such as *(das) Ausgehen* '(the) going-out' for 8b or *(das) Aufstehen* '(the) getting-out' for 8c).

Summarizing, what the morphological analysis of the data set shows is that for both *-mäßig* and *-technisch* nominal bases clearly predominate. Still, the suffixes display a significant different with respect to the word class of their bases: while *-mäßig* is almost exclusively denominal (98%, only 2 deverbal types, which are doubtful), *-technisch* must be categorized as denominal (88%) and deverbal (12%). With respect to morphology, the difference between the two suffixes is important insofar as derivation usually begins with nominal bases in the history of German (see Werner 2012 on nominal derivation, Kempf 2016 on adjectival derivation). Consider for example the nominalizing suffix *-ung* which is deverbal in present-day German (cf. *Drehung* 'turning' > *drehen* 'to turn' or *Hoffnung* 'hope' > *hoffen* 'to hope'), whereas the first attestations of the suffix are denominal (and to some minor extent deadjectival). This has been preserved in present-day German in formations such as *Stallung* 'stabling' (> *Stall* 'stable') or *Waldung* 'forest, woodland' (> *Wald* 'forest').

The two suffixes in question originated from simplex lexemes and are still attested in present-day German in their original semantics (*mäßig* 'moderate', *technisch* 'technical'). As regards their further morphological development as (semi-)suffixes, this means that the first formations, where the two morphemes became serial and semantically bleached, were, in the light of the synchronic distribution, presumably denominal. This is synchronically reflected in our data by the higher amount of denominal formations as compared to deverbal formations. Furthermore, the ability of deriving nominals is a formal prerequisite for the next step in the development of the suffixes, namely deriving verbs – a step that is also reflected by our synchronic data: only the suffix *-technisch* shows also deverbal formations, which means that it is further developed in its distribution as regards the word class selection of the base. This is surprising given the shorter lifespan of the suffix as compared to *-mäßig* (see Inghult 1975, Ruge 2004: 39–40). In terms of language dynamics, the cases in our data which were contextually ambiguous between a denominal and a deverbal interpretation (such as

---

8 This nicely illustrates the parallelism between DAs and RAs, since RAs cannot occur as predicatives, because predicative constructions denote states.

vorspieltechnisch in 4c in section 2) may serve as the basis for widening the original pattern from denominal to deverbal derivation. However, further research is needed in this regard. This also holds for the productivity of deverbal DAs which has not been described in the literature on DAs from a typological perspective yet, which may open the floor for further investigations reconsidering the morphology of DAs more deeply. In addition, future research could bring some light in the nature of different connotations between the two suffixes since, from a native speaker's perspective, *-technisch* is a bit more colloquial and stylistically more marked. As opposed to *-mäßig*, the suffix *-technisch* has a slightly humoristic touch, which might be due to the divergent, but still co-existing semantics of its lexical homonym *technisch* 'technical', which synchronically may open the floor for an unconscious pun.

4 Conclusion and outlook

The aim of the paper was to identify potential differences between the two most productive morphological patterns of forming DAs in present-day German. Through generalization (section 3) drawn from a corpus-based investigation (outlined in section 2), it provides new insights into the morphology of the suffixes *-mäßig* and *-technisch* as well as their relation to each other: while *-mäßig* has been considered to be the most productive suffix within DAs in the previous research on that topic, the generalization received from the "Falterkorpus" data of present-day German (see section 2) suggests that *-technisch* is actually slightly more productive and fulfills the function of encoding DAs more exclusively. In contrast to *-mäßig*, which functions as a marker for QAs in 15% of the analyzed cases, *-technisch* is never attestable with qualitative readings in any of the examples. Furthermore, the results show different formal properties between the two morphemes of present-day German as already observed by the literature (e.g. Salfner 2018: 63–71) but had never been quantified empirically. Formally, differences between the two suffixes concern the particular word class of the base involved (verbs vs. nouns): while *-technisch* forms deverbal as well as denominal DAs, *-mäßig* is nearly exclusively denominal. In other words, *-technisch* is more widely distributed with respect to the word class of the base which, synchronically, points to its stronger productivity as a marker for DAs, also because only these two suffixal patterns can generate new ad-hoc-formations (Salfner 2018: 63–71). This is surprising given its lower prominence in the description of present-day German (see section 1) and its shorter historical development than *-mäßig* (see Inghult 1975, Ruge 2004: 39–40).

What can be further seen from the generalizations drawn from our data is that a qualitative semantics of DAs as a certain type of adverb(ial) is not necessarily a primary concept of the word class 'adverb' given the syntactic as well as morphological distribution as seen by -*technisch* (cf. parallel discussion about relational adjectives in Hotzenköcherle 1968, Schmidt 1993, Frevel/Knobloch 2005). Instead, derived formations are highly underspecified and receive their individual meaning (such as qualitative vs. frame-related semantics) by their individual contextualization at an interplay of morphology and syntax. Syntactically for instance, non-qualitative usage is excluded in a predicative construction, whereas, morphologically, a qualitative semantics is, inter alia, automatically triggered by modifying affixes or in the context of *un*-negation (cf. section 1). As our study illustrated, a deeper morphological perspective on DAs (see section 4), i.e. by investigating differences between the two suffixes as regards distributions and morphological structure (e.g. the word-class of the base), shows that semantic properties that have proven to be characteristic for syntax are perfectly in parallel with the structure building principles of morphology, and vice versa. From a bottom-up perspective starting at the word-level, morphology, as this paper wanted to argue for, can provide innovative ideas for syntax and its sometimes covert linkages to semantics.

As regards further research on language dynamics focusing on this special type adverb(ial) with specific morphological and syntactic properties, it would be important to see of what sort of word-formation types the first formations with -*technisch* and -*mäßig* were based on historically, especially in the light of the synchronic predominance of denominal formations for both suffixes. Especially since compounding and derivation are the major word formation processes in German, it would be important to see what word formation process is prior for initiating a word class change of the base (such as from denominal to deverbal). The detection of a potential logic behind the emergence and development of the DAs in question could also bring some light into the dynamics of their synchronic distribution in present-day German, also in the light of language variation (e.g. in different genres or differences in oral vs. written language). For morphological theory and the interplay of morphology and syntax, it would be important to know whether certain syntactic constructions might also facilitate the morphological development of a certain pattern (e.g. towards being deverbal) and their respective markers.

Sources

Corpus *Falter* (*flt*) in the archive of written language of DeReKo (cosmas II) [Archiv der geschriebenen Sprache]. Permanent URL: https://cosmas2.ids-mannheim.de/cosmas2-web/ (28.03.2021)

References

Dalton-Puffer, Christiane & Ingo Plag. 2000. Categorywise, some compound-type morphemes seem to be rather suffix-like: On the status of -ful, -type, and -wise in present day English. *Folia Linguistica* 34(3–4). 225–244.
De Cesare, Anna-Maria, Ana Albom, Doriana Cimmino & Marta Lupica Spagnolo. 2020. Domain adverbials in the news. A corpus-based contrastive study of English, German, French, Italian and Spanish. *Languages in Contrast* 20(1). 31–57.
Decroos, Nancy & Torsten Leuschner. 2008. Wortbildung zwischen System und Norm. Affixoide im Deutschen und im Niederländischen. *Sprachwissenschaft* 33(1). 1–34.
Diepeveen, Ariane. 2012. Modifying words. Dutch adverbial morphology in contrast. PhD thesis FU Berlin. Permanent URL: https://refubium.fu-berlin.de/handle/fub188/9301?show=full&locale-attribute=en (14.03.2021).
Duden. 1995. *Grammatik der deutschen Gegenwartssprache*. 5th edition. Mannheim / Berlin: Bibliographisches Institut.
Duden. 2016. *Die Grammatik*. 9th edition. Mannheim / Berlin: Bibliographisches Institut.
Erben, Johannes. 2000. *Einführung in die deutsche Wortbildungslehre*. 4th edition. Berlin: Erich Schmidt.
Fábregas, Antonio. 2007. The internal structure of relational adjectives. *Probus* 19(1). 1–36.
Fleischer, Wolfgang & Irmhild Barz. 1992. *Wortbildung der deutschen Gegenwartssprache*. Tübingen: Niemeyer.
Frevel, Claudia & Clemens Knobloch. 2005. Das Relationsadjektiv. In Clemens Knobloch & Burkhard Schaeder (eds.), *Wortarten und Grammatikalisierung. Perspektiven in System und Erwerb*, 151–175. (Linguistik – Impulse & Tendenzen 12.) Berlin/ Boston: de Gruyter.
Frey, Werner & Karin Pittner. 1998. Zur Positionierung der Adverbiale im deutschen Mittelfeld. *Linguistische Berichte* 176. 489–534.
Ganslmayer, Christine. 2012. *Adjektivderivation in der Urkundensprache des 13. Jahrhunderts: Eine historisch-synchrone Untersuchung anhand der ältesten deutschsprachigen Originalurkunden*. Berlin/Boston: de Gruyter.
Gunkel, Lutz & Gisela Zifonun. 2008. Constraints on relational-adjective noun constructions. A comparative view on English, German and French. *Zeitschrift für Anglistik und Amerikanistik* 56(3). 283–302.
Hahnfeld, Andrea. 2015. *Produktivität deverbaler Substantive auf -(er)ei: Quantitative Untersuchung in einem diachronischen Zeitungstext-Korpus*. Hamburg: Disserta.
Hartmann, Stefan. 2016. *Wortbildungswandel: Eine diachrone Studie zu deutschen Nominalisierungsmustern*. Berlin/ Boston: de Gruyter.
Holzer, Peter. 1996. *Das Relationsadjektiv in der spanischen und deutschen Gegenwartssprache*. Wilhelmsfeld: Egert.

Hotzenköcherle, Rudolf. 1968. Gegenwartsprobleme im deutschen Adjektivsystem. *Neuphilologische Mitteilungen* 69. 1–28.
Inghult, Göran. 1975. *Die semantische Struktur desubstantivischer Bildungen auf "-mässig": eine synchronisch-diachronische Studie.* Stockholm: Almqvist & Wiksell.
Kann, Hans-Joachim. 1974. Belege zum Wortbildungsmuster Substantiv + technisch. *Muttersprache* 84. 309–313.
Kempf, Luise. 2016. *Adjektivsuffixe in Konkurrenz. Wortbildungswandel vom Frühneuhochdeutschen zum Neuhochdeutschen.* Berlin/Boston: de Gruyter.
Krifka, Manfred & Renate Musan. 2012. Information structure: overview and linguistic issues. In Manfred Krifka & Renate Musan (eds.), *The expression of information structure*, 1–44. Berlin/New York: de Gruyter.
Lenker, Ursula. 2002. Is it, stylewise or otherwise, wise to use-wise? In Teresa Fanego (ed.), *English Historical Syntax and Morphology*, 157–180. Amsterdam, Philadelphia: Benjamins.
Maienborn, Claudia. 2001. On the position and interpretation of locative modifiers. *Natural Language Semantics* 9(2). 191–240.
Maienborn, Claudia & Martin Schäfer. 2011. Adverbs and adverbials. In Claudia Maienborn, Klaus von Heusinger & Paul Portner (eds.), *Semantics. An international handbook of natural language meaning.* Volume 1, 1390–1420. (Handbooks of Linguistics and Communication Science, HSK 33.2.) Berlin/New York: de Gruyter.
Marchand, Hans. 1969. *The Categories and Types of Present-Day English Word Formation: A Synchronic-Diachronic Approach.* 2nd, completely revised and enlarged edition. München: Beck.
Marchis Moreno, Mihaela. 2010. On the morpho-syntactic properties of relational adjectives in Romanian and Spanish. *Bucharest Working Papers in Linguistics* 12(1). 77–92.
Marchis Moreno, Mihaela. 2015. Relational adjectives as interfaces. *Studia Linguistica* 69(3). 304–332.
Mravlag, Hedwig. 2013. *Relationsadjektive im Deutschen, Französischen und Russischen.* Innsbruck: University Press.
Müller, Peter O. 2005. Einführung. In Peter O. Müller (ed.), *Fremdwortbildung. Theorie und Praxis in Geschichte und Gegenwart*, 11–45. Frankfurt am Main/Wien: Lang.
Pittner, Karin. 1999. *Adverbiale im Deutschen: Untersuchungen zu ihrer Stellung und Interpretation.* Tübingen: Stauffenburg.
Ramaglia, Francesca. 2011. *Adjectives at the Syntax-Semantics Interface.* München: Lincom.
Ruge, Nikolaus. 2004. Das Suffixoid „-technisch" in der Wortbildung der deutschen Gegenwartssprache. *Muttersprache* 114. 29–41.
Salfner, Fabienne. 2018. *Semantik und Diskursstruktur. Die mäßig-Adverbiale im Deutschen.* Tübingen: Stauffenburg.
Schäfer, Martin. 2013. *Positions and Interpretations. German Adverbial Adjectives at the Syntax-Semantics Interface.* Berlin/Boston: de Gruyter.
Schmidt, Jürgen Erich. 1993. *Die deutsche Substantivgruppe und die Attribuierungskomplikation.* Tübingen: Niemeyer.
Seibicke, Wilfried. 1963. Wörter auf -mäßig. Sprachkritik und Sprachbetrachtung. *Muttersprache* 73. 33–47; 73–78.
Ten Hacken, Pius. 2019. Relational adjectives between syntax and morphology. *SKASE Journal of Theoretical Linguistics* 16(1). 77–92.
Werner, Martina. 2012. *Genus, Derivation und Quantifikation. Zur Funktion der Suffigierung und verwandter Phänomene im Deutschen.* Berlin/Boston: de Gruyter.

Werner, Martina. 2016. Genus und Fugenelemente. Zur Herleitung einer motivierten Relation. In Peter Ernst & Martina Werner (eds.), *Linguistische Pragmatik in historischen Bezügen*, 285–311. (Lingua Historica Germanica 9.) Berlin/Boston: de Gruyter.

Zifonun, Gisela. 2011. Relationale Adjektive – ein „klassisches" Muster im europäischen Vergleich. *Deutsche Sprache* 9(2). 98–112.

Anna-Maria De Cesare
Framing, segmenting, indexing: Towards a functional account of Romance domain adverbs in written texts

Abstract: This contribution provides a functional account of adverbs such as Fr. *politiquement*, It. *politicamente*, and Sp. *políticamente* (E. 'politically'), which can be interpreted as manner or domain adverbs. Based on theoretical frameworks devised to model discourse, specifically the information units of written texts, we offer a detailed account of the functional spaces that these adverbs occupy in the Utterance. Special attention is then devoted to the occurrence of these adverbs in the functional left periphery of the Utterance, where they most clearly work as domain adverbs. We show that, in this pragmatic area, domain adverbs have framing, segmenting, and indexing discourse functions and that these functions can be predicted by the interplay between the meaning of these adverbs and the scoping properties of the left-peripheral discourse space they occupy in the Utterance.

Keywords: domain adverbs, syntax-pragmatics interface, functional left periphery, information structure, text linguistics

1 Introduction

The goal of this study[1] is to describe the functional properties of adverbs such as Fr. *politiquement* 'politically', *financièrement* 'financially', *légalement* 'legally' etc.), which are underspecified in the lexicon, as they can function (at least) as manner or domain adverbs. In the literature on the Romance languages, it is generally claimed that these adverbs most typically function as domain adverbs when they occur in detached initial position, as in (1):[2]

---

[1] I would like to thank Olivier Duplâtre, Klaus Grübl, Martina Werner as well as two anonymous readers for their valuable feedback and constructive comments on a previous version of this contribution.
[2] In our examples, we highlight the adverb (or other relevant content) in italics.

Anna-Maria De Cesare, Technische Universität Dresden, anna-maria.decesare@tu-dresden.de

https://doi.org/10.1515/9783110767971-010

(1) Fr. *Politiquement*, c'est un inconnu.
 'Politically, he is unknown.'

Domain adverbs (henceforth DAs) have received increasing attention in the literature, including in the Romance languages (see, among others, Molinier 1984; van Raemdonck 1999; Molinier & Lévrier 2000: 218–237; Hermoso Mellado-Damas 2015; De Cesare et al. 2020; Lupica Spagnolo 2021). Taking a historical perspective, several studies have shown that DAs arose recently in the European languages, pointing to a new and global communicative need (for a historical account of DAs, see Klump 2007 on French and Spanish and Grübl 2018 on Italian). Other studies provide a detailed description of the form and uses of DAs in present-day varieties of one or more Romance languages (cf. De Cesare et al. 2020 for a contrastive, corpus-based study of DAs in Italian, French and Spanish, as well as English and German; see also Lupica Spagnolo in press, who offers a corpus-based description of Italian and German DAs[3]). From a theoretical point of view, the questions addressed in the literature include classificatory problems, related to both the macro-class to which DAs belong (see, among many others, Mørdrup 1976; Guimier 1996; Nølke 1990, 1993; Zampese 1994; Ramat & Ricca 1998; Garcés Gómez 2003) and the sub-classes which are identified within the class of DAs (Molinier 1984, Ramat & Ricca 1998: 191–193). An important theoretical issue yet to be solved also concerns the nature of the structural position occupied by DAs in the left periphery of the clause: a problem that is addressed in cartographic syntax (see, e.g., Cinque 1999 and Haumann 2007 on English).

In this contribution, we pursue another line of research: our aim is to determine the functional properties and textual functions of DAs. Specifically, our aim is threefold. First, we want to describe the distribution of adverbs such as Fr. *politiquement* 'politically' in different 'discourse spaces', rather than syntactic positions (in the same vein as Borreguero Zuloaga 2014; De Cesare & Borreguero Zuloaga 2014, as well as De Cesare 2016, 2018). Secondly, we want to show that the interpretation of adverbs such as Fr. *politiquement* as DAs clearly depends on the nature of the discourse space they occupy. Thirdly, we want to highlight the textual functions DAs can play when occurring in the position illustrated in ex. (1), which we conceive as the *functional left periphery of the Utterance*.[4] While our

---

3 Also see Werner & Rastinger (in this vol.) on domain adverbs formed with *-mäßig* and *-technisch* in present-day German.
4 While the term *left periphery* is conventionally associated to the generative framework, in particular to Rizzi's 1997 cartographic account of the initial area of the clause, it is also used in functionally oriented studies modeling the initial area of the Utterance (in connection to adverbs,

study is mainly descriptive, it also offers interesting theoretical outputs concerning the central concepts attached to DAs, namely *Topic* and *Frame*.

Our contribution is divided into three parts. We first provide a general definition of DAs, based on the main grammatical and semantic properties identified in the literature on French, Italian and Spanish (section 2). In the second and most important part of the contribution (section 3), we describe the functional properties of DAs, which are widely neglected in the literature reviewed in section 2. After a short presentation of our reference theoretical model, called *Basel Model* (see Ferrari et al. 2008 and Ferrari 2014), we show that there is a clear correlation between the interpretation of adverbs such as *politiquement* as DAs and their distribution in different functional spaces of the Utterance (called *Frame*, *Nucleus* and *Appendix*). Focusing on their distribution in the Frame, the discourse space corresponding to the functional left periphery of the Utterance (as in ex. 1), we then provide a detailed description of their textual functions in journalistic prose by drawing on the multi-faceted notion of *Cadre* proposed in Charolles 1997 and 2002. We conclude with a brief summary of our results and by highlighting the descriptive and theoretical outputs of our study (section 4).

2 Domain adverbs: General definition

In the literature on the Romance languages, domain adverbs (DAs) are mainly defined by considering their morpho-syntactic, semantic, and syntactic properties. In the first part of this section (sections 2.1–2.2), we describe these properties based on the literature on French, Italian and Spanish and show how and where these features interface with pragmatic properties. In the last part of this section (section 2.3), we review the classes to which adverbs like Fr. *politiquement*, It. *politicamente*, and Sp. *políticamente* have been assigned, highlighting again how they are connected to pragmatic properties. Two notions play an important role in defining DAs: *Topic* and *Frame*.

---

adverbials and discourse markers, see Rodríguez Ramalle 2009, Borreguero Zuloaga 2014 and De Cesare 2018).

2.1 Form and meaning of DAs

Based on the literature reviewed, the prototypical examples of DAs include adverbs like Fr. *politiquement*, It. *politicamente*, and Sp. *políticamente* 'politically', as in (1), repeated in (2):[5]

(2) Fr. *Politiquement*, c'est un inconnu.
 'Politically, he is unknown.'

In the three Romance languages under scrutiny, DAs are derived adverbs, formed by attaching the adverb-marking suffix MENTE (Fr. -*ment*, It./Sp. -*mente*) to relational adjectives (Molinier & Lévrier 2000: 225; Scalise et al. 1990; Ricca 2004: 476), i.e., adjectives that are morphologically derived from a common noun, as shown in (3):

(3) N. *politique* > Adj. *politique* > Adv. *politiquement*
 'N. *politics* > Adj. *political* > Adv. *politically*'

DAs generally retain a clear semantic relation with their basis (noun and adjective; cf. Molinier & Lévrier 2000: 224). One of the most common ways to describe the meaning conveyed by DAs is through the PP 'from an Adj. point of view' (Fr. *d'un point de vue Adj.* / It. *da un/dal punto di vista Agg.* / Sp. *desde el punto de vista Adj.*):

(4) Fr. *Politiquement*, c'est une décision inacceptable.
 ~ *D'un point de vue politique*, c'est une décision inacceptable.
 'Politically, this decision is unacceptable.'
 ~ From a political point of view, this decision is unacceptable.

Another way of capturing the meaning of DAs is through the expressions *as far as N is concerned* and *as for N* (Fr. *en ce qui concerne NP*, It. *per quanto riguarda NP*, Sp. *en cuanto a NP, en lo relativo a NP, en lo que respecta a NP*; see, among others, Grossmann 1999: 414). In (5), the meaning of It. *politicamente* can be paraphrased by 'as far as politics is concerned' or 'as for politics':

---

5 For space reasons and given that the defining properties of DAs are similar across the three Romance languages, we mainly provide examples with Fr. *politiquement*.

(5) It. *Politicamente*, Piero ha chiuso.
~ *Per quanto riguarda la politica*, Piero ha chiuso.
Lit. 'Politically, Peter has closed'
~ As far as politics is concerned, Peter is no longer involved.

In addition to clarifying the meaning of DAs, the prepositional expressions *as far as N is concerned* and *as for N* also point to a specific pragmatic function of DAs in sentence initial position. These adverbs are *thematic markers* (Klump 2002: 207): they provide the thematic frame of the Utterance. Specifically, given their meaning, DAs "anchor the content of their Utterance in a specific domain" (Gezundhajt 2000: 192). In examples (2), (4) and (5), the content of the Utterance – i.e., respectively, *he is unknown; this decision is unacceptable; Peter is no longer involved* – must be interpreted as being valid in the domain of politics, expressed by the DA functioning as thematic marker.

2.2 The syntactic positions of DAs in the clause

French, Italian and Spanish DAs can occupy different 'sentence slots' (for French, see Molinier & Lévrier 2000: 231–232 and Nøjgaard 1993: 280–281). In non-formal accounts describing the linear position of adverbs in the sentence, these slots are generally defined based on main clauses with canonical word order: 'Subject [or Null Subject in Italian and Spanish] – Verb – Object'. Three main slots are identified, to which we refer via the capitals I, II, and III:

(6) **I** Subject **IIa** Verb **IIb** Object(s) **III**

Adverbs such as Fr. *politiquement* can occur in the sentence slots I, II and III, which are defined topologically as initial-medial-final and in relation to other clause elements (e.g., adverbs placed between the Subject and the Verb). Additionally, the "slot" occupied by these adverbs is described by considering its syntactic (and prosodic) integration in the clause. An adverb such as Fr. *politiquement* can be detached (or parenthetical) or non-detached (i.e., integrated).

Based on the claims made in the literature, the canonical position of DAs is in detached initial position (position I), as in (7), also referred to as the "syntactic frame of the sentence" (see Guimier 1996: 142; Molinier & Lévrier 2000: 227, 231). The position of Fr. *politiquement* in ex. (7) is claimed to be the one most in line with the core function of DAs, by which they specify "the conditions allowing the predication" (Guimier 1996: 142) and "a domain in which a proposition is true" (Molinier & Lévrier 2000: 221).⁶

(7) Fr. *Politiquement*, elle est très engagée.
 'Politically, she is very involved.'

Importantly, a recent corpus study based on written texts (Lupica Spagnolo 2021) shows that the preferential distribution of DAs in Italian (and German) is in fact not in initial but in medial position. A frequency count of the syntactic distribution of DAs in the three sentence slots (initial, medial, and final) allows observing that these adverbs are most common in mid-clause positions, as in (8), where the DA is integrated in the clause and occurs between the verb and a final locative complement (position IIb), and (9), where it is detached between the subject and the verb (position IIa). What this corpus-based study also shows is that the final detached position of DAs (position III), illustrated in (10), is rare overall.

(8) Fr. Ce candidat satisfait *politiquement* surtout à Paris.
 'This candidate pleases politically above all in Paris.'

(9) Fr. Ce candidat, *politiquement*, est un inconnu.
 'This candidate, politically, is unknown.'

(10) Fr. Ce candidat est un inconnu, *politiquement*.
 'This candidate is unknown, politically.'

The sentence distribution of Fr. *politiquement* in detached initial position is also clearly distinct from its occurrence in final integrated position, as in (11). In fact, in a position such as (11), the adverb is most likely to be interpreted as a manner adverb, in the sense of 'in an Adj. manner'. The impact of the syntactic position and clause integration on the interpretation of the adverb is particularly transparent in ex. such as (12), drawn from Grossmann (1999: 414).

(11) Fr. Elle est très engagée *politiquement*.
 'She is very involved politically.'

---

6 Interestingly, one reviewer pointed out that in Brazilian Portuguese, the initial detached position of the adverb in ex. (7) would only license a manner adverbial interpretation. In French and Italian, by contrast, the adverb in initial detached position is less likely to have a manner reading if it can be interpreted as a domain adverb.

(12) a. *Filosoficamente* la teoria non è interessante.
'Philosophically, the theory is not interesting.'
b. Vive *filosoficamente*.
'[S/he] lives philosophically.'

Besides their distribution between the main sentence constituents (as in the examples provided above), DAs can also occur within a clause constituent, typically a noun phrase. In this case, they occupy an integrated position, which can be either before or after an adjective, as shown respectively in (13) and (14). A DA can even occur before an adjective that is part of a manner adverbial expression, as shown in ex. (15).[7]

(13) Fr. Ce candidat a un programme *politiquement* intéressant.
'This candidate has a program [that is] politically interesting.'

(14) Fr. Ce candidat a un programme intéressant *politiquement*.
'This candidate has a program [that is] interesting politically.'

(15) Fr. Ce candidat recueille des informations de manière *politiquement* peu correcte.
'This candidate collects information in a politically questionable manner'

As far as their functional properties are concerned, few studies link the linear syntactic positions occupied by DAs to their information structural properties and discourse functions. From an information structural point of view, detached initial adverbs such as Fr. *politiquement* are generally described in opposition to their final integrated distribution. The main claim is that, while adverbs such as Fr. *politiquement* in (11) and It. *filosoficamente* in (12b) are rhematic, and constitute the focus of the sentence, they are non-rhematic and non-focal in (7) and (12a) (cf. Wandruszka 1982: 158; Nølke 1990). Instead, they function as *thematic operators* (Wandruszka 1982: 158) or as *frames* (Guimier 1996: 151).

A description of the functional properties of DAs in the other sentence positions is rarely provided. Nøjgaard (1993: 281), for instance, only describes position II, claiming it is parenthetical ("en parenthèse"), and thus hinting at a backgrounded status of the content of the DA. As a result, nothing specific is said about the functional properties distinguishing DAs in the different sentence slots they can occupy. Guimier 1996, for example, claims that the function of a DA in final detached position (*Cet exemple est intéressant, linguistiquement.* 'This example is

---

[7] For a discussion on the differences between DAs and manner adverbs, see, e.g., Guimier (1996: 144–145) as well as Molinier & Lévrier (2000: 219–221, 227–228).

interesting, linguistically') is the same as in detached initial position (*Linguistiquement, cet exemple est intéressant.* 'Linguistically, this example is interesting.'), but in the latter case it is to be interpreted as delayed. In his view, the adverb arrives later than expected as a repair mechanism on the part of the speaker ("il arrive tardivement pour réparer un oubli de la part du locuteur"; Guimier 1996: 142).

In sum, the description of the functional properties of DAs provided in non-formal accounts is rather sketchy. Moreover, there is a general lack of clarity concerning the definitions of the central concepts used to describe the functional properties of DAs, namely *theme, rheme, focus,* and *frame*. Given that these notions are notoriously problematic to define, we are left to wonder how they differ and should be interpreted (on the relation between DAs and Topics, see section 3.2.1).

2.3 Some considerations on the conceptualization of the class of DAs

In the literature on the Romance languages (but not exclusively, as we will clarify below as well), adverbs such as Fr. *politiquement*, It. *politicamente*, and Sp. *políticamente* are assigned to a wide array of classes, labeled in different ways. Table 1 presents an overview of these classes, overlooking the manner interpretation of these adverbs.

Table 1: Classes including adverbs such as *politically* in French, Italian and Spanish.

French: *adverbes de domaine* (Nølke 1990; Guimier 1996; van Raemdonck 1999; Hermoso Mellado-Damas 2015); *adverbes de point de vue* (Nølke 1990; van Raemdonck 1999; Gezundhajt 2000; Molinier & Lévrier 2000); *adverbes de cadre* (Schlyter 1977); *adverbes limitatifs* (Nøjgaard 1993, 414); *adverbes de limitation* and *adverbes de restriction* (Nilsson-Ehle 1941, 213)
Italian: *avverbi di dominio* (Lonzi 1991; Cinque 1998; Ricca 2010); *avverbi di punto di vista* (Lonzi 1991); *avverbi di inquadramento* (Zampese 1994, Ricca 2010)
Spanish: *adverbios de ámbito* (Burguera Serra & Vidal Díez 2013); *adverbios nocionales* (Kovacci 1999); *adverbios de topicalización* (Garcés Gómez 2003); *adverbios de marco o tópico* (Rodríguez Ramalle 2003), *adverbios de punto de vista* (Kovacci 1999; Porroche Ballesteros 2006); *adverbios limitativos* (Garcés Gómez 2003)

Clearly, these classes do not have the same extension. *Viewpoint adverbs* (Fr. *adverbes de point de vue* / It. *avverbi di punto di vista* / Sp. *adverbios de punto de vista*, calqued on the E. label *viewpoint* proposed in Quirk et al. 1985), for instance, subsume a broader set than *domain adverbs* (Fr. *adverbes de domaine* / It. *avverbi di dominio* / Sp. *adverbios de ámbito* or *nocionales*, possibly all based on the term *domain adverbs* used in Bellert 1977). The latter class includes forms expressing a 'notional domain' such as politics, law, and/or sports. The former class, in addition, comprises forms such as Fr. *personnellement* 'personally', as well as the adverbial expressions *de mon (ton/son) point de vue* 'from my (your/his/her) point of view' (i.e., their Romance counterparts), which express the subjective point of view of the speaker/writer (Beaulieu-Masson 2006: 79–80).

Broader than the class of domain adverbs are also the classes labeled with an expression referring to a *limiting, restricting* property of adverbs (see Fr. *adverbes limitatifs, de limitation, de restriction*) / Sp. *limitativos*, named after the German class *limitierende Adverbiale*, proposed in Bartsch 1972). These classes in fact incorporate sets of adverbials that are semantically quite heterogeneous. Besides domain adverbs such as Fr. *politiquement*, It. *politicamente*, and Sp. *políticamente*, they include adverbial expressions as diverse as Fr. *essentiellement* 'essentially', *globalement* 'globally', *intrinsèquement* 'intrinsically', *strictement* 'strictly' (see Nøjgaard 1993: 414) and It. *sotto questo profilo* 'under this profile', *in questo senso* 'in this sense', *in teoria* 'in theory', *in pratica* 'in practice', *in sostanza* 'overall', *in considerazione di* 'in consideration of', *in relazione a* 'in relation to'; *agli occhi di* 'in the eyes of', *nella nostra valutazione* 'in our evaluation'; *secondo + NP* 'according + NP'; *quanto a* 'as for', *a proposito di* 'as far as' (see Wandruszka 1982: 160).[8]

More interesting for the purpose of our study is the fact that the class labels listed in Table 1 highlight different linguistic and pragmatic properties of Fr. *politiquement*, It. *politicamente*, and Sp. *políticamente*. While the term *domain* refers to the meaning conveyed by these adverbs (for details, see section 2.1), other labels point to their functional properties. On the one hand, they are defined through the notion of *topic* and reference is made to a *topicalization* function (Sp. *adverbios de tópico* or *topicalización*). On the other hand, they are related to the notion of *frame* and associated to a *framing* function (Fr. *adverbes de cadre* or *cadrage*, used in Schlyter 1977 and Chircu 2008; It. *avverbi di inquadramento* and Sp. *adverbios de marco*). Following a proposal made in Schlyter 1977, several studies consider that the framing function can be performed by domain adverbs as well as other semantic subsets of adverbs and adverbials (see Table 2).

Table 2: Framing adverbs/adverbials (Guimier 1996: 141–154; van Raemdonck 1999: 105).

- domain (*légalement* 'legally'; *anatomiquement* 'anatomically')
- space and time (*ici* 'here', *hier* 'yesterday', *intérieurement* 'internally')
- habit (*normalement* 'usually')
- cause . . .

---

[8] All these expressions cannot be translated directly: the English counterparts we provide are thus to be interpreted primarily as working translations.

Again, two main notions are employed to define the functional properties of DAs and the classes to which they belong: *Topic* and *frame*. As we pointed out earlier in relation to the interface between the syntactic position and pragmatic properties of DAs (section 2.2), in most of the studies considered it is not clear how these notions are understood and, consequently, differ.

3 Towards a functional account of domain adverbs

In this section we describe the functional properties of DAs relying on a theoretical model of discourse known as the *Basel Model for paragraph segmentation* (Ferrari et al. 2008; Ferrari 2014). We start by defining the *Utterance*, corresponding to the main reference unit of written paragraphs (section 3.1). We then outline the functional spaces that DAs can occupy within an Utterance, clarifying what distinguishes our account from other proposals (section 3.2). In a third step, based on the conception of *Cadre* 'Frame' outlined in Charolles 1997, 2002, we describe in more detail the discourse functions DAs play when they occur in the *Frame Information Unit*, corresponding to the functional left periphery of the Utterance (section 3.3). Since our reference framework has been devised to describe written texts, the data we use is drawn from newspaper articles available on the Sketch Engine platform.[9] Again, for reasons of space, we only provide French examples.

3.1 Defining *Utterances* and their internal organization

The *Basel Model* (in short: BM) has been conceived to both describe and explain the organization of written textual units, mainly matching the size of a paragraph. In the BM, the most important functional unit of the paragraph is the *Utterance*. This unit performs two types of acts: a speech act (as defined by Austin 1962) and an act of textual composition, defined in relation to the previous and subsequent text (for more details, see Ferrari 2014: 25–26 and below). As shown in (16), written paragraphs typically include several Utterances (by convention, we segment the Utterances – abbreviated U1, U2, U3 etc. – composing a paragraph by using the double slash):

---

[9] We mainly used the data available in the Timestamped JSI web corpus 2020-10 French. For details on the Timestamped corpora, see www.sketchengine.eu/jozef-stefan-institute-newsfeed-corpus/

(16) // Il est nécessaire d'étudier l'évolution de l'environnement socio-économique du sport professionnel en général et du football en particulier pour comprendre à quoi est due la mauvaise réputation de l'agent de joueurs. //**U1** Aujourd'hui, la France est un marché atypique car nous manquons cruellement de pluralisme au niveau des médias sportifs, ce qui implique un manque d'investigation global sur un sujet complexe comme celui des relations entre clubs et agents. //**U2** [. . .] (https://blogs.mediapart.fr/)
// It is necessary to study the evolution of the socio-economic environment of professional sport in general and soccer in particular to understand the reasons for the bad reputation of the players' agent. //**U1** Today, France is an atypical market because we cruelly lack pluralism in sports media, which implies a lack of global investigation on a complex subject such as the relations between clubs and agents. //**U2** [. . .][10]

An Utterance can be broken down into smaller functional units, the nature of which depends on the layer of information structure (IS) considered. For the purpose of this study, we identify three main logically independent layers (see Table 3).

Table 3: Layers of information structure.

Layers of IS	Definition	Main functions/units
I. *Psycho-cognitive* layer (Prince 1981)	Layer structured according to the recoverability of the information in relation to the discourse, the context and/or the encyclopedic memory of the participants.	**Given—New** (De Cesare 2011)
II. *Aboutness*-layer (Lambrecht 1994)	Layer structured according to "what we talk about" (Topic) and "what we say about it" (Comment).	**Topic—Comment** (Reinhart 1981)
III. *Hierarchico-informational* layer (Ferrari et al. 2008; Ferrari 2014)	Layer structured according to the information that accomplishes a speech act and/or an act of textual composition (Nucleus) and the information that optionally accompanies it (Frame and Appendix).	**Frame—Nucleus-Appendix** (Ferrari 2014)

As is widely known, besides containing *given* and *new* information (see layer I in Table 3), an Utterance can generally also be broken down into a Topic and a Comment (as defined in layer II):

---

[10] The English translations of the examples provided in this section are revised versions of the suggestions provided by www.DeepL.com/Translator.

(17) // Aujourd'hui, la France[Aboutness Topic] est un marché atypique[Comment] [...]. //
// Today, France[Aboutness Topic] is an atypical market [Comment] [...]. //

In addition, an Utterance can be broken down into other smaller functional units (see layer III in Table 3), globally referred to in the BM as *Information Units* (Ferrari 2014: 37). The Information Units of the Utterance are the *Nucleus*, the *Frame* and the *Appendix*. These Information Units (in short: IUs) are hierarchically organized. The Nucleus (also called *nuclear Unit*) is the most important IU of the Utterance. It determines both the illocutionary force (i.e., speech act: assertive, interrogative, commissive etc.) and the textual function (i.e., act of textual composition: motivation, concession, illustration etc.) performed by the Utterance as a whole. In written texts, Utterances are mostly assertive. As a result of their illocutionary monotony, in written communication the main function of nuclear Units is defined in textual terms: their role is to ensure continuity and coherence between the Utterances forming larger textual units, such as the paragraph.

Let us illustrate the functional units conceived in the BM and, more specifically, the properties of the Nucleus based on ex. (18), where the nuclear content of each Utterance is highlighted in bold (in the annotation system adopted in the BM, IU boundaries are signaled by a single slash):

(18) // / Il est nécessaire d'étudier l'évolution de l'environnement socio-économique du sport professionnel en général et du football en particulier pour comprendre à quoi est due la mauvaise réputation de l'agent de joueurs /^{Nucleus}. //U1 Aujourd'hui, / **la France est un marché atypique car nous manquons cruellement de pluralisme au niveau des médias sportifs,** /^{Nucleus} ce qui implique un manque d'investigation global sur un sujet complexe comme celui des relations entre clubs et agents. //U2 [...] (https://blogs.mediapart.fr/)

The first Utterance of (18) only includes one IU, which is the Nucleus. Given its central role in defining the functional properties of an Utterance, the Nucleus is the only IU that must be present in all Utterances. We therefore also find it in Utterance 2. Both Nuclei determine that the Utterances to which they belong are assertive. Moreover, given that U2 provides a special case with respect to the content expressed in U1, we can consider that the logical relation between U1 and U2 is that of specification.

As can be observed, the second Utterance of (18) includes additional information (conveyed by the text not marked in bold), which plays a secondary role. Secondary information is realized in 'discourse spaces' that are hierarchically subordinated to the Nucleus. In the second Utterance of (18), we find two types of subordinated (or backgrounded) information. The first information, corresponding to the temporal adverb *aujourd'hui* 'today', is realized in a Frame IU, which necessarily precedes the Nucleus. The second information, *ce qui implique* [. . .] 'which implies [. . .]', is realized in an Appendix IU, the main function of which is to "complete *a posteriori* or *in medias res* the content of the IU [Nucleus, Frame or another Appendix] to which it is attached" (Ferrari 2014: 39). In the second Utterance of (18), the Appendix completes *a posteriori* the Nucleus. Utterance 2 in (18) thus includes three IUs: a Frame, the Nucleus, and an Appendix. This is shown in (19):

(19) // / Aujourd'hui, /[Frame] **la France est un marché atypique car nous manquons cruellement de pluralisme au niveau des médias sportifs,** / [Nucleus] ce qui implique un manque d'investigation global sur un sujet complexe comme celui des relations entre clubs et agents /[Appendix]. //U2 [. . .]

All IUs (Nucleus, Frame, Appendix) are recursive. This means that an Utterance can include two or more identical IUs. In (20), for instance, the Utterance is opened by two Frames:

(20) // / *Autrement dit*, /[Frame1] *politiquement*, /[Frame2] Navalny ne présente pas plus de danger que la mouche du coche /[Nucleus] . // (comite-valmy.org)
// / In other words, /[Frame1] politically, /[Frame2] Navalny is no more dangerous than a gadfly/[Nucleus] . //

3.2 The distribution of DAs in functional spaces

3.2.1 Preliminary remarks on the relation between DAs and Topics

In the literature on the Romance languages (but not exclusively), DAs such as Fr. *politiquement* are commonly associated to Topics (or Themes). As we mentioned earlier (in section 2.1), their meaning and function is captured through linguistic expressions such as the prepositional phrases *as far as N is concerned* and *as for N*, called *thematic markers*. Moreover, notably when they occur in detached initial position, these adverbs are claimed to function as *thematic operators* (section 2.2.). The widely held belief that DAs are associated to topicality is also reflected by the labels used to refer to adverbs such as *politically*: in several studies, they are called *adverbs of topic* or *topicalization* (see section 2.3).

To clarify the relation between adverbs such as Fr. *politiquement* and the concept of Topic/Theme, we must first recall how this notion is defined in different frameworks and disentangle a semantic, syntactic and discourse conception of Topic:[11]

1. *Aboutness Topic* (Reinhart 1981; Lambrecht 1994), defined within a semantic proposition as "What we talk about"; this notion of Topic is structurally related to the concept of *Comment*, defined as "What we say about the Topic". The *aboutness Topic* (and the related *Comment*) is an information structural notion (see layer II in Table 3).
2. *Structural Topic* (Cinque 1999; Rizzi & Bocci 2017), referring to the structural position of an *aboutness Topic*. The Topic, in the cartographic understanding of the notion, is located in the left periphery, i.e., in the functional portion of the clause situated at the interface between the propositional content and the articulation of discourse (Rizzi 1997: 283).
3. *Discourse Topic*, defined at the discourse level; in the framework known as *Question under discussion* (in short QuD), this notion corresponds to the general question that one can reconstruct based on a given sentence and/or the presence of a certain linguistic expression (see Krifka & Musan 2012).

The relation between an adverb such as *politically* (and its Romance counterparts) in initial detached position and the notion of Topic can be clarified based on the following example:

(21)   *Politically*, this issue is sensitive.
   1. Aboutness Topic: *this issue* (Comment: *is sensitive*)
   2. Structural Topic: *politically*
   3. Discourse Topic: *What do you think about this issue?* (Comment: *this issue is sensitive*). According to Grübl 2020, the function of the adverb *politically* is to break down the QuD and, specifically, to indicate that the Utterance (*this issue is sensitive*) only refers to a particular aspect of the QuD (namely politics).

As can be observed, a DA such as *politically* does not function as an *aboutness-Topic*: it does not correspond to what we talk about. As a logical conse-

---

[11] It is also worthwhile pointing out that the need to identify different types of Topics has been recognized very early in functionally oriented accounts (see, *inter alia*, Chafe 1976) and is an important contribution of cartographic syntax (see the three Topics proposed in Frascarelli & Hinterhölzl 2007: *aboutness Topic, contrastive Topic* and a *familiar Topic*). Moreover, there is a wide body of studies that reflect on the functional differences between Romance expressions working as *aboutness-Topics* and *frames* (defined syntactically or pragmatically), cf. Charolles 1997, 2002, Zampese (2005: 208–213), Beaulieu-Masson 2006 as well as Velghe & Lahousse 2015.

quence, from a syntactic point of view, it is also difficult to maintain that DAs occupy the structural position of Topic in the left periphery, a proposal that was made in earlier accounts on DAs (see Cinque 1998). In recent proposals based on cartographic syntax, DAs in ex. such as (21) are instead claimed to occur in a functional projection called *Frame setting* (see Maienborn 2001: 194; this view is shared by Grübl 2020) or *Scene* (Haumann 2007: 382).[12] Finally, a DA neither corresponds to the general discourse Topic. What it corresponds to, in the framework of the QuD model, is to a specific discourse-Topic, to be reconstructed based on the sentence hosting the DA (for details on this proposal, see again Grübl 2020).

In conclusion, given that DAs cannot be considered Topics at any level of analysis (semantics, syntax, and discourse), we need to refrain from associating them to this notion.

3.2.2 The functional spaces available to DAs in the Utterance

In what follows, we describe the distribution of adverbs such as Fr. *politiquement* (It. *politicamente* and Sp. *políticamente*) by considering the Utterance and paying attention to their occurrence in the Information Units defined in the layer called *hierarchico-informational* in the BM (see layer III in Table 3).

Adverbs such as Fr. *politiquement* (It. *politicamente* and Sp. *políticamente*) can occur in different functional spaces of the Utterance, i.e., the Frame, Nucleus and Appendix:

(22) // *Politiquement*, /^{Frame} il s'agit d'une position qui considère que l'égalité s'obtient par l'abstraction des différences et des conditions [. . .] /^{Nucleus}. //
(www.contretemps.eu)
// Politically, /^{Frame} it is a stance that sees equality as being achieved by abstracting differences and conditions [. . .] /^{Nucleus}. //

(23) // / Toute ma vie, /^{Frame} j'ai été engagée *politiquement* /^{Nucleus}. //
(journaldequebec.com)
// / All my life, /^{Frame} I have been politically involved /^{Nucleus}. //

---

[12] In cartographic syntax, the position of DAs is still object of discussion. The same holds true for the position hosting linguistic expressions associated to topicality and/or, more generally, prominence. Rizzi (2004: 239, 242) proposes a position called *Modifier*.

(24)   // C'est un moment fondamental, /^Nucleus *politiquement* /^Appendix . // (lepoint.fr)
       // It's a crucial moment, /^Nucleus politically /^Appendix . //

Their interpretation as domain adverbs is clear in ex. such as (22), where *politiquement* is realized in the Frame IU, which necessarily precedes the Nucleus (also see ex. 20, where the DA is in the second Frame of the Utterance). The same interpretation is favored in (24), as well as (25), where *politiquement* occurs in an Appendix IU. In (24), the adverb is in an Appendix that follows the Nucleus, and in (25) in one that interrupts it.

(25)   // / Cette infection tombe donc, /^Nucleus- *politiquement*, /^Appendix au pire des moments pour le républicain /^-Nucleus . //(rtl.fr)
       // / This infection thus comes, /^Nucleus- politically, /^Appendix at the worst of times for the republican/^-Nucleus . //

By contrast, when the adverb occurs in the Nucleus, in particular at the end of it, its most natural interpretation is as manner adverb. The difference between the distribution of an adverb in the Frame and at the end of the Nucleus is very transparent in the pair of examples (12a) and (12b), repeated below for the sake of clarity:

(26)   a.   // / *Filosoficamente* /^Frame la teoria non è interessante /^Nucleus //.
            'Philosophically, the theory is not interesting.'
       b.   // / Vive *filosoficamente* /^Nucleus //. (ex. from Grossmann 1999: 414)
            '[S/he] lives philosophically.'

There are important functional differences between a DA realized in the Frame (22/26a), the Nucleus (23/26b) and in an Appendix IU (24, 25). From an information structural point of view, a DA in the Nucleus is foregrounded information, while it is backgrounded in both the Frame and the Appendix. In fact, in (23) and (26b), given that it occurs at the end of the Nucleus, the adverb coincides with the Focus of the nuclear IU and conveys the most important information of the whole Utterance (for a definition of *Focus* within the BM, see Ferrari et al. 2008: 95–99).

There are also important differences between a DA occurring in a Frame and in an Appendix IU (for details on the different natures of these Units, cf. Ferrari 2014: 46–50). While in both cases the DA conveys a content that is backgrounded in the Utterance, a DA in the Appendix has a lower degree of prominence and is strongly restricted in terms of its scoping properties. The domain expressed by a DA in Appendix is only valid for the content of the IU to which it is attached. This is true for ex. 25, as well as (27):

(27) Je résume ma candidature comme ça: J'ai voté pour rien pendant longtemps. Les autres en tout cas ont fait comme moi, ils ont voté pour rien. // / Aujourd'hui, /^Frame on va voter pour quelqu'un qui, /^Nucleus- politiquement, /^Appendix n'est rien /^-Nucleus // . Ils nous prennent pour des imbéciles, votons pour un imbécile. (www.franceculture.fr)
'I summarize my candidacy like this: I voted for nothing for a long time. The others, in any case, did the same as me, they voted for nothing. Today, we are going to vote for someone who, politically, is nothing. They take us for fools, let's vote for a fool.'

The scope of a DA in Appendix is local, which has important implications on its functions: a DA in Appendix can only be used to specify a content in its immediate vicinity, occurring in the same Utterance. By contrast, as we will show in more detail in section 3.3, an important feature of the Frame IU is discourse permanence.

3.3 DAs in the Frame

While it might not be their most typical distribution, at least in written (journalistic) texts (see section 2.2), it is when DAs occur in the Frame IU of the Utterance that they show the most interesting textual functions. In this section, we thus provide a detailed account of the properties of DAs in the functional left periphery of the Utterance. After a more detailed definition of the Frame IU (section 3.3.1), we show that, besides their core function, consisting of specifying a semantic domain valid for interpreting the content of the Utterance in which they occur, DAs can have a segmenting and indexing functions. These functions depend first and foremost on the scoping properties of the Frame in which DAs are realized, i.e., whether they occur in a Frame having discourse-scope over multiple Utterances (section 3.3.2) or local scope over one Utterance (section 3.3.3).

3.3.1 General definition of Frame

The Frame is an optional, recursive functional Information Unit, which linearly precedes the main IU of the Utterance, the Nucleus (see sections 3.1 and 3.2.2.). From a linguistic point of view, the Frame IU does not have a predefined format. As a result, it can host a variety of linguistic expressions, including temporal adverbs such as *aujourd'hui* 'today' (see ex. 18), reformulative expressions such as *autrement dit* 'in other words' (ex. 20), or DAs such as *politiquement* 'politically' (ex. 20 and 22). From a semantic point of view, the Frame IU is defined as follows (for details, cf. Ferrari et al. 2008: 99–105 and Zampese 2005):

> The **Frame**[13] provides the framework for the Nucleus by offering denotative content, propositional attitude content or procedural content (e.g., connectors). By means of these types of content, the Frame supplies the semantic co-ordinates for a vericonditional interpretation of the Nucleus and/or specifies the illocutionary or textual (logic, thematic, polyphonic) *raison d'être* of the Nucleus. (Ferrari 2014: 38)

As is clear from this definition, the Frame IU plays an important role in relation to the nuclear Unit of the Utterance as it specifies the "framework for the Nucleus". Besides non-denotational (procedural) contents, expressed, e.g., by connectors (Fr. *donc, par conséquent* 'consequently' etc.), the Frame IU hosts the denotational domain that is pertinent to interpret the Nucleus (Ferrari et al. 2008: 46). In the framework of the BM, the "domain of pertinence" is to be understood broadly, as it includes the spatio-temporal coordinates to interpret the Nucleus (cf. again the content of the first Frame in ex. 20), but also the semantic domain expressed by DAs.

The definition provided above highlights the important role played by the Frame IU for the interpretation of the Nucleus and thus for the local understanding of the Utterance. However, as mentioned earlier, one important property of the Frame is discourse permanence (Zampese 2005: 173; Ferrari 2014: 48). This means that, as far as the scoping properties of this UI are concerned, a Frame has by default *textual* (i.e., wide, discourse) scope. It opens a "textual space" that is valid to interpret more than one Utterance (Charolles 1997[14]) and "remains active until the locutor decides to deactivate it" (Ferrari 2014: 48). The difference between a Frame with textual (i.e., multiple Utterances) scope and a Frame with Utterance scope is exemplified in ex. (28) and (29), respectively:

(28) // / *Aujourd'hui* /^{Frame} elle doit sortir /^{Nucleus}. // / Il fait beau /^{Nucleus}. //
// / Today /^{Frame} she must go out /^{Nucleus}. // / The weather is nice /^{Nucleus}. //

(29) // *Aujourd'hui* /^{Frame} elle doit sortir /^{Nucleus}. // / Demain, /^{Frame} on verra / ^{Nucleus}. //
// Today /^{Frame} she must go out /^{Nucleus}. // / Tomorrow, /^{Frame} we will see /^{Nucleus}. //

---

[13] The concept of *Frame* used in the BM is inspired by the notion of *Cadre* as defined in Charolles 1997 (see Ferrari 2014: 38). However, as we will see in section 3.3.3, Charolles 1997's conception of the Frame is more restricted than the one adopted in the BM.

[14] Note that Charolles (1997: 15) refers to propositions (i.e., syntactico-semantic units) rather than Utterances.

3.3.2 DAs in a Frame IU with textual scope

When DAs occur in a Frame IU, they generally have textual scope, extending their meaning over multiple Utterances. Given their meaning component (section 2.1), the core function of framed DAs with textual scope is to express a semantic domain valid for interpreting the nuclear content of the Utterance hosting the DA and, additionally, the nuclear content of at least one more adjacent Utterance. In ex. (30), for instance, the domain expressed by *politiquement* in the Frame of the third Utterance constrains the interpretation of the nuclear content of the Utterance hosting the DA (*les débats sont tout aussi vifs* 'the debates are just as lively'), as well as the Nucleus of the following Utterance (*Les islamistes et l'opposition ont trouvé le coupable* 'Islamists and the opposition have found the culprit').

(30) // Dans les mêmes colonnes un autre spécialiste objecte: //**U1** " Sur le plan scientifique, l'effet psychologique consécutif à la prise d'une substance est prépondérant si la personne croit en ses réelles capacités ". //**U2** / *Politiquement*, /^{Frame} les débats sont tout aussi vifs /^{Nucleus} . //**U3** / Les islamistes et l'opposition ont trouvé le coupable ... /^{Nucleus} //**U4** (Paris Match 01/08/96 ; ex. cited in Charolles 1997: 28)
// In the same columns, another specialist objects: //**U1** "On a scientific level, the psychological effect following the intake of a substance is preponderant if the person believes in his or her real abilities". //**U2** / Politically, /^{Frame} the debates are just as lively. /^{Nucleus} //**U3** / Islamists and the opposition have found the culprit ... /^{Nucleus} //

When the DA is in a Frame IU having multiple Utterances scope, it also serves important textual functions. One of them is the segmenting function. As can be observed again based on (30), the framed DA carves out from the paragraph in which it occurs a smaller portion of text, comprising U3 and U4. Framed DAs with scope over multiple Utterances, by definition, also have an indexing, or classificatory function (this function, associated with a wide array of linguistic expressions, is outlined in Charolles 1997: 31–32). The Utterances indexed by the DA form a semantically homogeneous discourse unit, called *block* by Charolles 1997 and *Textual Movement* in the BM (see Ferrari 2014: 26). The indexing (classificatory) function of DAs is also present in ex. such as (31), where the domain expressed by Fr. *politiquement* in the Frame of the first Utterance is valid for interpreting the whole text block:

(31) // / *Politiquement,* /^Frame lors des dernières élections municipales, / la présence de Vincent Mirande dans l'entourage du candidat Thierry Nadal n'est pas passée inaperçue /^Nucleus . //**U1** Notamment auprès du maire d'Agde, Gilles D'Ettore, qui avait fustigé ce supposé mélange des genres, dont l'intéressé se défend. //**U2** "J'assume tout, dit-il. //**U3** D'autant que les colonnes de L'Agathois sont restées ouvertes à tout le monde pendant la campagne. //**U4** J'ai publié les articles de Thierry Nadal, mais aussi de Jean-Louis Cousin, Bertrand de Pontual et Thierry Gaubert. //**U5** J'avais aussi contacté la mairie d'Agde, mais ils n'ont pas souhaité communiquer dans le journal." //**U6** (midilibre.fr, 1.10.2020)

// / Politically, /^Frame during the last municipal elections, / the presence of Vincent Mirande in the entourage of candidate Thierry Nadal did not go unnoticed ^Nucleus . //**U1** Notably with the mayor of Agde, Gilles D'Ettore, / who had castigated this supposed mixture of genres, which the interested party defends itself. //**U2** "I assume everything, he says. //**U3** Especially since the columns of L'Agathois remained open to everyone during the campaign. //**U4** I published articles by Thierry Nadal, but also by Jean-Louis Cousin, Bertrand de Pontual and Thierry Gaubert. //**U5** I had also contacted the town hall of Agde, but they did not wish to communicate in the newspaper". //**U6**

Indexes such as Fr. *politiquement* in (30) and (31) occur in a special type of Frame, called *Discourse Frame* (Fr. *Cadre du discours*, or simply *Cadre* 'Frame', in Charolles 1997: 27, 33). A Discourse Frame is defined by two properties, related to its scope and directionality:

a) It has *textual scoping properties*, extending beyond the Utterance hosting the Frame.
b) It is *forward-looking*, extending its meaning to the text to follow.

In line with Charolles 1997, we consider that when a DA occurs in a Discourse Frame, as does Fr. *politiquement* in (30) and (31), it indexes a special semantic domain referred to as *Discourse Universe* (Fr. *univers du discours* by Charolles 1997: 28), which is defined as follows:

> Discourse universes group together propositions [in our view: Utterances] that behave in the same way with respect to certain criteria that restrict their scope of validity. These criteria can sometimes specify not, strictly speaking, circumstances but rather sectors of activity, areas of knowledge in which certain assertions are verified.
> (Charolles 1997: 28; our translation)

Discourse Universes must be distinguished from other possible indexes, in particular *thematic fields* (Fr. *champs thématiques*; Charolles 1997: 26), occurring in Discourse Frames hosting linguistic expressions such as Fr. *en ce qui concerne NP / concernant NP* 'concerning NP', *pour ce qui est de NP* 'as for NP', *à propos de NP* 'with regards to NP'. In (32), the text block is opened by the thematic field *en ce qui concerne la politique* 'as far as politics is concerned':

(32) // / « *En ce qui concerne la politique* », /^{Frame} explique T-Dubb-O, / « ça va se jouer selon une des deux issues possibles /^{Nucleus} . //**U1** Actuellement on a une opportunité qui se referme très rapidement, où nous pouvons soit recréer nous-mêmes un système qui soit réellement juste pour tous les gens, ou bien ils vont recréer un système dans lequel on sera plus jamais capables de les faire trembler comme on l'a fait à Ferguson. » //**U2** (eburnienews.net)
// / "As far as politics is concerned," /^{Frame} explains T-Dubb-O, "it's going to come down to one of two possible outcomes /^{Nucleus} . //**U1** Right now we have an opportunity that is closing very quickly, where we can either recreate ourselves a system that is really fair to all people, or they're going to recreate a system where we're never going to be able to shake them down like we did in Ferguson." //**U2**

3.3.3 DAs in a Frame IU with Utterance scope

Framed DAs, as we have seen, have textual scope by default. However, in special conditions, they can also have local scope, extending their meaning only to the nuclear Unit of the Utterance. Framed DAs have Utterance scope for instance in textual configurations such as (33), where they occur in the Frame Unit of the last Utterance of the paragraph or even, as is the case in (34), in the whole text. Given this special textual configuration, it is obvious why the framed DAs (in 33, *économiquement et politiquement* 'economically and politically') only have local scope over the Nucleus of the Utterance in which they occur (*ce n'est jamais bon* 'it's never good'). In discourse contexts such as (33), the function of the framed DAs is its most basic: it consists of identifying a semantic domain valid for interpreting the content of the Nucleus.

(33) Constatant son échec, Bruno Le Maire a annoncé se désengager du dossier Veolia-Suez. C'est sa deuxième erreur. Elle est classique chez les responsables politiques qui réagissent trop souvent à chaud, y compris sur des sujets d'une immense complexité. Si l'État ne veut pas être un actionnaire qui se contente d'éponger les pertes et de percevoir des dividendes, il est indispensable qu'il ait une stratégie globale en matière d'investissements et de gestion de ses actifs. Ce n'est pas le cas aujourd'hui. Tant que les pouvoirs publics n'auront pas une vision d'ensemble à moyen et long terme, ils ne pourront que réagir au gré du vent et des circonstances. // / *Économiquement et politiquement,* /[Frame] ce n'est jamais bon /[Nucleus]. // (www.lalsace.fr, 7.10.2020)

Noting its failure, Bruno Le Maire announced his withdrawal from the Veolia-Suez project. This is his second mistake. It is a classic mistake by politicians who too often react too quickly, even on subjects of immense complexity. If the State does not want to be a shareholder that simply absorbs losses and receives dividends, it is essential that it has a global strategy for investing and managing its assets. This is not the case today. As long as the public authorities do not have an overall vision for the medium and long term, they will only be able to react to the wind and circumstances. // / Economically and politically, /[Frame] this is never good /[Nucleus]. //

Framed DAs have Utterance scope also in textual configurations such as (34), where a different DA opens two consecutive Utterances (U2 is opened by *politiquement*, U3 by *scientifiquement*; a similar case is in ex. 30). In cases like these, the first DA opens a Frame that is immediately closed by the one occurring in the next Utterance.

(34) // L'enjeu est alors de montrer comment le fait d'échapper à l'expérience des assignations racialisantes parce qu'on est blanc·he·s se traduit en même temps par une posture qui est politique et scientifique. //**U1** / *Politiquement,* /[Frame] il s'agit d'une position qui considère que l'égalité s'obtient par l'abstraction des différences et des conditions /[Nucleus] – alors que cela sert surtout à taire les revendications des minoritaires, tout en les particularisant pour les disqualifier. //**U2** / *Scientifiquement,* /[Frame] cette attitude se traduit par le fait d'ignorer délibérément ce que les travaux issus des expériences minoritaires apportent sur le plan du contenu des savoirs comme sur la manière même de concevoir leur validité /[Nucleus]. //**U3** (Timestamped JSI web corpus 2020)

// The challenge is then to show how escaping from the experience of racializing assignments because one is white translates at the same time into a posture that is both political and scientific. //**U1** / *Politically*, /^Frame it is a stance that sees equality as being achieved by abstracting differences and conditions /^Nucleus – whereas this serves primarily to silence the claims of minorities, while at the same time particularizing them in order to disqualify them. //**U2** / *Scientifically*, /^Frame this attitude translates into deliberately ignoring what the work resulting from minority experiences contributes in terms of both the content of knowledge and the very way of conceiving its validity /^Nucleus //**U3** .

Following Charolle's 1997/2002 conception of Frame, consecutive framed DAs with Utterance scope, as in (34), have two functions. Besides the core function of framed DAs, consisting of identifying a semantic domain valid for interpreting the content of the nuclear Unit, they have a segmenting function, consisting in partitioning the text in which they occur in smaller information chunks (in this case, corresponding to single Utterances). Given their local scope over single Utterances, these DAs do not work as indexes.

4 Conclusions

Based on the theoretical framework known as *Basel Model*, devised to model written texts (Ferrari et al. 2008; Ferrari 2014), we offered a functional account of adverbs such as Fr. *politiquement*, It. *politicamente*, and Sp. *políticamente*, paying special attention to their interpretation as *domain adverbs*. While the Basel model allows proposing a detailed picture of the functional discourse spaces that DAs occupy in the Utterance (Frame and Appendix), Charolles' 1997 discourse-oriented notion of *Frame* allows highlighting the main functions of these adverbs when they occur in the "functional left periphery of the Utterance". An overview of our account is in Table 4 below.

We believe that the approach and methodology chosen in this contribution, which differs from other proposals (such as the one adopted by Grübl 2020), present several descriptive and theoretical advantages. From a descriptive point of view, our account is based on the observation of stretches of discourses extending beyond the Utterance hosting the DA, which allows paying close attention to the discourse context in which DAs occur and in which they have also been originally produced. Highlighting their framing, segmenting, and indexing functions might have proven more difficult, if not impossible, had we chosen the *Question*

Table 4: Preferred interpretation, scope, and discourse functions of adverbs such as *politically* in the functional spaces of the Utterance.

	Frame (Background)	Nucleus (Foreground)	Appendix (Background)
Interpretation	Domain	Manner	Domain
Scope	I. Textual scope (= Discourse Frame) II. Utterance scope (= Utterance Frame)		Information Unit: scope over the IU to which the Appendix is attached (Nucleus, Frame or another Appendix)
Functions	I. Discourse Frame: – identification of a semantic domain valid for interpreting multiple Utterances – segmenting – indexing II. Utterance Frame – identification of a semantic domain valid for interpreting the Utterance – segmenting	Focus (when occurring at the end of the Nucleus)	Identification of a semantic domain valid for interpreting the IU to which the Appendix is attached

under discussion/QuD framework, based on the reconstruction of general implicit questions.

From a theoretical point of view, our study leads to important notional distinctions. First, we show that DAs cannot be understood as Topics at any given level of analysis (semantics, syntax, and pragmatics). Secondly, we clarify the differences between the information structural notions of *Topic* and *Frame*, the boundaries of which are often fuzzy in the literature on DAs. In our understanding, *Topic* is to be defined in terms of *aboutness* (as "what we talk about", following Lambrecht 1994), while *Frame* is defined at a logically distinct level of information structure (called *hierarchico-informational* in our theoretical reference model). When it is present, the *Frame* is the starting point of the Utterance, providing denotational or instructional content to interpret the main part of the Utterance, i.e., the Nucleus. Since *Frames* and *Topics* belong to two logically distinct layers of information structure, they can overlap, giving rise to *Framed Topics* (a concept that differs from the structural notion of *Frame Topic*, to which we refer again below). Framed Topics are Frames hosting *bona fide* aboutness Topics (*Lui vuole andare in Francia. / Lei, /*Frame *invece, preferisce l'Italia.* 'He wants to go to France. / She, /Frame by contrast, prefers Italy.'), but also adverbial expressions in initial detached position (see ex. 32) like *as far as N is concerned* and *as for N* (called *thematic fields* by Charolles 1997). Finally, considering their scoping properties, we highlighted the necessity to distinguish two types of *Frames*: a *Discourse Frame* and an *Utterance Frame*, the second one occurring in special textual configurations.

Given that the focus of our study primarily lies on the functional properties of DAs, we resorted to a discourse model rather than a syntactically oriented one. This explains why we consider the left periphery of the Utterance, rather than the clause, and assign DAs to a discourse space (the *Frame*), rather than a syntactic position (referred to – *inter alia* – as *Topic*, *Scene*, *Frame setter* or *Frame Topic*; the latter label is used in Grübl 2020). Theoretically, the main space hosting DAs in the functional left periphery of the Utterance is defined first and foremost based on its role in the discourse, considering its scope with respect to the rest of the text; in formal syntax, the position occupied by DAs in the left periphery is defined, instead, mainly by considering the syntactic properties of other adverbs and adverbials.

All in all, simplifying the issue to some degree, we can say that while our study focused on the second component of the 'syntax-pragmatics' interface, syntactic accounts tend to devote more attention to the first component. In our view, both accounts are equally needed, as they complement each other and allow achieving a comprehensive understanding of the properties of adverbs in general and DAs in particular.

References

Austin, John Langshaw. 1962. *How to Do Things with Words*. Oxford: Oxford University Press.
Bartsch, Renate. 1972. *Adverbialsemantik. Die Konstitution logisch-semantischer Repräsentationen von Adverbialkonstruktionen*. Frankfurt: Athenäum.
Beaulieu-Masson, Anne. 2006. Cadres et points de vue dans le discours journalistique. *Travaux neuchâtelois de linguistique* 44. 77–89.
Bellert, Irena. 1977. On semantic and distributional properties of sentential adverbs. *Linguistic Inquiry* 8(2). 337–351.
Borreguero Zuloaga, Margarita. 2014. Left periphery in discourse: Frame Unit and discourse markers. Andreas Dufter & Álvaro Octavio de Toledo (eds.), *Left Sentence Peripheries in Spanish: Diachronic, Variationist and Comparative Perspectives*, 345–382. Amsterdam: John Benjamins.
Burguera Serra, Joan G. & Mónica Vidal Díez. 2013. Usos y valores de los adverbios de ámbito en español. In María Pilar Garcés (ed.), *Los adverbios con función discursiva. Procesos de formación y evolución*, 43–64. Madrid/Frankfurt: Iberoamericana/Vervuert.
Chafe, William. 1976. Givenness, contrastiveness, definiteness, Subjects, topics and point of view. In Charles N. Li (ed.), *Subject and Topic*, 27–55. London/New York: Academic Press.

Charolles, Michel. 1997. L'encadrement du discours. Univers, champs, domaines et espaces. *Cahier de Recherche Linguistique* 6. 1–73.

Charolles, Michel. 2002. Les adverbiaux cadratifs et leur fonctionnement textuel. Unpublished. Archived URL: https://web.archive.org/web/20051217073614/http://www.lattice.cnrs.fr/article.php3?id_article=164 (18.11.2021)

Chircu, Adrian. 2008. *L'adverbe dans les langues romanes. Études étymologique, lexicale et morphologique: français, roumain, italien, espagnol, portugais, catalan, provençal*. Cluj Napoca: Casa Cărţii de Ştiinţă.

Cinque, Guglielmo. 1998. L'ordine relativo degli avverbi di frase in italiano (e in altre lingue). In Giuliano Bernini, Pierluigi Cuzzolin & Piera Molinelli (eds.), *Ars linguistica. Studi offerti da colleghi ed allievi a Paolo Ramat in occasione del suo 60° compleanno*, 141–149. Roma: Bulzoni.

Cinque, Guglielmo. 1999. *Adverbs and Functional Heads: A Cross-Linguistic Perspective*. New York: Oxford University Press.

De Cesare, Anna-Maria. 2011. Dato-Nuovo, Struttura. In Raffaele Simone (ed.), *Enciclopedia dell'italiano*, 338–343. Roma: Treccani.

De Cesare, Anna-Maria. 2016. Per una tipologia semantico-funzionale degli avverbiali. Uno studio basato sulla distribuzione informativa degli avverbi (in -*mente*) negli enunciati dell'italiano parlato. *Linguistica e Filologia* 36. 27–68.

De Cesare, Anna-Maria. 2018. Italian sentence adverbs in the left periphery: Modeling their functional properties in online daily newspapers. In Margarita Borreguero Zuloaga, Vahram Atayan & Sybille Grosse (eds.), 96–120. *Models of Discourse Units in Romance Languages* [special issue] *Revue Romane* 53 (1).

De Cesare, Anna-Maria & Margarita Borreguero Zuloaga. 2014. The contribution of the Basel Model to the description of polyfunctional discourse markers. The case of It. *anche*, Fr. *aussi* and Sp. *tambièn*. In Salvador Pons Bordería (ed.), *Discourse Segmentation in Romance Languages*, 55–94. Amsterdam-Philadelphia: John Benjamins.

De Cesare, Anna-Maria, Ana Albom, Doriana Cimmino & Marta Lupica Spagnolo. 2020. Domain adverbials in the news. A corpus-based contrastive perspective on English, German, French, Italian and Spanish. *Languages in Contrast* 20(1). 31–57.

Ferrari, Angela. 2014. The Basel Model for paragraph segmentation: the construction units, their relationships and linguistic indication. In Salvador Pons Bordería (ed.), *Discourse Segmentation in Romance Languages*, 23–54. Amsterdam, John Benjamins.

Ferrari, Angela, Luca Cignetti, Anna-Maria De Cesare, Letizia Lala, Magda Mandelli, Claudia Ricci & Carlo Enrico Roggia. 2008. *L'interfaccia lingua-testo. Natura e funzioni dell'articolazione informativa dell'enunciato*. Alessandria: Edizioni dell'Orso.

Frascarelli, Mara & Roland Hinterhölzl. 2007. Types of Topics in German and Italian. In Susanne Winkler & Kerstin Schwabe (eds.), *On Information Structure, Meaning and Form*, 87–116. Amsterdam: Benjamins.

Garcéz Gómez, María Pilar. 2003. Adverbios de topicalización y marcadores de topicalización. *Romanistisches Jahrbuch* 53. 355–382.

Gezundhajt, Henriette. 2000. *Adverbes en -ment et opérations énonciatives*. Bern etc.: Lang.

Grossmann, Maria. 1999. Gli aggettivi denominali come basi di derivazione in italiano. In Paola Benincà, Alberto A. Mioni & Laura Vanelli (eds.), *Fonologia e morfologia dell'italiano e dei dialetti d'Italia*. Atti del XXXI Congresso internazionale della Società di linguistica italiana (Padova, 25-27.9.1997), 401–422. Roma: Bulzoni.

Grübl, Klaus. 2018. On the rise of domain adverbials in Italian: the history of the *-mente parlando* construction. In Anna-Maria De Cesare, Ana Albom, Doriana Cimmino & Marta Lupica Spagnolo (eds.), *Formal and Functional Perspectives on Sentence Adverbials in the Romance Languages and Beyond* [Special issue] *Linguistik Online* 92(5). 65–86. https://bop.unibe.ch/linguistik-online/article/view/4505 (18.11.2021)

Grübl, Klaus. 2020. What are 'domain adverbs' and what functions do they have? Paper presented in the online Conference "Adverbs and Adverbials: Categorial Issues", org. by Olivier Duplâtre and Pierre-Yves Modicom, 2.10.2020.

Guimier, Claude. 1996. *Les adverbes du français, le cas des adverbes en* -ment. Paris: Ophrys.

Haumann, Dagmar. 2007. *Adverb Licensing and Clause Structure in English*. Amsterdam-Philadephia: Benjamins.

Hermoso Mellado-Damas, Adelaida. 2015. Les adverbes de domaine et l'expression de la modalité assertive. *Anales de Filología Francesa* 23. 109–123.

Klump, Andre. 2007. Zur Funktion und Verwendung der gemeinromanischen Adverbialbestimmung vom Typ *économiquement parlant* am Beispiel des Französischen und Spanischen. *Zeitschrift für Romanische Philologie* 123(2). 204–212.

Kovacci, Ofelia. 1999. El adverbio. In Ignacio Bosque & Violeta Demonte (eds.), *Gramática descriptiva de la lengua española*, vol. I, 705–786. Madrid: Espasa.

Krifka, Manfred & Renate Musan. 2012. Information structure: Overview and linguistic issues. In Manfred Krifka & Renate Musan (eds.), *The Expression of Information Structure*, 1–43. Berlin-Boston: De Gruyter.

Lambrecht, Knud. 1994. *Information Structure and Sentence Form. Topic, Focus and the Mental Representations of Discourse Referents*. Cambridge: Cambridge University Press.

Lonzi, Lidia. 1991. Il sintagma avverbiale. In Lorenzo Renzi & Giampaolo Salvi (eds.), *Grande grammatica italiana di consultazione*. Vol. 2, 341–412. Bologna: il Mulino.

Lupica Spagnolo, Marta. 2021. *Politically (speaking)*: Form, position, and function of domain adverbials in Italian and German. *Vox Romanica* 80. 133–173.

Maienborn, Claudia. 2001. On the position and interpretation of locative modifiers. *Natural Language Semantics* 9. 191–240.

Molinier, Christian. 1984. Remarques sur les adverbes de point de vue. *Cahiers de grammaire* 7. 55–75.

Molinier, Christian & Françoise Lévrier. 2000. *Grammaire des adverbes. Description des formes en* -ment. Genève-Paris: Droz.

Mørdrup, Ole. 1976. *Une analyse non-transformationelle des adverbes en* -ment. Copenhagen: Akademisk Forlag.

Nilsson-Ehle, Hans. 1941. *Les adverbes en* -ment *compléments d'un verbe en français moderne*. Munksgaard: Copenhague.

Nøjgaard, Morten. 1993. *Les adverbes français. Essai de description fonctionnelle*. 3 vols. Historisk-filosofiske Meddelelser 66: 2. Copenhagen: Munksgaard.

Nølke, Henning. 1990. Les adverbes contextuels: problèmes de classification. *Langue française* 88. 12–27.

Nølke, Henning. 1993. *Le regard du locuteur*. Paris: Kimé.

Porroche Ballesteros, Margarita. 2006. Sobre los adverbios enunciativos españoles: caracterización, clasificación y funciones pragmáticas y discursivas fundamentales. *Revista Española de Lingüística* 35(2). 495–522.

Prince, Ellen F. 1981. Toward a taxonomy of given-new information. In Peter Cole (ed.), *Radical Pragmatics*, 223–255. New York: Academic Press.

Quirk, Randolph, Sidney Greenbaum, Geoffrey Leech & Jan Svartvik. 1985 [1972]. *A Comprehensive Grammar of the English Language*. London: Longman.
Ramat, Paolo & Davide Ricca. 1998. Sentence adverbs in the languages of Europe. In Johan van der Auwera & Dónall P. Ó Baoill (eds.), *Adverbial Constructions in the Languages of Europe*, 187–275. Berlin-New York: De Gruyter.
Reinhart, Tanya. 1981. Pragmatics and linguistics. An analysis of sentence topics. *Philosophica* 27: 53–94.
Ricca, Davide. 2004. Derivazione avverbiale. In Maria Grossmann & Franz Rainer (eds.), *La formazione delle parole in italiano*, 472–489. Tübingen: Niemeyer.
Ricca, Davide. 2010. Il sintagma avverbiale. In Giampaolo Salvi & Lorenzo Renzi (eds.), *Grammatica dell'italiano antico*, 715–754. Bologna: il Mulino.
Rizzi, Luigi. 1997. The fine structure of the left periphery. In Liliane Haegeman (ed.), *Elements of Grammar*. 281–337. Dordrecht: Kluwer.
Rizzi, Luigi. 2004. Locality and the left periphery. In Adriana Belletti (ed.), *Structures and Beyond. The Cartography of Syntactic Structures*. Vol. 3, 104–131. Oxford: Oxford University Press.
Rizzi, Luigi & Giuliano Bocci. 2017. Left periphery of the clause: Primarily illustrated for Italian. In Martin Everaert & Henk C. van Riemsdijk (eds.), *The Wiley Blackwell Companion to Syntax*. 2nd edn. Wiley Online-Library. https://onlinelibrary.wiley.com/doi/full/10.1002/9781118358733.wbsyncom104 (18.11.2021)
Rodríguez Ramalle, Teresa María. 2003. *Gramática de los adverbios en -mente: cómo expresar maneras, opiniones y actitudes a través de la lengua*. Madrid: UAM Ediciones.
Rodríguez Ramalle, Teresa María. 2009. Sobre la estructura discursiva de la oración y su proyección sintáctica: el caso de los adverbios oracionales y otros constituyentes de la periferia oracional. ELUA. *Estudios de Lingüística* 23. 265–288.
Scalise, Sergio, Federica Bevilacqua, Andrea Buoso & Giovanna Piantini. 1990. Il suffisso -mente. *Studi Italiani di Linguistica Teorica ed Applicata* 19(1). 61–88.
Schlyter, Suzanne. 1977. *La place des adverbes en -ment en français*. Konstanz: Universität Konstanz Dissertation.
van Raemdonck, Dan. 1999. L'adverbe de domaine-point de vue est-il un adverbe de phrase? *Orbis Linguarum* 11. 101–112.
Velghe, Tom & Karen Lahousse. 2015. Thematic markers in informal written French: *Pour ce qui est de*, *au niveau (de)* and *en matière de*. *Journal of French Language Studies* 25(3). 423–444. doi:10.1017/S0959269514000283
Wandruszka, Ulrich. 1982. *Studien zur italienischen Wortstellung: Worstellung – Semantik – Informationsstruktur*. Tübingen: Narr.
Werner, Martina & Nina C. Rastinger. In this vol. Domain adverbials and morphology: The rivalry between -*mäßig* and -*technisch* in German. In Olivier Duplâtre & Pierre-Yves Modicom (eds.), Adverbs and Adverbials. Categorial Issues. Berlin, de Gruyter. 232–249.
Zampese, Luciano. 1994. Un frammento di grammatica italiana: Gli avverbi di frase. In Emilio Manzotti & Angela Ferrari (eds.), *Insegnare l'italiano: principi, metodi, esempi*, 237–268. Brescia: La Scuola.
Zampese, Luciano. 2005. La struttura informativa degli articoli di cronaca: natura e funzioni dell'Unità di Quadro. In Angela Ferrari (ed.), *Rilievi. Le gerarchie semantico-pragmatiche di alcuni tipi di testo*, 173–216. Firenze: Cesati.

List of contributors

Albers, Marius
Universität Siegen
albers@germanistik.uni-siegen.de

De Cesare, Anna-Maria
Technische Universität Dresden
anna-maria.decesare@tu-dresden.de

Delhem, Romain
Université Clermont Auvergne
romain.delhem@uca.fr

Duplâtre, Olivier
Sorbonne Université
olivier-duplatre@wanadoo.fr

Kakoyianni-Doa, Fryni
University of Cyprus
frynidoa@ucy.ac.cy

Mirto, Ignazio Mauro
Università di Palermo
ignazio.mirto@libero.it

Modicom, Pierre-Yves
Université Bordeaux-Montaigne
pymodicom.ling@yahoo.fr

Rastinger, Nina C.
Österreichische Akademie der Wissenschaften
ninaclaudia.rastinger@oeaw.ac.at

Sanchez-Stockhammer, Christina
Universität Chemnitz
christina.sanchez@phil.tu-chemnitz.de

Tescari Neto, Aquiles
University of Campinas
tescari@unicamp.br

Unwin, Antony
Universität Augsburg
unwin@math.uni-augsburg.de

Werner, Martina
Universität Wien
martina.werner@univie.ac.at

Zhang Courteaud, Jian
Université Jean Moulin Lyon 3
jianzhzh@gmail.com

Index

adjunct 21–22, 51, 57, 143–146, 149, 162–163, 209–210, 237

Bartsch 22, 168, 257
Bellert 22, 140, 144, 155, 168, 256

cartography 139–149, 162–165, 250, 262–263
Chomsky 8, 100, 102, 144, 168
Cinque 4, 17, 19, 139–151, 156–162, 250, 256, 262–263
comparative 48–51, 55–56, 74–79, 128
conjunction 34–40, 49–51, 182, 188
connective adverb 8, 68–69, 222

De Cesare 22–25, 89, 229–233, 242, 249–276
degree 34–35, 38, 40, 43–48, 69
Dik 2–4, 19–20, 140, 148–149, 204
Dionysius Thrax 1–2, 8, 34
domain adverb 14–15, 21–26, 229–247, 249–276

English 10–11, 22–23, 33–54, 55–83, 97, 143–146
Ernst 9, 17–19, 22, 144–146, 222–223

flat adverb 33, 43, 51
frame 230–238, 250–273
French 16–20, 141–142, 159, 167–194, 195–226, 250–258
frequency 33–34, 44–53, 55–58, 63–69, 74–83, 176, 182, 185–190

German 10–13, 21–28, 109–133, 229–247, 250
Geuder 214, 212–223
Greek 10, 16, 24, 167–194
Greenbaum 15, 17, 168
Guimier 18, 22, 168, 174–176, 199–201, 212, 214, 253–257

Hallonsten Halling 6, 56
Haspelmath 1, 6, 7, 10, 34
Hengeveld 5–7, 121, 140, 148–149

high adverb 14–15, 142–143, 151–163
Hummel 11–12

inflected adverb 109–111, 121–122
inflection 10, 41–42, 49–51, 79–80, 87–95, 102–103, 121–126, 169
information structure 246, 255, 259, 262, 272
intensifier 48, 55–56
Italian 12, 87–108, 142, 148–150, 158–159, 250–256

Jackendoff 16–17, 139, 144, 148, 222
Jespersen 35, 39, 40

Laenzlinger 141–142, 149
left periphery 149, 162–165, 249–251, 262–265, 273
low adverb 151–162

Maienborn 8, 21–22, 99–100, 230, 263
Mandarin Chinese 19, 23–24, 195–226
manner 6–22, 33–36, 42–43, 47–48, 55–56, 77, 114, 155–156, 195–205, 209–213, 219–225, 249, 254
modality 10–11, 16, 22, 24, 37, 42, 47–48, 58–60, 68–69, 77, 167–194
Molinier/ Lévrier 22, 168–171, 177–179, 200–203, 211–214, 250–256
Mørdrup 22, 168, 198–203, 211–213, 250

Nilsson–Ehe 20, 22, 205, 256
Nøjgaard 22, 201, 253–257
Nølke 7–8, 167, 250, 255–256

orientation 14–19, 23, 102–104, 155–156, 168, 172, 194–225

part of speech 5–6, 23–27, 55–65, 95, 97, 100–101, 122
Pittner 10, 56, 230
place 33–35, 46–52, 68
Portuguese 139–165, 254
preposition 11–12, 33–40, 43–44, 49–60, 87–92, 98, 121–126, 129–130

Quirk 4, 33, 35–39, 47, 56–57, 75–81, 256

Ramat/ Ricca 7, 56, 140, 148, 250
relational adjective 229–231, 244–247
Rizzi 140, 148–153, 162–165, 250, 262–263

Schäfer 8, 10, 21–22, 99–100, 230, 235
Schlyter 22, 168, 199–203, 256–257

secondary predication 12–13, 22–24, 116–119
sentence adverb 14–16, 19, 23, 139–165, 195–207, 211–216, 223

time 20, 22, 43, 47, 68, 77

verb particle 12–13, 43, 109–133

www.ingramcontent.com/pod-product-compliance
Lightning Source LLC
Chambersburg PA
CBHW050518170426
43201CB00013B/1996